MANIFEST DESTINY

THE AMERICAN HERITAGE SERIES

THE AMERICAN HERITAGE SERIES

Under the general editorship of
Leonard W. Levy and Alfred Young

MANIFEST DESTINY

Edited by

Norman A. Graebner

University of Virginia

THE BOBBS-MERRILL COMPANY, INC.
INDIANAPOLIS · NEW YORK

Foreword

On a visit to the University of Indonesia in 1962, Robert F. Kennedy, then Attorney General, was asked for his opinion on the United States' War with Mexico. He replied, "Some from Texas might disagree, but I think we were unjustified. I do not think we can be proud of that episode." Some from Texas, of course, did disagree with Kennedy's remark—a Senator asked for an apology and the Governor expressed outrage—all of which illustrates that Americans in the 1960's are as divided over the moral implications of American expansion as were Americans in the 1840's.

This anthology assembles representative statements by the proponents and critics of "manifest destiny," the ideology which Americans used to justify the acquisition of Texas, California, the Southwest, and Oregon, and which beckoned others to "all of Mexico," Cuba, Central America, and beyond. Here are the articles of such famous ideologues of expansion as John L. O'Sullivan and Walt Whitman, the overblown oratory of congressmen and senators, the state papers of Tyler, Polk, Buchanan, John Quincy Adams, and Seward. Arrayed against the expansionists are their critics, ranging from caustic Whig editors who pronounced manifest destiny "political clap-trap," to trenchant conservatives like John C. Calhoun and abolitionists whose moral conscience was outraged by "a war of conquest." Their ideas are certainly of interest to students of American intellectual history as well as to students of foreign policy, frontier expansion, and American diplomacy.

It is fitting that these selections were assembled by a scholar who has already made clear his skepticism of the influence of manifest destiny on American diplomacy. In *Empire on the Pacific* (1955) Professor Graebner made a convincing case for the tug of commercial interests as opposed to ideology. In his Introduction and headnotes to this volume the knowledgeable editor again emphasizes the forces shaping foreign policy and the realities of diplomacy which enable the reader to grasp the often heady rhetoric of the documents.

While it was not the editor's purpose to draw contemporary analogies, many Americans may find that the critics of manifest destiny articulate the uneasiness that perplex critics of American foreign policy in the twentieth century. "Morality among nations," Professor Graebner observes, "often served as a cloak for self-aggrandizement." Democratic idealism was "easily transformed into an agency of imperialism." Thus, as an effort to analyze the American ideology of "mission" which so often beclouded the understanding of realistic national interest, this volume might help to explain the continuing dilemmas that beset American foreign policy.

This book is one of a series whose aim is to provide the essential primary sources of the American experience, especially of American thought. The series, when completed, will constitute a documentary library of American history, filling a need long felt among scholars, students, libraries, and general readers for authoritative collections of original materials. Some volumes will illuminate the thought of significant individuals, such as James Madison or Louis Brandeis; some will deal with movements, such as the Antifederalists or the Populists; others will be organized around special themes, such as Puritan political thought, or American Catholic thought on social questions.

Many volumes will take up the large number of subjects traditionally studied in American history for which surprisingly there are no documentary anthologies; others will pioneer in introducing new subjects of increasing importance to scholars as to the contemporary world. The series aspires to maintain the high standards demanded of contemporary editing, providing authentic texts, intelligently and unobtrusively edited. It will also have the distinction of presenting pieces of substantial length which give the full character and flavor of the original. The series will be the most comprehensive and authoritative of its kind.

Alfred Young
Leonard W. Levy

Contents

PART TWO   TEXAS

PART THREE   OREGON

PART FIVE   ALL OF MEXICO

PART SIX CUBA

Introduction

Manifest destiny, a phrase used by contemporaries and historians to describe and explain the continental expansion of the United States in the 1840's, expressed merely a national mood. The belief in a national destiny was neither new nor strange; no nation or empire in history has ever been totally without it. But for its proponents of the 1840's the meaning conveyed by the phrase was clearly understood and peculiarly American. It implied that the United States was destined by the will of Heaven to become a country of political and territorial eminence. It attributed the probability and even the necessity of this growth to a homogeneous process created by certain unique qualities in American civilization—the energy and vigor of its people, their idealism and faith in their democratic institutions, and their sense of mission now endowed with a new vitality. It assigned to the American people the obligation to extend the area of freedom to their less fortunate neighbors, but only to those trained for self-government and genuinely desirous of entering the American Union. Expansionists of the forties saw this self-imposed limitation on forceful annexation as no serious barrier to the Republic's growth. It was inconceivable to them that any neighboring population would decline an invitation to enter the realm of the United States. Eventually editors and politicians transformed the idea of manifest destiny into a significant expression of American nationalism.

Such convictions of destiny came easily to the American people in the mid-forties, for they logically emerged from the sheer size and dramatic achievements of the young Republic. From New England and Pennsylvania, reaching on into the Ohio Valley and the Great Lakes region, an industrial revolution was multiplying the productive resources of the United States. New forms of transportation, made possible by the efficient application of steam, rendered the national economy greater than the sum of its parts. Steamboats transformed the Mississippi and Ohio rivers—with their many tributaries—into a mighty inland system of commercial and human traffic. Railroads had long since left the Atlantic seaboard and were, by the forties, creeping toward the burgeoning cities of the Middle West. Asa Whitney had already projected a railroad line from Lake Michigan to the Pacific Northwest. Samuel F. B. Morse's successful demonstration of the magnetic telegraph in 1844 assured almost instantaneous communication across the entire continent. "What mighty distances have been overcome by railroads," exclaimed the *Southern Quarterly Review* (October, 1844), "and, stranger than all, is the transmission of intelligence with the speed and with the aid of lightning!"

The purchase of Louisiana, forty years earlier, enabled the United States to leap the Mississippi and extended its territorial claims westward to the shores of the Pacific. But, in the forties, the land resources of the nation no longer appeared as boundless as they once did to Thomas Jefferson. Augmented by Europe's ceaseless outpouring of humanity, the population of the United States had quadrupled in less than fifty years. Immigrants from Ireland and northern Europe flowed into the little settlements dotting the Mississippi Valley, and from these centers of trade they fanned out across the countryside, creating new markets and stimulating the region's industrial and agricultural expansion. Settlements extended as far west as the lower Missouri; beyond them stretched the treeless prairies inhabited by Indians and buffalo. Restless farmers, always reaching for the farthest frontiers, had begun the grand overland trek to the inland valleys of Oregon and California. The easy identification of sufficient land with opportunity and the absence of oppression quickly converted manifest destiny into a major reform movement. Through territorial expansion the Republic would guarantee humanity's future. "Long may our country prove itself the asylum of the oppressed," pleaded Congressman James Belser of Alabama in January, 1845. "Let its institutions and its people be extended far and wide, and when the waters of despotism shall have inundated other portions of the globe, and the votary of liberty be compelled to betake himself to his ark, let this government be the Ararat on which it shall rest."[1]

This visible evidence of the nation's expanding power contrasted markedly with the relative absence of such progress elsewhere on the North American continent, and assured the Republic that one day it would surpass in strength and grandeur the great nations of Europe. As one British traveler warned his countrymen in the late forties:

We cannot conceal from ourselves that in many of the most important points of national capabilities they beat us; they are more energetic, more enterprising, less embarrassed with class interests, less burthened by the legacy of debt. This country, as a field for increase of power, is in every respect so infinitely beyond ours that comparison would be absurd. . . . They only wait for material power, to apply the incendiary torch of Republicanism to the nations of Europe.

However, manifest destiny's existence, as an organized body of thought, required more than a recognition and appreciation

[1] *Congressional Globe* (28th Cong., 2nd Sess., 1845), Appendix, p. 43.

of national power and energy. It demanded above all a sense of mission, one anchored to political idealism. Americans of the early forties viewed their political system with a messianic consciousness, convinced that they held the future of republican government in their hands. Andrew Jackson asserted in his Farewell Address that Providence had selected the American people to be "the guardians of freedom to preserve it for the benefit of the human race."[2] Even more grandiloquent was the phraseology of John L. O'Sullivan, editor of the *Democratic Review,* who reminded the American people in July, 1840, that to them much had been given and much would be required. Continued O'Sullivan:

> We have been placed in the forefront of the battle in the cause of Man against the powers of evil which have so long crushed him to the dust. The problem of his capacity for self-government is to be solved here. . . . he [Man] should be left to the individual action of his own will and conscience. Let us but establish this, and the race will have made an advance from which nothing short of the hand of Omnipotence can force it to recede. To no other has been committed the ark of man's hopes. . . . Surely we cannot fail of success in such a cause! Surely we cannot falter when so much depends upon our perseverance to the end![3]

O'Sullivan, always in the vanguard of American expansionist thinking, had helped to found the *Review* in 1837 and remained its editor until 1846. With Samuel J. Tilden he founded the New York *Morning News* in 1844, and for the following two years as editor filled its pages with expansionist sentiment. It

[2] James D. Richardson, ed., *Messages and Papers of the Presidents,* (Washington: Government Printing Office, 1896), III, 308.

[3] "The Progress of Society," *The United States Magazine and Democratic Review,* VIII (July, 1840), 87.

was O'Sullivan who, during the summer of 1845, first used the phrase "manifest destiny."[4]

That the American creed, as embodied in the Declaration of Independence, would not fail appeared obvious enough, for its foundation lay in human reason. "Democracy must finally reign," promised the *Democratic Review* in March, 1840. "There is in man an eternal principle or progress which no power on earth may resist. Every custom, law, science, or religion, which obstructs its course, will fall as leaves before the wind." Few Americans even in that ebullient age would have denied that the nation's economic superiority rested on elements unique to the North American environment—its raw materials and climate as well as a wide spectrum of productive and commercial advantages—which existed on only a small portion of the earth's surface. Perhaps its democratic and free institutions, reflecting as they did specific historic and environmental conditions, might be no less endemic. But the propagandists for national expansion seldom dwelt on the possible limitations to the universal extension of their notions of sound and humane government. "The march of the Anglo-Saxon race is onward," boasted the Washington *Union* (June 2, 1845). "They must . . . accomplish their destiny, spreading far and wide the great principles of self-government, and who shall say how far they will prosecute the work?"

America's mission to humanity was not new, but the generation of the forties was the first to attach it to territorial expansion. The Founding Fathers had limited the nation's democratic mission to the creation and perpetuation of a model republic which might be worthy of emulation. Expansion, they feared, might disturb the federal structure of government by dispersing

---

[4] O'Sullivan's role in promulgating the phrase, "manifest destiny," has been developed in Julius W. Pratt, "The Origins of 'Manifest Destiny,'" *American Historical Review*, XXXII (July, 1927), 795–798.

political authority too widely. The outspoken southern conservative of the Jeffersonian era, John Randolph, once observed, "We are the first people that ever acquired provinces . . . not for us to govern, but that they might *govern us*—that we might be ruled to our ruin by people bound to us by no common tie of interest or sentiment."[5] With the passage of time, however, even conservative Easterners accepted the inevitability of American expansion and ceased to regard the westward-moving center of political power a threat to their estate. "We look forward to that event without alarm," the noted Massachusetts scholar and orator, Edward Everett, could assure a Tennessee audience in 1829, "as in the order of the natural growth of this great Republic. We have a firm faith that our interests are mutually consistent, that if you prosper, we shall prosper. . . ."[6]

By the forties the addition of new states from the Louisiana Purchase, all without subverting the American federal system, had dispelled completely such earlier fears of expansion. The reestablishment of the states-rights principle under Jacksonian rule destroyed what remained of the older institutional arguments against national growth. In January, 1838, the *Democratic Review* affirmed the compatibility between expansion and the basic principles of American government: "The peculiar characteristic of our system,—the distinctive evidence of its divine origin . . . is, that it may, if its theory is maintained pure in practice, be extended, with equal safety and efficiency, over any indefinite number of millions of population and territory." Similarly Stephen A. Douglas of Illinois asserted in January, 1845, that "our federal system is admirably adapted to the whole

[5] Quoted in Russell Kirk, *Randolph of Roanoke: A Study in Conservative Thought* (Chicago: University of Chicago Press, 1951), p. 145.

[6] Edward Everett, *Orations and Speeches on Various Occasions* (Boston: Little, Brown, and Company, 1870), I, 196.

continent."[7] Indeed, to states-rights Democrats there was no better guarantee against federal consolidation than the addition of new states.

In essence, then, manifest destiny suggested that the American people were destined to extend their democratic principles over the North American continent. This vision was not lost on Senator James Buchanan, the Pennsylvania Democrat, who declared in March, 1844: "Providence has given to the American people a great and important mission, and that mission they were destined to fulfill—to spread the blessings of Christian liberty and laws from one end to the other of this immense continent. . . . To talk of confining the American spirit of emigration within limits," he added, "was like talking of limiting the stars in their courses, or bridling the foaming torrent of Niagara."[8] Two years later Congressman John S. Chipman of Michigan predicted with equal assurance, "This continent will be our own; the gentlemen may say it is by manifest destiny, or by Adams' will, or by whatever else they will. That destiny was found written in every page of our history. . . ."[9]

Such rhetoric was more than an expression of purpose; it was a search for justification. Historically, national ambition demanded no vindication beyond the demonstration of interest and the possession of the strength to achieve the objective. But no nation had ever embarked on a career of expansion so completely at the price of its own national ideology as did the United States in the 1840's. Its sense of mission collided

[7] "The Texas Question," *Democratic Review*, XIV (April, 1844), 429; *Congressional Globe* (28th Cong., 2nd Sess., 1844), Appendix, p. 68.

[8] Buchanan's speech on the mission of the United States, March 12, 1844, *Congressional Globe* (28th Cong., 1st Sess., 1844), p. 380.

[9] Chipman's address of January 14, 1846, *Congressional Globe* (29th Cong., 1st Sess., 1846), p. 207.

sharply with its democratic doctrine of self-determination as well as its ideals of amity and peace. Morality among individuals is a rationale for self-sacrifice; among nations it often serves as a cloak for self-aggrandizement. Democratic idealism is easily transformed into an agency of imperialism when it attempts to deny opposing governments—because of their alleged corruption or immorality—the right to territories which they possess. It seeks to rationalize the removal of those who stand in the path of destiny by declaring them politically and morally inferior. Such an approach to the achievement of external ambitions may assure popular support for specific foreign policies formulated by the national government; it can do no more. National sentiment, unsupported by force or the threatened use of force, can wield no measurable influence in affairs among nations.

MANIFEST DESTINY: THE ABSENCE OF ENDS AND MEANS

Never in history could a people more readily accept and proclaim a sense of destiny, for never were a people more perfectly situated to transform their whims into realities. Expansion was rationalized so effectively at each point of conflict that it seemed to many Americans an unchallangeable franchise. Confronted by problems neither of conscience nor of extensive countering force, the American people could claim as a natural right boundaries that seemed to satisfy the requirements of security and commerce. Expanding as they did into a vacuum—vast regions almost devoid of population—they could conclude that they were simply fulfilling the dictates of manifest destiny. For them the distinctions between sentiment and action, between individual purpose and national achievement, appeared inconsequential.

Historians, emphasizing the expansive mood of the forties, have tended to identify the westward extension of the United States to the Pacific with the concept of destiny itself. Such identifications are misleading, for they ignore all the genuine elements of successful policy. Those regions into which the nation threatened to expand were under the legal jurisdiction of other governments. Their acquisition required the formulation of policies which encompassed both the precise definition of ends and the creation of adequate means. Manifest destiny doctrines—a body of sentiment and nothing else—avoided completely the essential question of *means,* and it was only the absence of powerful opposition on the North American continent that permitted the fallacy that power and its employment were of little consequence. Occupying a wilderness created the illusion that power was less important than moral progress, and that expansion was indeed a civilizing, not a conquering, process.

Jeremy Bentham once termed the concept of natural right pure nonsense, for the claims of nations were natural only when supported by superior force. The natural right of the United States to a continental empire lay in its power of conquest, not in the uniqueness of its political institutions. American expansionism could triumph only when the nation could bring its diplomatic and military influence to bear on specific points of national concern. What created the easy victory of American expansion was not a sense of destiny, however widely and dramatically it was proclaimed, but the absence of powerful competitors which might have either prevented the expansion entirely or forced the country to pay an exorbitant price for its territorial gains. The advantages of geography and the political and military inefficiency of the Indian tribes or even of Mexican arms tended to obscure the elements of force which were no less real, only less obtrusive, than that employed by other nations in their efforts at empire building. It was no wonder that British and French critics concluded that the American conquest of the continent was by pick and shovel.

Concepts of manifest destiny were as totally negligent of *ends* as they were of means. Expansionists agreed that the nation was destined to reach its natural boundaries. But what were these natural frontiers? For Benjamin Franklin and John Adams they comprised the Mississippi River. But when the United States, through the purchase of Louisiana, crossed the Mississippi, there was no end in sight. Expansionists now regarded Florida as a natural appendage—belonging as naturally to the United States, declared one Kentucky newspaper, as Cornwall did to England. John Quincy Adams observed in his diary that the acquisition of Florida in 1819 "rendered it still more unavoidable that the remainder of the continent should ultimately be ours." Eventually Europe would discover, he predicted, that the United States and North America were identical. But President James Monroe revealed no more interest in building a state on the Pacific than had Jefferson. Equally convinced that the distances to Oregon were too great to be bridged by one empire, Thomas Hart Benton of Missouri in 1825 defined the natural boundary of the United States as "the ridge of the Rocky Mountains. . . . Along the back of this ridge, the Western limit of this republic should be drawn, and the statue of the fabled god, Terminus, should be raised upon its highest peak, never to be thrown down."[10] President John Tyler, in his message of December, 1843, perpetuated this limited view of the nation's future. And as late as 1845 Daniel Webster continued to refer to an independent republic along the distant Pacific coast. Meanwhile expansionists could never agree on the natural boundaries of Texas. Representative C. J. Ingersoll of Pennsylvania found them in the vast deserts between the Rio Grande and the Nueces. For others they comprised the Rio Grande itself, but James Gadsden discovered in the Sierra Madre mountains "a natural territorial boundary, imposing in its Mountain and Desert outlines."[11]

[10] Benton's remarks of March 1, 1825, *Register of Debates in Congress* (18th Cong., 2nd Sess., 1825), col. 711–712.

[11] Gadsden, quoted in Albert K. Weinberg, *Manifest Destiny: A Study of Nationalist Expansionism in American History* (Baltimore: The Johns Hopkins Press, 1935), p. 56.

Yet geographical predestination alone seemed sufficient to assure the sweep of the nation to the Pacific. As Lord Curzon once wrote, "Of all natural frontiers the sea is the most uncompromising, the least alterable, and the most effective."[12] As early as 1823 Francis Baylies warned the nation not to terminate its westward march at the Rockies. "Sir, our natural boundary is the Pacific Ocean," he declared. "The swelling tide of our population must and will roll on until the mighty ocean interposes its waters, and limits our territorial empire."[13] By the mid-forties the true proponents of manifest destiny had become continentalists. Stephen Douglas voiced these sentiments when he declared in January, 1845:

He would blot out the lines on the map which now marked our national boundaries on this continent, and make the area of liberty as broad as the continent itself. He would not suffer petty rival republics to grow up here, engendering jealousy at each other, and interfering with each others domestic affairs, and continually endangering their peace. He did not wish to go beyond the great ocean —beyond those boundaries which the God of nature had marked out. . . .[14]

Similarly the New York *Herald* prophesied that the American Republic would, in due course, embrace all the land from the Isthmus of Panama to the polar regions and from the Atlantic to the Pacific. One Texas correspondent of that newspaper wrote (August 9, 1845) that "the fact must be no longer disguised, that we, the people of the United States, must hold, and govern, under free and harmonious institutions, the continent we inhabit." John L. O'Sullivan noted in the New York *Morning News* (December 27, 1845) that it had become "our mani-

[12] Quoted in Weinberg, p. 64.

[13] Debate of January 24, 1823, *Annals of Congress* (17th Cong., 2nd Sess., 1823), col. 682–683.

[14] Speech of January 31, 1845, *Congressional Globe* (28th Cong., 2nd Sess., 1845), pp. 226–227.

fest destiny to occupy and to possess the whole of the Continent which Providence has given us. . . ."

If the ultimate vision of American destiny in the forties comprised a vast federal republic that boasted continental dimensions and a government based on the principle of states rights, the future boundaries of the United States, as determined by the standards of geographical predestination, never seemed to possess any ultimate logic. Boundaries that appeared natural to one generation were rejected as utterly inadequate by the next. It was left for Robert Winthrop, the conservative Massachusetts Whig, in January, 1846, to reduce the doctrine of geographical predestination to an absurdity:

> It is not a little amusing to observe what different views are taken as to the indication of "the hand of nature" and the pointings of "the finger of God," by the same gentlemen, under different circumstances and upon different subjects. In one quarter of the compass they can descry the hand of nature in a level desert and a second-rate river, beckoning us impatiently to march up to them. But when they turn their eyes to another part of the horizon the loftiest mountains in the universe are quite lost upon their gaze. There is no hand of nature there. The configuration of the earth has no longer any significance. The Rocky Mountains are mere molehills. Our destiny is onward.[15]

Democratic idealism was even less precise as a guide to national action than the doctrine of geographical predestination. By 1845 such goals of reaching the waters of the Pacific were far too limited for the more enthusiastic exponents of the new expansionism. As they interpreted the expression of democratic idealism, the dogma represented an ever-expanding force. Indeed, for some it had no visible limit at all. It looked beyond the North American continent to South America, to the islands of the Pacific, and to the Old World itself. One editorial in the New York *Herald* (September 15, 1845), declared, "American

[15] *Congressional Globe* (29th Cong., 1st Sess., 1846), Appendix, p. 294.

patriotism takes a wider and loftier range than heretofore. Its horizon is widening every day. No longer bounded by the limits of the confederacy, it looks abroad upon the whole earth, and into the mind of the republic daily sinks deeper and deeper the conviction that the civilization of the earth—the reform of the governments of the ancient world—the emancipation of the whole race, are dependent, in a great degree, on the United States." This was a magnificent vision for a democratic purpose, but it hardly explains the sweep of the United States across the continent. It bears no relationship whatever to the actual goals which the Tyler and Polk administrations pursued in their diplomacy with Texas, Mexico, and England.

TEXAS ANNEXATION: A POLITICAL ISSUE

Texas provided the necessary catalyst which fused all the elements of manifest destiny into a single national movement. When, in 1844, the annexation issue suddenly exploded on the national scene, the expansionist front had been quiescent for a full generation. The twenties and thirties had been years of introspection. The changing structure of American political and economic life had absorbed the people's energies and directed their thoughts inward. Yet the same inner-directed concerns which rendered the country generally oblivious to external affairs promoted both the sense of power and the democratic idealism which, under the impetus of expansionist oratory, could easily transform the nation's mood and forge a spirit of national destiny.

As a public issue, Texas's annexation could provoke a national response only as the occasion demanded. Yet as early as the 1820's American pioneers had decreed that one day the occasion for a national decision would arise. Responding to the Mexican government's generous offer of free land, American frontiersmen surged into Texas in such overwhelming numbers that soon they dominated much of the province. In 1828 the Tèran Commission, despatched to Texas by the Mexican government, rendered an alarming report on the number and quality of Americans residing in Texas. Thereupon, Lucas Alamán, Secretary of Foreign Relations, warned the Mexican Congress that American settlers were simply the advance agents of United States imperialism. Their techniques, he charged, were well established:

They commence by introducing themselves into the territory which they covet, upon pretence of commercial negotiations, or of the establishment of colonies, with or without the assent of the Government to which it belongs. These colonies grow, multiply, become the predominant party in the population; . . . These pioneers excite, by degrees, movements which disturb the political state of the country . . . and then follow discontents and dissatisfaction, calculated to fatigue the patience of the legitimate owner, and to diminish the usefulness of the administration and of the exercise of authority. When things have come to this pass, which is precisely the present state of things in Texas, the diplomatic management commences: the inquietude they have excited in the territory, . . . the interests of the colonists therein established, the insurrections of adventurers, and savages instigated by them, and the pertinacity with which the opinion is set up as to their right of possession, . . . [and] with the aid of other incidents, which are never wanting in the course of diplomatic relations, the desired end is attained of concluding an arrangement as onerous for one party as it is advantageous to the other. Sometimes more direct means are resorted to; and taking advantage of the enfeebled state, or domestic difficulties, of the possessor of the soil, they proceed, upon the most extraordinary pretexts, to make themselves masters of the country, as was the case in the Floridas; leaving the question to be decided afterwards as to the legality of the possession, which force alone could take from them.[16]

In 1830 an aroused Mexican government attempted to prohibit further American migration into Texas, but to no avail. The resultant tension between the Americans and their Mexican

[16] *House Ex. Doc. No. 351* (25th Cong., 2nd Sess., 1838), Serial 332, pp. 313–314.

rulers erupted into open warfare which culminated in 1836 with the establishment of the Republic of Texas and its immediate request for admission into the American Union. Such Northerners as John Quincy Adams, however, viewing events in Texas as a Southern conspiracy designed to extend the area of slavery, managed to prevent any action by Congress.

That Texas finally kindled the nation's expansionist tendencies resulted less from the pressure of pioneers or the simple urge to expand than from the scheming and ambition of politicians. President John Tyler, urged on by such Southern advisers as Duff Green, R. M. T. Hunter, and Thomas W. Gilmer, commenced his promotion of the Texas issue as early as 1843, convinced that it would grip the country's imagination and help to repair his battered political fences. Tyler believed the issue powerful enough, if properly handled, to unhinge Henry Clay from the titular headship of the Whig Party and perhaps secure for himself a second term in the White House. Tyler's personal efforts to control the Texas question culminated in a treaty of annexation, negotiated with the Lone Star Republic, which he submitted to the Senate in April, 1844. Even before the Senate rejected the treaty, however, the annexation issue had passed into other hands.

For an influential group of Southern Democrats, Texas comprised a purely sectional challenge upon which hinged the very existence of the South's institutions. As Secretary of State in 1844, John C. Calhoun, now approaching the end of his long career as the special defender of Southern causes, promoted the annexation of Texas with the sectional fervor expected of him. "I only ask the South to stand by me," he wrote in May, 1844. "Now is the time to vindicate and save our institutions."[17] For

---

[17] Calhoun to James H. Hammond, May 17, 1844, J. Franklin Jameson, ed., *The Correspondence of John C. Calhoun, Annual Report of the American Historical Association, 1899* (Washington: Government Printing Office, 1900), II, 589.

Calhoun and his Southern colleagues it was British abolitionism that rendered annexation so essential for Southern security.
Lord Aberdeen, the British Foreign Minister, had made clear
the attitudes of the British government toward slavery. Reassuring the United States in December, 1843, of Britain's honorable intentions toward Texas, Aberdeen added the disturbing
comment that "Great Britain desires and is constantly exerting
herself to promote the general abolition of slavery throughout
the world." Whereas England would do nothing secretly or un-
derhandedly to accomplish it, continued Aberdeen, she hoped
to see that institution abolished in the United States. In his
reply Calhoun not only defended the right of the United States
to annex Texas but also reminded the Foreign Minister that
slavery was a Southern question and beyond the jurisdiction of
the Federal government.[18] Indeed, Southern Democrats hoped
that the Texas issue would upset the hegemony of Martin Van
Buren over their party and secure the nomination of Calhoun.

Southern politicians soon discovered that they could control
the Texas question with no greater success than could the President. Eventually it was the agrarian Democrats, centered in the
lower Midwest, with their allies in the Southwest and East, who
captured the issue, nationalized it, carried expansionism to its
highest pitch of the decade, and eventually rode into power on
its emotional impact. It was their control of the Baltimore Convention of 1844 that upset the hopes of Van Buren and secured
the nomination of James K. Polk of Tennessee. This faction, led
by Lewis Cass of Michigan, Stephen Douglas of Illinois, and
Robert Walker of Mississippi, had no interest in the expansion
of slavery. These men emerged rather as the true proponents
of manifest destiny, defending the westward extension of the

[18] See Calhoun to Richard Pakenham, April 18, 1844, William
R. Manning, ed., *Diplomatic Correspondence of the United States:
Inter-American Affairs, 1831–1860* (Washington: Government Print-
ing Office, 1936), VII, 18–22.

United States on broad national grounds. It was their oratory that fused the American concept of mission, traditionally limited to the creation of a model republic, with expansion itself. Through annexation, not merely through exemplary government, they agreed, the United States was destined to extend the area of freedom over the North American continent.

What compelled the identification of freedom with expansion in the American mind was the dread of European encroachment. Continental expansionism in the forties was in large measure a defensive maneuver in which the superior claims of the United States to contested lands was rationalized in terms of manifest destiny. In his message of transmittal President Tyler warned the Senate that if it rejected the Texas treaty, Texas would seek the friendship of other nations. "In contemplating such a contingency," he continued, "it cannot be overlooked that the United States are already almost surrounded by the possessions of European powers. The Canadas, New Brunswick, and Nova Scotia, the islands in the American seas, with Texas trammeled by treaties of alliance or of a commercial character differing in policy from that of the United States, would complete the circle." (Document 6.) Similarly Andrew Jackson, in his famous letter to Aaron V. Brown in 1843, advocated extending "the area of freedom" to Texas to terminate British ambition and intrigue along the southwestern frontier of the United States. Polk's inaugural address of March 4, 1845, reminded the nation that annexation alone would preserve American democracy from the encroachments of European monarchy.

Ultimately the proponents of manifest destiny justified the annexation of Texas in terms of its contribution to the American system of government. Annexation would perfect the Union and guarantee the blessings of liberty to the American people. Thomas W. Gilmer declared that "our union has no danger to apprehend from those who believe that its genius is expansive and progressive, but from those who think that the limits of the United States are already too large and the principles of 1776 too old-fashioned for this fastidious age."[19] For states-rights Democrats expansion was the surest defense against the country's great internal enemy: a federal government that would encroach on the liberties of the states and the people. "The dangers that an American patriot ought to apprehend," warned the *Southern Quarterly Review* in October, 1844, "do not find their source in the growth of our people, the increase of our territory, or the power of foreign competitors. They originate in the sordid, grasping and rapacious spirit of our legislation, . . . in the usurpations of power, the shortness of memory and laxity of conscience in our public men. . . . Such rulers as these have elevated the government above the Constitution they were sworn to defend, and above the people who entrusted it to them to preserve." Those who opposed annexation, the writer noted bitterly, were likewise the defenders of centralization in government. They cared nothing for the nation's destiny. For them, he concluded, nothing "can be well ordered and sure but the pitiful present that they can command."

What removed all taint of injustice and oppression from the Texas question was the knowledge that the vast majority of Texans favored annexation to the United States. Indeed, the expanionists of the day denied any interest in annexing anyone but Anglo-Saxon peoples. They questioned the capacity of others for self-government. The expansionist, Levi Woodbury of New Hampshire, opened fraternization to all who would willingly partake of American institutions. He had no interest in the forceful annexation of distant lands and alien peoples.

When gentlemen talked about Patagonia and the Celestial Empire coming into the Union [he said] . . . let them look back into our constitutional history, and see if it is possible for this government to embrace any nation, unless that nation be willing to come in and adopt our republican institutions, and are conquered not by our swords, but by our liberal example and systems of equal rights, en-

[19] *Niles' National Register,* LXIV (July 1, 1843), 285.

nobling liberties and well-regulated laws. We must thus affiliate together—they with us and we with them—before a single step for amalgamation is likely to be taken on either side, however much gentlemen may appear to apprehend so many kinds of heterogeneous mixtures. . . .[20]

Whig leaders condemned the expansionist oratory as a dangerous appeal to American nationalism, perpetrated as much to elevate Democrats to public office as to secure the annexation of Texas. These conservatives harbored no fears of British encroachment. They regarded the identification of freedom with expansion as revolutionary and unsound. Representative George P. Marsh of Vermont ridiculed the idea of extending freedom into Texas as "an argument addressed to the ear and not to the understanding—a mere jingle of words without meaning, or, if significant, false in the only sense which the words will fairly bear. . . ."[21] E. S. Hanlin of Ohio wondered how men could talk of extending the area of freedom when annexation was designed to prevent the abolition of slavery in Texas. "Were it not for perpetuating slavery in that country," he charged, "we should hear no more of this measure."[22]

For the Whig Party and its abolitionist allies in the North Texas annexation posed a dual challenge of major proportions. The first source of anxiety was the contest for political power. Would the agrarianism of the West and South or the industrialism of the East and the Great Lakes dominate national policy? Philip Hone, the New York merchant, detected clearly why the Texas issue was rocking the Republic to its foundations. Southern demagogues, he said, were promoting their personal objec-

[20] Woodbury's speech in the Senate, February 17, 1845, *Congressional Globe* (28th Cong., 2nd Sess., 1845), Appendix, p. 233.

[21] Speech of January 20, 1845, *Congressional Globe* (28th Cong., 2nd Sess., 1845), Appendix, p. 316.

[22] Hanlin's speech in the House, January 9, 1845, *Congressional Globe* (28th Cong., 2nd Sess., 1845), Appendix, p. 375.

tives, and those of the South, by solidifying their power through the addition of four or five slave states. Antislavery Whigs maintained that the second challenge was inherent in the first—the expansion and strengthening of the hated institution of slavery. Joshua Giddings, the Ohio abolitionist and Whig, held forth, both in and out of Congress, on the dual nature of the struggle over Texas. In a noted address before the House of Representatives in May, 1844, Giddings demanded to know why the New England and Pennsylvania Democrats would support annexation while the Texans in Congress voted down their system of tariffs. Would Western Democrats, he added, willingly give up their harbor improvements and the dredging of their rivers merely to improve the Southern slave trade and perpetuate slavery in Texas?[23] Thomas Corwin, the conservative Ohio Whig, saw two prospects as disturbing—a divided country and the demise of Whig ascendency. Perhaps a combination of Whigs and Democrats, he wrote, might still "keep *in* the Tariff and keep *out* Texas."[24]

Texas upset the calculations of its opponents. "It is the greatest question of the *age*," wrote the Alabama expansionist, Dixon H. Lewis, "and I predict will agitate the country more than all the other public questions ever have. Public opinion will boil and effervesce . . . more like a volcano than a cider barrel—but at last it will settle down with *unanimity* for annexation in the South and West and a large majority in the North."[25] To Andrew Davezac, the New York Democrat, the issue was equally

[23] See Gidding's speech of May 21, 1844, *Congressional Globe* (28th Cong., 1st Sess., 1844), Appendix, pp. 704–707.

[24] Corwin to Oran Follett, February 22, 1845, March 7, 13, 1845, L. Belle Hamlin, ed., "Selections from the Follett Papers, II," *Quarterly Publication of the Historical and Philosophical Society of Ohio*, IX (July-September, 1814), 80–81, 84.

[25] Lewis to Richard Cralle, March 19, 1844, Cralle Papers, Manuscripts Division, Library of Congress.

productive of change. "It has been the entering wedge," he admitted in July, 1844, "that has opened, both the ears and throats of my auditors everywhere—from Baltimore to Buffalo."[26]

National expansionism ultimately tipped the political scales in favor of the Democrats and thus assured the annexation of Texas. When Congress convened in December, 1844, the Democratic leadership brought a joint resolution of annexation before both houses. Convinced that Mexico would react violently to annexation, Benton proposed negotiation with Mexico prior to annexation for the purpose of defining the boundary. By January, 1845, however, Benton had agreed to immediate annexation, with the question of the boundary being left to future diplomacy. The House passed the resolution for annexation late in January; and, by the end of February, by a vote of 27 to 25, the Senate approved an amended resolution. Tyler, anxious to proceed under the authority granted by Congress, directed the American chargé in Texas on March 3 to invite Texas to join the Union. Polk, upon entering office the following day, upheld Tyler's action. Texas responded favorably to the American invitation, and entered the Union when Congress approved its new constitution the following December.

Needless to say, the doctrines of manifest destiny, as a powerful Democratic appeal in the 1844 campaign, played a significant role in the annexation of Texas. However this does not demonstrate the relevance of national sentiment to the successful conduct of diplomacy. Texas confronted the United States with a purely internal political question. The Lone Star Republic was not only a free agent in complete control of its own destiny but it was also determined to enter the American Union at the first opportunity. Whatever barrier still existed in 1844 to Texas's annexation lay not in the opposing power and interest of another nation, but in the configuration of sectional and party

[26] Davezac to Polk, July 11, 1844, Polk Papers, Manuscripts Division, Library of Congress.

alignments in Congress. To the extent that concepts of manifest destiny strengthened the proannexationist forces in Congress they also contributed to American expansion, for no one would deny the relevance of public opinion to the actions of Congress.

THE NATIONAL DEBATE OVER OREGON

Even as Texas, its annexation assured, receded from its commanding position in American thought and politics, American expansionism shifted its focus beyond the summit of the Rockies to the regions of Oregon and California. "The Rio Grande has no more efficacy as a permanent barrier against the extension of Anglo-Saxon power than the Sabine possessed," predicted the Baltimore *American* in March, 1845. "The process by which Texas was acquired may be repeated over and over again. . . ."[27] The New York *Sun* assured its readers that the United States, with its system of self-governing states and homogeneous civilization, would, unlike Rome, increase in strength and durability as it expanded. "Who shall say," observed the *Sun* (March 7, 1845), "there is not room at the family altar for another sister like Texas, and in the fullness of time for many daughters from the shores of the Pacific."

Expansionism, focusing in 1845 on regions beyond Texas, reached a new level of rhetorical extravagance. The notion of a continental destiny was not new, but editors now proclaimed it with a sense of finality. No longer, by September, 1845, did the New York *Herald* recognize any clear limitation to the nation's future growth:

The minds of men have been awakened to a clear conviction of the destiny of this great nation of freemen. No longer bounded by those limits which nature had in the eye of those of little faith [in] the last generation, assigned to the dominion of republicanism on

[27] Baltimore *American* quoted in *Niles' National Register*, March 15, 1845.

this continent, the pioneers of Anglo-Saxon civilization and Anglo-Saxon free institutions, now seek distant territories, stretching even to the shores of the Pacific; and the arms of the republic, it is clear to all men of sober discernment, must soon embrace the whole hemisphere, from the icy wilderness of the North to the most prolific regions of the smiling and prolific South.[28]

How this destiny was to be achieved rested lightly on the shoulders of those who proclaimed it. Texas had established the pattern which, in the course of time, would annex what remained of the continent to the American Union. American pioneers who had built a civilization in Texas and then applied for admission to the United States would repeat the process elsewhere. Already American settlers in the Willamette Valley of Oregon were creating a mature society. At Champoeg in 1843 they adopted a frame of government. Next they made it clear that they desired and anticipated the extension of American law and institutions into the Oregon country. Other American pioneers, entering Mexican California, had by 1845 converted the Sacramento Valley into an American settlement. Clearly even in California the processes of annexation were at work. "Once let the tide of emigration flow toward California," predicted Alfred Robinson, a long-time American resident of that province, "and the American population will soon be sufficiently numerous to play the Texas game."[29]

By what process the United States would acquire the heavily-peopled and politically backward regions of Mexico and Central America was less clear, for the doctrines of manifest destiny assumed that only qualified populations, desiring admittance, would enter the Republic. Levi Woodbury had rationalized the

[28] New York *Herald,* September 25, 1845.

[29] Alfred Robinson to Thomas O. Larkin, May 29, 1845, George P. Hammond, ed., *The Larkin Papers* (Berkeley: University of California Press, 1952), III, 205.

antiimperialist nature of American policy toward Texas in such terms, and even the arch expansionist O'Sullivan would recognize no other principle. His New York *Morning News* stressed this limitation when it declared on October 13, 1845:

> Public sentiment with us repudiates possession without use, and this sentiment is gradually acquiring the force of established public law. It has sent our adventurous pioneers to the plains of Texas, will carry them to the Rio del Norte, and even that boundary, purely nominal and conventional as it is, will not stay them on their march to the Pacific, the limit which nature has provided. In like manner it will come to pass that the confederated democracies of the Anglo-American race will give this great continent as an inheritance to man. Rapacity and spoliation cannot be the features of this magnificent enterprise, not perhaps, because we are above and beyond the influence of such views, but because circumstances do not admit of their operation. We take from no man; the reverse rather—we give to man. This national policy, necessity or destiny, we know to be just and beneficent, and we can, therefore, afford to scorn the invective and imputations of rival nations.

Oregon, the immediate objective of expansionism after March, 1845, challenged the easy assumptions that lands along the Pacific would succumb through osmosis to the centripetal force of American civilization. Texas was a political issue and its resolution lay generally within the competence of Congress. Oregon was a diplomatic question to be resolved, if at all, through successful negotiations with the London government. England's legal claims demanded that American expansionists either admit the irrelevance of national sentiment when confronted by the will and claims of another nation, or support its pretensions with superior argumentation or force. Argumentation promised to be far less demanding or disagreeable than war. What placed such a tremendous burden on American rhetoric, however, was the determination of Western expansionists, supported officially by the Baltimore platform of 1844, to achieve no less than the whole of Oregon up to the Alaska line of 54° 40′. United States claims, based on discovery, settlement, and the Spanish treaty of 1819 were substantial enough as far north as the Columbia River and were recognized as such by the British government. North of the Columbia, where the British Hudson's Bay Company was completely dominant, the American claims were inconclusive or nonexistent.

Clearly the American claims to Oregon, if only to prevent compromise negotiations by the United States government, required augmentation. Unable to sustain their demands through historic claims or diplomatic precedent, the proponents of 54-40 discovered the true title to Oregon in a higher law. O'Sullivan defined the American claim in his editorial of December 27, 1845: "Away, away with all these cobweb tissues of rights of discovery, exploration, settlement, contiguity. . . . [The American title] is by the right of our manifest destiny to overspread and to possess the whole of the continent which Providence has given us. . . ." Edward D. Baker of Illinois informed the House of Representatives in January, 1846, that he had little regard for "musty records and the voyages of old sea captains, or the Spanish treaties, because we had a higher and better title under the law of nature and of nations. . . ." Some members of Congress pushed the American title back to Adam's will. To William Sawyer of Ohio it was even older. "We received our rights from high Heaven," he shouted, "from destiny, if you please."[30]

Fundamentally the true title of the United States to all of Oregon lay in the doctrine of geographical predestination. Such higher law claims had been used before to justify the abrogation of Indian titles to unoccupied lands. Lewis Cass cited such claims when, as Secretary of War under Jackson, he demanded the removal of the Georgia Indians to the West. "There can be no doubt . . . ," ran one observation which appeared in the January, 1830, issue of the *North American Review*, "that the Creator intended that the earth should be reclaimed from a state

[30] *Congressional Globe* (29th Cong., 1st Sess., 1846), pp. 136, 301.

of nature and cultivated; that the human race should spread over it, procuring from it the means of comfortable subsistence, and of increase and improvement." That the Indians of Georgia had attained a high level of cultivation and of culture mattered little. The land was destined for Anglo-American occupation.

America's higher law claims to Oregon lay in the proximity of the region to the United States, especially when contrasted to the vast distances that separated it from England. Several lines of poetry in the February, 1846, issue of the *Democratic Review* summarized the American contention:

> Why clamor in the question, "whose the right
>   By conquest or discovery?—what eye,
> Briton or Apalachian, had first sight
>   Of the great wastes that now disputed lie?"
>   The right depends on the propinquity,
> The absolute sympathy of soil and place,
>   Needful against the foreign enemy,
> And for the due expansion of our race;
> And this expansion, certain as the light,
> Makes the right sure, in progress of the might!

What gave the right of propinquity its essential force was the related question of land utilization. "There is . . . no such thing as title to the wild lands of the new world," declared the New York *Morning News* in November, 1845, "except that which actual possession gives. They belong to whoever will redeem them from the Indian and the desert, and subjugate them to the use of man. Title by discovery is nothing unless sustained by occupancy. . . . And such a shadowless title is all that Great Britain makes to Oregon." In the House of Representatives John Quincy Adams called upon the clerk to read from Genesis: "Be fruitful, and multiply, and replenish the earth, and subdue it. . . ."[31] To Adams this Biblical command gave the American

[31] For Adams' remarks see *Congressional Globe* (29th Cong., 1st Sess., 1846), p. 342.

people better right to the region than the Hudson's Bay Company. England desired Oregon merely for navigation and hunting while the United States wished to carry out the behest of the Almighty and "to make the wilderness blossom as the rose."

Finally Democratic expansionists based the American title to Oregon on the nation's right to guarantee the future welfare and security of its citizens. O'Sullivan, in the New York *Morning News*, December 27, 1845, pointed to the "duty and the right of providing the necessary accommodation for all this stupendous future of the American destiny." Similarly Baker observed that the United States had a continent before it in which to "spread our free principles, our language, our literature, and power; and we had the present right to provide for the future progress. To do this was to secure our safety, in the widest and highest sense; and thus our destiny had become so manifest that it could not fail but by our own folly."[32] Herein lay the right of vital necessity.

Armed by such allegedly uncontestable claims to Oregon, the ultras in Congress condemned every tendency toward compromise with Britain at the 49th parallel. "Away with the siren cry of concession and compromise," cried John C. McClernand in January, 1846, "inexorable *destiny* interposes her iron sceptre to forbid it. Shame! Why should we *recede* to the 49th parallel while Britain *advances* to the same line?"[33] Some Democrats openly declared that they preferred war to compromise. "Shall we pause in our career, or retrace our steps," demanded Andrew Kennedy of Indiana, in January, 1846, "because the British lion has chosen to place himself in our path? Has our blood already become so pale that we should tremble at the roar of the King of Beasts? We will not go out of our way to seek a conflict with

[32] Baker's speech of January 3, 1846, *Congressional Globe* (29th Cong., 1st Sess., 1846), p. 136.

[33] *Congressional Globe* (29th Cong., 1st Sess., 1846), Appendix, p. 277.

him; but if he crosses our path, and refuses to move at a peaceful command, he will run his nose in the talons of the American eagle, and his blood will spout as from a harpooned whale."[34]

Whatever the American dreams of empire along the Pacific's shores, they would be fulfilled by President Polk or not at all. Polk's accession to the White House seemed to assure the force of executive leadership behind the nation's expansionist program. His professed adherence to both the Texas and the whole-of-Oregon issues in the 1844 campaign seemed to place him in the camp of the true believers in manifest destiny. Yet his expansionism was less clearly expressed and far less boisterous than that of such enthusiasts as Cass and Douglas. His natural reserve was accentuated after his election by the burden of responsibility. However, Polk entered the White House at least outwardly committed to the acquisition of Oregon up to the Alaska line. In his inaugural address he insisted that the American title was "clear and unquestionable."[35]

When Polk assumed command of America's external relations in the spring of 1845 the United States had uncontested claims on the Pacific only up to that commercially impractical, but undeniably beautiful, coast which lay between 42° and the Columbia River. North of the Columbia the United States was in conflict with an expanding British Empire, supported by the Hudson's Bay Company. As late as the forties Oregon remained in a state of equilibrium between two westward-moving empires struggling for mastery of the Northwest coast. Almost thirty years of diplomacy had produced no boundary settlement for the simple reason that no American diplomatist, beginning with John Quincy Adams, would accept the Columbia River line. The reason was clear: such a settlement would not achieve for the United States any of its essential interests in the Pacific Northwest.

[34] *Congressional Globe* (29th Cong., 1st Sess., 1846), p. 180.

[35] Richardson, ed., *Messages and Papers of the Presidents*, IV, 381.

Diplomacy would dispose of rival claims to Oregon only after it had resolved the deeper struggle for commercial position on the Pacific coast. Traders and seamen who had visited the Pacific coast of North America during the decade before 1845 had created a precise vision of the benefits to be gained from acquiring the region. Whatever their mission on that great ocean, they were without exception struck by the excellent quality of an Oregon waterway which ultimately would guide American expansion in the Far Northwest. All agreed that the Columbia River, which marked the northern extremity of American settlements in Oregon, was useless as an ocean port. Running the bar at its entrance was at best hazardous. By contrast, travelers agreed that the Fuca Strait and the sea arms to the east of it comprised one of the finest harbors in the world. Charles Wilkes, the American naval officer, presented this characteristic description in his *Narrative,* "Nothing can exceed the beauty of these waters, and their safety: not a shoal exists within the Straits of Juan de Fuca, Admiralty Inlet, Puget Sound, or Hood's Canal, that can in any way interrupt their navigation by a seventy-four gun ship. I venture nothing in saying there is no country in the world that possesses waters equal to these."[36] Here were the harbors of Oregon that could be entered or left under any wind or during any season. These waters were the objective of every American diplomatist—from John Quincy Adams to James K. Polk—who carried responsibility for the Oregon negotiations.

To achieve this traditional objective of American diplomacy required no less than a settlement at the 49th parallel, a settlement made possible by the decision of the Hudson's Bay Company to withdraw its chief post from Fort Vancouver on the Columbia to Vancouver Island north of Fuca Strait. Lord Aber-

[36] Charles Wilkes, *Narrative of the United States Exploring Expedition During the Years 1838, 1839, 1840, 1841, 1842* (Philadelphia: Lea and Blanchard, 1845), IV, 305.

deen admitted privately in 1844 that a settlement at the 49th parallel would comprise an acceptable division of ocean frontage between the United States and Great Britain. Whig Party leaders in the United States, convinced that a compromise at 49° was possible without force or the threat of force, clamored that the Oregon question be treated as a commercial interest, to be resolved by diplomacy without benefit of any overdemanding and ultimately meaningless references to manifest destiny.

Polk as President was the official spokesmen for two conflicting concepts of a feasible and proper settlement of the Oregon question. As titular head of the Democratic Party he was obligated to pursue nothing less than 54–40; as President of the United States he was the recipient of an established diplomatic tradition which favored a settlement along the 49th parallel as the best available without war. His choices were clear. He could assert the American claims to the whole of Oregon and demand an immediate settlement, or he could await the occasion for a satisfactory compromise arrangement with England, confident, as Calhoun had been, that time favored a British retreat from the Columbia River line. Addressing the Senate in January, 1843, Calhoun had defined and upheld the American policy of inaction. *"Time,"* he said, "is acting for us; and, if we shall have the wisdom to trust its operation, it will assert and maintain our right with resistless force, without costing a cent of money, or a drop of blood. There is often, in the affairs of government, more efficiency and wisdom in nonaction than in action. All we want to effect our object in this case, is 'a wise and masterly inactivity.' Our population is rolling toward the shores of the Pacific with an impetus greater than what we realize."[37]

Polk maintained the bold exterior required to coexist with

[37] Calhoun's speech of January 24, 1843, *Congressional Globe* (27th Cong., 3rd Sess., 1843), Appendix, p. 139. See also Calhoun to Pakenham, September 3, 1844, quoted in *Congressional Globe* (29th Cong., 1st Sess., 1846), Appendix, p. 26.

his Democratic colleagues, but privately accepted the conservative precedent which anchored American interests to waterways rather than to land. In July, 1845, he offered a settlement at 49°, for, he added, "the entrance of the Straits of Fuca, Admiralty Inlet, and Puget's Sound, with their fine harbors and rich surrounding soil, are all south of this parallel." (Document 10.) Polk accepted without question the verdict of American travelers that the Columbia River could never serve satisfactorily as an ocean port, that the Strait of Fuca and Puget Sound comprised one of the world's best harbors, and that the country north of 49° was unfit for agriculture and incapable of sustaining anything but the fur trade. With his advisers Polk doubted "whether the judgment of the civilized world would be in our favor in a war waged for a comparatively worthless territory north of 49°, which his predecessors had over and over again offered to surrender to Great Britain, provided she would yield her pretentions to the country south of that latitude." (Document 10.)

To assure the vocal Western Democratic leadership that he would remain true to the Baltimore platform, Polk in his message of December, 1845, requested from Congress the year's notice needed to terminate the British-American joint occupancy of Oregon, established as early as 1818. Through this request the President provoked another massive debate over Oregon's future, but his heart was not in it. In White House discussions with Congressional leaders Polk refused to take a stand. He understood well enough that the continued pursuit of the whole of Oregon would result in either interminable diplomatic drift, or war. Compromise, he acknowledged privately, would serve the national interest better than adherence to the alliterative abstraction of "54-40 or fight." In favoring compromise, Polk had the support of the entire Whig Party and two powerful factions of his own Democratic Party—those led by Calhoun and Van Buren. Through the practical, if unprecedented, device of submitting the British compromise proposal of the spring of 1846 to Congress for its prior advice,

Polk both gained a compromise at the 49th parallel and still managed to escape his political obligations to those who demanded that he acquire the whole of Oregon in the name of manifest destiny.

California no less than Oregon demanded its own peculiar expansionist rationale, for its acquisition confronted the United States with a series of problems not present in either the Texas or Oregon issues. If the government in Mexico City lacked the energy to control, much less develop, this remote province, its title was still as clear as its hold was ephemeral. The annexation of this outpost required bargaining with its owner. Even that possibility seemed remote in 1845, for the Mexican government had carried out its threat to break diplomatic relations with the United States rather than condone the American annexation of Texas. For a decade American citizens had drifted into the inland valleys and coastal villages of California, but in 1845 they still comprised an infinitesimal number, even when compared to the small Mexican and Indian population.

Obviously the United States could not achieve its continental destiny without embracing California. Yet this Mexican province had never been an issue in American politics; its positive contribution to American civilization had scarcely been established. California, moreover, because of its alien population, was by the established principles of American expansion less than acceptable as a territorial objective. American acquisitiveness toward Texas and Oregon had been ethnocentric; it rejected the notion of annexing allegedly inferior peoples. "There seems to be something in our laws and institutions," Alexander Duncan of Ohio reminded the House of Representatives early in 1845, "peculiarly adapted to our Anglo-Saxon-American race, under which they will thrive and prosper, but under which all others wilt and die."[38] He pointed to the decline of the French and Spanish on the North American continent when American laws had been extended to them. It was their unfitness for "liberal and equal laws, and equal institutions," he assumed, that accounted for this inability to prosper under the United States.

Such inhibitions toward the annexing of Mexican peoples gradually disintegrated under the pressure of events. The decision to annex Texas itself encouraged the process by weakening the respect which many Americans held for Mexico's territorial integrity, and thus pointed the way to further acquisitions in the Southwest. Having, through the annexation of Texas, passed its arm "down to the waist of the continent," observed the *Dublin Freeman,* the nation would certainly "not hesitate to pass it round."[39] That the United States was destined to annex additional portions of Mexican territory seemed apparent enough, but only when its population had been absorbed by the Anglo-Saxons now overspreading the continent. As early as 1845 the rapid migration of pioneers into California promised to render the province fit for eventual annexation. In July, 1845, the *Democratic Review* noted that Mexican influence in California was nearing extinction, for the Anglo-Saxon foot was on its border.

American acquisitiveness toward California, like that displayed toward Texas and Oregon, progressed at two levels—that of abstract rationalization and that of concrete national interest. Polk alone carried the responsibility for United States diplomacy with Mexico, and interpreted American objectives in the Southwest—like those in Oregon—as precise and deter-

---

[38] *Congressional Globe* (28th Cong., 2nd Sess., 1845), Appendix, p. 178.

[39] *Dublin Freeman* quoted in Frederick Merk, *Manifest Destiny and Mission in American History: A Reinterpretation* (New York: Alfred A. Knopf, 1963), p. 83.

mined by the sea. Travelers and sea captains of the early forties agreed that two inlets gave special significance to the California coast—the bays of San Francisco and San Diego. These men viewed San Francisco harbor with wonderment. Charles Wilkes assured the readers of his *Narrative* (Vol. V, p. 162) that California could boast "one of the finest, if not the very best harbor in the world." It was sufficiently extensive, he added, to shelter the combined navies of Europe. Thomas J. Farnham, the American traveler and writer, called it simply "the glory of the Western world."[40] All who had visited the bay observed that it was the unqualified answer to American hopes for commercial greatness in the Pacific. To the south lay San Diego Bay—the rendezvous of the California hide trade. Here, all Boston firms maintained their coastal depots for cleaning, drying, and storing the hides until a full cargo of thirty to forty thousand had been collected for the long journey to Boston. The processing and storing of hides required a warm port, free from rain, fog, and heavy surf. San Diego alone met all these requirements. This beautiful bay, so deep and placid that ships could lie a cable's length from the smooth, hard-packed, sandy beach, became the chief point of New England's interest on the California coast. The bay was exposed to neither wind nor surf, for it was protected for its entire fifteen-mile length and possessed a narrow, deep entrance. Richard Henry Dana observed in *Two Years Before the Mast* (1840) that San Diego harbor was comparable in value and importance to San Francisco Bay. The noted sea captain, Benjamin Morrell, once termed San Diego "as fine a bay for vessels under three hundred tons as was ever formed by Nature in her most friendly mood to mariners."[41]

During the autumn of 1845, even before his administration

[40] Thomas J. Farnham, *Life and Adventures in California* (New York: William H. Graham, 1846), pp. 352, 355.

[41] Captain Benjamin Morrell, *A Narrative of Four Voyages to the South Sea* (New York: J. & J. Harper, 1832), p. 200.

had disposed of the Oregon question, Polk embarked on a dual course to acquire at least a portion of California. English activity in that distant province convinced him that, in Great Britain, the United States faced a strong and determined competitor for possession, in particular, of San Francisco Bay. Thomas O. Larkin, an American merchant at Monterey, reported that the French and British governments maintained consuls in California although neither nation had any commercial interests along the Pacific coast. "Why they are in Service their Government best know and Uncle Sam will know to his cost," Larkin warned in July, 1845.[42] Larkin's reports produced a wave of excitement in the administration. "The appearance of a British Vice Consul and French Consul in California at this present crisis without any apparent commercial business," Secretary of State James Buchanan answered Larkin, "is well calculated to produce the impression that their respective governments entertained designs on that country. . . ." On October 17, 1845, Buchanan drafted special instructions to Larkin:

The future destiny of that country is a subject of anxious solicitude for the government and people of the United States. The interests of our commerce and our whale fisheries on the Pacific Ocean demand that you should exert the greatest vigilance in discovering and defeating any attempts which may be made by foreign governments to acquire a control over that country. . . . On all proper occasions, you should not fail prudently to warn the government and people of California of the danger of such an interference to their peace and prosperity; to inspire them with a jealousy of European domination, and to arouse in their bosoms that love of liberty and independence so natural to the American continent.[43]

[42] Larkin to the New York *Journal of Commerce*, July, 1845, Hammond, ed., *The Larkin Papers*, III, 266–267, 292–293.

[43] Buchanan to Larkin, October 17, 1845, John Bassett Moore, ed., *The Works of James Buchanan* (Philadelphia: J. B. Lippincott Company, 1909), VI, 275.

Polk appointed Larkin as his confidential agent in California to encourage the Californians, should they separate from Mexico, to cast their lot with the United States. "While the President will make no effort and use no influence to induce California to become one of the free and independent states of the Union, yet," continued Buchanan's instructions, "if the people should desire to unite their destiny with ours, they would be received as brethren, whenever this can be done without affording Mexico just cause of complaint." Larkin was told to let events take their course unless Britain or France should attempt to take California against the will of its residents.

During November, 1845, Polk initiated the second phase of his California policy—an immediate effort to purchase the province from Mexico. On November 9, William S. Parrott, a long-time resident of Mexico now serving as Polk's special agent at the Mexican capital, returned to Washington with confirming information that the officials in Mexico City would receive an American envoy. As early as September Polk and his cabinet had agreed to tender such a mission to John Slidell of Louisiana. In his instructions to Slidell, dated November 10, Buchanan clarified the administration's objectives in California. In a variety of boundary proposals Polk was adamant only on one—the Rio Grande. Those that applied to California were defined solely in terms of Pacific ports. They started with San Francisco and Monterey, the capital of the province, but they included also a suggested boundary line which would reach westward from El Paso along the 32nd parallel to the Pacific, this extended as far as the harbor of San Diego. Unfortunately Slidell was not received by the Mexican government. The administration's program of acquiring at least one of the important harbors along the California coast by purchase from Mexico had failed.

From the defeat of their diplomacy to achieve a boundary settlement with Mexico Polk and his cabinet moved early in May, 1846, toward a recommendation of war, employing as the immediate pretext the refusal of the Mexican government to pay the claims of American citizens against it for their losses in Mexico. Before the cabinet could agree on such a drastic course of action, Polk received word that a detachment of General Zachary Taylor's forces stationed along the disputed Rio Grande boundary of Texas had been fired upon by Mexican forces. Armed with such intelligence, the President now phrased his message to obtain an immediate and overwhelming endorsement for a policy of force. Mexico, he charged, "has passed the boundary of the United States, has invaded our territory and shed American blood upon American soil."[44] War existed, in short, by act of Mexico. Polk explained that his action of stationing Taylor on the Rio Grande was not an act of aggression, but merely the attempt to occupy a disputed territory. Yet the possibility that the President had sought to provoke a clash of arms left sufficient doubt in the minds of his Whig opponents to permit them to make the Mexican War the most bitterly criticized in American history.

During the summer of 1846 the rapid American conquest of California quickly crystallized the expansionist arguments for the retention of the province. Indeed, California suddenly appeared totally satisfactory as a territorial addition. Amalgamation of the Mexican population no longer caused anxiety, for, as Andrew J. Donelson predicted, within five years the Anglo-American people would be dominant in the province. Lewis Cass in February, 1847, still believed any amalgamation between Americans and Mexicans quite deplorable. "We do not want the people of Mexico either as citizens or subjects," he warned, but then he added reassuringly with special reference to California, "all we want is a portion of territory which they nominally hold, generally uninhabited, or, where inhabited at

---

[44] War Message, *Congressional Globe* (29th Cong., 1st Sess., 1846), p. 782.

all, sparsely so, and with a population which would soon recede or identify itself with ours."[45] Buchanan, opposing the extension of the United States to the Sierra Madre Mountains, asked: "How should we govern the mongrel race which inhabit it?" Like Donelson and Cass, he harbored no fear of annexing California, for, he added, "The Californias are comparatively uninhabited and will therefore be almost exclusively colonised by our own people."[46]

There was little sentimentality in the *Democratic Review*'s prediction in March, 1847, that American pioneers in California would dispossess the inhabitants as they had the American Indians. It declared that evidently "the process which has been gone through at the North of driving back the Indians, or annihilating them as a race, has yet to be gone through at the south." Similarly the *American Review* that same month saw Mexicans giving way to "a superior population, insensibly oozing into her territories, changing her customs, and out-living, out-trading, exterminating her weaker blood. . . ."

California's immense potential as the seat of a rich empire, contrasted to its backwardness under Mexican rule, added a new dimension to the doctrine of manifest destiny—the regeneration of California's soil. As early as September, 1845, the St. Louis *Daily Missourian* observed that, despite the wonders of the region, under its present government it was "doomed to desolation and a barren waste, instead of the garden of the world." In a sublime passage the editor noted the need for its acquisition by the United States:

That Mexico shall domineer over it, merely for the sake of domineering, without calling forth its resources, to contribute to the comfort and happiness of man—that enterprise shall be prevented from

[45] Cass's speech of February 10, 1847, *Congressional Globe* (29th Cong., 2nd Sess., 1847), Appendix, 215.

[46] Buchanan to General James Shields, April 23, 1847, Buchanan Papers, Pennsylvania Historical Society.

entering, exploring and bringing forth the fruits of that rich field—that this delightful land should only be a theatre for robbery and plunder, instead of being devoted to the uses which nature and nature's God designed it, we cannot believe. But that it can become other than it now is, we cannot see, unless settled by our countrymen —which we believe, is inevitable, as it seems to be a law of nature, as a western statesman has well remarked, "that the children of Adam follow the sun;" or, as the poet has it, "Westward the star of empire holds its way."[47]

In its January, 1846, issue the *American Review* expanded this theme. After three centuries of Spanish and Mexican rule, California, despite its natural advantages, possessed no commerce, little agriculture, and no industry. In every respect, asserted the writer, the region was as devoid of wealth, cultivation, and power as when the Spaniards first sailed its coasts. But to him such conditions could not continue, for "No one who cherishes a faith in the wisdom of an overruling Providence, and who sees, in the national movements which convulse the world, the silent operation of an invisible but omnipotent hand, can believe it to be for the interest of humanity, for the well-being of the world, that this vast and magnificent region should continue forever in its present state. . . ." The assurance of expanding migration into California after the outbreak of the Mexican War merely emphasized the burgeoning American role of regeneration. Queried the *Illinois State Register* on July 10, 1846: "Shall this garden of beauty be suffered to lie dormant in its wild and useless luxuriance . . . ?" As United States territory, predicted the editor, "it would almost immediately be made to blossom like a rose; myriads of enterprising Americans would flock to its rich and inviting prairies; the hum of Anglo-American industry would be heard in its vales; cities would rise upon its plains and seacoast, and the resources and wealth of the nation be increased in an incalculable degree."

[47] St. Louis *Missouri Reporter*, September 1, 1845.

Polk, adequately supported by the Democratic expansionists in Congress, rationalized the American retention of California, not with references to the doctrine of regeneration, but with the principle of indemnity. "No terms can . . . be contemplated," O'Sullivan argued in July, 1846, "which will not require from [Mexico] indemnity . . . for the many wrongs which we have suffered at her hands. And if, in agreeing upon those terms, she finds it more for her interest to give us California than to satisfy our just demands in any other way, what objection can there be to the arrangement . . . ?"[48] Unfortunately for the President, indemnity, clearly recognized as a legitimate fruit of victory by the law of nations, was acceptable to only those Americans who placed responsibility of the war on Mexico. To those Whigs who attacked the war California constituted conquest, not indemnity, and therefore was scarcely an acceptable objective to be pursued through the agency of war. To achieve his wartime purpose—that of forcing territorial concessions from Mexico through a vigorous military policy—Polk was compelled to ask for increasing military appropriations from Congress. To shield himself from charges of conquest he defined, in his message of December 8, 1846, his objective as one to obtain "a honorable peace and thereby secure *ample indemnity* for the expenses of the war, as well as to our much-injured citizens. . . ."[49] He avoided assiduously any precise definition of the indemnification he sought. Not until December, 1847, did Polk explain his policy fully. He reminded Congress that "the doctrine of no territory is the doctrine of no indemnity; and, if sanctioned, would be a public acknowledgment that our country was wrong, and that the war declared by Congress with extraordinary unanimity was unjust, and should be abandoned."[50] The

[48] New York *Morning News,* July 10, 1846.

[49] Polk's message, *Congressional Globe* (29th Cong., 2nd Sess., 1847), p. 9.

[50] *Congressional Globe* (29th Cong., 2nd Sess., 1847), pp. 9, 305; *Congressional Globe* (30th Cong., 1st Sess., 1848), Appendix, p. 2.

indemnity he sought—and now made public—comprised the two Mexican provinces of California and New Mexico.

Polk maintained control of United States military and diplomatic policy throughout the course of the Mexican War, despite the persistent opposition and ridicule that he faced. But his initial purpose of exerting vigorous, if limited, pressure on the Mexican government—just enough to gain his precise territorial objectives—ended in miscalculation simply because no Mexican government would come forth to treat with the agents of a victorious United States. By the autumn of 1847 this growing conviction that the ephemeral nature of the Mexican government might prolong an expensive war indefinitely convinced the expansionist press that the United States had no choice but to meet her destiny and annex the entire Mexican republic.

New manifest destiny doctrines swept aside the older arguments against the annexation of other than Anglo-Saxon peoples. Now Mexico, like California, would be rescued from inefficient and corrupt rule, and regenerated by an infusion of American power and influence. The regeneration that could not be achieved by the United States armed forces would be accomplished by a rapid migration of settlers into Mexico. Here, indeed, were the essential agents of destiny. As the *Democratic Review* observed in October, 1847: "This occupation of territory by the people, is the great movement of the age, and until every acre of the North American continent is occupied by citizens of the United States, the foundation of the future empire will not have been laid." Expansionists were certain that the Mexican natives would quickly lose their identity before the onrush of American pioneers. "The Mexican race now see, in the fate of the aboriginees of the North, their own inevitable destiny," declared the *Democratic Review* (February, 1847). "They must amalgamate and be lost, in the superior vigor of the Anglo-Saxon race, or they must utterly perish." In December the New

York *Evening Post* charged that the Mexican people did not possess the elements to exist independently alongside the United States. "Providence has so ordained it," the *Post* continued, "and it is folly not to recognize the fact. The Mexicans are *Aboriginal Indians*, and they must share the destiny of their race." Similarly the Philadelphia *Public Ledger*, recalling Mexico's dismal past, predicted in November, 1847, that "the most intelligent and moral of the Mexican people will accommodate themselves to American, as far better than Mexican rule, and will insist . . . upon continuing American. Thus will annexation be forced upon us as the inevitable result of a long military occupation whether we want it or not."[51]

For expansionists the annexation of all Mexico was right because it was humane. The United States had no choice, warned the *Evening Post,* but to continue its military occupation to save Mexico from "the *uncontrolled* dominance of the mongrel barbarians, who, for a quarter of a century, have degraded and oppressed her." The New York *Sun* reminded its readers that the American mission was to liberate and ennoble. "Well may the Mexican nation, whose great masses have never yet tasted liberty," ran its editorial of October 22, "prattle over their lost phantom of nationality. . . . If they have not . . . the intelligence and manhood to accept the ranks and rights of freemen at our hands, we must bear with their ignorance."

During December and January, with Congress in session, Democratic orators seized control of the all-of-Mexico movement and carried this new burst of expansionism to greater heights of grandeur and extravagance. Their speeches rang with appeals to the nationalism of war and the cause of liberty. Cass observed that annexation would sweep away the abuses of generations. Senator Ambrose Sevier of Arkansas pointed to the progress that awaited the most degenerate Mexican population

[51] Philadelphia *Public Ledger* quoted in Merk, *Manifest Destiny and Mission in American History*, p. 116.

from the application of American law and education. In January, 1848, the Democratic Party of New York, in convention, adopted resolutions favoring annexation. The new mission of regeneration was proclaimed everywhere in the banquet toasts to returning officers. At one Washington dinner in January Senator Daniel Dickinson of New York offered a toast to "A more perfect Union: embracing the entire North American continent."[52] In Congress that month Senator R. M. T. Hunter of Virginia commented on the fever annexationism had stirred up. "Schemes of ambition, vast enough to have tasked even a Roman imagination to conceive," he cried, "present themselves suddenly as practical questions."[53] Both Buchanan and Walker of the cabinet, as well as Vice President George M. Dallas, openly embraced the all-of-Mexico movement.

That conservative coalition which had upheld the Oregon compromise combined again early in 1848 to oppose and condemn this new crusade. This powerful and well-led group feared that the United States, unless it sought greater moderation in its external policies, would drift into a perilous career of conquest which would tax the nation's energies without bringing any commensurate advantages. Its spokesmen doubted that the annexation of Mexico would serve the cause of humanity or present a new world of opportunity for American immigrants. Waddy Thompson, the South Carolina Whig who had spent many years in Mexico, warned in October against annexation: "We shall get no land, but will add a large population, aliens to us in feeling, education, race, and religion—a people unaccustomed to work, and accustomed to insubordination and resis-

[52] For such all-of-Mexico sentiment see *Niles' National Register*, LXXIII (January 22, 1848), 334–335; *Congressional Globe* (30th Cong., 1st Sess., 1848), Appendix, p. 446.

[53] See speech of R. M. T. Hunter in the Senate, January 3, 1848, Historical Pamphlets, Durrett Collection, University of Chicago Library.

tance to law, the expense of governing whom will be ten times as great as the revenues derived from them."[54] Thompson, joined by Calhoun and other Southern antiannexationists, warned the South that no portion of Mexico was suitable for slavery. Mexico's annexation would merely endanger the South's interests with a new cordon of free states. In Congress Calhoun acknowledged the dilemma created by the thoughtless decision to invade Mexico and recommended that the United States withdraw all its military forces to a defensive line across northern Mexico and maintain that line until Mexico chose to negotiate a permanent and satisfactory boundary arrangement with the United States.

Neither the mission of regeneration nor its rejection by conservatives determined the American course of empire. The great debate between those who anticipated nothing less than the achievement of a continental destiny and those who, in the interest of morality or from fear of a bitter controversy over slavery expansion, opposed the further acquisition of national territory, was largely irrelevant. Polk and his advisers pursued a precise vision, shared by those expansionists who searched the Mexican borderlands for the American interest. In the mid-forties, when the nation's agricultural frontier was still pushing across Iowa and Missouri, the concern of those who knew California lay less in land than in the configuration of the coastline and its possible relationship to America's future in the entire world of the Pacific. If American continentalism during the war years provided a substantially favorable climate for the acquisition of Mexican lands, it contributed nothing to the actual formulation of the administration's expansionist program.

During the early weeks of the Mexican War the President noted repeatedly in his diary that he would accept no treaty which did not transfer New Mexico and Upper California to the

[54] Thompson quoted in *The National Intelligencer*, October 21, 1847.

United States. It was left only to hammer out his precise war aims. Initially, Polk and his cabinet were attracted to San Francisco and Monterey. Several days after the outbreak of war George Bancroft, Secretary of the Navy, assured the Marblehead merchant, Samuel Hooper, that by mid-June the United States flag would be floating over these two northern California ports. "I hope California is now in our possession, never to be given up," he added. "We were driven reluctantly to war; we must make a solid peace. . . ."[55]

But Hooper did not rest at Bancroft's promise. He prodded the administration to look southward along the California coast. Settlement at the thirty-second parallel, Hooper informed Bancroft, would secure both Los Angeles and the bay of San Diego. Such a boundary, moreover, would encompass all the Anglo-American population in the province and remove future annoyance by leaving a barren wilderness between Upper California and the larger Mexican cities to the south. Should the United States acquire San Diego as well as Monterey and San Francisco, continued Hooper, "it would insure a peaceful state of things through the whole country and enable [the Americans] to continue their trade as before along the whole coast. . . ." Thereafter the administration looked to San Diego. Bancroft assured Hooper in June, 1846, that the administration would accede to New England's wishes. "If Mexico makes peace this month," he wrote, "the Rio del Norte and the Parallel of 35° may do as a boundary; after that 32° which will include San Diego."[56] This harbor remained the ultimate and unshakable territorial objective of Polk's wartime diplomacy.

Eventually the President achieved this goal through the efforts of Nicholas P. Trist. Unable after almost a year of success-

[55] Bancroft to Hooper, June 19, 1846, George Bancroft Papers, Massachusetts Historical Society.

[56] Bancroft to Hooper, June 22, 1846; Hooper to Bancroft, June 25, 1846, George Bancroft Papers.

ful fighting in Mexico to force the Mexican government to sue for terms, Polk, in April, 1847, dispatched Trist as a secret diplomatic agent to join General Winfield Scott's army in Mexico and await any sudden shift in Mexican politics. Trist's official baggage contained detailed instructions and the *projet* for a treaty which aimed pointedly at the acquisition of the entire coast of California to San Diego Bay. Trist's subsequent negotiations secured not only a treaty of peace with Mexico which terminated the war but also the administration's precise territorial objectives. Manifest destiny fully revealed itself in the Mexican War only when it clamored for the whole of Mexico, but even that final burst of agrarian nationalism was killed effectively by the Treaty of Guadalupe Hidalgo. American victories along the road to Mexico City were important only in that they created the force which permitted the President to secure through war what he had once hoped to achieve through diplomacy alone. It was Trist, working alone and unobserved, who in the final analysis defined the southern boundary of California.

CUBA AND THE DOCTRINE OF NATURAL GROWTH

After the acquisition of California the nation's expansionist activities went into momentary eclipse. Mexico was a dead issue, beyond resurrection, since American expansion into the Southwest was grounded on clearly-conceived interests that were now achieved. To the north, Canada had never completely escaped the encircling arm of destiny, for that area also comprised part of the continent. It was not that expansionists cared to challenge the British title, but rather that they anticipated the time when the Canadians, as lovers of freedom, would have the good judgment to cast off the British yoke and, in accordance with the American principle of expansion through consent, clamor for admission to the American Union. In 1853 the United States acquired the Gadsden Purchase, a strip of desert land south of the Gila River, for purposes of building railroads.

But if the notion of manifest destiny faltered for lack of an immediate territorial objective, Democratic orators soon discovered additional subjects for sustaining the American mission to humanity. One new object of their concern lay in Europe where the flame of revolution, which they boastfully attributed to the spark of American liberty, commenced in France early in 1848, spread quickly across the continent, and culminated finally in the Hungarian uprising against Hapsburg rule. Those who had proclaimed the vision of a continental Union, governed under free institutions, now identified American destiny with the cause of Europe's freedom from tyranny. From the beginning they lacked both the means and the intention to transform sentiment into action, and eventually the new crusade sputtered out as the revolutionary movements themselves ultimately failed. Even then the expansionist Democrats, attributing the collapse of the great revolutions of 1848 to the conservative Whig leadership, formed the Young America movement in 1852 to rekindle the nation's humanitarian emotions, capture control of the Democratic Party, secure the nomination of Stephen A. Douglas, and return the government to Democratic control. However, they failed to nominate their hero when the Democratic convention selected Franklin Pierce. Yet their persistent reiteration of the American mission to relieve the suffering of downtrodden humankind set the stage for the immediate revival of manifest destiny sentiment.

Cuba provided a controversy for politicians in search of an issue, for its proximity to the United States rendered its status, whenever it appeared to be under challenge, a matter of deep public concern. Southern politicians and editors had sustained a peculiar interest in the island, reminding the country periodically of the dismal state of Spanish colonial rule and demanding its acquisition by the United States. Much of the Cuban population was Negro, but its slave condition eliminated the problem of absorbing another colored population into the American Republic. Southern Democrats campaigned openly for the annexation of Cuba in 1852, and after November they anticipated a stronger and more purposeful foreign policy under the new Democratic administration.

Strangely, it was the conservative Whig Secretary of State, Edward Everett, who transformed Cuba into a question of immediate manifest destiny. In rejecting a British-French proposal for a three-power convention in which each nation would eschew permanently all designs on Cuba, Everett disclaimed any American intention to acquire the island. Cognizant of the nation's political realities, however, he refused to bind the United States for all time. In his long dispatch of December 1, 1852, he reminded British and French officials that American expansion had not resulted from any grasping spirit, but rather from the "law of American growth and progress," which was achieved either through peaceful agreements with other nations or through the irresistible movement of United States citizens into undeveloped territory.[57] Immediately Everett became a hero in the eyes of the Democratic expansionists. The *Democratic Review* deemed Everett's rejection "the best paper that has ever appeared on the subject from the State Department."[58] Douglas declared that no other document had ever received such universal acclaim from the American people.

Everett's doctrine of natural growth was not new. O'Sullivan had developed the thesis in the New York *Morning News* as early as January 5, 1846, when he observed that the United States had "reached a period which, like the marked physical transition in the human frame from the age of childhood to the noble stature and vigor of young manhood, is stamped with distinct features of expansion, change, development." The

[57] Everett to Count Sartiges, December 1, 1852, John Bassett Moore, *A Digest of International Law* (Washington: Government Printing Office, 1906), VI, 469.

[58] *Democratic Review,* XXXI (November-December, 1852), p. 433.

Democratic Review restated this proposition in May, 1848. Nations were living organisms, declared the writer, always on the increase or the decrease. When they ceased to grow they began to die.

This identification of American expansion with natural growth conformed to the requirements of the fifties and evolved into the decade's chief rationale for further territorial acquisitions. Douglas insisted that the law of natural growth sanctioned the breaking of treaties that might otherwise limit the possessions of the United States. The nation, he said, "must obey the law of increase, must multiply, and as fast as we multiply we must expand."[59] The *United States Review* asserted that whether the country's foreign affairs were "directed by a sot or a simpleton they will continue to grow and expand by a law of nature and a decree of Providence."[60] Again, in 1859, during that rebirth of expansionism directed toward Cuba, the *United States Democratic Review* reasserted the doctrine of natural growth: "We are governed by the laws under which the universe was created; and therefore, in obedience to those laws, we must of necessity move forward in the paths of destiny shaped for us by the great Ruler of the Universe."[61]

What made the dogma of natural growth so reassuring was the inevitability it derived from the working of natural law. Thus the fulfillment of American destiny in the Caribbean required neither conquest nor force. Milton S. Latham, Representative from California, commented that the laws of nature were "silent and secret, not boisterous and noisy, by fits and starts." (Document 36.) Parke Godwin recognized this inexorable work-

[59] *Congressional Globe*, (32nd Cong., 3rd Sess., 1853), Appendix, p. 273.

[60] Quoted in Weinberg, pp. 201–202.

[61] Quoted in Weinberg, p. 207.

ing of nature in behalf of the United States when he wrote
in 1854:

Precisely . . . because this tendency to the assimilation of foreign
ingredients, or to the putting forth of new members, is an inevitable
incident of our growth . . . there is no need that it should be especially fostered or stimulated. It will thrive of itself; it will supply the
fuel of its own fires; and all that it requires is only a wise direction.
. . . The fruit will fall into our hands when it is ripe, without an
officious shaking of the tree. Cuba will be ours, and Canada and
Mexico, too—if we want them—in due season, and without the
wicked imperative of a war.[62]

Expansionists proclaimed the doctrine of natural growth to
emphasize the peaceful quality of American progress. Yet their
persistent, if futile, search for the means to destroy Spanish
authority in Cuba illustrated their doubt that time alone would
fulfill the nation's destiny toward the coveted island. Cass in
December, 1852, admitted the limits of national action. He
would, he declared in the Senate, resist the transfer of Cuba to
another power; he would willingly pay Spain a reasonable price
for it. Should Cuba fight for her independence, she would have
his sympathy. Should she achieve independence he would, of
course, recognize it. In the meantime the United States had no
choice but to respect the existing colonial relationship. "So long
as Spain retains Cuba, or till the island becomes independent—
truly and honorably," he concluded, "we have no right to
interfere with it."[63]

Other expansionists, more determined, argued that the United
States had the right, if not the obligation, to break the Spanish
hold on Cuba. The rationale for freeing Cuba lay partially in
the American mission to humanity. "Has the whole circle of

[62] Parke Godwin, *Political Essays* (New York: Dix, Edwards and
Company, 1856), p. 169.

[63] "The Cuban Debate," *Democratic Review*, XXXI (November-
December, 1852), 436–437.

humanity, which looks on with astonishment and mortification at Spanish misrule of her last remaining colony," asked the *Democratic Review* in December, 1852, "no interest in the speedy and total overthrow of Spanish sovereignty and tyranny?" The second and clinching argument for terminating Spanish authority lay in the alleged outrages of the Spanish officials in Cuba against American citizens and the American flag. For such arbitrary treatment, moreover, there was no diplomatic recourse, since the American consul at Havana was permitted no direct communication with local Spanish authorities but only with the government in Madrid. The *Democratic Review* in October, 1852, anticipated a Democratic administration in Washington which would defend American interest in Cuba. Senator Stephen R. Mallory of Florida reminded his Congressional colleagues that only the policies of the United States had permitted Spain to maintain her possession of Cuba. The time had come, he declared, to terminate Spain's atrocious government in Cuba as well as her impudent behavior toward American seamen and ship captains. Late in January, 1853, Senator Pierre Soulé of Louisiana denied that Spain had any right at all to Cuba, and that to purchase the island would be tantamount to buying stolen goods. Spain, he warned, would not sell anyway. What remained for the United States, therefore, was a military conquest of the island. It was anticipated that with Spain's authority broken, Cuba would automatically enter the Union. "Once we are in possession," predicted the *Democratic Review* in 1852, "the public will of Cuba can be ascertained at once by an impartial and universal vote of the whites. But one result is possible, or credible. Cuba would rush under the folds of our flag, and blaze for ever in the circle of our stars."

Franklin Pierce entered the White House in March, 1853, determined to convert the burgeoning demand for Cuba into official policy. In his inaugural address he assured his supporters that his administration would not be controlled by any "timid forebodings of evil from expansion." Still, the times were not propitious for action. Pierce and his Secretary of State, William L. Marcy, agreed with Soulé that Spain would not sell the island. To exert direct force on the Spanish government might arouse a bitter reaction in England and France. Thus Marcy instructed Soulé, now the new American minister at Madrid, to make no proposal for the purchase of Cuba. However, in April, 1854, because of continuing pressure from Democratic expansionists, the Pierce administration instructed Soulé to offer Spain 130 million dollars for the island. If Spain refused, Soulé was to direct his efforts "to the next most desirable object which is to detach that island from the Spanish dominion. . . ."[64] At that moment, however, the Madrid government was in such a state of chaos that no Spanish official could possibly treat with an American diplomat on a matter as important as the permanent disposal of Cuba. Pierce now instructed Soulé to confer with John Y. Mason and James Buchanan, ministers to France and Britain respectively, and recommend a course of action for the United States.

In October, 1854, the three American diplomats, Soulé, Buchanan, and Mason, submitted their report from Aix-la-Chapelle —the notorious "Ostend Manifesto." The document was scarcely helpful. It repeated the old arguments for acquiring Cuba and declared that, if Spain refused to sell, "then by every law human and divine, we shall be justified in wresting it from Spain. . . ."[65] The reaction in both Europe and America was violent. Cass condemned any seizure of Cuba as an act of unacceptable rapacity. Even Marcy was shocked. Such a robbery, he wrote, "would degrade us in our own estimation and disgrace us in the eyes of the world."[66] The Secretary instructed Soulé to press the Spanish government no further.

[64] Marcy to Soulé, April 3, 1854, quoted in Allan Nevins, *Ordeal of the Union* (New York: Charles Scribner's Sons, 1947), II, 354.

[65] *House Ex. Doc. No. 93* (33rd Cong., 2nd Sess., 1854–1855) Serial 790, pp. 131–132.

[66] Marcy to Buchanan, July 2, 1853, quoted in Nevins, *Ordeal of the Union*, II, 363.

Spain was not the only impediment to the fulfillment of manifest destiny in the Caribbean. Cuba, as a territorial objective, defied the essential principles of American expansion. *DeBow's Review* in January, 1853, reminded its readers that the Cuban question had nothing in common with the acquisition of Texas:

We have never been able to see any good reason why Cuba should be annexed to the United States, even with the consent of Spain, and without the hazard of war. Texas furnished an outlet for overgrowing population. Cuba is already full, and would afford no homes for the enterprising emigrants from the United States. The present slave population, with its annual increase under the humane system of slavery which would follow its annexation, would be amply sufficient for all its wants. It would not, then, give us an outlet for our rapidly increasing slave population. The people of Texas had laws, institutions, manners and feelings similar to our own. In fact, Texas was colonized from this country. Such is not the case with Cuba. . . . Though under the same government, they would remain a distinct people.[67]

American conservatives subjected the doctrine of natural growth to persistent ridicule. Senator Jacob Collamer of Vermont noted that the Spanish title to Cuba was at least as good as the United States' title to Indian lands, and that it could be broken only by first provoking a quarrel with the Madrid regime. He denied that natural growth required territorial expansion. "A nation," he charged, "may grow in numbers, in wealth, in civilization, may grow for centuries, and never enlarge its territory one inch."[68] Others questioned the popular contention that America's future greatness and security required the annexation of Cuba. "The plea of an interest amounting to a *necessity* is false . . . ," observed *Hunt's Merchant's Magazine* in February, 1853. "We can be safe and great *without* Cuba. Our Gulf and

[67] "Cuba and the United States," *DeBow's Review*, XIV (January, 1853), 64–65.

[68] *Congressional Globe* (35th Cong., 2nd Sess., 1859), p. 1180.

Mississippi trade is likely, under the ability of self-protection we have now attained, to have just as free passage, inwardly and outwardly, if we do not acquire Cuba, as if we do—and might not be greatly disturbed, even were England its proprietor. With fortifications at Key West and other points on the Florida shore, and a fleet, if need be, in the channel, our merchant vessels would be tolerably secure of a way, at all times— quite as much so probably, as if we owned Cuba." Throughout the fifties such proponents of conservatism had their way.

SUMMARY AND CONCLUSION

Manifest destiny, in its evolution as a body of American thought, expressed a spirit of confidence and a sense of power. It set forth in extravagent language a vision of national greatness in territorial, political, or diplomatic concerns. It proclaimed a national mission to the downtrodden and oppressed, designed to rationalize in terms of a higher good the nation's right, and even its duty, to dispossess neighboring countries of portions of their landed possessions. But whatever its form and strength, manifest destiny was purely the creation of editors and politicians, expounded to churn the public's nationalistic emotions for the purpose of reaping larger political harvests. Those who preached the crusade created fanciful dreams of the Republic's future; they ignored specifics and were unmindful of means. They were ideologues, not statesmen.

Even their success in converting the nation to the wisdom or feasibility of their views was doubtful. It was the consideration of national interest alone that carried the annexations of the forties through Congress. In the case of Texas, where the final decision conformed to the will of the expansionists, the victory came hard. The Senate overwhelmingly rejected the Texas treaty of 1844, and only after months of intense party and sectional maneuvering—during which time the Texas issue became nationalized—was the joint resolution of annexation adopted by the narrow vote of 27 to 25. Where the nation would expand after Texas was the business of the national executive as the wielder of the nation's diplomacy, and the territory which the United States opened up across the continent to the Pacific satisfied a series of traditional and limited national interests. National growth itself had little or no connection with the continentalism which dominated the language of manifest destiny in the forties and which cloaked American expansionism with universal goals—abstract rather than precise. Manifest destiny created the sentiment that would underwrite governmental policies of expansion; it could not and did not create the policies themselves.

The Senate approved the Oregon Treaty of 1846 with an ample margin, but it was the minority of fourteen senators—the die-hard proponents of the whole-of-Oregon movement—who represented the cause of manifest destiny. The Oregon Treaty was a triumph for the moderates. Again, in 1848, the Senate agreed to the nation's expansion by accepting the Treaty of Guadalupe Hidalgo. But the Senate resolution which demanded more than California and New Mexico from the defeated enemy represented a futile effort to convert the all-of-Mexico sentiment into policy. It lost by eleven votes. The persistent failure of Democratic orators to achieve their declared political and diplomatic goals with appeals to both the emotions of patriotism and the actual record of American expansion culminated in their inability to elect their leading expansionist, Lewis Cass, to the White House in 1848.

Except for the Gadsden Purchase in 1853, a quiet transaction that responded to the needs of railroad building, the nation failed to expand between 1848 and 1860. However, manifest destiny suffered one last and glorious revival when, as late as 1859, James Buchanan sparked another burst of expansionism toward Cuba. But whatever the appeal of such sentiment in Washington, it had no influence in Madrid. Without the physical coercion of Spain there could be no expansion, and even those Americans who would accept the doctrine that the ends justified the means could not discover the "occasion"—at least one acceptable to the majority of United States citizens—for bringing the overwhelming power of the United States to bear on the weakening Spanish rule in Cuba.

American expansion before the Civil War, like all successful national action abroad, required specific and limited objectives, totally achievable within the context of diplomacy or force, whether that force be displayed or merely assumed. After national interest and diplomatic advantage combined, during the forties, to carry the United States to the Pacific, the necessary elements of policy and policy formulation never reoccurred to extend boundaries further. Perhaps it mattered little. The decade of the fifties—for the United States a decade of unprecedented internal development—amply proved the contention of the antiexpansionists that the country's material growth was not dependent upon its further territorial advancement.

Urbana, Illinois   *Norman A. Graebner*
February 1, 1967

Chronology

1836   Republic of Texas established.

1837   August: United States refuses Texas petition for annexation.

1843   Oregon settlers petition for territorial government.
       June: National convention at Cincinnati demands occupation of Oregon.

1844   May: Democratic Party Convention platform calls for "reoccupation of Oregon and the reannexation of Texas;" campaigns on slogan of "Fifty-Four Forty or Fight."
       June 8: Senate rejects treaty to annex Texas, 35–10.
       December 8: James K. Polk, Democrat, defeats Henry Clay, Whig for the presidency; popular vote: 1,337,243 to 1,299,068; electoral vote: 170 to 105.

1845   January 25: Congress annexes Texas by joint resolution. The vote was the House, 120–98; the Senate, 27–25.
       March 1: President John Tyler signs resolution of annexation.
       March 4: President Polk in his inaugural address asserts United States title to Oregon as "clear and unquestionable," and insists that the question of Texas belongs "exclusively to the United States and Texas."
       March 28: Mexico breaks diplomatic relations with the United States.
       June 15: General Zachary Taylor ordered to occupy a point "on or near the Rio Grande River" to defend the Texas territory.

July–August: John L. O'Sullivan first uses phrase, "Manifest Destiny," in the *United States Magazine and Democratic Review.*

October: General Taylor stations 3500 troops on the South Bank of the Nueces River, about 150 miles from the Rio Grande.

November 7: John L. Slidell dispatched on secret mission to Mexico to purchase Upper California and New Mexico and settle Texas boundary dispute.

December 2: In First Annual Message to Congress, Polk asks for power to abrogate convention of joint occupation of Oregon.

December 16: Mexican government informs Slidell that it will not receive him.

December 29: Texas admitted to the Union.

1846   January 12: Slidell's report reaches Washington.

January 13: General Taylor ordered to advance to the Rio Grande.

March: Slidell leaves Mexico after new Mexican government refuses to receive him.

April 23: Senate, 42–10; and House, 142–46, by joint resolution, authorize Polk to terminate joint occupation of Oregon.

April 25: Skirmish at Matamoros between troops of General Arista and General Taylor.

May 9: General Taylor's report reaches Washington that "hostilities may now be considered as commenced."

May 11: President Polk delivers war message to congress, asserting that "Mexico . . . has shed American blood on American soil."

May 11–12: Declaration of War passes House, 174–14; Senate, 40–2.

May 21: Polk serves notice on Britain of intention to abrogate joint treaty over Oregon.

June 6: British offer reaches Washington proposing Oregon boundary at 49°.

June 15: Senate ratifies Oregon treaty, 41–14.

June 15–July 5: Bear Flag Revolt in California.

July 7–August 17: Naval expedition to California.

August 17: Commodore Robert F. Stockton declares the annexation of California.

August 8: David Wilmot (Democrat, Penn.) introduces proviso to appropriations bill banning slavery in any territory to be acquired from Mexico.

1847   April 15: Nicholas Trist dispatched as Peace Commissioner.
August 27–September 6: Trist's negotiations with Mexico fail.
September 14: American capture of Mexico City.

1848   February 2: Treaty of Guadalupe Hidalgo negotiated.
March 10: Senate ratifies Treaty, 38–14.

1850   April 19: Clayton Bulwer Treaty signed with England over a canal in the Isthmus.

1851   August: failure of fillibustering expedition to Cuba led by General Narciso Lopez.

1852   December 1: Edward Everett's letter on Cuba.

1853   December 30: U.S. negotiates treaty with Mexico for Gadsden Purchase.

1854   October 18: Ostend Manifesto on Cuba.

1855   June–October: William Walker fillibustering expedition to Nicaragua.

1860   September: William H. Seward's speech, St. Paul, Minnesota.

Bibliographical Essay

Manifest destiny, as a body of national sentiment, poses a series of questions for students of history. What elements gave it birth? What objectives did it seek? To what extent did it determine the actual policies pursued by the United States government? For some historians the relationship between private opinion and public action is a matter of primary concern; for others it is not. Some significant writings on manifest destiny view it as a branch of American thought—nothing more or less than one important aspect of the intellectual history of the United States. Other studies attempt to relate the various territorial objectives encompassed by the doctrines of manifest destiny to the formulation of American diplomatic policy, and thereby account for the nation's success or failure in pursuing the goals of its expansionists. A third category of pertinent historical literature regards public opinion as irrelevant to national decisions and limits its analysis to the conflicting claims, interests, arguments, and proposals of rival governments in their negotiations over questions of American expansion. Much of the essential writing on American expansion, 1844–1860, has been general in scope, working largely with abstractions and ideas rather than with matters of concrete national interest; much of it has been specific and purely monographic, centering on single episodes, issues, or movements.

Of those volumes concerned with expansionism as a national sentiment, not as a guide for policy, the standard account is Albert K. Weinberg, *Manifest Destiny: A Study of Nationalist Expansionism in American History* (Baltimore: The Johns Hopkins Press, 1935). Ephraim D. Adams, *The Power of Ideals in American History* (New Haven: Yale University Press, 1913) contains a perceptive chapter on manifest destiny. Julius W. Pratt has contributed a useful introduction to American expansionist thought with "The Ideology of American Expansion," in Avery Craven (ed.), *Essays in Honor of William E. Dodd* (Chicago: University of Chicago Press, 1935). Pratt discovers the first use of the term "manifest destiny" in "The Origin of 'Manifest Destiny,'" *American Historical Review*, XXXII (July, 1927). A more recent study of American expansionism is Frederick Merk, *Manifest Destiny and Mission in American History: A Reinterpretation* (New York: Alfred A. Knopf, 1963). Merk, unlike most writers on manifest destiny, is concerned with the relationship between national expansionist thought and governmental policy. He concludes that the importance of manifest destiny has been vastly overrated, that it played no determining role in American expansion. Merk suggests that the United States, in its expansion across the continent, pursued clearly-conceived territorial objectives, defined by national interest and tradition. This theme has been more fully explored in Norman A. Graebner, *Empire on the Pacific: A Study in American Continental Expansion* (New York: The Ronald Press Company, 1955).

Many writers have left an indelible impression on the historiography of American expansion in the 1840's. General works on the diplomacy involving Texas, Oregon, and California are Jesse S. Reeves, *American Diplomacy under Tyler and Polk* (Baltimore: The Johns Hopkins Press, 1907); Eugene I. McCormac, *James K. Polk: A Political Biography* (Berkeley: University of California Press, 1922); and St. George L. Sioussat, "James Buchanan," in Samuel F. Bemis (ed.), *The American Secretaries of State and Their Diplomacy*, V (New York: Alfred A. Knopf, 1928). A more laudatory view of Buchanan's diplomacy can be found in P. S. Klein, *President James Buchanan* (University Park, Pa.: Pennsylvania State University Press, 1962). Richard W. Van Alstyne, *The Rising American Empire* (New York: Oxford University Press, 1960) contains a brief but highly perceptive account of the 1840's.

On the annexation of Texas the standard work remains Justin H. Smith, *The Annexation of Texas* (New York: The Baker and Taylor Company, 1911). A briefer account is Stanley Siegel, *A Political History of the Texas Republic* (Austin: University of Texas Press, 1956). Ephraim D. Adams has developed one important aspect of the question in his book, *British Interests and Activities in Texas, 1838–1846* (Baltimore: The Johns Hopkins Press, 1910). Downgrading the interest of France and Britain in an independent Texas are Henry Blumenthal, *A Reappraisal of Franco-American Relations, 1830–1871* (Chapel Hill: The University of North Carolina Press, 1959) and W. D. Jones, *Lord Aberdeen and the Americas* (Athens, Ga.: University of Georgia Press, 1958). On Texan diplomacy see Joseph M. Schmitz, *Texan Statecraft, 1836–1845* (San Antonio, Texas: Naylor Company, 1941). On land speculation as a factor in American activity see Elgin Williams, *The Animating Pursuits of Speculation* (New York: Columbia University Press, 1949). President Tyler's policy is surveyed in Oliver P. Chitwood, *John Tyler: Champion of the Old South* (New York: Appleton-Century-Crofts, 1939). Walker H. Donaldson describes the actions of another noted expansionist in "A Politician of Expansion: Robert J. Walker," *Mississippi Valley Historical Review*, XIX (December, 1932).

Writings on the Fifty-Four Forty movement regarding Oregon include Daniel W. Howe, "The Mississippi Valley in the Movement for Fifty-Four Forty or Fight," *Proceedings* of the Mississippi Valley Historical Association (1911–1912); Thomas Hart Benton, *Thirty Years' View*, II (New York: D. Appleton and Company, 1856); Robert L. Schuyler, "Polk and the Oregon Compromise," *Political Science Quarterly,* XXVI (September, 1911); and John Hope Franklin, "The Southern Expansionists of 1846," *Journal of Southern History,* XXV (August, 1959). Stressing the problems confronting Polk because of pressures within the Democratic Party are Norman A. Graebner, "Polk, Politics, and Oregon," The East Tennessee Historical Society's *Publications,* XXIV (1952) and "Politics and the Oregon Compromise," *Pacific Northwest Quarterly,* LII (January, 1961). Correcting some earlier misconceptions regarding the Fifty-Four Forty movement is E. A. Miles, " 'Fifty-four Forty or Fight'—An American Political Legend," *Mississippi Valley Historical Review,* XLIV (September, 1957).

Most historians have accepted the view that England alone retreated in the Oregon negotiations. Their writings, therefore, tend to analyze the British rather than the American position. A good general survey of the British view is Joseph Schafer, "The British Attitude toward the Oregon Question, 1815–1846," *American Historical Review,* XVI (January, 1911). Several useful studies which attribute the British inclination to compromise to the American pioneers are Frederick Merk, "Oregon Pioneers and the Boundary Settlement," *American Historical Review,* XXIX (July, 1924); Melvin C. Jacobs, *Winning Oregon: A Study of an Expansionist Movement* (Caldwell, Idaho: The Caxton Printers, 1938); Richard W. Van Alstyne, "International Rivalries in the Pacific Northwest," *Oregon Historical Quarterly,* XLVI (September, 1945); and Leslie M. Scott, "Influence of American Settlement upon the Oregon Boundary Treaty of 1846," *Oregon Historical Quarterly,* XXIX (March, 1928). The free-trade thesis in the Oregon compromise is developed by Thomas P. Martin, "Free Trade and the Oregon Question, 1842–1846," *Facts and Factors in Economic History: Articles by Former Students of Edwin Francis Gay* (Cambridge, Mass.: Harvard University Press, 1932). This thesis is challenged by Merk in "The British Corn Crisis of 1845–1846 and the Oregon

Treaty," *Agricultural History*, VIII (1934). On Aberdeen's leadership and British opinion are Merk, "British Government Propaganda and the Oregon Treaty," *American Historical Review*, XL (October, 1934) and his "British Party Politics and the Oregon Treaty," *American Historical Review*, XXXVII (July, 1932). Developing the view that Aberdeen thought little of Oregon and compromised readily is W. D. Jones, *Lord Aberdeen and the Americas* (Athens, Ga.: University of Georgia Press, 1958). That Polk favored compromise because of his fear of war is seen in Julius W. Pratt, "James K. Polk and John Bull," *The Canadian Historical Review*, XXIV (December, 1943). On the American rejection of arbitration and British opinion of Oregon see James O. McCabe, "Arbitration and the Oregon Question," *The Canadian Historical Review*, XLI (December, 1960). For the importance of ports in Oregon diplomacy challenging the traditional view see Merk, *Albert Gallatin and the Oregon Problem: A Study in Anglo-American Diplomacy* (Cambridge, Mass.: Harvard University Press, 1950) and Graebner, "Maritime Factors in the Oregon Compromise," *Pacific Historical Review*, XX (November, 1951). On French neutrality see Henry Blumenthal, *A Reappraisal of Franco-American Relations, 1830-1871* (Chapel Hill: The University of South Carolina Press, 1959). Some aspects of these questions are touched upon in Ray Allen Billington, *The Far Western Frontier, 1830–1860* (New York: Harper and Brothers, 1956).

On the early American interest in California the basic survey is Robert Glass Cleland, *Early Sentiment for the Annexation of California 1835–1846* (Austin: Texas State Historical Association, 1915). A somewhat different analysis can be found in Graebner, "American Interest in California, 1845," *Pacific Historical Review*, XXII (February, 1953). Noting the limited American infiltration into California before 1846 is John A. Hawgood, "The Pattern of Yankee Infiltration in Mexican Alta California, 1821–1846," *Pacific Historical Review*, XXVII (February, 1958). For the British interest in California see Ephraim D. Adams, "English Interest in the Annexation of California,"

American Historical Review, XIV (July, 1909) and Lester G. Engelson, "Proposals for the Colonization of California by England in Connection with the Mexican Debt to British Bondholders, 1837–1846," *California Historical Society Quarterly,* XVIII (June, 1939). On the French interest see Rufus Kay Wyllys, "French Imperialists in California," *California Historical Society Quarterly,* VIII (June, 1929); of some value on this theme is also George Vern Blue, "France and the Oregon Question," *Oregon Historical Quarterly,* XXXIV (March–June, 1933). Of special importance on French activities in California are Abraham P. Nasatir (ed.), *French Activities in California: An Archival Calendar-Guide* (Stanford: Stanford University Press, 1945) and "The French Consulate in California, 1843–1856," *California Historical Society Quarterly,* XI (September, 1932).

Polk's Mexican policy is traced in the writings of Jesse S. Reeves, Eugene I. McCormac, and St. George L. Sioussat, and has already been noted. Such standard works on the Mexican War as Justin H. Smith, *The War with Mexico,* 2 vols. (New York: The Macmillan Company, 1919) and George Lockhart Rives, *The United States and Mexico, 1821–1848,* 2 vols. (New York: C. Scribner's Sons, 1913) also contain material on Polk's diplomacy and the coming of the Mexican War. Presenting brief, but valuable, accounts of United States-Mexican relations are Samuel F. Bemis, *The Latin American Policy of the United States* (New York: Harcourt, Brace and Company, 1943) and James M. Callahan, *American Foreign Policy in Mexican Relations* (New York: The Macmillan Company, 1932). A brief and readable account of the military campaigns of the Mexican War is Otis A. Singletary, *The Mexican War* (Chicago: University of Chicago Press, 1960). Polk's techniques in pursuing his wartime goals amid enormous political opposition at home are analyzed in Graebner, "James K. Polk's Wartime Expansionist Policy," East Tennessee Historical Society's *Publications,* XXIII (1951).

General studies of the Treaty of Guadalupe Hidalgo are

Julius Klein, *The Making of the Treaty of Guadalupe Hidalgo on February 2, 1848* (Berkeley: University of California Press, 1905) and Jesse S. Reeves, "The Treaty of Guadalupe Hidalgo," *American Historical Review*, X (January, 1905). Two excellent accounts of the all-of-Mexico movement are Edward G. Bourne, "The United States and Mexico, 1847–1848," *American Historical Review*, V (April, 1900) and John D. P. Fuller, *The Movement for the Acquisition of All Mexico, 1846–1848* (Baltimore: The Johns Hopkins Press, 1936). Historians have generally been critical of Nicholas P. Trist in his conflict with the Polk administration. Louis M. Sears made an effort to rehabilitate Trist in his "Nicholas P. Trist, a Diplomat with Ideals," *Mississippi Valley Historical Review*, XI (June, 1924). Tracing Trist's relations with the Polk administration and his rejection for political reasons is Graebner, "Party Politics and the Trist Mission," *Journal of Southern History*, XIX (May, 1953). Explaining why Trist did not acquire Lower California is E. K. Chamberlin, "Nicholas Trist and Baja California," *Pacific Historical Review*, XXXII (February, 1963). The standard work on the Gadsden Purchase of 1853 is Paul Neff Garber, *The Gadsden Treaty* (Philadelphia: University of Pennsylvania Press, 1923).

The European revolutions of 1848 did not create any American territorial objectives in Europe, but they did stimulate the latent sense of democratic mission—always an essential element in the concept of manifest destiny. Several key writings on the American reaction to events in France and Central Europe after 1848 reveal the extent of revolutionary enthusiasm in the United States. On the American response to the revolutionary movement within Germany is J. G. Gazley, *American Opinion of German Unification, 1848–1871* (New York: Columbia University Press, 1926). Merle E. Curti deals with Austrian affairs in his "Austria and the United States, 1848–1852," *Smith College Studies in History*, XI, No. 3 (1926). Analyzing the impact of the European revolutions on American politics is Curti's "Young America," *American Historical Review*, XXXII (October, 1926).

A more detailed account of American reaction to Central European affairs is Arthur J. May, *Contemporary American Opinion of the Mid-Century Revolutions in Central Europe* (Philadelphia: University of Pennsylvania Press, 1927). The American view of the revolutions in France is treated in E. N. Curtis, "American Opinion of the French Nineteenth-Century Revolutions," *American Historical Review*, XXIX (January, 1924). Also useful are J. W. Oliver, "Louis Kossuth's Appeal to the Middle West—1852," *Mississippi Valley Historical Review*, XIV (December, 1928) and F. A. Golder, "Russian-American Relations during the Crimean War," *American Historical Review*, XXXI (April, 1926).

Historians have by no means neglected the region of the Caribbean; rather their writings reveal the importance of Cuba and Central America, especially, to the United States. Demonstrating the nature and extent of American acquisitiveness toward Cuba, especially after 1848, are P. S. Foner, *A History of Cuba and Its Relations with the United States*, 2 vols. (New York: International Publishers, 1963); Basil Rauch, *American Interest in Cuba: 1848–1855* (New York: Columbia University Press, 1948); two studies by Amos A. Ettinger, *The Proposed Anglo-Franco-American Treaty of 1852 to Guarantee Cuba to Spain*, in Royal Historical Society, London, *Transactions*, 4th series, Vol. 13 (1930) and *The Mission to Spain of Pierre Soulé, 1853–1855* (New Haven: Yale University Press, 1932); Henry L. Janes, "The Black Warrior Affair," *American Historical Review*, XII (January, 1907); Robert G. Caldwell, *The Lopez Expeditions to Cuba, 1848–1851* (Princeton: Princeton University Press, 1915); and G. B. Henderson, "Southern Designs on Cuba, 1854–1857, and Some European Opinions," *Journal of Southern History*, V (November, 1939). A perceptive analysis of one aspect of the question is John A. Logan, Jr., *No Transfer* (New Haven: Yale University Press, 1961). For the French view of the Cuba problem see Henry Blumenthal, *A Reappraisal of Franco-American Relations, 1830–1871* (Chapel Hill: The University of North Carolina Press, 1959). For additional study of the Ostend Manifesto episode the following two volumes are helpful: P. S. Klein, *President James Buchanan* (University Park, Pa.: Pennsylvania State University Press, 1962) and Ivor D. Spencer, *The Victor and the Spoils: A Life of William L. Marcy* (Providence: Brown University Press, 1959). C. S. Urban analyzes the role of the Cuban Negro in American thought in "The Africanization of Cuba Scare, 1853–1855," *Hispanic American Historical Review*, XXXVII (February, 1957).

On the American interest in the isthmian question the standard work is Mary W. Williams, *Anglo-American Isthmian Diplomacy, 1815–1915* (Washington: American Historical Association, 1916). Dexter Perkins, *The Monroe Doctrine, 1826–1867* (Baltimore: The Johns Hopkins Press, 1933) contains valuable material on the Isthmus. For a study of William Walker see William O. Scroggs, *Filibusters and Financiers: The Story of William Walker and His Associates* (New York: The Macmillan Company, 1916). Also essential for any study of the British-American rivalry in Central America after 1848 are a number of articles by Richard W. Van Alstyne: "The Central American Policy of Lord Palmerston, 1846–1848," *Hispanic American Historical Review*, XVI (August, 1936); "British Diplomacy and the Clayton-Bulwer Treaty, 1850–1860," *Journal of Modern History*, XI (June, 1939); and "Anglo-American Relations, 1853–1857: British Statesmen on the Clayton-Bulwer Treaty and American Expansion," *American Historical Review*, XLII (April, 1937).

PART ONE

THE ELEMENTS OF DESTINY

1   Ralph Waldo Emerson
"America is the country
of the future"

Manifest destiny conveyed a vision of greatness in all aspects of American life, from the immensity of the nation's territory open for exploration and extension, to its internal development and the quality of its government and civilization. The vision had well-grounded roots, for Americans of the 1840's had merely to observe their burgeoning population and economy to conclude that the United States was destined to become an increasingly powerful and influential member of the family of nations. Americans everywhere sensed the country's potential, and through essays, speeches, and editorials expressed their pride in its significant past and confidence in its limitless future.

Perhaps no American intellectual captured the spirit of the expanding nation more succinctly than did Ralph Waldo Emerson—the sensitive and penetrating critic of American society. In the following essay, delivered as a lecture before the Mercantile Library Association of Boston on February 7, 1844, he analyzed the elements of power and growth which gave such profound promise to the nation's future. He noted the impact of improving transportation facilities, especially railroads, on the tempo of American life, on education, engineering, architecture, agriculture, and commerce. He observed the relationship between the opportunities afforded by the size and resources of the United States and the imaginativeness of its people. He saw the relationship between the nation's political institutions and the unending flow of Europeans to American shores. "America," Emerson wrote, "is the country of the Future." But to

3

Emerson the nation's proper destiny lay in beneficence, not power, and in the country's ability to find in its science and productivity the relief of poverty and other human ills.

IT is remarkable, that our people have their intellectual culture from one country, and their duties from another. Our books are European. We were born within the frame and sphere of Shakespeare and Milton, of Bacon, Dryden and Pope; our college text-books are the writings of Butler, Locke, Paley, Blackstone, and Stewart; and our domestic reading has been Clarendon and Hume, Addison and Johnson, Young and Cowper, Edgeworth and Scott, Southey, Coleridge and Wordsworth, and the Edinburgh and Quarterly Reviews. We are sent to a feudal school to learn democracy. A gulf yawns for the young American between his education and his work. We are like the all-accomplished banker's daughter, who, when her education was finished, and her father had become a bankrupt, and she was asked what she could do for him in his sickness and misfortunes,—could she make a shirt, mix bread, scald milk pans? No, but she could waltz, and cut rice-paper, and paint velvet, and transfer drawings, and make satin stitch, and play on the clavichord, and sing German songs, and act charades, and arrange tableaux, and a great many other equally useful and indispensable performances. It has seemed verily so with the education of our young men; the system of thought was the growth of monarchical institutions, whilst those that were flourishing around them were not consecrated to their imagination nor interpreted to their understanding.

This false state of things is newly in a way to be corrected. America is beginning to assert itself to the senses and to the imagination of her children, and Europe is receding in the same degree. Thus their reaction on education gives a new importance

---

From Ralph Waldo Emerson, "The Young American," *Dial*, IV (April, 1844), 484–507, *passim*.

to the internal improvements and to the politics of the country.

There is no American citizen who has not been stimulated to reflection by the facilities now in progress of construction for travel and the transportation of goods in the United States. The alleged effect to augment disproportionately the size of cities, is in a rapid course of fulfillment in this metropolis of New England.

The growth of Boston, never slow, has been so accelerated since the railroads have been opened which join it to Providence, to Albany, and to Portland, that the extreme depression of general trade has not concealed it from the most careless eye. The narrow peninsula, which a few years ago easily held its thirty or forty thousand people, with many pastures and waste lands, not to mention the large private gardens in the midst of the town, has been found too strait when forty are swelled to a hundred thousand. The waste lands have been fenced in and builded over, the private gardens one after the other have become streets. Boston proper consisted of seven hundred and twenty acres of land. Acre after acre has been since won from the sea, and in a short time the antiquary will find it difficult to trace the peninsular topography. Within the last year, the newspapers tell us, from twelve to fifteen hundred buildings of all sorts have been erected, many of them of a rich and durable character. And because each of the new avenues of iron road ramifies like the bough of a tree, the growth of the city proceeds at a geometrical rate. Already a new road is shooting northwest towards the Connecticut and Montreal; and every great line of road that is completed makes cross sections from road to road more practicable, so that the land will presently be mapped in a network of iron.

This rage for road building is beneficent for America, where vast distance is so main a consideration in our domestic politics and trade, inasmuch as the great political promise of the invention is to hold the Union staunch, whose days seemed already numbered by the mere inconvenience of transporting representatives, judges, and officers, across such tedious distances of land and water. Not only is distance annihilated, but when, as now, the locomotive and the steamboat, like enormous shuttles, shoot every day across the thousand various threads of national descent and employment, and bind them fast in one web, an hourly assimilation goes forward, and there is no danger that local peculiarities and hostilities should be preserved. . . .

In an uneven country the railroad is a fine object in the making. It has introduced a multitude of picturesque traits into our pastoral scenery. The tunneling of mountains, the bridging of streams, the bold mole carried out into a broad silent meadow, silent and unvisited by any but its own neighbors since the planting of the region; the encounter at short distances along the track of gangs of laborers; the energy with which they strain at their tasks; the cries of the overseer or *boss;* the character of the work itself, which so violates and revolutionizes the primal and immemorial forms of nature; the village of shanties, at the edge of beautiful lakes until now the undisturbed haunt of the wild duck, and in the most sequestered nooks of the forest, around which the wives and children of the Irish are seen; the number of foreigners, men and women, whom now the woodsman encounters singly in the forest paths; the blowing of rocks, explosions all day, with the occasional alarm of frightful accident, and the indefinite promise of what the new channel of trade may do and undo for the rural towns, keep the senses and imagination active; and the varied aspects of the enterprise make it the topic of all companies, in cars and boats, and by firesides. . . .

The railroad is but one arrow in our quiver, though it has great value as a sort of yard-stick, and surveyor's line. The bountiful continent is ours, state on state, and territory on territory, to the waves of the Pacific sea;

> "Our garden is the immeasurable earth,
> The heaven's blue pillars are Medea's house,"

and new duties, new motives await and cheer us. The task of planting, of surveying, of building upon this immense tract, requires an education and a sentiment commensurate thereto. A consciousness of this fact, is beginning to take the place of the purely trading spirit and education which sprang up whilst all the population lived on the fringe of sea-coast. And even on the coast, prudent men have begun to see that every American should be educated with a view to the values of land. The arts of engineering and of architecture are studied; scientific agriculture is an object of growing attention; the mineral riches are explored; limestone, coal, slate, and iron; and the value of timber-lands is enhanced.

Columbus alleged as a reason for seeking a continent in the West, that the harmony of nature required a great tract of land in the western hemisphere, to balance the known extent of land in the eastern; and it now appears that we must estimate the native values of this immense region to redress the balance of our own judgment, and appreciate the advantages opened to the human race in this country, which is our fortunate home. The land is the appointed remedy for whatever is false and fantastic in our culture. The great continent we inhabit is to be physic and food for our mind, as well as our body. The land, with its tranquillizing, sanative influences, is to repair the errors of a scholastic and traditional education, and bring us into just relations with men and things. . . .

I look on such improvements, also, as directly tending to endear the land to the inhabitant, and give him whatever is valuable in local attachment. Any relation to the land, the habit of tilling it, or mining it, or even hunting on it, generates the feeling of patriotism. He who keeps shop on it, or he who merely uses it as a support to his desk and ledger, or to his manufactory, values it very little. The vast majority of the people of this country live by the land, and carry its quality in their manners and opinions. We in the Atlantic states, by position, have been commercial, and have, as I said, imbibed easily an European culture.

Luckily for us, now that steam has narrowed the Atlantic to a strait, the nervous, rocky West is intruding a new and continental element into the national mind, and we shall yet have an American genius. How much better when the whole land is a garden, and the people have grown up in the bowers of a paradise. Without looking, then, to those extraordinary social influences which are now acting in precisely this direction, but only at what is inevitably doing around us, I think we must regard the *land* as a commanding and increasing power on the American citizen, the sanative and Americanizing influence, which promises to disclose new powers for ages to come.

In the second place, the uprise and culmination of the new and anti-feudal power of Commerce, is the political fact of most significance to the American at this hour.

We cannot look on the freedom of this country, in connexion with its youth, without a presentiment that here shall laws and institutions exist on some scale of proportion to the majesty of nature. To men legislating for the vast area betwixt the two oceans, betwixt the snows and the tropics, somewhat of the gravity and grandeur of nature will infuse itself into the code. A heterogenous population crowding on all ships from all corners of the world to the great gates of North America, namely, Boston, New York, and New Orleans, and thence proceeding inward to the prairie and the mountains, and quickly contributing their private thought to the public opinion, their toll to the treasury, and their vote to the election, it cannot be doubted that the legislation of this country should become more catholic and cosmopolitan than that of any other. It seems so easy for America to inspire and express the most expansive and humane spirit; new-born, free, healthful, strong, the land of the laborer, of the democrat, of the philanthropist, of the believer, of the saint, she should speak for the human race. America is the country of the Future. From Washington, its capital city, proverbially 'the city of magnificent distances,' through all its cities, states, and territories, it is a country of beginnings, of projects, of vast designs, and expectations. It has no past: all has an onward and prospective look. And herein is it fitted to receive more readily every generous feature which the wisdom or the fortune of man has yet to impress.

Gentlemen, there is a sublime and friendly Destiny by which the human race is guided,—the race never dying, the individual never spared,—to results affecting masses and ages. Men are narrow and selfish, but the Genius, or Destiny, is not narrow, but beneficent. It is not discovered in their calculated and voluntary activity, but in what befalls, with or without their design. Only what is inevitable interests us, and it turns out that love and good are inevitable, and in the course of things. That Genius has infused itself into nature. It indicates itself by a small excess of good, a small balance in brute facts always favorable to the side of reason. All the facts in any part of nature shall be tabulated, and the results shall indicate the same security and benefit; so slight as to be hardly observable, and yet it is there. The sphere is found flattened at the poles, and swelled at the equator; a form flowing necessarily from the fluid state, yet *the* form, the mathematician assures us, required to prevent the great protuberances of the continent, or even of lesser mountains cast up at any time by earthquakes, from continually deranging the axis of the earth. The census of the population is found to keep an invariable equality in the sexes, with a trifling predominance in favor of the male, as if to counterbalance the necessarily increased exposure of male life in war, navigation, and other accidents. Remark the unceasing effort throughout nature at somewhat better than the actual creatures: *amelioration in nature,* which alone permits and authorizes amelioration in mankind. The population of the world is a conditional population; these are not the best, but the best that could live in the existing state of soils, of gases, animals, and morals: the best that could *yet* live; there shall be a better, please God. This Genius, or Destiny, is of the sternest administration, though rumors exist of its secret tenderness. It may be styled a cruel kindness, serving the whole even to the ruin of the member; a terrible communist, reserving all profits to the community, without dividend to individuals. Its law is, you shall have every thing as a member, nothing to yourself. For Nature is the noblest engineer, yet uses a grinding economy, working up all that is wasted today into tomorrow's creation;—not a superfluous grain of sand, for all the ostentation she makes of expense and public works. It is because Nature thus saves and uses, laboring for the general, that we poor particulars are so crushed and straitened, and find it so hard to live. She flung us out in her plenty, but we cannot shed a hair, or a paring of a nail, but instantly she snatches at the shred, and appropriates it to the general stock. Our condition is like that of the poor wolves: if one of the flock wound himself, or so much as limp, the rest eat him up incontinently. . . .

I pass in the third place to speak of the signs of that which is the sequel of trade.

It is in consequence of the revolution in the state of society wrought by trade, that Government in our times is beginning to wear so clumsy and cumbrous an appearance. We have already seen our way to shorter methods. The time is full of good signs. Some of them shall ripen to fruit. All this beneficent socialism is a friendly omen, and the swelling cry of voices for the education of the people, indicates that Government has other offices than those of banker and executioner. Witness the new movements in the civilized world, the Communism of France, Germany, and Switzerland; the Trades' Unions; the English League against the Corn Laws; and the whole *Industrial Statistics,* so called. In Paris, the blouse, the badge of the operative, has begun to make its appearance in the saloons. Witness too the spectacle of three Communities which have within a very short time sprung up within this Commonwealth, beside several others undertaken by citizens of Massachusetts within the territory of other States. These proceeded from a variety of motives, from an impatience of many usages in common life, from a wish for greater freedom than the manners and opinions of society permitted, but in great part from a feeling that the true offices of the State, the State had let fall to the ground; that in the scramble of parties for the public purse, the main duties of government were omitted,—the duty to instruct the ignorant, to supply the poor with work and with good guidance. These communists preferred the agricultural life as the most favorable condition for human culture; but they thought that the farm, as we manage it, did not satisfy the right ambition of man. The farmer, after sacrificing pleasure, taste, freedom, thought, love, to his work, turns out often a bankrupt, like the merchant. This result might well seem astounding. All this drudgery, from cockcrowing to starlight, for all these years, to end in mortgages and the auctioneer's flag, and removing from bad to worse. It is time to have the thing looked into, and with a sifting criticism ascertained who is the fool. It seemed a great deal worse because the farmer is living in the same town with men who pretend to know exactly what he wants. On one side, is agricultural chemistry, coolly exposing the nonsense of our spendthrift agriculture and ruinous expense of manures, and offering, by means of a teaspoonful of artificial guano, to turn a sandbank into corn; and, on the other, the farmer, not only eager for the information, but with bad crops and in debt and bankruptcy, for want of it. Here are Etzlers and countless mechanical projectors, who, with the Fourierists, undoubtingly affirm that the smallest union would make every man rich;—and, on the other side, is this multitude of poor men and women seeking work, and who cannot find enough to pay their board. The science is confident, and surely the poverty is real. If any means could be found to bring these two together! . . .

Gentlemen, the development of our American internal resources, the extension to the utmost of the commercial system, and the appearance of new moral causes which are to modify the state, are giving an aspect of greatness to the Future, which the imagination fears to open. One thing is plain for all men of common sense and common conscience, that here, here in America, is the home of man. After all the deductions which are to be made for our pitiful and most unworthy politics, which stake every gravest national question on the silly die, whether James or whether Jonathan shall sit in the chair and hold the purse, after all the deduction is made for our frivolities and insanities, there still remains an organic simplicity and liberty, which, when it loses its balance redresses itself presently, which offers opportunity to the human mind not known in any other region.

It is true, the public mind wants self-respect. We are full of vanity, of which the most signal proof is our sensitiveness to foreign and especially English censure. One cause of this is our immense reading, and that reading chiefly confined to the productions of the English press. But a more misplaced sensibility than this tenderness to fame on the subject of our country and civil institutions, I cannot recall. Could we not defend and apologize for the sun and rain. Here are we, men of English blood, planted now for five, six, or seven generations on this immense tract in the temperate zone, and so planted at such a conjuncture of time and events, that we have left behind us whatever old and odious establishments the mind of men had outgrown. The unsupportable burdens under which Europe staggers, and almost every month mutters 'A Revolution! a Revolution!' we have escaped from as by one bound. No thanks to us; but in the blessed course of events it did happen that this country was not open to the Puritans until they had felt the burden of the feudal system, and until the commercial era in modern Europe had dawned, so that without knowing what they did, they left the whole curse behind, and put the storms of the Atlantic between them and this antiquity. And the felling of the forest, and the settling, in so far of the area of this continent, was accomplished under the free spirit of trading communities with a complete success. Not by our right hand, or foresight, or skill, was it done, but by the simple acceptance of the plainest road ever shown men to walk in. It was the human race, under Divine leading, going forth to receive and inhabit their patrimony. And now, if any Englishman, or Frenchman, or Spaniard, or Russian, or

German, can find any food for merriment in the spectacle, make him welcome to shake his sides. There never was a people that could better afford to be the subject of a little fun, than we. An honest man may, perhaps, wonder how, with so much to call forth congratulation, our lively visitors should be so merry and critical. Perhaps they have great need of a little holiday and diversion from their domestic cares, like other house-keepers who have a heavy time of it at home, and need all the refreshment they can get from kicking up their feet a little now that they have got away on a frolic.

It is also true, that, to imaginative persons in this country, there is somewhat bare and bald in our short history, and unsettled wilderness. They ask, who would live in a new country, that can live in an old? Europe is to our boys and girls, what novels and romances are; and it is not strange they should burn to see the picturesque extremes of an antiquated country. But it is one thing to visit the pyramids, and another to wish to live there. Would they like tithes to the clergy, and sevenths to the government, and horse-guards, and licensed press, and grief when a child is born, and threatening, starved weavers, and a pauperism now constituting one-thirteenth of the population? Instead of the open future expanding here before the eye of every boy to vastness, would they like the closing in of the future to a narrow slit of sky, and that fast contracting to be no future? One thing, for instance, the beauties of aristocracy, we commend to the study of the travelling American. The English, the most conservative people this side of India, are not sensible of the restraint, but an American would seriously resent it. The aristocracy, incorporated by law and education, degrades life for the unprivileged classes. It is a questionable compensation to the embittered feeling of a proud commoner, the reflection that the worthless lord who, by the magic of title, paralyzes his arm, and plucks from him half the graces and rights of a man, is himself also an aspirant excluded with the same ruthlessness from higher circles, since there is no end to the wheels within wheels of this spiral heaven. Something may be pardoned to the spirit of loyalty when it becomes fantastic; and something to the imagination, for the baldest life is symbolic. Philip II of Spain rated his ambassador for neglecting business of great importance in Italy, whilst he debated some point of honor with the French ambassador; "You have left a business of importance for a ceremony." The ambassador replied, "How? for a ceremony? your majesty's self is but a ceremony." In the East, where the religious sentiment comes in to the support of the aristocracy, and in the Romish church also, there is a grain of sweetness in the tyranny; but in England, the fact seems to me intolerable, what is commonly affirmed, that such is the transcendent honor accorded to wealth and birth, that no man of letters, be his eminence what it may, is received into the best society, except as a lion and a show. It seems to me, that with the lights which are now gleaming in the eyes of all men, residence in that country becomes degradation to any man not employed to revolutionize it. The English have many virtues, many advantages, and the proudest history of the world; but they need all, and more than all the resources of the past to indemnify a heroic gentleman in that country for the mortifications prepared for him by the system of society, and which seem to impose the alternative to resist or to avoid it. That there are mitigations and practical alleviations to this rigor, is not an excuse for the rule. Commanding worth, and personal power must sit crowned in all companies, nor will extraordinary persons be slighted or affronted in any company of civilized men. But the system is an invasion of the sentiment of justice and the native rights of men, which, however decorated, must lessen the value of English citizenship. It is for Englishmen to consider, not for us: we only say, let us live in America, too thankful for our want of feudal institutions. Our houses and towns are like mosses and lichens, so slight and new; but youth is a fault of which we shall daily mend. And really at last all lands are alike. Ours, too, is as old as the Flood, and wants no ornament or privilege which nature could bestow. Here stars, here woods, here hills, here animals, here men abound, and the vast tendencies concur of a new order. If only the men are well employed in conspiring with the designs of the Spirit who led us hither, and is leading us still, we shall quickly enough advance out of all hearing of other's censures, out of all regrets of our own, into a new and more excellent social state than history has recorded.

2   John L. O'Sullivan

"The Great Nation of Futurity"

Under the editorship of John L. O'Sullivan, the *Democratic Review*, in the years following 1838, became a powerful mouthpiece for the varying notions that eventually evolved into the idea of manifest destiny. The following essay was almost revolutionary in its conceptualization of the nation's destiny, for as early as November, 1839, it identified the American mission to humanity with the need for territorial expansion. What dictated the course of American destiny, the essay proposed, was the principle of equality which underlay the country's social and political system and distinguished it from that of the European monarchies. In fulfilling its mission the United States would enjoy a boundless future, becoming, in time, a nation of many nations, a union of many republics. O'Sullivan urged the people of the United States to have less exchange with Europe and develop instead those business and intellectual pursuits that would strengthen the American principle of equality.

THE American people having derived their origin from many other nations, and the Declaration of National Independence

From "The Great Nation of Futurity," *The United States Magazine and Democratic Review*, VI (November, 1839), 426–430.

being entirely based on the great principle of human equality, these facts demonstrate at once our disconnected position as regards any other nation; that we have, in reality, but little connection with the past history of any of them, and still less with all antiquity, its glories, or its crimes. On the contrary, our national birth was the beginning of a new history, the formation and progress of an untried political system, which separates us from the past and connects us with the future only; and so far as regards the entire development of the natural rights of man, in moral, political, and national life, we may confidently assume that our country is destined to be *the great nation* of futurity.

It is so destined, because the principle upon which a nation is organized fixes its destiny, and that of equality is perfect, is universal. It presides in all the operations of the physical world, and it is also the conscious law of the soul—the self-evident dictate of morality, which accurately defines the duty of man to man, and consequently man's rights as man. Besides, the truthful annals of any nation furnish abundant evidence, that its happiness, its greatness, its duration, were always proportionate to the democratic equality in its system of government.

How many nations have had their decline and fall, because the equal rights of the minority were trampled on by the despotism of the majority; or the interests of the many sacrificed to the aristocracy of the few; or the rights and interests of all given up to the monarchy of one? These three kinds of government have figured so frequently and so largely in the ages that have passed away, that their history, through all time to come, can only furnish a resemblance. Like causes produce like effects, and the true philosopher of history will easily discern the principle of equality, or of privilege, working out its inevitable result. The first is regenerative, because it is natural and right; the latter is destructive to society, because it is unnatural and wrong.

What friend of human liberty, civilization, and refinement, can cast his view over the past history of the monarchies and aristocracies of antiquity, and not deplore that they ever existed? What philanthropist can contemplate the oppressions, the cruelties, and injustice inflicted by them on the masses of mankind, and not turn with moral horror from the retrospect?

America is destined for better deeds. It is our unparalleled glory that we have no reminiscences of battle fields, but in defence of humanity, of the oppressed of all nations, of the rights of conscience, the rights of personal enfranchisement. Our annals describe no scenes of horrid carnage, where men were led on by hundreds of thousands to slay one another, dupes and victims to emperors, kings, nobles, demons in the human form called heroes. We have had patriots to defend our homes, our liberties, but no aspirants to crowns or thrones; nor have the American people ever suffered themselves to be led on by wicked ambition to depopulate the land, to spread desolation far and wide, that a human being might be placed on a seat of supremacy.

We have no interest in the scenes of antiquity, only as lessons of avoidance of nearly all their examples. The expansive future is our arena, and for our history. We are entering on its untrodden space, with the truths of God in our minds, beneficent objects in our hearts, and with a clear conscience unsullied by the past. We are the nation of human progress, and who will, what can, set limits to our onward march? Providence is with us, and no earthly power can. We point to the everlasting truth on the first page of our national declaration, and we proclaim to the millions of other lands, that "the gates of hell"— the powers of aristocracy and monarchy—"shall not prevail against it."

The far-reaching, the boundless future will be the era of American greatness. In its magnificent domain of space and time, the nation of many nations is destined to manifest to mankind the excellence of divine principles; to establish on earth the noblest temple ever dedicated to the worship of the Most High—the Sacred and the True. Its floor shall be a hemisphere —its roof the firmament of the star-studded heavens, and its congregation an Union of many Republics, comprising hundreds of happy millions, calling, owning no man master, but governed by God's natural and moral law of equality, the law of brotherhood—of "peace and good will amongst men."

But although the mighty constituent truth upon which our social and political system is founded will assuredly work out the glorious destiny herein shadowed forth, yet there are many untoward circumstances to retard our progress, to procrastinate the entire fruition of the greatest good to the human race. There is a tendency to imitativeness, prevailing amongst our professional and literary men, subversive of originality of thought, and wholly unfavorable to progress. Being in early life devoted to the study of the laws, institutions, and antiquities of other nations, they are far behind the mind and movement of the age in which they live: so much so, that the spirit of improvement, as well as of enfranchisement, exists chiefly in the great masses— the agricultural and mechanical population.

This propensity to imitate foreign nations is absurd and injurious. It is absurd, for we have never yet drawn on our mental resources that we have not found them ample and of unsurpassed excellence; witness our constitutions of government, where we had no foreign ones to imitate. It is injurious, for never have we followed foreign examples in legislation; witness our laws, our charters of monopoly, that we did not inflict evil on ourselves, subverting common right, in violation of common sense and common justice. The halls of legislation and the courts of law in a Republic are necessarily the public schools of the adult population. If, in these institutions, foreign precedents are legislated, and foreign decisions adjudged over again, is it to be wondered at that an imitative propensity predominates amongst professional and business men. Taught to look abroad for the highest standards of law, judicial wisdom, and literary excellence, the native sense is subjugated to a most obsequious idolatry of the tastes, sentiments, and prejudices of Europe. Hence our legislation, jurisprudence, literature, are more reflective of foreign aristocracy than of American democracy.

European governments have plunged themselves in debt, designating burthens on the people "national blessings." Our State Legislatures, humbly imitating their pernicious example, have pawned, bonded the property, labor, and credit of their constituents to the subjects of monarchy. It is by our own labor, and with our own materials, that our internal improvements are constructed, but our British-law-trained legislators have enacted that we shall be in debt for them, paying interest, but never to become owners. With various climates, soils, natural resources, and products, beyond any other country, and producing more real capital annually than any other sixteen millions of people on earth, we are, nevertheless, borrowers, paying tribute to the money powers of Europe.

Our business men have also conned the lesson of example, and devoted themselves body and mind to the promotion of foreign interests. If States can steep themselves in debt, with any propriety in times of peace, why may not merchants import merchandise on credit? If the one can bond the labor and property of generations yet unborn, why may not the other contract debts against the yearly crops and daily labor of their contemporary fellow citizens?

And our literature!—Oh, when will it breathe the spirit of our republican institutions? When will it be imbued with the God-like aspiration of intellectual freedom—the elevating principle of equality? When will it assert *its* national independence, and speak the soul—the heart of the American people? Why cannot our literati comprehend the matchless sublimity of our position amongst the nations of the world—our high destiny— and cease bending the knee of foreign idolatry, false tastes, false doctrines, false principles? When will they be inspired by the magnificent scenery of our own world, imbibe the fresh enthusiasm of a new heaven and a new earth, and soar upon the ex-

panded wings of truth and liberty? Is not nature as original—
her truths as captivating—her aspects as various, as lovely, as
grand—her Promethean fire as glowing in this, our Western
hemisphere, as in that of the East? And above all, is not our
private life as morally beautiful and good—is not our public life
as politically right, as indicative of the brightest prospects of
humanity, and therefore as inspiring of the highest conceptions?
Why, then, do our authors aim at no higher degree of merit, than
a successful imitation of English writers of celebrity?

But with all the retrograde tendencies of our laws, our judica-
ture, our colleges, our literature, still they are compelled to follow
the mighty impulse of the age; they are carried onward by the
increasing tide of progress; and though they cast many a longing
look behind, they cannot stay the glorious movement of the
masses, nor induce them to venerate the rubbish, the prejudices,
the superstitions of other times and other lands, the theocracy of
priests, the divine right of kings, the aristocracy of blood, the
metaphysics of colleges, the irrational stuff of law libraries. Already the brightest hopes of philanthropy, the most enlarged
speculations of true philosophy, are inspired by the indications
perceptible amongst the mechanical and agricultural population. There, with predominating influence, beats the vigorous
national heart of America, propelling the onward march of the
multitude, propagating and extending, through the present and
the future, the powerful purpose of soul, which, in the seven-
teenth century, sought a refuge among savages, and reared in
the wilderness the sacred altars of intellectual freedom. This
was the seed that produced individual equality, and political
liberty, as its natural fruit; and this is our true nationality. American patriotism is not of soil; we are not aborigines, nor of ancestry, for we are of all nations; but it is essentially personal
enfranchisement, for "where liberty dwells," said Franklin, the
sage of the Revolution, "there is my country."

Such is our distinguishing characteristic, our popular instinct,
and never yet has any public functionary stood forth for the

rights of conscience against any, or all, sects desirous of predominating over such right, that he was not sustained by the people. And when a venerated patriot of the Revolution appealed to his fellow-citizens against the over-shadowing power of a monarch institution, they came in their strength, and the moneyed despot was brought low. Corporate powers and privileges shrink to nothing when brought in conflict against the rights of individuals. Hence it is that our professional, literary, or commercial aristocracy, have no faith in the virtue, intelligence or capability of the people. The latter have never responded to their exotic sentiments, nor promoted their views of a strong government irresponsible to the popular majority, to the will of the masses.

Yes, we are the nation of progress, of individual freedom, of universal enfranchisement. Equality of rights is the cynosure of our union of States, the grand exemplar of the correlative equality of individuals; and while truth sheds its effulgence, we cannot retrograde, without dissolving the one and subverting the other. We must onward to the fulfilment of our mission—to the entire development of the principle of our organization—freedom of conscience, freedom of person, freedom of trade and business pursuits, universality of freedom and equality. This is our high destiny, and in nature's eternal, inevitable decree of cause and effect we must accomplish it. All this will be our future history, to establish on earth the moral dignity and salvation of man—the immutable truth and beneficence of God. For this blessed mission to the nations of the world, which are shut out from the life-giving light of truth, has America been chosen; and her high example shall smite unto death the tyranny of kings, hierarchs, and oligarchs, and carry the glad tidings of peace and good will where myriads now endure an existence scarcely more enviable than that of beasts of the field. Who, then, can doubt that our country is destined to be *the great nation* of futurity?

3

"Democracy must finally reign"[1]

Manifest Destiny captured the nation with the possibilities of expansion only after it had identified territorial expansion with a sense of mission. This mission demanded some appreciation of the unique qualities of American civilization, the relationship of those qualities to human reason and character, and the human requirements for individual development and expression. The editor of the *Democratic Review* saw that American society lacked nothing in making a profound contribution to governmental progress all over the world, and that the essence of the nation's uniqueness lay in its democratic system. The following essay establishes the bases of good government—that it be founded on personal representation, that it seek the good of its members, and that it permit those whom it serves the right to change it. Democracy, the writer concludes, must finally reign. But he discovers the power of democracy to expand in the appeal of that governmental system to human reason. He is, therefore, not concerned with the precise role that the United States should or must play in the expansion of democratic principles.

DEMOCRACY must finally triumph in human reason, because its foundations are deep in the human heart. The great mass, whose souls are bound by a strong fraternal sympathy, once relieved from ancient prejudice, will stand forth as its moveless champions. It fastens the affections of men, as the shield of their present liberties and the ground of their future hopes. They perceive

From "Democracy," *Democratic Review*, VII (March, 1840), 215–229.

[1] This editorial was very likely written by John L. O'Sullivan.

in it a saving faith, a redeeming truth, a regenerating power. It is the only creed which does justice to man, or that can bind the entire race in eternal chains of brotherhood and love. Nothing sinks so deep into the hearts of the multitude, for nothing else is so identified with their moral and social good. Though the high and mighty of the earth may deride its simple truths, these are willing to die in their defence. Those truths are blended too closely with all for which it is worthy to live and glorious to perish, to be relinquished without a struggle or a pang. They are too firmly allied to the imperishable hopes, the deathless aspirations, the onward triumphant march of humanity, ever to be deserted. The fortunes of individuals may change—empires be born and blotted out—kings rise and fall—wealth, honor, distinction, fade as the dying pageant of a dream—but Democracy must live. While man lasts it must live. Its origin is among the necessary relations of things, and it can only cease to be when eternal truth is no more. . . .

Democracy, in its true sense, is the last best revelation of human thought. We speak, of course, of that true and genuine Democracy which breathes the air and lives in the light of Christianity—whose essence is justice, and whose object is human progress. We have no sympathy with much that usurps the name, like that fierce and turbulent spirit of ancient Greece, which was only the monstrous misgrowth of faction and fraud, or that Democracy whose only distinction is the slavelike observance of party usages—the dumb repetition of party creeds; and still less for that wild, reckless spirit of mobism which triumphs, with remorseless and fiendish exultation, over all lawful authority, all constituted restraint. The object of our worship is far different from these; the present offering is made to a spirit which asserts a virtuous freedom of act and thought— which insists on the rights of men—demands the equal diffusion of every advantage—asks the impartial participation of every gift of God—sympathizes with the down-trodden—rejoices in their elevation—and proclaims to the world the sovereignty, not of the people barely, but of immutable justice and truth. . . .

That man has some rights, we say, is a fact beyond the limits of a lawful doubt; it is a fact presupposed in some sense in all political ratiocination; it is a fact of universal consciousness, which can no more be disbelieved than the existence of self; it is a fact which admits no formal demonstration, for itself is the groundwork and first-truth of demonstration. The best proof of its legitimacy is the appeal to each individual truth. It rests on instincts which are broad, bursting manifestations of Nature—on convictions which spring up spontaneously with the earliest as well as mightiest unfoldings of human thought which are developed in the child and the savage, and ever wield, under every sky, despotic influence over the volitions of human will. The spirit of resistance is never more instantly or violently aroused, than when these spontaneous convictions of right are infringed. No people, how stupid in mind or degraded in morals soever, which has not felt their might—so inseparable are they from human existence, so powerfully active over all the movings of human impulse. Years of oppression cannot wholly eradicate or dim their force, whilst they grow stronger and firmer with intellectual progress and moral elevation. Man has rights. To every faculty of his organization there is annexed the consciousness of a right to its use, of a right to invigorate and expand it, to multiply its objects and unfold its power. . . .

Government is the agent of society, the organ through which its purposes are declared and its will executed. It is the instrument by which the few exert the delegated power of the many. Its origin is in the weakness or wickedness of men. To protect the feeble from the strong, the good from the bad, each from all and all from each, is its prominent design. Would all conform to the natural laws of their being, its functions would be exceedingly simple and few. Vice, intolerance, precipitancy, crime of all sorts, create the necessity for complex forms and strong powers of government. The best government is that whose rule of action is simple justice to all. Justice is the supreme, sovereign arbiter of the world—of higher authority than either the edict of royalty, the decrees of party, or the injunctions of law. The state's most indispensable duty is to provide for its impartial administration. Thus fastening to it, by indissoluble bonds, the affinities of every individual and class, it will establish a social union more stable than the hills, and more harmonious than the spheres.

If it be true, then, that men are equal in respect to their rights —that they enter society on common ground—that government is the agent of all—there are momentous inferences which the truth plainly involves.

I. The basis of representation is the person. Neither birth, wisdom nor wealth confers on its possessor an exclusive right to legislative control, or, what is the same thing, an exclusive right to select those in whom the legislation is placed. Power emanates from the people: it is transiently delegated by society to be wielded for its benefit. It is transferred to representatives to guard and facilitate its exercise. Every individual is interested in its use or abuse; for it is his own power relinquished for a moment, with a view to his higher security and good. Property qualifications are but little regarded in these States. The prevailing theoretical doctrine is, the majority of the whole number must rule. Objections to this principle, however sturdily advanced, have fallen, one after another, before the triumphant experiment of our free people. . . . The majority of a free populace has no inducement to go wrong. They cannot be long deluded. They have no exclusive affinities to cloud their perceptions or warp their judgments. Their whole interest is on the side of order and right. They have no partial or unjust laws to sustain, no privileges to perpetuate, no selfish relations to protect, and no corrupting ambition to gratify. They cannot live at the expense of the few. Their dependence must be upon themselves. Their resources and strength must be drawn from themselves; whilst their frantic excesses, if any, must fall with full severity upon their own heads. Privileged classes, on the other hand, whether their exclusiveness be founded on birth or acquisition of any sort, have always plans of their own to accomplish. Their very existence depends upon the maintenance of their assumed superiority. Their entire interest is centered in the retention of power already possessed, and the usurpation of as much more as can be gained. . . . The stability and safety of a people corresponds with the extent of their freedom from unequal legislation or unjust control.

II. Again: As government is the agent of society, its operation must be directed to the good of all its members. In this we include more than is commonly meant by that very indefinite phrase, "the general good"—a phrase to which the lives and fortunes of millions have been wantonly sacrificed. The great object of government is to secure every man in the enjoyment of his rights. Beyond this, it should not meddle with the affairs of men. There is provision for the existence and growth of society in our very constitution. It seems to be imagined by many that human nature must be fostered, fondled, or stimulated to exertion by legislative interposition. They forget those great principles at the bottom of that nature which compel the use of every faculty. The injunction to labor there written is far more imperative than human law could make it; for its motives are ever vigilant and active. While a thousand clamorous desires reign in the human breast; while man shall seek his highest happiness; while he shall delight in advancement and conquest; while industry will add to his comfort, and indolence prove the inevitable source of misery and death; no mode of exertion, no means of production, no road to improvement, will be left untried. The movements of human thought are not more tireless than the springs of human action. A curiosity which is never satisfied, an instinct ever effective, appetites more importunate than death, impulses like steeds restlessly panting and champing for the race, are ever urging the human being to additional, accumulated effort. Under this influence, no benefit will be allowed to elude his grasp; every prospect of personal advantage will be readily embraced; every hope of gain will be realized; he will traverse distant seas, explore the wildest woods, face every difficulty, and only cease to act when he has ceased to live. We may rest assured that labor will be put forth whenever it will meet with success, and capital will be applied where it shall command the best return. The agency of government is obviously not required here. The movings of self-interest are too powerful to need extraneous aid. The interference of legislation will only blind its eyes, and diminish its strength. It will infallibly prove a burden and a curse. From the necessity of the case, it must ever be partial; and if so, it is an infringement of natural right, an abandonment of the first principles of social union, a perversion of the clearest doctrines of science, a usurpation of power, and the infliction of the grossest wrong. The form in which it is manifested cannot alter the fact. Whether it be done by granting monopolies of any branch of trade, by conferring reward and distinction on a chosen few, by deputing privileges of an honorable or commercial sort, by yielding facilities to any department of business, by forcing industry into unusual channels, by imposing restraints on particular interests, by subjecting certain men to liabilities from which other men are exempt, or by fostering the wealth of some classes at the expense of the rest, it is equally odious and unjust. In every shape, these restrictions are hostile to the plainest rights of person and property, prejudicial to the growth and destructive of the peace of society. We conceive that every man has a right to employ his productive means, in whatever they consist, in a mode to ensure the largest returns, or most consistent with his notions of propriety. His only limit is the regard which is due to the rights of his fellow men. . . .

III. As the will of the whole people is the source, and their good the end, of government, it is manifest they may at any time effect its change. They may accomplish any revolution which their growing civilization demands. They may adapt the structure of all its departments to whatever state public morality and intelligence requires. Their naked right none but the sturdiest adherents of unrelenting despotism will deny. But in the practical determination of a change, parties will inevitably arise; they will arrange themselves under the operation of necessary influences and principles springing from the diversity of human nature. The interests fostered by established systems, through the natural instinct of selfishness, will speedily form themselves into conservative bands. Their dependents, through all the ramifications of society, will hasten to swell the same ranks; while the naturally timid, dubious as to the virtue of their fellow-men, averse to change, conjuring up dismal prospects of future anarchy and misrule, will enlist under the same banners. To these will be gathered the wealth and fashion which draws its existence from old customs and laws—the privilege which subsists on ancient error—and the talent which, accustomed to profound veneration, never travels beyond a beaten track. They will be met, on the other hand, by the untutored yet unsophisticated mass, and those bold, independent men of genius who intuitively seize the right, and labor with fearless self-denying energy for human progress. The contest will be intense, as the interests and principles involved are great. As it embraces the great doctrines of science, the first-truths of government, the welfare of nations, and the destinies of a race, a long warfare will infringe on the civilities of life, will break the restraints of law, will estrange friends, will throw the sword into families, and give rein to the wildest excesses of passion. Yet it is not difficult to tell where victory will perch. The rights and happiness of the many will prevail. Democracy must finally reign. There is in man an eternal principle of progress which no power on earth may resist. Every custom, law, science, or religion, which obstructs its course, will fall as leaves before the wind. Already it has done much, but will do more. The despotism of force, the absolutism of religion, the feudalism of wealth, it has laid on the crimson field; while the principle, alive, unwounded, vigorous, is still battling against nobility and privilege with unrelaxing strength. It is contending for the extinction of tyranny, for the abolition of prerogative, for the reform of abuse, for the amelioration of government, for the destruction of monopoly, for the establishment of justice, for the elevation of the masses, for the progress of humanity, and for the dignity and worth of the individual man. . . .

4   Charles Wilkes

Commercial Destiny in the Pacific

As an expanding nation, the destiny of the United States pointed westward—across the continent to the Pacific and thence across the Pacific to the Orient. Even Thomas Jefferson foresaw that the United States would some day become a major Pacific power, with ports along the Pacific joined to the Mississippi Valley with important avenues of commerce. Senator Thomas Hart Benton of Missouri, in his noted Senate speech of March, 1825, predicted a close relationship between the United States and the countries of eastern Asia. He saw, at that early date, that the United States would provide the Asians with access to American commerce and institutions, and that the Asians would support the United States against the more ambitious powers of Europe.

Ultimately, the nation would be forced to define concrete and achievable objectives along the Pacific coast that might serve its interests in the regions bordering the great ocean. These objectives would, of necessity, be defined in physical, not idealistic, terms. Among those objectives which excited the vision of American expansionists were several known ports along the Pacific coast. With the exception of the noted overland explorer, John Charles Fremont, the literary travelers of the forties approached the regions of Oregon and California from the sea. What they saw was so clear and dramatic that their writings bore a marked resemblance. They were concerned with four waterways—the Strait of Juan de Fuca, the Columbia River, San Francisco Bay, and the harbor of San Diego. Charles Wilkes, captain of the official United States exploring expedition in the Pacific during the years 1838 to 1842, visited the first three of these inlets, and his varying impressions were typical of all who saw them. Wilkes, no less than others, detected the natural connection between the American possession of the two great harbors of Juan de Fuca Strait and San Francisco Bay and the extension of American influence in the Pacific sea trade.

on the 28th of April, at 6 A. M., we made Cape Disappointment, which we soon came up with. A heavy sea, caused by the strong winds that had prevailed for several days, was running. I, notwithstanding, stood for the bar of the Columbia river, after making every preparation to cross it; but on approaching nearer, I found breakers extending from Cape Disappointment to Point Adams, in one unbroken line.

I am at a loss to conceive how any doubt should ever have existed, that here was the mouth of the mighty river, whose existence was reported so long before the actual place of its discharge was known, or how the inquiring mind and talent of observation of Vancouver could have allowed him to hesitate, when he must have seen the evidence of a powerful flood of fresh water contending with the tides of the ocean, in a bar turbulent with breakers, in turbid waters extending several miles beyond the line of the shore, and in the marked line of separation between the sea and river water. Such appearances must be constant, and if seen, the inferences could hardly be

---

From Charles Wilkes, *Narrative of the United States Exploring Expedition During the Years 1838, 1839, 1840, 1841, 1842* (Philadelphia, 1845), IV, 293–296, 305, 320–321, V, 145, 148, 151–152, 157, 158, 171–172.

questionable, that the great river of the west poured into the ocean at this point.

Mere description can give little idea of the terrors of the bar of the Columbia: all who have seen it have spoken of the wildness of the scene, and the incessant roar of the waters, representing it as one of the most fearful sights that can possibly meet the eye of the sailor. The difficulty of its channel, the distance of the leading sailing marks, their uncertainty to one unacquainted with them, the want of knowledge of the strength and direction of the currents, with the necessity of approaching close to unseen dangers, the transition from clear to turbid water, all cause doubt and mistrust.

Under such feelings I must confess that I felt myself laboring; and, although I had on board a person from the Sandwich Islands who professed to be a Columbia river pilot, I found him at a loss to designate the true passage, and unable to tell whether we were in a right way or not. I therefore, at once, determined to haul off with the tide, which was running ebb with great rapidity, and which soon carried us back into the blue water of the ocean, to wait there until the sea on the bar had in some measure subsided. . . .

During the night, I took into consideration the loss of time that must arise from awaiting an opportunity to cross the bar, and after due reflection came to the conclusion that it would be better to proceed at once to the Straits of Juan de Fuca, and there begin my work on this coast. . . .

The coast of Oregon, to the south of Cape Flattery, is rocky, much broken, and affords no harbours, except for very small vessels. It may therefore be considered as extremely dangerous, and particularly on account of its outlying rocks. The soundings on this coast, however, I afterwards discovered, may serve as a sure indication by which danger may be avoided, and safety may be insured by not approaching the coast into soundings of less than seventy fathoms.

On the morning of the 1st of May, we found ourselves well

into the straits; and as I proposed to defer the survey of this part of them until my return, we hastened to reach Port Discovery, where we anchored at half-past 6 p. m. on the 2d of May; just forty-nine years after Vancouver, pursuing the track of De Fuca, had visited the same harbour.

The Straits of Juan de Fuca may be safely navigated. The wind will for the greater part of the year be found to blow directly through them, and generally outwards: this wind is at times very violent. The shores of the strait are bold, and anchorage is to be found in but few places. We could not obtain bottom in some places with sixty fathoms of line, even within a boat's length of the shore.

The south shore is composed of perpendicular sandy cliffs, that run back into high and rugged peaks, and is covered with a forest of various species of pines, that rises almost to the highest points of the range of mountains. The highest points themselves are covered with snow; and among them Mount Olympus was conspicuous, rising to an altitude of eight thousand one hundred and thirty-eight feet. . . .

Nothing can exceed the beauty of these waters, and their safety: not a shoal exists within the Straits of Juan de Fuca, Admiralty Inlet, Puget Sound, or Hood's Canal, that can in any way interrupt their navigation by a seventy-four gun ship. I venture nothing in saying, there is no country in the world that possesses waters equal to these. . . . [Later Wilkes and his party explored the valley of the Columbia and then moved down the river to Astoria in preparation for their voyage along the coast to California.]

In point of beauty of situation, few places will vie with Astoria. It is situated on the south side of the Columbia river, eleven miles from Cape Disappointment, as the crow flies. From Astoria there is a fine view of the high promontory of Cape Disappointment, and the ocean bounding it on the west; the Chinook Hills and Point Ellice, with its rugged peak, on the north; Tongue Point and Katalamet Range on the east; and a high background, bristling with lofty pines, to the south. The ground rises from the river gradually to the top of a ridge five hundred feet in elevation. This was originally covered with a thick forest of pines: that part reclaimed by the first occupants is again growing up in brushwood. From all parts of the ground the broad surface of the river is in view. The stillness is remarkable, and makes it evident that one is yet far removed from civilized life: the distant though distinct roar of the ocean is the only sound that is heard: this, however, is almost incessant; for the stream, though rushing onwards in silence to meet the ocean, keeps up an eternal war with it on the bar, producing at times scenes of great grandeur, but which, as we had already experienced, renders the bar wholly impassable for days together. . . .

The Columbia, opposite to Astoria, is four miles wide, but in the middle of the river is an extensive sand-bar, with only a few feet water on it, and at extreme low tides it is bare: the channel is very narrow on each side and difficult to navigate. At Astoria there is only space for a dozen vessels to lie at anchor, and it would therefore be difficult to accommodate any extensive trade. The point of land extends about half a mile below its site, where Young's river joins the Columbia, and forms a bay, on the banks of which Lewis and Clarke wintered. The position of their hut is still pointed out, but the building has long since gone to decay. . . .

On the 5th, the prospect of passing the bar was favourable, and at 2^h 30^m P. M. the Company's bark Columbia, which had been lying off and on for the last week, entered. On passing the vessels she saluted us, and proceeded up to river to Astoria. At 3^h 30^m, I determined on making the attempt to get to sea. We quickly got the vessels under way, and in an hour afterwards we had passed the bar in safety.

The Cadborough followed our example, and went to sea also. Her master, before we got under way, had strong misgivings as to undertaking the risk at so late an hour both of the day and tide. The vessels of the Hudson Bay Company never attempt to pass either in or out, unless the opportunity is such as will warrant the master in making the attempt. They consider that there is sufficient risk at the best of times, and are unwilling to increase it. I have already stated that the entrance to the Columbia is impracticable for two-thirds of the year. This arises from the fact that it can never be entered at night, and in the day only at particular times of the tide and direction of the wind. Unlike all known ports, it requires both the tide and wind to be contrary, to insure any degree of safety. . . .

The coast south of the Columbia river I regretted we had not an opportunity more particularly to examine: the attempt of the Flying-Fish was unsuccessful; the season had advanced so far as to make it next to impossible to accomplish it in the manner I desired. I have no reason to doubt the correctness of the examinations that have been already made. No ports exist along any part of it, that are accessible to any class of vessels, even those of but very small draught of water; and the impediment that the constant and heavy surf offers, along the whole coast, to a landing in boats, makes this part of our territory comparatively valueless in a commercial point of view. Along a great part of it is an iron-bound shore, rising precipitately from the water. Anchorage in a few places may be had, but only in fair weather, and during the fine season. . . .

On approaching the coast in the neighborhood of San Francisco, the country has by no means an inviting aspect. To the north, it rises in a lofty range, whose highest point is known as the Table Hill, and forms an iron-bound coast from Punto de los Reyes to the mouth of the harbour.

To the south, there is an extended sandy beach, behind which rise the sand-hills of San Bruno, to a moderate height. There are no symptoms of cultivation, nor is the land on either side fit for it; for in the former direction it is mountainous, in the latter sandy, and in both barren. The entrance to the harbour is striking; bold and rocky shores confine the rush of the tide, which bore us on and through a narrow passage into a large estuary: in this, several islands and rocks lie scattered around: some of the islands are clothed with vegetation to their very tops; others are barren and covered with guano, having an immense number of sea-fowls hovering over, around, and alighting upon them. The distant shores of the bay extend north and south far beyond the visible horizon, exhibiting one of the most spacious, and at the same time safest ports in the world. To the east rises a lofty inland range, known by the name of La Sierra, brilliant with all the beautiful tints that the atmosphere in this climate produces.

Yerba Buena is the usual though by no means the best anchorage. The town, as is stated, is not calculated to produce a favourable impression on a stranger. Its buildings may be counted, and consist of a large frame building, occupied by the agent of the Hudson Bay Company, a store, kept by Mr. Spears, an American, a billiard-room and bar, a poop cabin of a ship, occupied as a dwelling by Captain Hinckley, a blacksmith's shop, and some out-buildings. These, though few in number, are also far between. With these, I must not forget to enumerate an old dilapidated adobe building, which has a conspicuous position on the top of the hill overlooking the anchorage. When to this we add a sterile soil and hills of bare rock, it will be seen that Yerba Buena and the country around it are any thing but beautiful. This description holds good when the tide is high, but at low water it has for a foreground an extensive mud-flat, which does not add to the beauty of the view.

Although I was prepared for anarchy and confusion, I was surprised when I found a total absence of all government in California, and even its forms and ceremonies thrown aside.

After passing through the entrance, we were scarcely able to distinguish the Presidio; and had it not been for its solitary flagstaff, we could not have ascertained its situation. From this staff no flag floated; the building was deserted, the walls had fallen to decay, the guns were dismounted, and every thing around it lay in quiet. . . .

Upper California may boast one of the finest, if not the very best harbour in the world,—that of San Francisco, as before described. Few are more extensive or could be as readily defended as it; while the combined fleets of all the naval powers of Europe might moor in it. This is, however, the only really good harbour which this country possesses; for the others so called may be frequented only during the fine season, being nothing more than roadsteads, affording little safety and but few supplies to vessels.

Among these bays are that of Monterey, the capital of Upper California, and that of Santa Barbara and San Pedro. The two last are partly protected from the swell of the Pacific Ocean by the islands that cover them. They are, however, but seldom used, there being comparatively little trade upon all this coast; for the hides and tallow which formerly abounded and made the business profitable for vessels, are no longer to be procured. The destruction of the missions, and the onerous laws, duties, and prohibitions, have nearly destroyed the little traffic that once existed, and it is now all transferred to the bay of San Francisco. There a few hulks may be seen lying, furnished with every needful article: these keep up an illicit intercourse by the connivance of the officers of the customs, by whose cupidity the revenue laws are openly infringed, and what of right belongs to the government, goes to enrich the governor and his officers. . . .

The situation of Upper California will cause its separation from Mexico before many years. The country between it and Mexico can never be anything but a barren waste, which precludes all intercourse except that by sea, always more or less interrupted by the course of the winds, and the unhealthfulness of the lower or seaport towns of Mexico. It is very probable that this country will become united with Oregon, with which it will perhaps form a state that is destined to control the destinies of the Pacific. This future state is admirably situated to become a powerful maritime nation, with two of the finest ports in the world,—that within the straits of Juan de Fuca, and San Francisco. These two regions have, in fact, within themselves every thing to make them increase, and keep up an intercourse with the whole of Polynesia, as well as the countries of South America on the one side, and China, the Philippines, New Holland, and New Zealand, on the other. Among the latter, before many years, may be included Japan. Such various climates will furnish the materials for a beneficial interchange of products, and an intercourse that must, in time, become immense; while this western coast, enjoying a climate in many respects superior to any other in the Pacific, possessed as it must be by the Anglo-Norman race, and having none to enter into rivalry with it but the indolent inhabitants of warm climates, is evidently destined to fill a large space in the world's future history. . . .

PART TWO

TEXAS

5 William E. Channing

"With Texas, we shall have no peace"

National sentiment, especially that which results in governmental action, can erupt only as precise circumstances might warrant. Manifest destiny was no exception. Whether one attributes the rise of this aspect of American nationalism to the logical projection of the country's past achievements or to a traditional sense of mission, the transformation of such convictions from a mood of quiet and uncomprehended acceptance into a broad and purposeful national movement required some concrete issue that could be easily exploited by the makers of public opinion. Because Texas, after it achieved independence from Mexico in 1836, was occupied and managed by former citizens of the United States, and because it shared an extensive border with the United States, it was totally natural that some Americans would anticipate that region's eventual incorporation into the American Union. Perhaps the Philadelphia *Evening Star* spoke the sentiments of all such Americans when it declared as early as 1836, "Texas sooner or later from its position must become the property of the United States."[1]

As one of his final acts as President, Andrew Jackson recognized the Texas Republic on March 3, 1837. Already Texas leaders had broached the subject of annexation on the basis of similarity of blood, language, and institutions. Provoking a firm rejection from the gov-

[1] Philadelphia *Evening Star* quoted in J. E. Winston, "The Attitude of the Newspapers of the United States Towards Texan Annexation," Mississippi Valley Historical Association *Proceedings*, VIII, 1914–1915, p. 170.

ernment of the United States, the Texas Republic embarked on its own diplomatic career. Before the end of 1840 France, Holland, and Belgium had recognized the young nation; Britain followed in July, 1842. On August 23 Captain Charles Elliot arrived in Texas as the British chargé d'affaires. Thereafter British and French diplomacy sought the perpetuation of Texas independence from the United States, for the union of the two republics would endanger the balance of power in the Western world. Eventually American expansionists would interpret this British interest in Texan independence as part of a general European plot to prevent the normal growth of the United States.

It was obvious why many Americans hesitated to annex Texas in 1837 or even opposed its acquisition totally as an acceptable national objective. Jackson regarded the problems confronting the United States with respect to Texas as *largely* diplomatic ones. He recognized both the possibility of war with Mexico—either over annexation itself or over a subsequent boundary dispute—as well as the possibility that annexation would create the suspicion among the nations of Europe that the United States was directly implicated in the Texas independence movement. But for other Americans the objections were more fundamental, and focused on the possible impact of annexation on American traditions and American civilization itself. Opponents of the slavery expansion such as John Quincy Adams viewed the entire Anglo-American movement into Texas as American aggression in behalf of slavery. Such misgivings he recorded in his *Diary:* "The annexation of Texas to this Union is the first step to the conquest of all Mexico, of the West Indies, of a maritime, colonizing, slavetainted monarchy, and of extinguished freedom." No American critic summarized better the arguments against annexation than did the noted Boston clergyman, William E. Channing. Channing, a leading Unitarian philosopher, commented frequently in his essays and sermons on the significant issues of the day. The following essay, written in 1837, took the form of a long letter to Henry Clay. Channing opposed annexation as an inexcusable aggression toward Mexico, as an effort of Southerners with influence in the federal government to extend the institution of slavery, and, above all, as a dangerous aberration from a firmly established, closely calculated, and conservative course of national action.

My Dear Sir:

. . . IT is with great reluctance that I enter on the topic of this letter. My tastes and habits incline me to very different objects of thought and exertion. I had hoped, that I should never again feel myself called to take part in the agitations and exciting discussions of the day, especially in those of a political character. I desire nothing so much as to devote what remains of life to the study and exposition of great principles and universal truths. But the subject of Texas weighs heavily on my mind, and I cannot shake it off. To me, it is more than a political question. It belongs eminently to morals and religion. I have hoped, that the attention of the public would be called to it by some more powerful voice. I have postponed writing, until the national legislature is about to commence the important session, in which, it is thought, this subject may be decided. But no one speaks, and therefore I cannot be silent. Should Texas be annexed to our country, I feel that I could not forgive myself, if, with my deep, solemn impressions, I should do nothing to avert the evil. . . .

I. We have a strong argument against annexing Texas to the United States, in the Criminality of the revolt which threatens to sever that country from Mexico. On this point our citizens need light. The Texan insurrection is seriously regarded by many among us as a struggle of the oppressed for freedom. The Texan revolution is thought to resemble our own. Our own is contaminated by being brought into such relationship, and we owe to our fathers and ourselves a disclaimer of affinity with this new republic. The Texan revolt, if regarded in its causes and its means of success, is criminal; and we ought in no way to become partakers in its guilt. . . .

From Channing to Henry Clay, 1837, in *The Works of William E. Channing* (Boston, 1848), II, 184–248.

I have no disposition to deny that Texas had grievances to justify complaint. In proof of this I need no documents. That she was not always wisely governed, that her rights were not always respected, who can doubt? What else could be excepted? Mexico is not wise. Mexico is not skilled in the science of human rights. Her civilization is very imperfect, as we and the Texans have always known; and a good government is one of the slowest fruits of civilization. In truth a good government exists nowhere. The errors and vices of rulers entail evils on every state. Especially in an extensive community, some districts will always suffer from unwise, partial, unjust legislation. If every town or county may start up into a sovereign state, whenever it is wronged, society will be given up to perpetual convulsion, and history be one bloody record of revolt. The right of insurrection is to be exercised most rarely, fearfully, reluctantly, and only in cases of fixed, pronounced, persevering oppression, from which no relief can be found but in force. Nothing is easier than for any and every people to draw up a list of wrongs; nothing more ruinous than to rebel because every claim is not treated with respect. The United States did not throw off the British yoke, because every human right, which could be demonstrated by moral science, was not granted them; but because they were denied the rights which their fathers had enjoyed, and which had been secured to the rest of the empire. . . .

Having thus considered the grievances of the Texans, I now proceed to consider the real and great causes of the revolt. These are matters of notoriety, so as to need no minute exposition. The first great cause was the unbounded, unprincipled spirit of land speculation, which so tempting a prize as Texas easily kindled in multitudes in the United States, where this mode of gambling is too common a vice. . . .

Texas, indeed, has been regarded as a prey for land speculators within its own borders and in the United States. To show the scale on which this kind of plunder has been carried on, it may be stated, that the legislature of Coahuila and Texas, in open violation of the laws of Mexico, were induced "by a company of land speculators, never distinctly known, to grant them, in consideration of twenty thousand dollars, the extent of four hundred square leagues of the public land. This transaction was disavowed, and the grant annulled, by the Mexican government, and led to the dispersion of the legislature, and the imprisonment of the governor, Viesca. And yet this unauthorized, and, perhaps, corrupt, grant of public lands formed the basis of new speculation and frauds. A new scrip was formed; and, according to the best information we have been able to obtain, four hundred leagues became, in the hands of speculators, as many thousands. The extent of these frauds is yet to be ascertained; for such is the blindness of cupidity, that any thing which looks fair on paper passes without scrutiny for a land-title in Texas." The indignation excited in the Mexican government by this enormous grant, and the attempt to seize the legislators who perpetrated it, were among the immediate excitements to the revolt. In consequence of these lawless proceedings, great numbers in this country and Texas have nominal titles to land, which can only be substantiated by setting aside the authority of the General Congress of Mexico, and are, of consequence, directly and strongly interested in severing this province from the Mexican confederacy. Texan independence can alone legalize the mighty frauds of the land speculator. Texas must be wrested from the country to which she owes allegiance, that her soil may pass into the hands of cheating and cheated foreigners. We have here one explanation of the zeal, with which the Texan cause was embraced in the United States. From this country the great impulse has been given to the Texan revolution; and a principal motive has been, the unappeasable hunger for Texan land. An interest in that soil, whether real or fictitious, has been spread over our country. Thus "the generous zeal for freedom," which has stirred and armed so many of our citizens to fight for Texas, turns out to be a passion for unrighteous spoil. . . .

Had this country resisted with its whole power the lawlessness of its citizens; had these, notwithstanding such opposition, succeeded in extorting from Mexico a recognition of independence; and were their sovereignty acknowledged by other nations; we should stand acquitted, in the sight of the civilized world, of participating in their crime, were considerations of policy to determine us to admit them into our Union. Unhappily, the United States have not discharged the obligations of a neutral state. They have suffered, by a culpable negligence, the violation of the Mexican territory by their citizens; and if now, in the midst of the conflict, whilst Mexico yet threatens to enforce her claims, they should proceed to incorporate Texas with themselves, they would involve themselves, before all nations, in the whole infamy of the revolt. The United States have not been just to Mexico. Our citizens did not steal singly, silently, in disguise, into that land. Their purpose of dismembering Mexico, and attaching her distant province to this country, was not wrapped in mystery. It was proclaimed in our public prints. Expeditions were openly fitted out within our borders for the Texan war. Troops were organized, equipped, and marched for the scene of action. Advertisements for volunteers, to be enrolled and conducted to Texas at the expense of that territory, were inserted in our newspapers. The government, indeed, issued its proclamation, forbidding these hostile preparations; but this was a dead letter. Military companies, with officers and standards, in defiance of proclamations, and in the face of day, directed their steps to the revolted province. We had, indeed, an army near the frontiers of Mexico. Did it turn back these invaders of a land with which we were at peace? On the contrary, did not its presence give confidence to the revolters? After this, what construction of our conduct shall we force on the world, if we proceed, especially at this moment, to receive into our Union the territory, which, through our neglect, has fallen a prey to lawless invasion? Are we willing to take our place among robber-states? As a people, have we no self-respect? Have we no reverence for national morality? Have we no feeling of responsibility to other nations, and to Him by whom the fates of nations are disposed?

II. Having unfolded the argument against the annexation of Texas from the criminality of the revolt, I proceed to a second very solemn consideration, namely, that by this act our country will enter on a career of encroachment, war, and crime, and will merit and incur the punishment and woe of aggravated wrongdoing. The seizure of Texas will not stand alone. It will darken our future history. It will be linked by an iron necessity to long-continued deeds of rapine and blood. Ages may not see the catastrophe of the tragedy, the first scene of which we are so ready to enact. It is strange that nations should be so much more rash than individuals; and this, in the face of experience, which has been teaching, from the beginning of society, that, of all precipitate and criminal deeds, those perpetrated by nations are the most fruitful of misery.

Did this country know itself, or were it disposed to profit by self-knowledge, it would feel the necessity of laying an immediate curb on its passion for extended territory. It would not trust itself to new acquisitions. It would shrink from the temptation to conquest. We are a restless people, prone to encroachment, impatient of the ordinary laws of progress, less anxious to consolidate and perfect than to extend our institutions, more ambitious of spreading overselves over a wide space than of diffusing beauty and fruitfulness over a narrower field. We boast of our rapid growth, forgetting that, throughout nature, noble growths are slow. Our people throw themselves beyond the bounds of civilization, and expose themselves to relapses into a semi-barbarous state, under the impulse of wild imagination, and for the name of great possessions. Perhaps there is no people on earth, on whom the ties of local attachment sit so loosely. . . .

It is full time, that we should lay on ourselves serious, resolute restraint. Possessed of a domain, vast enough for the growth of ages, it is time for us to stop in the career of acquisition and conquest. Already endangered by our greatness, we cannot advance without imminent peril to our institutions, union, prosperity, virtue, and peace. Our former additions of territory have been justified by the necessity of obtaining outlets for the population of the South and West. No such pretext exists for the occupation of Texas. We cannot seize upon or join to ourselves that territory, without manifesting and strengthening the purpose of setting no limits to our empire. We give ourselves an impulse, which will and must precipitate us into new invasions of our neighbours' soil. Is it by pressing forward in this course that we are to learn self-restraint? Is cupidity to be appeased by gratification? Is it by unrighteous grasping, that an impatient people will be instructed how to hem themselves within the rigid bounds of justice?

Texas is a country conquered by our citizens; and the annexation of it to our Union will be the beginning of conquests, which, unless arrested and beaten back by a just and kind Providence, will stop only at the Isthmus of Darien. Henceforth, we must cease to cry, Peace, peace. Our Eagle will whet, not gorge its appetite on its first victim; and will snuff a more tempting quarry, more alluring blood, in every new region which opens southward. To annex Texas is to declare perpetual war with Mexico. That word, *Mexico*, associated in men's minds with boundless wealth, has already awakened rapacity. Already it has been proclaimed, that the Anglo-Saxon race is destined to the sway of this magnificent realm, that the rude form of society, which Spain established there, is to yield and vanish before a higher civilization. Without this exposure of plans of rapine and subjugation, the result, as far as our will can determine it, is plain. Texas is the first step to Mexico. The moment we plant our authority on Texas, the boundaries of those two countries will become nominal, will be a little more than lines on the sand of the sea-shore. In the fact, that portions of the Southern and

Western States are already threatened with devastation, through the impatience of multitudes to precipitate themselves into the Texan land of promise, we have a pledge and earnest of the flood which will pour itself still further south, when Texas shall be but partially overrun. . . .

. . . It is sometimes said, that nations are swayed by laws, as unfailing as those which govern matter; that they have their destinies; that their character and position carry them forward irresistibly to their goal; that the stationary Turk must sink under the progressive civilization of Russia, as inevitably as the crumbling edifice falls to the earth; that, by a like necessity, the Indians have melted before the white man, and the mixed, degraded race of Mexico must melt before the Anglo-Saxon. Away with this vile sophistry! There is no necessity for crime. These is no Fate to justify rapacious nations, any more than to justify gamblers and robbers, in plunder. We boast of the progress of society, and this progress consists in the substitution of reason and moral principle for the sway of brute force. It is true, that more civilized must always exert a great power over less civilized communities in their neighbourhood. But it may and should be a power to enlighten and improve, not to crush and destroy. We talk of accomplishing our destiny. So did the late conqueror of Europe; and destiny consigned him to a lonely rock in the ocean, the prey of an ambition which destroyed no peace but his own.

Hitherto I have spoken of the annexation of Texas in embroiling us with Mexico; but it will not stop here. It will bring us into collision with other states. It will, almost of necessity, involve us in hostility with European powers. Such are now the connexions of nations, that Europe must look with jealousy on a country, whose ambition, seconded by vast resources, will seem to place within her grasp the empire of the new world. And not only general considerations of this nature, but the particular relation of certain foreign states to this continent, must tend to destroy the peace now happily subsisting between us and the kingdoms of Europe. England, in particular, must watch us with suspicion, and cannot but resist our appropriation of Texas to ourselves. She has at once a moral and political interest in this question, which demands and will justify interference. . . .

III. I proceed now to a consideration of what is to me the strongest argument against annexing Texas to the United States. This measure will extend and perpetuate slavery. I have necessarily glanced at this topic in the preceding pages; but it deserves to be brought out distinctly. I shall speak calmly, but I must speak earnestly; and I feel, and rejoice to feel, that, however you may differ from some of my views, yet we do not differ as to the great principle on which all my remarks and remonstrances are founded. Slavery seems to you, as to me, an evil and a wrong. Your language on this subject has given me a satisfaction, for which I owe you thanks; and if, in what I am now to say, I may use expressions which you may think too strong, I am sure your candor will recognise in them the signs of deep conviction, and will acquit me of all desire to irritate or give pain.

The annexation of Texas, I have said, will extend and per-petuate slavery. It is fitted, and, still more, intended to do so. On this point there can be no doubt. As far back as the year 1829, the annexation of Texas was agitated in the Southern and Western States; and it was urged on the ground of the strength and extension it would give the slave-holding interest. In a series of essays, ascribed to a gentleman now a senator in Congress, it was maintained, that five or six slave-holding States would by this measure be added to the Union; and he even intimated that as many as nine States as large as Kentucky might be formed within the limits of Texas. In Virginia, about the same time, calculations were made as to the increased value which would thus be given to slaves, and it was even said, that this acquisition would raise the price fifty per cent. Of late the language on this subject is most explicit. The great argument for annexing Texas is, that it will strengthen "the peculiar institutions" of the South, and open a new and vast field for slavery. . . .

The annexation of Texas, if it should be accomplished, would do much to determine the future history and character of this country. It is one of those measures, which call a nation to pause, reflect, look forward, because their force is not soon exhausted. Many acts of government, intensely exciting at the moment, are yet of little importance, because their influence is too transient to leave a trace on history. A bad administration may impoverish a people at home, or cripple its energies abroad, for a year or more. But such wounds heal soon. A young people soon recruits its powers, and starts forward with increased impulse, after the momentary suspension of its activity. The chief interest of a people lies in measures, which, making, perhaps, little noise, go far to fix its character, to determine its policy and fate for ages, to decide its rank among nations. A fearful responsibility rests on those who originate or control these pregnant acts. The destiny of millions is in their hands. The execration of millions may fall on their heads. Long after present excitements shall have passed away, long after they and their generation shall have vanished from the earth, the fruits of their agency will be reaped. Such a measure is that of which I now write. It will commit us to a degrading policy, the issues of which lie beyond human foresight. In opening to ourselves vast regions, through which we may spread slavery, and in spreading it for this, among other ends, that the Slave-holding States may bear rule in the national councils, we make slavery the predominant interest of the state. We make it the basis of power, the spring or guide of public measures, the object for which the revenues, strength, and wealth of the country are to be exhausted. Slavery will be branded on our front, as the great Idea, the prominent feature of the country. We shall renounce our high calling as a people, and accomplish the lowest destiny to which a nation can be bound. . . .

IV. I now proceed to another important argument against the annexation of Texas to our country, the argument drawn from the bearings of the measure on our National Union. Next to liberty, union is our great political interest, and this cannot but be loosened, it may be dissolved, by the proposed extension of our territory. I will not say that every extension must be pernicious, that our government cannot hold together even our present confederacy, that the central heart cannot send its influences to the remote States which are to spring up within our present borders. Old theories must be cautiously applied to the institutions of this country. If the Federal government will abstain from minute legislation, and rigidly confine itself within constitutional bounds, it may be a bond of union to more extensive communities than were ever comprehended under one sway. Undoubtedly, there is peril in extending ourselves, and yet the chief benefit of the Union, which is the preservation of peaceful relations among neighbouring States, is so vast, that some risk should be taken to secure it in the greatest possible degree. The objection to the annexation of Texas, drawn from the unwieldiness it would give to the country, though very serious, is not decisive. A far more serious objection is, that it is to be annexed to us for the avowed purpose of multiplying slaveholding States, and thus giving political power. This cannot, ought not to be borne. It will justify, it will at length demand, the separation of the States. . . .

In other ways the annexation of Texas is to endanger the Union. It will give new violence and passion to the agitation of the question of slavery. It is well known, that a majority at the North have discouraged the discussion of this topic, on the ground, that slavery was imposed on the South by necessity, that its continuance was not of choice, and that the States in which it subsists, if left to themselves, would find a remedy in their own way. Let slavery be systematically proposed as the policy of these States, let it bind them together in efforts to establish political power, and a new feeling will burst forth through the whole North. It will be a concentration of moral, religious, political, and patriotic feelings. The fire, now smothered, will blaze out, and, of consequence, new jealousies and exasperations will be kindled at the South. Strange, that the South should think of securing its "pecular institutions" by violent means. Its violence necessarily increases the evils it would suppress. For example, by denying the right of petition to those who sought the abolition of slavery within the immediate jurisdiction of the United States, it has awakened a spirit, which will overwhelm Congress with petitions till this right be restored. The annexation of Texas would be a measure of the same injurious character, and would stir up an open, uncompromising hostility to slavery, of which we have seen no example, and which would produce a reaction very dangerous to union. . . .

V. I proceed now to the last head of this communication. I observe, that the cause of Liberty, of free institutions, a cause more sacred than union, forbids the annexation of Texas. It is plain from the whole preceding discussion, that this measure will exert a disastrous influence on the moral sentiments and principles of this country, by sanctioning plunder, by inflaming cupidity, by encouraging lawless speculation, by bringing into the confederacy a community whose whole history and circumstances are adverse to moral order and wholesome restraint, by violating national faith, by proposing immoral and inhuman ends, by placing us as a people in opposition to the efforts of philanthropy, and the advancing movements of the civilized world. It will spread a moral corruption, already too rife among us, and, in so doing, it will shake the foundations of freedom at home, and bring reproach on it abroad. It will be treachery to the great cause which has been confided to this above all nations.

The dependence of freedom on morals is an old subject, and I have no thought of enlarging on the general truth. I wish only to say, that it is one which needs to be brought home to us at the present moment, and that it cannot be trifled with but to our great peril. There are symptoms of corruption amongst us, which show us that we cannot enter on a new career of crime without peculiar hazard. I cannot do justice to this topic without speaking freely of our country, as freely as I should of any other; and unhappily we are so accustomed, as a people, to receive incense, to be soothed by flattery, and to account reputation as a more important interest than morality, that my freedom may be construed into a kind of disloyalty. But it would be wrong to make concessions to this dangerous weakness. I believe that morality is the first interest of a people, and that this requires self-knowledge in nations, as truly as in individuals. He who helps a community to comprehend itself, and to apply to itself a higher rule of action, is the truest patriot, and contributes most to its enduring fame.

I have said, that we shall expose our freedom to great peril by entering on a new career of crime. We are corrupt enough already. In one respect, our institutions have disappointed us all. They have not wrought out for us that elevation of character, which is the most precious, and, in truth, the only substantial blessing of liberty. Our progress in prosperity has indeed been the wonder of the world; but this prosperity has done much to counteract the ennobling influence of free institutions. The peculiar circumstances of the country and of our times have poured in upon us a torrent of wealth; and human nature has not been strong enough for the assault of such severe temptation. Prosperity has become dearer than freedom. Government is regarded more as a means of enriching the country, than of securing private rights. We have become wedded to gain, as our chief good. That, under the predominance of this degrading passion, the higher virtues, the moral independence, the simplicity of manners, the stern uprightness, the self-reverence, the respect for man as man, which are the ornaments and safeguards of a republic, should wither, and give place to selfish calculation and indulgence, to show and extravagance, to anxious, envious, discontented strivings, to wild adventure, and to the gambling spirit of speculation, will surprise no one who has studied human nature. The invasion of Texas by our citizens is a mournful comment on our national morality. Whether without some fiery trial, some signal prostration of our prosperity, we can rise to the force and self-denial of freemen, is a question not easily solved. . . .

That the cause of republicanism is suffering abroad, through the defects and crimes of our countrymen, is as true, as that it is regarded with increased skepticism among ourselves. Abroad, republicanism is identified with the United States, and it is certain that the American name has not risen of late in the world. It so happens, that, whilst writing, I have received a newspaper from England, in which Lynch law is as familiarly associated with our country, as if it were one of our establishments. We are quoted as monuments of the degrading tendencies of popular institutions. When I visited England fifteen years ago, republican sentiments were freely expressed to me. I should probably hear none now. Men's minds seem to be returning to severer principles of government; and this country is responsible for a part of this change. It is believed abroad, that property is less secure among us, order less stable, law less revered, social ties more easily broken, religion less enforced, life held less sacred, than in other countries. Undoubtedly, the prejudices of foreign nations, the interests of foreign governments, have led to gross exaggeration of evils here. The least civilized parts of the country are made to represent the whole, and occasional atrocities are construed into habits. But who does not feel, that we have given cause of reproach? and shall we fix this reproach, and exasperate it into indignation and hatred, by adopting a policy against which the moral sentiments of the Christian world revolt? . . .

I have alluded to the want of wisdom with which we are accustomed to speak of our destiny as a people. We are *destined* (that is the word) to overspread North America; and, intoxicated with the idea, it matters little to us how we accomplish our fate. To spread, to supplant others, to cover a boundless space, this seems our ambition, no matter what influence we spread with us. Why cannot we rise to noble conceptions of our destiny? Why do we not feel, that our work as a nation is, to carry freedom, religion, science, and a nobler form of human nature over this continent? and why do we not remember, that to diffuse these blessings we must first cherish them in our own borders; and that whatever deeply and permanently corrupts us will make our spreading influence a curse, not a blessing, to this new world? It is a common idea in Europe, that we are destined to spread an inferior civilization over North America; that our slavery and our absorption in gain and outward interests mark us out, as fated to fall behind the old world in the higher improvements of human nature, in the philosophy, the refinements, the enthusiasm of literature and the arts, which throw a lustre round other countries. I am not prophet enough to read our fate. I believe, indeed, that we are to make our futurity for ourselves. I believe, that a nation's destiny lies in its character, in the principles which govern its policy and bear rule in the hearts of its citizens. I take my stand on God's moral and eternal law. A nation, renouncing and defying this, cannot be free, cannot be great. . . .

6   John Tyler

The National Advantages
of Annexation

After years of quiet evolution as an independent nation, Texas, in 1843, confronted Southern leaders in the United States with an unprecedented and undeniable challenge. Convinced that Britain, in its role of world champion of abolitionism, was seeking the end of slavery in Texas, Ashbel Smith, Texan chargé in London, warned John C. Calhoun on June 19: "I sincerely believe that the ultimate purpose [of England] is to make Texas a refuge for runaway slaves from the United States, and eventually a negro nation . . . under the protection of Great Britain. . . . It is regarded as infinitely important as an entering wedge . . . for operating against the institutions of the Southern States."[1] In July Louis Tappan, the noted New York abolitionist, while attending the convention of the British and Foreign Antislavery Society in London, successfully pressed the British government for a declaration that it would "employ all legitimate means to attain so great and desirable an object as abolition in Texas."[2] On January 12, 1844, Aberdeen reminded the French government that the two European powers shared a mutual interest in preventing the annexation of Texas by the United States. Four days later the French Foreign Minister, Francois Guizot, replied that "it would be for the advantage of all Maritime States, for France and Great Britain in particular, that the independence of Texas should be maintained, and that a barrier should thus be opposed to the encroachments of the United States. . . ."[3]

President John Tyler needed little encouragement, beyond the knowledge that British and French diplomacy seemed to reflect an unnatural and threatening interest in Texas, to inaugurate a movement for the annexation of the former Mexican province. As J. Fred Rippy has written, "manifest destiny never pointed to the acquisition of a region so unmistakably as when undemocratic, conservative Europe revealed an inclination to interfere or to absorb. . . ."[4] Tyler,

---

[1] Ashbel Smith to Calhoun, June 19, 1843, in Harriet Smithers, "English Abolitionism and the Annexation of Texas," *Southwestern Historical Quarterly*, XXXII (October, 1928), 200.

[2] Louis Tappan to the British Government in Smithers, *Ibid.*, p. 195.

[3] Ephraim Douglass Adams, *British Interests and Activities in Texas 1838–1846* (Baltimore: The Johns Hopkins Press, 1910), pp. 158–160.

[4] J. Fred Rippy, *The United States and Mexico* (New York: A. A. Knopf, 1926), p. 29.

although a Virginian and under direct Southern influence, cast his appeal in national terms. With his message to Congress of April 22, 1844, he transmitted the annexation treaty which his Secretary of State, Calhoun, had negotiated with the Texas Republic ten days earlier. In his appeal the President made it clear that Texas, as a part of the United States, would serve all sections of the nation.

. . . THE country thus proposed to be annexed has been settled principally by persons from the United States, who emigrated on the invitation of both Spain and Mexico, and who carried with them into the wilderness which they have partially reclaimed the laws, customs, and political and domestic institutions of their native land. They are deeply indoctrinated in all the principles of civil liberty, and will bring along with them in the act of reassociation devotion to our Union and a firm and inflexible resolution to assist in maintaining the public liberty unimpaired—a consideration which, as it appears to me, is to be regarded as of no small moment. The country itself thus obtained is of incalculable value in an agricultural and commercial point of view. To a soil of inexhaustible fertility it unites a genial and healthy climate, and is destined at a day not distant to make large contributions to the commerce of the world. . . .

A new and powerful impulse will thus be given to the navigating interest of the country, which will be chiefly engrossed by our fellow-citizens of the Eastern and Middle States, who have already attained a remarkable degree of prosperity by the partial monopoly they have enjoyed of the carrying trade of the Union, particularly the coastwise trade, which this new acquisition is destined in time, and that not distant, to swell to a magnitude which can not easily be computed, while the addition made to the boundaries of the home market thus secured to their mining, manufacturing and mechanical skill and industry

From James D. Richardson, ed., *Messages and Papers of the Presidents* (Washington, 1897), IV, 308–313.

will be of a character the most commanding and important. Such are some of the many advantages which will accrue to the Eastern and Middle States by the ratification of the treaty—advantages the extent of which it is impossible to estimate with accuracy or properly to appreciate. Texas, being adapted to the culture of cotton, sugar, and rice, and devoting most of her energies to the raising of these productions, will open an extensive market to the Western States in the important articles of beef, pork, horses, mules, etc., as well as in breadstuffs.

At the same time, the Southern and Southeastern States will find in the fact of annexation protection and security to their peace and tranquillity, as well against all domestic as foreign efforts to disturb them, thus consecrating anew the union of the States and holding out the promise of its perpetual duration. Thus, at the same time that the tide of public prosperity is greatly swollen, an appeal of what appears to the Executive to be of an imposing, if not of a resistless, character is made to the interests of every portion of the country. Agriculture, which would have a new and extensive market opened for its produce; commerce, whose ships would be freighted with the rich productions of an extensive and fertile region; and the mechanical arts, in all their various ramifications, would seem to unite in one universal demand for the ratification of the treaty.

But important as these considerations may appear, they are to be regarded as but secondary to others. Texas, for reasons deemed sufficient by herself, threw off her dependence on Mexico as far back as 1836, and consummated her independence by the battle of San Jacinto in the same year, since which period Mexico has attempted no serious invasion of her territory, but the contest has assumed features of a mere border war, characterized by acts revolting to humanity. In the year 1836 Texas adopted her constitution, under which she has existed as a sovereign power ever since, having been recognized as such by many of the principal powers of the world; and contemporaneously with its adoption, by a solemn vote of her people, embracing all her population but ninety-three persons, declared her anxious desire to be admitted into association with the United States as a portion of their territory. This vote, thus solemnly taken, has never been reversed, and now by the action of her constituted authorities, sustained as it is by popular sentiment, she reaffirms her desire for annexation. This course has been adopted by her without the employment of any sinister measures on the part of this Government. No intrigue has been set on foot to accomplish it. Texas herself wills it, and the Executive of the United States, concurring with her, has seen no sufficient reason to avoid the consummation of an act esteemed to be so desirable by both. . . .

The documents now transmitted along with the treaty lead to the conclusion, as inevitable, that if the boon now tendered be rejected Texas will seek for the friendship of others. In contemplating such a contingency it can not be overlooked that the United States are already almost surrounded by the possessions of European powers. The Canadas, New Brunswick, and Nova Scotia, the islands in the American seas, with Texas trammeled by treaties of alliance or of a commercial character differing in policy from that of the United States, would complete the circle. Texas voluntarily steps forth, upon terms of perfect honor and good faith to all nations, to ask to be annexed to the Union. As an independent sovereignty her right to do this is unquestionable. In doing so she gives no cause of umbrage to any other power; her people desire it, and there is no slavish transfer of her sovereignty and independence. She has for eight years maintained her independence against all efforts to subdue her. She has been recognized as independent by many of the most prominent of the family of nations, and that recognition, so far as they are concerned, places her in a position, without giving any just cause of umbrage to them, to surrender her sovereignty at her own will and pleasure. The United States, actuated evermore by a spirit of justice, has desired by the stipulations of the treaty to render justice to all. They have made provision for the payment of the public debt of Texas. We look to her ample and fertile domain as the certain means of accomplishing this; but this is a matter between the United States and Texas, and with which other Governments have nothing to do. Our right to receive the rich grant tendered by Texas is perfect, and this Government should not, having due respect either to its own honor or its own interests, permit its course of policy to be interrupted by the interference of other powers, even if such interference were threatened. The question is one purely American. In the acquisition, while we abstain most carefully from all that could interrupt the public peace, we claim the right to exercise a due regard to our own. This Government can not consistently with its honor permit any such interference. With equal, if not greater, propriety might the United States demand of other governments to surrender their numerous and valuable acquisitions made in past time at numberless places on the surface of the globe, whereby they have added to their power and enlarged their resources.

To Mexico the Executive is disposed to pursue a course conciliatory in its character and at the same time to render her the most ample justice by conventions and stipulations not inconsistent with the rights and dignity of the Government. It is actuated by no spirit of unjust aggrandizement, but looks only to its own security. It has made known to Mexico at several periods its extreme anxiety to witness the termination of hostilities between that country and Texas. Its wishes, however, have been entirely disregarded. It has ever been ready to urge an adjustment of the dispute upon terms mutually advantageous to both. It will be ready at all times to hear and discuss any claims Mexico may think she has on the justice of the United States and to adjust any that may be deemed to be so on the most liberal terms. There is no desire on the part of the Executive to wound her pride or affect injuriously her interest, but at the same time it can not compromit by any delay in its action the essential interest of the United States. Mexico has no right to ask or expect this of us; we deal rightfully with Texas as an independent power. The war which has been waged for eight years has resulted only in the conviction with all others than herself that Texas can not be reconquered. . . .

In full view, then, of the highest public duty, and as a measure of security against evils incalculably great, the Executive has entered into the negotiation, the fruits of which are now submitted to the Senate. Independent of the urgent reasons which existed for the step it has taken, it might safely invoke the fact (which it confidently believes) that there exists no civilized government on earth having a voluntary tender made it of a domain so rich and fertile, so replete with all that can add to national greatness and wealth, and so necessary to its peace and safety that would reject the offer. Nor are other powers, Mexico inclusive, likely in any degree to be injuriously affected by the ratification of the treaty. The prosperity of Texas will be equally interesting to all; in the increase of the general commerce of the world that prosperity will be secured by annexation.

But one view of the subject remains to be presented. It grows out of the proposed enlargement of our territory. From this, I am free to confess, I see no danger. The federative system is susceptible of the greatest extension compatible with the ability of the representation of the most distant State or Territory to reach the seat of Government in time to participate in the functions of legislation and to make known the wants of the constituent body. Our confederated Republic consisted originally of thirteen members. It now consists of twice that number, while applications are before Congress to permit other additions. This addition of new States has served to strengthen rather than to weaken the Union. New interests have sprung up, which require the united power of all, through the action of the common Government, to protect and defend upon the high seas and in foreign parts. Each State commits with perfect security to that common Government those great interests growing out of our relations with other nations of the world, and which equally involve the good of all the States. Its domestic concerns are left to its own exclusive management. But if there were any force in the objection it would seem to require an immediate abandonment of territorial possessions which lie in the distance and stretch to a far-off sea, and yet no one would be found, it is believed, ready to recommend such an abandonment. Texas lies at our very doors and in our immediate vicinity.

7

Joshua Giddings *versus*
Slavery and Southern Power

To such opponents of Texas annexation as Congressman Joshua Giddings of Ohio's Western Reserve, the central question of sectional power and slavery expansion raised by the Texas issue could not be buried away under the cloak of destiny. Giddings, like many Northern Whigs and all Northern abolitionists, denounced annexation on two counts: the extension of Democratic power and the expansion of slavery. Nowhere did he demonstrate the dual nature of the expansionist conflict in American politics more clearly and with more vehemence than in his speech before the House of Representatives on May 21, 1844.

. . . THE President and his cabinet, and the southern democrats, aver that this nation shall take upon itself the support and perpetuation of slavery in Texas, and of the slave trade between our slave-breeding States and the people of that government.

———————

From *Congressional Globe* (28th Cong., 1st Sess., 1844), Appendix, pp. 704–705, 707.

They urge that our army and navy shall be employed, and our national energies put forth; our character disgraced before the civilized world, in order to attain that object. They insist that we shall violate our treaty stipulations with Mexico; that we shall abandon our principles in favor of human liberty; acknowledge ourselves a nation of political hypocrites; bring dishonor upon the memory of our revolutionary patriots; turn traitors to the sacred cause of freedom; and wage an unceasing war upon humanity itself. These are the matters urged on one side, and objected to by the other. This is the issue to be determined by the people—by the electors of the North and of the South, of the East and of the West. On this issue the whigs, the democrats, and liberty men are to pass judgment.

It is true that the annexation of Texas to these United States is brought forward as the proposed means by which we may extend and perpetuate slavery, and continue the slave trade; but that object is merely collateral to the great and ulterior design of supporting slavery and the slave trade. The object and purpose for which it is now sought to annex Texas to the United States is clearly and unequivocally set forth in the official correspondence between the Secretary of State and Mr. Everett, our minister at the court of St. James; between said Secretary and our "chargé de affaires" in Texas, and between him and the British minister resident in this city. In every letter of that correspondence the object is frankly avowed, without any apparent delicacy or attempt at concealment. The same object of maintaining the slave trade between the slave-breeding States of this Union and Texas, and the perpetuating slavery in Texas, is the avowed object of nearly every democratic paper south of Mason and Dixon's line, by nearly every address upon that subject, and by the proceedings of nearly all the public meetings held in the slave States for the purpose of promoting the cause of annexation. . . .

And now what say our democrats of New England, and New York, and Ohio? I call upon them to come forth and show their colors; play the man, meet the issue, and let us have no dodging. We shall soon return to our constituents, and must meet this question before the people. Will the gentleman from Indiana then stand forth frankly and say to the democrats of this district "you must work hard, and live cheap, and be economical, for we have agreed to pay the debts of Texas, and every laboring man in the nation must contribute a portion of his earnings?" And then suppose the honest farmer, in the true Yankee fashion, should inquire for the benefits which this nation is to derive from the payment of this twenty millions of Texas debts; will that gentleman frankly and boldly declare to him, that, by paying that amount of money, we have established true democratic slavery in Texas, and have secured a first rate market for the democratic slave dealers of the South? . . .

It is well known, Mr. Chairman, that, since the formation of this confederacy, there has long been a supposed conflict between the interests of free labor and of slave labor, between the southern and northern States. I do not say that the conflict is real; I only say that in the minds of the people, both north and south, and in this hall, such conflict exists. This supposed conflict has given rise to difference of policy in our national councils. I refer to the tariff in particular, as being a favorite measure of the North, while free trade is advocated by the South. I refer also to our harbor improvements, and the improvement of our river navigation, as another measure in which the Northwest and West have felt great interest and much anxiety, and to which the South have been constantly opposed. But so equally balanced has been the political power between these opposing interests, that for five years past our lake commerce has been entirely abandoned; and such were the deficits of the tariff, that for many years our revenues were unequal to the support of government. Time eventually gave the friends of northern interests power to amend the tariff, and, by the fixed order of nature's law, our population at the north has increased so much faster than it has in the slave States, that under the late census, the

North and West now hold the balance of political power; and at the present session we have passed a bill for the protection of our lake and river commerce, which now awaits the action of the Senate, and will soon become a law. But let us admit Texas, and we shall place the balance of power in the hands of the Texans themselves. They, with the southern states, will then be held at the will of the Texan advocates of free trade. Are our friends of the North prepared to deliver over this great national policy to the people of Texas? Are the liberty-loving democrats of Pennsylvania ready to give up our tariff?—to strike off all protection from the articles of iron, and coal, and other productions of the State, in order to purchase a slave market for their neighbors, who, in the words of Thomas Jefferson Randolph, "breed men for the market like oxen for the shambles?" . . .

And I appeal to the whole population of the western States —of all classes and conditions, and political parties—to say whether they are willing to give up their harbor improvements, and the improvement of our river navigation, for the purpose of improving the southern slave trade, and of perpetuating slavery in Texas? What say my democratic colleagues on this point— will they go it? Will the democracy of Ohio march up to that point with firm and unflinching step? I think not. If they do, they had better settle their political affairs, and make their political bequests before election, or they will take their departure from the political world unprepared. . . .

Mr. Chairman, we at this moment appear before the civilized world in the disgraceful attitude of making war upon Mexico, an unoffending nation, in the obvious violation of our treaty stipulations and our national faith solemnly pledged, for the purpose of extending slavery and perpetuating the slave trade. And I am exceedingly desirous of knowing whether any political party, or any respectable portion of any political party, intend to support and maintain this policy? What say our democratic friends? Has the gentleman from Indiana [Mr. Owen] spoken the sentiments of his party? Are the democrats of our free States prepared to follow his lead? Will they enter the field with "democracy and slavery, Texas and the slave-trade," inscribed upon their banners? If so, I ask them to come forth boldly, unfurl your banners, not to the breeze, but to that whirlwind of indignation which shall scatter you to the four winds of heaven, and which will leave no other memorial of you than the disgráceful cause that shall have exterminated your party. But, sir, I have too much respect for gentlemen of that party in our free States to indulge apprehensions of this kind. I hope, on the contrary, to see them treating this odious, this treasonable proposition, with that scorn and contempt which it justly merits. . . .

. . . I will now proceed to examine the proposed means of effecting the permanent establishment of slavery in Texas, and the slave trade between our slave States and the people of that government. To effect these objects the President proposes to annex Texas to the Union of these States. I, for one, deny the constitutional power of this government to amalgamate the political destinies of this people with those of Texas or any other foreign government. . . . The ability to purchase territory without inhabitants is one thing; but to annex a foreign government—that is, the people of a foreign government, with their habits, their moral and political views—is another and a different subject. . . .

The old thirteen States had each borne a portion of the burdens, and has shared in the dangers, of the revolution. Their people understood the objects for which they had contended. And I should like to find the man who will say, that he really believes the framers of that instrument intended to give authority to the federal government to annex the people of these States to Mexico, or to Brazil, or to Great Britain, by which our institutions would be subverted, and all the blood and treasure expended in the revolution would be lost to posterity? . . . Would the descendants of the pilgrim fathers—of those who had been driven from the land of their nativity by oppression, and who encountered the dangers of the sea, and sought freedom in the new world, amid the perils that awaited them; who, in the cabin of the Mayflower, while speeding her way from the land of oppression, concocted and arranged the first code of American popular government, and who carried it into practical operation at Plymouth, and inculcated its principles into the minds of their children? Would the descendants of those pilgrim heroes, reared and educated in the religious and political faith of their fathers, and who had manifested their unmitigated hatred of oppression, and their own devotion to the doctrines of civil liberty at Concord, at Lexington, at Bunker's hill, and on all the glorious battlefields of the revolution—would they have been likely to enter into any compact by which this federal government might transfer them or their descendants to the dominion of Texas, or Mexico, or Brazil, or to England itself? Sir, the assertion that such powers exist in the constitution is a reproach upon the New England character; it is offensive to New England feeling, an imputation upon New England honor; it is an insult to the common feelings of our people, and must inevitably call forth a corresponding indignation in the breast of every true son of the North.

But, Mr. Chairman, by adopting our federal constitution, a union was voluntarily formed of the old thirteen States. This was the act of each State; for each determined for itself upon the propriety of adopting the constitution. The compact made provisions for admitting by act of Congress new States, to be formed out of the territory included within the boundaries dividing our government from foreign nations. That union, formed by the wisdom of our fathers, and consecrated by the blood and suffering which had marked their recent struggle for independence we love and cherish. To it we shall adhere in all of its stipulations. We regard it as the sanctuary of American liberty. We shall defend it, if necessary, with our treasure and our lives. But we shall not surrender this Union, sanctioned and sanctified by half a century of national prosperity, in order to try a new union, and that, too, with slaveholding Texas! Sir, every school boy must see, that to form a new union with any foreign power, would be, ipso facto, a dissolution of our present Union. Now, I would say to an imbecile President, and a demented cabinet, that they have not the power to form a union between our people of the free States and Texas. If such a union be ever formed, it will be the voluntary acts of the people of our States and those of Texas. The President and his cabinet may enter into as many treaties as they please, and make such stipulations as they please, and form such unions for themselves as they please—we shall adhere to our present Union. If they wish to leave this Union and go to Texas, I, for one, will bid them "God speed." And if any of our southern sister States are desirous of leaving our present Union to form a new compact with Texas, let them say so with generous frankness. But if northern States prefer adhering to our present Union, and refuse to follow them into such new confederacy, do not let them attempt to charge us with dissolving the Union. I regret that any northern man should speak of dissolving the Union, if Texas be annexed. Such expressions are an abuse of language. The act of uniting with Texas would itself be the dissolution; and refusal to unite with that government would be to maintain the present Union. . . .

8   Chesselden Ellis

"Why wing the eagle
in his bold ascent towards the sun?"

During the final debate over Texas annexation in January and February, 1845, the speech by Chesselden Ellis, the Democratic Congressman from New York, in the House of Representatives comprised a major defense of the nationalist position on expansion. Ellis declared that Texas, by its very size and location, was a national, not a sectional, issue. Its value to the various regions of the United States, if not precisely equal to all, was still considerable. Ellis maintained that the "law of progressive improvement" decreed that the United States answer the request of American settlers in Texas with a decision for annexation. The American commitment to the extension of its democratic institutions alone gave the nation an interest in the affairs of Texas. Nothing should be permitted to stop the westward course of American civilization. "To arrest our peaceful and onward march," he cried, "would be treason to the cause of human liberty." (Document 8.) The annexation of Texas, moreover, would open the way for an "empire on the Pacific." Like other spokesmen of manifest destiny, Ellis denied the legitimacy or even the existence of any struggle for power between North and South in the controversy over expansion.

In this selection Ellis attempted to counter sectional arguments such as those used by Joshua Giddings. Slavery, as a legal institution, said Ellis, should be left to the compromises of the Constitution. Lastly, he insisted that Texas was a free agent, capable of determining its own destiny, and that the annexation of the republic by the United States could not furnish Mexico with any legitimate cause for war.

NO question has come before the Congress of the Union during the present generation, of so much importance to the welfare of our country, as the acquisition of Texas.

It is altogether national in its character; and though the blessings its consummation will bring with it, may be greater in some regions of the United States than in others, yet, sir, can it never be dwarfed down to the humble stature of a mere sectional measure. It is a movement which concerns the expansion of our institutions over a magnificent domain filling up the grand outline of a territory intended for the possession and destiny of the

---

From *Congressional Globe* (28th Cong., 2nd Sess., 1845), Appendix, pp. 138–139, 142–143.

American race—an outline drawn by the hand of the Creator himself, in deserts and mountains, around the southwestern border of this continent.

Sir, a momentary glance at the map of North America demonstrates the nationality of this question. Texas skirts the Gulf of Mexico hundreds of miles, spreads into the interior along the boundaries of our own country thousands of miles more, stretching north to a latitude beyond the queen city of the Mississippi, retreating far in the rear of the Indian nations collected upon our western borders, and extending to the verge of the southern pass of the Rocky mountains—that pass which opens to us the distant domain of Oregon and the shores of the Pacific. It embraces an area quintuple in size the empire State of the Union. It is washed, and drained, and fertilized, by the great streams which pour their tributary waters into the bosom of the "mighty father of floods." Rich and prolific, in the language of geography, in the productions of the most fertile soil of all climes, from the frozen North to the burning South, and in tropical staples surpassing the most favored regions of the earth. Sir, are we not all of us—the North, the South, the East, and the West—equally and together interested in advancing our noble race, our social and political system, our laws, our institutions over this territory not only thus conterminous with our own, but now a dismembered portion of that great valley which reaches from the lakes and the Alleghenies to the Rocky mountains and the deserts of Mexico?—a valley embracing an area of one million and a half of square miles, and containing an extent of navigable rivers unsurpassed in quadruple the same surface on the globe, proclaiming in characters impressed in creation itself, that here, upon this continent of North America, is the destined seat of power upon earth. And why withhold a participation in our blessings, from our own kindred in blood and neighbors in residence, seeking the benefits of union with us? Sir, the constitution itself declares, upon its face, our duty of progression. It was instituted "to form a more perfect union, to establish justice, insure domestic tranquility, provide for the common defence, promote the general welfare, and secure the blessings of liberty to ourselves and our posterity." It looks forward to an indefinite expansion of the great system, providing for the accession of new members to the confederacy. Shall we resist this noble spirit of progress, and strip our own posterity of their inheritance? an inheritance designed for their possession by the founders of the republic? . . . Can the benign object of the constitution be promoted by such restrictions by forcing up around us rival powers, instead of raising and embracing kindred friends? . . . No, sir. Its foundation, like that of Christianity, is laid upon the law of progressive improvement. Under this system, we have seen what the world has no where else seen in all its past history—liberty and law marching hand in hand; and as they marched forever harmonizing their conflicting claims. . . . How many empires of the earth are now larger than our own? And cannot our republic spread its blessings here, as far as monarchy its power abroad? The addition of new and adjacent regions to our dominion, instead of weakening, greatly strengthens the bonds of our Union. It augments the power against which the spirit of disunion must contend whenever it awakes. It multiplies counteracting interests, and lessens the danger of its influence. Has the voice of disloyalty been heard from our advancing population, in their conquest of the wilderness? The new States more than double their extent. Let me not be told that an increase of territory is an increase of adverse interests in our country. Under the operation of equal laws there can be no adverse interests. It is partial, unequal, monopolizing legislation that raises up a conflict of interests. The true interest of every living man is the true interest of the entire community, and of the world itself. It is an ultimate fact, and springs from the universal harmony of creation. . . .

. . . Why not rest where you now are, if patriotism dictates the cry of "the Union as it is," and not as its immortal founders intended it should be? Sir, away with this fettering system. Why wing the eagle in his bold ascent towards the sun? They sky was given for his dominion. Why strip him of his plumage, and fix him to the earth? Sir, you cannot, if you would, set bounds to the indomitable energy of our noble race. Where has the Creator raised mountains so high that we cannot scale them—ay, and subdue and cultivate them? or spread an ocean so broad and so deep that we cannot swim it, and whiten its bosom with our commerce? No, sir, To arrest our peaceful and onward march would be treason to the cause of human liberty. . . .

But, sir, this measure rises in magnitude when you look to Oregon, a territory you are now advancing to occupy. Texas approaches the verge of the mountain pass through which alone upon the South, you penetrate the grand rocky range, and reach the shores of the Pacific. Will you force the establishment of an independent power which, now as the ally of your enemy, or hereafter alone as your foe, may at once harass your commerce in the Gulf and your pathway to Oregon? Dare you permit the security of your intercourse with the new land of promise to be endangered? Sir, they are indissolubly united by the hand of nature, and must not be divided by the blind policy of man. Your course is onward. With Texas and Oregon, your brilliant destiny opens before you. The commerce of the great valley is then secured. The commerce of Northern Mexico is yours; and you lay the foundations of an empire on the Pacific, which in its consequences, will ere long revolutionize the most powerful kingdoms of the earth. There to Oregon your ever active population will press forward with intelligent and unconquerable energy. Your arts, your manufactures, your industry, your capital, whatever is American, will go with them. Connecting chains of steam communication must soon traverse the continent, and unite the two oceans that embrace it. Time and space are annihilated. The interchanges of commerce will speed thousands of miles from the shores of the Atlantic to the Pacific, far sooner than they could pass in the last generation to our inland lakes. Then, with the monopoly of the cotton product of the world in your hand, you will stand upon Oregon and look over upon the shores of Asia. Leaving England and the other nations of Europe behind you, you will have advanced thousands of miles nearer than they to China, to India, to the western coast of the Asiatic continent. The republics of South America, too, which skirt the Pacific, will lay within the embrace of your commerce on the West. Then shall we open in earnest the contest with England for commercial supremacy in the world. Competition will gradually undermine her prosperity. The distant markets for her manufacturers will, one by one, drop from her grasp, till American industry and skill will supplant her in them all. From the day when Texas and Oregon are brought under the sway of American enterprise, begins the decline, and its ultimate triumph comes the downfall of the British empire. . . .

Sir, a position has been taken in this debate that the annexation of Texas will disturb the relations of power between the North and the South, the free States and the slave. What relations of power? Are we then hostile rivals, under bonds to keep the peace? Sir, I thought we were a fraternity of States! Our origin, language, laws, institutions, history, and destiny the same. The war of the revolution was fought for all and by all. Through seven long years our fathers carried before them the declaration of independence, like the ark of the covenant of Jehovah, through fire and through blood. The constitution was the crown of their triumph. It was made for them and for us, and for posterity. And are we now here to carp and cavil at its provisions? It was made to embrace the continent. And are we to defeat the noble design of its founders? Is it their example we follow in agitating the breaking up of its compromises; awakening feelings calculated to estrange and divide us into imaginary adverse interests? What real interests are there, sir, of the South opposed to the North, or of the North opposed to the South, worthy to excite jealousies and array us in hostility among ourselves? Sir, in all this debate I have heard but one. In the midst of the lamentable efforts here calculated to arouse and exasperate sectional prejudices, against which the father of his country warned us so ardently in his parting benediction, no ground of diversity of interest has been named except the imputed hostility of the South to the protection of domestic manufactures. Is this not a question on which opinion differs at the North and the South, the East and the West, and on which political parties over the whole country more or less divide? But let me ask, in what State has the cause of protection been more uniformly sustained than in Louisiana? Texas is her neighbor, identical in interest and in products. But the security of protection, as far as it depends upon the character of a tariff or the action of Congress, is found in the wants of your government. . . .

But what is this pretence that the diffusion of slavery gives the representation from the South a preponderance? The reflection of an instant shows the error of the assertion. The diffusion of slavery does not increase the number of slaves, and cannot therefore the representation based upon them. . . . It is a false assumption, therefore, that the diffusion of slavery does itself affect in any way the question of political power in the Congress of the Union. But then the objection is made to the fact that the slaves are enumerated at all in estimating the number of the population to be entitled to a representative. THAT IS A BLOW AT THE CONSTITUTION ITSELF, AND TO ITS ORIGINAL CONSTRUCTION. Sir, that question was discussed and decided by our fathers. It cannot be opened. But look at the principle on which the objection is founded. If the slaves were emancipated, the objection would cease. Yet if such were the case, it would actually increase the representative power of the South in this hall, and could not lessen the senatorial. Yes, sir, if slavery were abolished in the South, that portion of the Union would have ten more representatives here. Three-fifths only of the slaves are embraced in the enumeration. If free, the whole would be embraced. Strange fancy and fallacy, indeed, that the abolition of slavery would diminish the political power of the South. It must increase it in the ratio of two-fifths of that whole population. It is true the increase of States in the South increases its political power in the Senate, as does the increase of States in other sections of the Union theirs in the Senate; but neither slavery nor the negro race augments the extent of that power. . . . Should we then desire to prevent the abolition of slavery? No, sir. But we should leave the institution to those with whom it exists, and who alone are responsible for its continuance. If the Union is to be extended, let the compromise in which it was formed be maintained. Without them, all efforts to preserve or enlarge it will be vain. . . .

Sir, suppose annexation be war: what then? It has not disturbed Texas in nine years, and unless Great Britain, with her aid, stimulates Mexico, will disturb us as little; and should our commercial enemy openly or secretly do that, who would hesitate for one moment as to the duty of an American Congress? Is it not notorious that Mexico cannot resubjugate Texas? "From the battle of San Jacinto," in the language of Mr. Webster, "the war was at an end." It is the truth. It was spoken by the Secretary of State to the minister of Mexico in 1842. Mere predatory incursions of banditti and sounding notes of preparation are all the demonstration of war which Mexico has made in years past, and even Whig nerves need not tremble at that. But, sir, were annexation out of the question, I hold it the duty of this government authoritatively to interpose its injunction, that the quiet of this quarter of the continent be no longer disturbed by the continuance of this controversy. It should say to Mexico: "This contest must now cease. You have long exhibited your utter inability to reinstate your authority in Texas, and you cannot be permitted, on the strength of a hopeless claim, for years unenforced, to keep our neighbor in a state of agitation by your threats and the depredations of marauders and pirates. The interests of nations demand peace. So long as you might assert your pretensions with any chance of success, or made an honest effort to try again the fortunes of actual conflict, we were content to let the contest remain open. But now it must end." . . .

Texas, sir, must be ours. Its acquisition is identified with the great interest of the country. It is constitutional. It can give no just grounds of complaint to any of the nations of the earth, on this continent or in Europe. . . .

Sir, in all our discussions, let us remember that Texas herself is a party to this measure, coequal with us. She must be consulted. We may dispute about the terms, but the decision is only our own. Let us remember, too, that we have much to gain by annexation, while Texas can obtain little else than mere security against Mexico. Though she even retain her lands, she surrenders her import revenue, with all its destined income, which would alone soon extinguish her debts. Instead of a supplanting rival, she becomes a competitor in the exchange of her staples on terms of equality with us. Her public men sink from eminent positions as the founders of an empire, to the level of State functionaries. . . .

9   Albert Gallatin

Annexation an Injustice

to Mexico

When expansionists denied that Mexico had any legitimate interest in the annexation question, they ignored a clearly-stated warning from Mexico City that annexation would mean war. American conservatives took such warnings seriously. Albert Gallatin, Secretary of the Treasury under Jefferson and Madison, diplomat, and statesman, now approaching the end of his long career, argued in the following brief essay that the United States, in annexing Texas, defied the established principles of diplomatic behavior. Thereafter, the nation could expect war as the only possible result.

AT the time when the annexation of Texas took place, Texas had been recognized as an independent power, both by the United States and by several of the principal European powers; but its independence had not been recognized by Mexico, and the two contending parties continued to be at war. Under those circumstances, there is not the slightest doubt that the annexation of Texas was tantamount to a declaration of war against Mexico. Nothing can be more clear and undeniable than that, whenever two nations are at war, if a third Power shall enter into a treaty of alliance, offensive and defensive, with either of the belligerents, and if such treaty is not contingent, and is to take effect immediately and pending the war, such treaty is a declaration of war against the other party. The causes of the war between the two belligerents do not alter the fact. Supposing that the third party, the interfering Power, should have concluded the treaty of alliance with that belligerent who was clearly engaged in a most just war, the treaty would not be the less a declaration of war against the other belligerent.

If Great Britain and France were at war, and the United States were to enter into such a treaty with either, can there be the slightest doubt that this would be actual war against the other party? that it would be considered as such, and that it must have been intended for that purpose? If at this moment, either France or England were to make such a treaty with Mexico, thereby binding themselves to defend and protect it with all their forces against any other Power whatever, would not the United States instantaneously view such a treaty as a declaration of war, and act accordingly?

But the annexation of Texas, by the United States, was even more than a treaty of offensive and defensive alliance. It embraced all the conditions and all the duties growing out of the

---

From Albert Gallatin, "Annexation of Texas," in *Peace with Mexico* (New York, 1847), pp. 7–9.

alliance; and it imposed them forever. From the moment when Texas had been annexed, the United States became bound to protect and defend her, so far as her legitimate boundaries extended, against any invasion, or attack, on the part of Mexico: and they have uniformly acted accordingly.

There is no impartial publicist that will not acknowledge the indubitable truth of these positions: it appears to me impossible, that they should be seriously denied by a single person.

It appears that Mexico was at that time disposed to acknowledge the independence of Texas, but on the express condition, that it should not be annexed to the United States; and it has been suggested, that this was done under the influence of some European Powers. Whether this last assertion be true or not, is not known to me. But the condition was remarkable and offensive.

Under an apprehension that Texas might be tempted to accept the terms proposed, the Government of the United States may have deemed it expedient to defeat the plan, by offering that annexation, which had been formerly declined, when the Government of Texas was anxious for it.

It may be admitted that, whether independent or annexed to the United States, Texas must be a slave-holding state, so long as slavery shall continue to exist in North America. Its whole population, with hardly any exception, consisted of citizens of the United States. Both for that reason, and on account of its geographical position, it was much more natural, that Texas should be a member of the United States, than of the Mexican Confederation. Viewed purely as a question of expediency, the annexation might be considered as beneficial to both parties. But expediency is not justice. Mexico and Texas had a perfect right to adjust their differences and make peace, on any terms they might deem proper. The anxiety to prevent this result indicated a previous disposition ultimately to occupy Texas: and when the annexation was accomplished; when it was seen, that the United States had appropriated to themselves all the advantages resulting from the American settlements in Texas, and from their subsequent insurrection; the purity of the motives of our Government became open to suspicion.

Setting aside the justice of the proceeding, it is true that it had been anticipated, by those who took an active part in the annexation, that the weakness of Mexico would compel it to yield, or at least induce her not to resort to actual war. This was verified by the fact: and had Government remained in the hands with whom the plan originated, war might probably have been avoided. But when no longer in power, they could neither regulate the impulse they had given, nor control the reckless spirits they had evoked.

Mexico, sensible of her weakness, declined war, and only resorted to a suspension of diplomatic intercourse; but a profound sense of the injury inflicted by the United States has ever since rankled in their minds. It will be found, through all their diplocatic correspondence, through all their manifestoes, that the Mexicans, even to this day, perpetually recur to this never-forgotten offensive measure. And, on the other hand, the subsequent administration of our Government seems to have altogether forgotten this primary act of injustice, and, in their negotiations, to have acted as if this was only an accomplished fact, and had been a matter of course.

PART THREE

OREGON

10 James Buchanan

The Historic American Interest

in Oregon

With the annexation of Texas assured, the expansionist interest during 1845 shifted quickly to the Rocky Mountains and beyond to the shores of the Pacific. Here was a vast region of immense contrasts and doubtful quality, but already the finger of destiny was upon it. The Pioneers who settled the distant valleys of Oregon and California were never to retrace their steps in another long journey across the continent. These pioneers established the direction of the nation's expansive tendencies and set the stage for a new burst of rhetoric which demanded its continued extension across the continent. United States claims, in 1845, were along the Pacific between the 42nd parallel and the Columbia River. To the north of this uncontested territory, however, the fulfillment of American destiny required whatever action—either negotiation or war—might deprive Britain of lands to which she had claims at least equal in quality to those of the United States. To the south, the Mexican title to California had unchallengeable validity. As in Oregon, the enlargement of the American empire south of 42° would require more than persevering pioneers or the phraseology of manifest destiny. It would demand a policy, conceived and executed by the national Executive, which recognized the Mexican interest in California and that nation's desire to defend its title, by war if necessary.

As early as 1844 the rapid movement of pioneers into Oregon had provoked a vigorous and even acrimonious debate in Congress over the American interest in that territory. The exchange revealed a clear division of opinion within the nation between the proponents of manifest destiny, who accepted the challenge that the United States must push its claims to 54° 40', and those who, in the interest of peace with England and the limited objective of securing access to the inlet of Puget Sound, favored compromise with Britain at the 49th parallel. Supporters of the whole-of-Oregon proposal professed no fear of war with England. Indeed, some Western Congressmen declared that they would welcome it.

As President, Polk not only hoped to avoid war with Britain but also recognized the limited American interest in Oregon. Faced with the necessity of resolving the Oregon question peacefully, Polk, in July, 1845, requested his Secretary of State, the noted Pennsylvania Democrat, James Buchanan, to repeat the traditional American offer —a settlement along the 49th parallel—to the British minister in Washington. This proposal denied Britain the free navigation of the Columbia River. The British minister rejected the proposal without forwarding it to London. Buchanan then prepared a full statement of the American position for Louis McLane, the American minister in London, to aid him in his conversations with British officials.

ALTHOUGH the President does not intend to transfer the Oregon negotiation from Washington to London, yet, as Her Britannic Majesty's Ministers will doubtless afford you frequent opportunities of conversing upon the subject, it is proper that you should be well informed of the present state of the question. For this purpose it is necessary to furnish you with a brief historical sketch of the propositions for its adjustment which have been heretofore made and rejected by the respective Governments.

The first negotiation was that of 1818, which terminated in the convention of the 20th October of that year. It was conducted by Messrs. Gallatin and Rush, as American Plenipotentiaries, in obedience to instructions from Mr. Adams, then Secre-

From Buchanan to Louis McLane, July 12, 1845, in John Bassett Moore, ed., *The Works of James Buchanan* (Philadelphia, 1909), VI, 186–194.

tary of State, under Mr. Monroe's administration. Our Plenipotentiaries inform us that they did not, on that occasion, "assert
that the United States had a perfect right to the country; but
insisted that their claim was at least good against Great Britain."
They, therefore, offered to compromise by adopting the parallel
of 49° as the dividing line between the two countries, and by
surrendering to Great Britain the free navigation of the rivers
(the Columbia of course included) which might be intersected
by this line. The British Plenipotentiaries, (Messrs. Robinson
and Goulburn) in answer, "did not make any formal proposition
for a boundary; but intimated that the river itself was the most
convenient that could be adopted, and that they would not
agree to any that did not give them the harbor at the mouth of
the river in common with the United States." But although they
did not propose a permanent boundary, they did make a most
extraordinary proposition to the American Plenipotentiaries,
which was instantly and properly rejected. This was no less in
effect than that the United States should surrender to Great
Britain the exclusive sovereignty over the whole territory north
of 49°, whilst that portion of it which lies between the 45th and
the 49th parallels, embracing the mouth, and nearly the whole
course of the Columbia river, should "be free and open to the
subjects and citizens of the two States respectively, for the purpose of trade and commerce," reserving the claims of the respective parties, not to the whole territory, but to this section of
it merely.

This negotiation resulted in the adoption of the third article
if the convention of the 20th October, 1818, under which the
United States so far yielded to the claims of Great Britain as to
agree that the whole territory should "be free and open for the
term of ten years from the date of the signature of the present
convention, to the vessels, citizens, and subjects of the two
Powers."

The second negotiation on this subject, during the administration of Mr. Monroe, was conducted in 1824 by Mr. Rush as

the American Plenipotentiary, under the instructions of Mr. Adams. In the meantime the United States had acquired the Spanish title, embracing the whole territory in dispute, under the Florida treaty of the 22d February, 1819; and Mr. Monroe had made his celebrated declaration to the world that the American continent should no longer be subject to colonization. Notwithstanding this change in the relative position of the parties, Mr. Monroe, anxious to settle the conflicting claims of Russia, Great Britain, and the United States to the territory on the Northwest Coast of America, and knowing that this could only be done by compromise, authorized Mr. Rush, through the instructions from Mr. Adams, dated the 22d July, 1823, "with a view to draw a definite line of demarcation for the future, to stipulate that no settlement shall be made on the Northwest Coast or on any of the islands thereto adjoining, by Russian subjects, south of latitude 55; by citizens of the United States north of latitude 51°, or by British subjects either south of 51 or north of 55. I mention, (says Mr. Adams,) the latitude of 51 as the bound within which we are willing to limit the future settlement of the United States because it is not to be doubted that the Columbia river branches as far north as 51." "As, however, the line already runs in latitude 49° to the Stony Mountains, should it be earnestly insisted upon by Great Britain, we will consent to carry it in continuance on the same parallel to the sea."

Mr. Rush, with great ability, attempted to execute his instructions. He first proposed 51°, and afterwards 49°; but in vain. . . .

The third negotiation in this subject took place in 1826–'7, during the administration of Mr. Adams, and was conducted by Mr. Gallatin, as American Plenipotentiary, under instructions from Mr. Clay, then Secretary of State. . . .

The next notice of this question will be found under the administration of General Jackson. It is contained in the instruction of Mr. Livingston to Mr. Van Buren, dated on the 1st August, 1831, with a copy of which, so far as they relate to this subject, you shall be furnished. From this you will perceive that General Jackson's administration, so far from objecting to the occupation of the whole territory by the British in common with ourselves, were entirely satisfied to suffer this state of things to continue. . . .

From the 1st of August, 1831, the date of Mr. Livingston's instructions to Mr. Van Buren, until the 9th of October, 1843, no further notice of the Oregon question was taken in any instructions from this Department. On that day, Mr. Upshur, then the Secretary of State under Mr. Tyler's administration, addressed instructions to Mr. Everett on the subject. Following in the course of compromise pointed out by his predecessors, Mr. Upshur says: "The offer of the 49th parallel of latitude, although it has once been rejected, may be again tendered, together with the right of navigating the Columbia, upon equitable terms. . . .

Next came the existing negotiation, which the President found pending on his accession to office.

This negotiation, like all which had preceded it, was based upon the principle of compromising the claims of the parties and not of demanding the whole territory for the United States. The first protocol signed by Messrs. Calhoun and Pakenham, on the 23d August last, states that it was instituted "to treat of the respective claims of the two countries to the Oregon territory with the view to establish a permanent boundary between the two countries westward of the Rocky Mountains to the Pacific Ocean."

The President, at a very early period of his administration, was called upon to decide whether he would break off or continue this negotiation. Placed in such a responsible position, he first inquired whether the national honor required that he should abruptly terminate it by demanding the whole territory in dispute. War before dishonor is a maxim deeply engraven upon the hearts of the American People; and this maxim ever shall regulate his conduct towards foreign nations. But it was impossible for him to conceive that there could be dishonor in pursuing the course which had been adopted by Mr. Monroe, his patriot Revolutionary predecessor, more than a quarter of a century ago, and had been either expressly sanctioned or acquiesced in by all succeeding administrations.

His next inquiry was, would a compromise of the claims of the parties, by adopting the parallel of 49°, materially injure the interest of the United States. The entrance of the Straits of Fuca, Admiralty Inlet, and Puget's Sound, with their fine harbors and rich surrounding soil, are all south of this parallel. We know but little of the country north of it; but, from all the information we have obtained, it is, with the exception of a few spots, wholly unfit for agriculture, and incapable of sustaining any considerable population. Its chief, indeed almost its only value consists in the furs which may yet be collected upon it; and, even in this particular, it is not of much importance.

Arbitration being out of the question, the alternatives which remained were either to compromise the claims of the parties upon terms similar to those which had often been proposed by the Government of the United States and rejected by that of Great Britain, or to demand the exclusive sovereignty over the whole territory in dispute, and thus to render war almost inevitable. In the present enlightened and Christian age, war ought to be the very last alternative of nations, and should never be resorted to unless for a cause which renders it imperatively necessary. To rush into hostilities, if this can be honorably avoided, would subject the United States to the condemnation of all Christendom. The President doubts whether the judgment of the civilized world would be in our favor in a war waged for a comparatively worthless territory north of 49°, which his predecessors had over and over again offered to surrender to Great Britain, provided she would yield her pretensions to the country south of that latitude. Besides, a war for such a cause, whilst it would doubtless be sustained by the patriotism, might not meet the approbation, of a large portion of our own fellow-citizens.

On the other hand, suppose the American proposition of the 49th degree of latitude should be again made by the United States and again rejected by Great Britain, and war then be the consequence, we might appeal to all mankind for the justice and moderation of our demand; the voice of an impartial world would pronounce our cause to be righteous, and our own citizens would be enthusiastically united in sustaining such a war. Should the negotiation end in disappointment, the President, having done all that can be required of him for the preservation of peace, will afterwards feel himself perfectly free to insist upon our rights in their full extent up to the Russian line.

Influenced by these important considerations, you will perceive, from my note to Mr. Pakenham, a copy of which I now enclose you, that the President has once more proposed to the Government of Great Britain that the territory west of the Rocky Mountains which has been, under existing treaties, "free and open" to the occupation of nations ever since 1818, shall now be divided between them by the forty-ninth parallel of north latitude, offering at the same time to make free to Great Britain any port or ports on Vancouver's Island, south of this parallel, which the British Government may desire.

You will observe that the proposition is silent in regard to the navigation of the Columbia river—a privilege which has heretofore been repeatedly offered to Great Britain in former attempts to settle this question. Such a privilege the President cannot concede, although he is well aware of the serious if not insuperable obstacles which this may present to the success of the negotiation. The tenacity with which Great Britain will adhere to the free navigation of the Columbia which she now enjoys is manifest from the note of Mr. Pakenham to Mr. Calhoun of the 12th September last, with a copy of which you have been furnished.

If the free navigation of the Columbia were granted to Great

Britain, this would be a perpetual source of strife and cause of collision between the citizens and subjects of the two nations in those remote regions. . . .

Whilst denying this privilege which has been hitherto so often offered, it may be asked what reason have we to hope that Great Britain may now accede to the naked parallel of 49°. There would be little or none, unless our proposition had contained such a concession in some other particular as to enable her to retreat with honor from her former demands. This will be found in our offer to make free to Great Britain any port or ports on Vancouver's Island south of 49°, which the British Government may desire. It is true this is but a trifling concession, considering the small portion of the cap of Vancouver's Island which lies south of that parallel; and although no equivalent, it is yet something, which may be a refuge for British pride, whilst surrendering the free navigation of the Columbia. Besides, as they have, in their last proposition, so far gone beyond that of 1827 as to offer to make free to the United States any port or ports which they might desire, either on the main land or Vancouver's Island south of latitude 49°, our offer to them of free ports on the southern cap of that island may be deemed a reciprocal concession. . . .

From what has been said, you will perceive how wholly impossible it is for the President to accept any terms of compromise which would bring the British south of the parallel of 49°; and this you may intimate to the British Ministers in conversation, should you deem it wise under all the circumstances. The only exception to this rule which could possibly be made might be the concession, for an adequate equivalent, of the small cap of Vancouver's Island south of this latitude, which would be of no importance to the United States, whilst it is of considerable value to Great Britain.

You will enforce our proposition upon the British Ministry with all the enlightened ability of which you are so eminently the master. Should it be rejected, the President will be relieved from the embarrassment in which he has been involved by the acts, offers, and declarations of his predecessors. Afterwards, if the difficulty can only be resolved by the sword, we may then appeal with confidence to the world for the equity and justice of our cause, and may anticipate the smiles of Heaven upon the right.

11   Frederick P. Stanton

Justification of American Claims
by Higher Law

Higher law principles that underlay the American title to the whole-of-Oregon worked on the assumption that God preferred to be on the side of morality rather than on the side of law. If the struggle for Oregon was between democracy and monarchy, the title of morality went to the United States because it was a democracy. Representative Frederick P. Stanton of Tennessee provided the twist that placed American claims on the chosen side. In his speech before the House on January 14, 1846, he denied that the Hudson's Bay Company or even England herself could establish a satisfactory claim to any portion of Oregon. The United States was destined to acquire the entire region, but destiny did not make the nation's action right. On the contrary, the United States was destined because it was right.

. . . I MUST acknowledge that, if England persists in attempting to hold all the territory north of the Columbia river, or any portion of it south of the 49th parallel of latitude, war must necessarily come. But this will not be on account of notice; war

---

From *Congressional Globe* (29th Cong., 1st Sess., 1846), pp. 199–200.

will ensue under these circumstances, with or without notice. We can never submit to such a claim on the part of England. The war which she may wage in asserting the claim will be a war of aggression and invasion—a war which we must meet, as we would surely meet the invader of this Capitol. I say it would be a war of invasion. And to show my exact meaning, I must be permitted to digress here for a while, to make some statements in reference to the title. I hold that England has no just title to any portion of Oregon. But her most plausible ground of pretension would be by that of contiguity, extending her possessions in North America by the 49th parallel to the Pacific. Now, if the Canadas actually extended on the line of 49° to the Rocky mountains, and the English Government were actually present with its people and its power on the north of that line, and the two nations stood upon equal footing in regard to other sources of title, then England might justly claim to extend her territory on that line to the ocean. But none of these conditions actually exist. The Canadas do not extend on that line to the Rocky mountains; England is not present with her people and her government on this continent; and she does not stand upon an equal footing as to other grounds of title. The country contiguous to that part of Oregon north of 49°, is the possession of the Hudson Bay Company, and cannot be extended by this principle of contiguity. The argument in this respect has lately been placed in a strong light. That company is a mere incorporation, and is subject to the limits prescribed by its charter, which is the law of its creation. That charter originally confined the company to Hudson's bay and its tributaries; and these limits cannot by any torture of construction be extended to those waters which fall over on the other side of the Rocky mountains into the Pacific ocean. An artificial person, a corporation, cannot overleap its prescribed powers; it cannot, therefore, extend its territories by the principle of contiguity. This is a well-settled principle of English common law; it is a principle which may well be adopted—indeed must be admitted—into the law of nations.

But I assume higher ground: I maintain, if this principle did not stand in the way—if the charter of the company as originally granted did not circumscribe its limits within that vast basin in the upper part of North America of which Hudson's bay is the centre, still it is not just, it never can be admitted, that a nation on another continent shall extend its possessions on this by contiguity. If the Canadas themselves bordered on this disputed country, and the circumstances of the two countries were otherwise equal, I should earnestly dispute the applicability of this principle. In the very nature of things it is wrong. Sir, the magnetic wires cannot be extended across the Atlantic ocean—the all pervading influence of electricity is stopped there, and its mysterious voice is drowned in the noise of the surge that beats our shore. Is the invisible power of England more penetrating and pervading than the universal agent I have named? Or rather, do the silent emanations of her power circulate around the whole globe, (like those mighty currents which gave polarity to the earth and direct the needle,) causing every interest in every land, to turn trembling upon its centre, and point to London as its pole? Are there no barriers? Do its intangible links extend through all oceans, over all lands, enabling her to grasp new countries, and divide them with contiguous powers, because she has a foothold by their side? The law which makes the ocean a barrier to instantaneous communication between nations—the law of nature, which has separated continents by interposing vast abysses, forbids that nations on one continent shall have rights on another by implication, extension, contiguity, or by any other invisible, intangible, metaphysical principle whatever. England has attempted to carry out on this continent, by diplomacy, the principles which she has established by the sword in her East India aggression. It remains to be seen whether, when diplomacy fails, she will attempt to use the same means here. The United States owe it to themselves— they owe it to this continent, and the world—to resist the application of those principles. The powers of the Old World, upon the discovery of this continent, adopted principles for its division among themselves; they may have been bound to each other for the maintenance of those principles. Nay, those principles may have been just and wise in their application to such nations, distant as they were from the wild and uncultivated countries which they sought to appropriate. Yet it does not follow that we are to be bound by these conventional arrangements. Our relations to this continent are widely different. We have arisen here, a mighty nation, fast approaching, and destined soon to surpass, the greatness of any European power. We have undisputed rightful possession of a large portion of this continent, and neither reason nor authority will admit that the government of any unappropriated portion of it should be transferred to a distant nation.

I hope I shall be understood. I do not mean to adopt that ground of title which had been assumed here by some gentlemen, under the imposing name of manifest destiny. It was the manifest destiny of England to spread her empire over a large portion of this continent, and of Asia. But that destiny, made manifest by complete fulfilment and perfect realization, neither commends itself to our minds as right, nor does it justify the arbitrary and oppressive measures by which it has been achieved. I believe it is our destiny to possess the whole of Oregon; but this destiny does not make it right; it is our destiny, because it is right. It is not necessary to name the principle I have attempted to state, nor does it require any course of reasoning to establish it. It is one of those propositions of which the bare statement carries conviction to the mind. It is an axiom in political science, as applied to this continent, and must receive universal assent, because it is based upon the law of nature. It is the same principle, in effect, which Mr. Monroe stated when he denied the right of European nations to make further colonies on this continent, and which the President, in his late Message, has again so appropriately and opportunely asserted in the face of the world.

If there be any force in my reasoning, Mr. Chairman, it

follows as a clear inference that a war prosecuted by Great Britain for any part of Oregon would be a war of aggression. And it would be a monstrous usurpation, a gross and blasting shame to humanity, surpassing all the bounds of ordinary crime, if England should determine to wage war upon us for any part of the territory below the 49th parallel. And, sir, I repeat, if such be the disposition of the British Government, if such be her foregone determination, the war must and will come, with or without notice. England would be responsible to the world—to Heaven, for the disastrous consequences of such a war. It would be but another crime of fearful magnitude added to that already mountainous mass of fraud and havoc by which England has heretofore extended her power, and by which she now maintains it. Did some gentleman say her crimes were represented by a vast pyramid of human skulls? I say, sir, rather by a huge pyramid of human hearts, living, yet bleeding in agony, as they are torn from the reeking bosoms of the toiling, fighting millions! . . .

12   Lewis C. Levin

Justification by "Contiguity"

On January 9, 1846, Lewis C. Levin, Congressman from Pennsylvania, established a further higher law claim to Oregon—that of contiguity. Britain he pointed out, occupied an island. Her expansion across the seas was by conquest, based upon her superior naval power. But the United States expanded not by force, but merely by occupying adjacent territory. Nearly a half-century before, this principle of contiguity had assured that the United States would possess Louisiana and Florida, whatever the will of France and Spain. They belonged to the United States by natural law—the law of contiguity.

British settlements in the far Northwest were the accidents of time; by the law of contiguity they were destined to give way to the superior claims of the United States. It was contiguity, declared Levin, that completed for the United States its valid title to the whole of Oregon.

. . . I WILL not fatigue the House by an examination of the title under which we claim to hold the Oregon territory. I consider that question settled on principles too broad and deep to be now doubted by the most infatuated advocate of foreign usurpation. On this point learning, statesmanship, and eloquences have exhausted their resources, and left no candid mind free from the conviction of the justice of our claim, and the insolence of the foreign pretention that attempts to invalidate it. . . .

Am I asked on what I found this principle of inherent and pre-existent right? I answer, on the genius of American institutions—on the spirit of republicanism, that permits not the contaminating proximity of monarchies upon the soil that we have consecrated to the rights of man, and the sublime machinery of the sovereign power of the people; on the eternal laws of God, which have given the earth to man for a habitation, and told him that the natural boundaries to a country only terminate where oceans intervene, and contiguity is obstructed by some formidable obstacle which separates nations and marks out their native home as distinctly as if drawn by the lines of military art. Natural boundaries and the genius of a people always harmonize. As their limits are expansive, so will their enterprise be boundless and their spirit swelling. The natives of an island, in the midst of wide oceans, or of mountains inaccessible to intruders, like those of Switzerland, will lie still, contented with their cribbed and narrow confines. But an island adjacent to an immense continent will aspire to grasp the continent, as does

From *Congressional Globe* (29th Cong., 1st Sess., 1846), Appendix, pp. 95–96.

England, whose natural features are so doubtfully defined by narrow channels separating her from a great continent. Her kings have been crowned in Paris, and Waterloo subjugated all France. Consequently, we have always seen her endeavoring to control the adjacent continent, and, when baffled in that object, throwing her armies and navies across distant oceans, to subjugate by conquest the helpless Hindoo, or exterminate by the sword the more warlike American. Her possessions, therefore, are possessions of conquest; the might of physical force, not the justice of claim, derived from treaty, occupation, cultivation, or any of the arts by which civilization imparts value to what she claims, and which constitutes the justice of our claim to the territory of Oregon to the extreme shores of the Pacific, as far north as 54° 40', to which Great Britain puts forth a doubtful claim of discovery subsequent to our own; the gradual encroachment of military posts, and the spurious authority of treaties dictated by her own ambition, and having no independent existence out of the sphere of her own interest. On our part, we start with the natural foundation of all legitimate claims to national territory; and if that principle pushes our adversary from every foot of soil upon our continent, it is a consequence that I neither fear nor regret; for, if the principle be sound, it will push its way into universal operation, in spite of the frail impediments incident to times, circumstances, and seasons, till it prevails, as it ever has done, by the irresistible power of its truth. I mean the principle of contiguity, free from the intervening barriers of formidable oceans, which, in the case of Great Britain, presents, at the outset, a fatal blow to her claim to any portion of the continent of North America.

In illustration of this obvious principle I must direct your gaze to Louisiana, held by France, and on the unnatural tenure of abstract right, which thousands of miles of intervening ocean exploded, upon grounds of impractical impossibility that sovereignty should exist upon a principle which violated the eternal barriers of nature and of God. Yet Louisiana was held by unquestionable titles, both on the part of France and Spain. It may be said we acquired Louisiana by purchase. I answer, that does not affect the natural principle on which she must inevitably have become ours, purchase or no purchase. Who can for a moment suppose that, if we had not acquired Louisiana by purchase, we should have acquired her by other means? Unquestionably we should. Louisiana is, by the eternal laws of nature, as much part and parcel of the United States as Ohio, or as Wales is of England, or Scotland or Ireland; all of which have come into the great national whirlpool of British central power by the force of the same inevitable law. Behold the Floridas, too; once the pride and boast of the Spanish crown—a gem that she would never surrender—a jewel that even protracted the sickly dream of her undying grandeur, even after King Joseph had despoiled her convents, and Napoleon had demonstrated her imbecility by bestriding her in her downfall, with her monarch, Ferdinand VII, for prisoner, and her crown twirling on his finger like a child's toy! Could Spain have retained the Floridas, even had she so resolved in the most rigid determination of a proud royalty? We know, we all know, that the mere idea is as visionary as the spectres that haunt a sick man's dream. Florida was ours by a natural law—the law of contiguity—the same law which marks out the limits of all nations on the lap of the earth, which gives identity to Spain, consolidation to France, individuality to the German empire, natural features to Italy and to Russia, and unity to Great Britain in England, Wales, Scotland, and Ireland.

And may I not bring this illustration down to the last point of national attraction, as seen in the annexation of Texas? Could there be a more decisive and clinching argument in favor of our claim to Oregon than the annexation of Texas? Not that I mean to say we had any claim to Texas, derived from treaty, or any means short of that natural law on whose irresistible power I lay an emphatic affirmative. We had recognised the independence of Texas. The great Powers of Europe had also recognised her as an independent republic; yet, behold the fatality of the natural law that so suddenly and by one blow, places an extinguisher upon all her national glory, and brings her into the bosom of the Federal Union—the "lone star," as has been so beautifully remarked by the Executive, "becoming one of the glorious constellation."

Let me not be misunderstood, sir. I do not speak as having been an advocate for the annexation of Texas *as a State,* though willing to see her come in as territory of the United States. When I cast my vote against the annexation of Texas, I fixed my eye upon Canada, the principle of whose annexation exists in nature; and I trembled as I thought of the day when Canada might point to the precedent you have established, and ask for an immediate representation on this floor—a representation based on the most uncompromising monarchists on the face of the globe! If, then, there was anything in my attitude on that question which might lead our southern friends to suppose that I was arraying myself against them, I trust they will do me the justice to believe that I was at least watching over their children's rights and interests. But, sir, I merely allude to Texas now to show the immense array of attractive interests that concentrated to a point to uphold Texas an independent empire, and all of which ingloriously failed before the all-subduing potency of an eternal law of Nature, that contiguous territory, however remote, must eventually melt into one government before the irresistible and expansive force of population, power, the social attraction of gravitation, and the intensity of the central influence to control the extremities, as in the human body, where the heart and the head govern all the members.

I am aware that this argument may be opposed by the fact of her Britannic Majesty now having actual possession of a portion of territory on the northern limb of our continent, and that a large tract of Maine has been ceded by our Government to that

Power. To this I answer that that fact is an accident of time and occasion, having no application to a principle in nature, which is eternal, and must eventually triumph.

Who can suppose for a moment that England will continue to retain through all future time her American possessions? Like France at one time, she now thinks she will never surrender them, but expend her last shilling and her last sigh in their defence. France throught the same of Louisiana; Spain thought the same of Florida. In five years England may be glad to rid herself of every foot of soil upon our continent, in order to concentrate her undivided energies to preserve her India provinces, or secure breathing space nearer the seat of her natural empire at home. I say natural empire, and I beg attention to this palpable distinction, so necessary to the present discussion. Nations have heretofore governed by natural and artificial empires; natural in their homestead or limits of continuity, and artificial when exercising assumed power over remote provinces. Nations of artificial grandeur commence their power with provinces remote and distant; they end their career by their timely surrender, if they survive the strangling embrace of their unnatural children. What has Spain dwindled to since she lost her provinces in North and South America? What Portugal? France, to compensate for similar losses, has established Algeria. Who believes she can retain it? Yet such is the fatalism of kings, who only flourish by aggression, and who are sure to breathe their last when confined to their homestead. Is England now acting on the lesson furnished by her royal predecessors in the road to ruin? It would really seem so.

But, to come back to the subject of claim, sir. There is one ground of title which no power on earth can controvert or take away from us. It is that memorial of the people of Oregon asking for the extension of our laws and constitution over that country. This brings the question directly to the principles of the American Revolution—self-government, the rights of man, and the sovereignty of the people. The people of Oregon are free, sovereign, and independent. They ask to be governed by American laws, which they have a right to adopt, and which we have a right to grant, and which, on no principle, have we a right to refuse. As we now stand in relation to Oregon, we never could agree that she should become a British province, even if England had an unquestionable right to that immense country, Without going into an elaborate argument on the details of claim set up by Great Britain, it is enough for us to know that she has no claim superior to our own. But, for the sake of argument, let us suppose them to be equal. On what ground can England lay claim to a territory peopled by emigrants from the United States—a territory contiguous to this Union, part of the continent of North America, and assigned by the fiat of nature to the same "manifest destiny?" Here, sir, we meet a claim to the whole of that territory which subtle diplomacy and international law in vain assail—the right of American born citizens to free government, and their liberty to choose their own laws, without the interference of a foreign monarch thousands of miles remote from their homestead. . . .

. . . American-born citizens have made a permanent settlement in that wild country. Not mere companies of trappers, with their military forts and garrisons, who only cultivate sufficient land for their present necessities, but the settlement of families who build and plant, and there abide forever to transmit the soil to their children. Now, sir, the British have no such settlements, and the Americans have. There is more title, sir, in a plain fact like this, than in all the treaties that ever were made by which the abstract right of discovery was sought to be transferred to another nation, who should also hold it as an abstract right. We recognise this principle, as far as it goes, in all our pre-emption laws. We make the labor and occupancy of the soil the consideration paid for its proprietorship. True, this does not reach to the disputed claims of nations for the same tract of territory; but it illustrates by analogy the true principle of property; for I mean to contend, sir, that discovery goes for nothing, unless followed by actual settlement, and on this ground I deny all foreign claims whatever; and if ours is not actual settlement, then was actual settlement never made in any country by any people.

To establish valid title to Oregon, on the part of Great Britain, she must show—first, title by discovery, acquired by treaty; second, actual settlement as a permanent abode by the subjects of her kingdom; third, contiguity. Now, England can show not even one of these titles. On our part we exhibit them all. First, discovery by Capt. Gray, of Boston; second, acquired by treaties with France and Spain from 42° up to 54° 40'; third, by actual settlement; and, fourth, by contiguity. A complete chain of valid title. . . .

13   John Quincy Adams

Justification by Scripture

John Quincy Adams stressed the last essential higher law claim to Oregon. The former Secretary of State and President propounded this claim in his noted address before the House of Representatives on February 9, 1846. Adams insisted that the American claim lay in the obvious contrast between the American desire to make the wilderness blossom, and the British purpose of reserving it for navigation and the hide trade. In all such higher law arguments there was an assumption that Britain would accept such doctrines in defiance of her own interests and claims along the Pacific coast of North America. Adams's defense of the whole-of-Oregon in 1846 appears strange for two reasons. First of all, he had helped to establish the historic American claim to the 49th parallel, both as Secretary of State and as President. Secondly, Adams understood diplomacy and national behavior too well to conclude that Britain would be swayed by such weak and unsubstantial arguments. In 1846, however, he was bitterly at odds with the Polk administration and was undoubtedly attempting to embarrass it by depriving the executive of moderate support in Congress in its effort to find a scapegoat to blame for its ultimate decision to compromise.

. . . SIR, there has been so much said on the question of title in this case, that I believe it would be a waste of time for me to say anything more about it, unless I refer to a little book you have there upon your table, which you sometimes employ to administer a solemn oath to every member of this House to support the Constitution of the United States. If you have it, be so good as to pass it to the Clerk, and I will ask him to read what I conceive to be the foundation of our title.

If the Clerk will be so good as to read the 26th, 27th, and 28th verses of the 1st chapter of Genesis, the committee will see what I consider to be the foundation of the title of the United States.

The Clerk read accordingly as follows:

"26. And God said, Let us make man in our image, after our likeness; and let them have dominion over the fish of the sea, and over the fowl of the air, and over the cattle, and over all the earth, and over every creeping thing that creepeth upon the earth.

"27. So God created man in his own image, in the image of God created he him: male and female created he them.

"28. And God blessed them, and God said unto them. Be fruitful and multiply, and replenish the earth, and subdue it; and have dominion over the fish of the sea, and over the fowl of the air, and over every living thing that moveth upon the earth."

That, sir, (continued Mr. A.) in my judgment, is the founda-

From *Congressional Globe* (29th Cong., 1st Sess., 1846), pp. 340–342.

tion not only of our title to the territory of Oregon, but the foundation of all human title to all human possessions. It is the foundation of the title by which you occupy that chair; it is the foundation of the title by which we are now called to occupy the territory of Oregon; and we cannot do it without putting a close to any agreement which we have made with Great Britain that we will not occupy it.

And here I beg leave to repeat an idea that I have already expressed before, and that is, that there is a very great misapprehension of the real merits of this case founded on the misnomer which declares that convention to be a convention of joint occupation. Sir, it is not a convention of joint occupation. It is a convention of non-occupation—a promise on the part of both parties that neither of the parties will occupy the territory for an indefinite space; first for ten years, then until the notice shall be given from one party to the other that the convention shall be terminated—that is to say, that the restriction, the fetter upon our hands shall be thrown off, which prevents occupation, and prevents the carrying into execution the law of God, which the Clerk has read from the Holy Scriptures. Now, if this controversy in relation to the territory of Oregon was with any other than a Christian nation, I could not cite that book. With the Chinese, and all nations who do not admit the canon of Scripture, it would be quite a different question. It would be a different question between us and the Indian savages, who occupy that country as far as there is any right of occupation, for they do not believe this book. I suppose the mass of this House believe this book. I see them go up and take their oath of office upon it; and many of the southern members kiss the book in token, I suppose, of their respect for it. It is between Christian nations that the foundation of title to land is laid in the first chapter of Genesis, and it is in this book that the title to jurisdiction, to eminent domain, to individual property, had its foundation—all of which flow from other sources subsequent to that which the Clerk read.

Now I will ask the Clerk to read another passage of that book; and that is, I think the 8th verse of the 2d Psalm.

The Clerk read:

"8. Ask of me, and I shall give thee the heathen for thine inheritance, and the uttermost parts of the earth for thy possession."

If the Clerk will read a verse or two before that which he has just read it will be seen to whom it is said He will give them.

The Clerk read:

"6. Yet have I set my king upon my holy hill of Zion.

"7. I will declare the decree: the Lord hath said unto me, Thou art my son; this day have I begotten thee.

"8. Ask of me, and I shall give thee the heathen for thine inheritance, and the uttermost parts of the earth for thy possession."

That (continued Mr. A.) is the Personage to whom the promise was made of giving the heathen for his inheritance, and the uttermost parts of the earth for his possession. Now, the promise contained in that verse was understood by all commentators upon the Bible, and by the Christian nations of all denominations, certainly before the reformation of Luther, to apply to the Lord Jesus Christ. Then, sir, without entering into any long historical detail, by the Christians and Christian nations, (for he spoke now of international law,) the Pope, or the Bishop of Rome, was considered as the representative of Christ upon earth; and this verse from the Psalm promising the heathen for his inheritance and the uttermost parts of the earth for his possession, together with another verse at the close of one of the gospels, (which he would not detain the committee by asking the Clerk to read at the desk,) in which the Lord Jesus Christ, after rising from the dead, said to his disciples, (in substance,) "Go forth and preach to all nations my Gospel; and I will be with you to the end of the world." From these three several passages of the Scriptures, the Pope of Rome asserted, and for many ages it was admitted that he had, the power of giving to any king or sovereign to whom he pleased, the power of going and subduing all barbarous nations, and subduing and conquering all territory, either not subdued at all, or subdued by barbarous nations, for the purpose of converting them to Christianity. At the time of the discovery of the continents of North and South America by Christopher Columbus, this was the law of nations between Christians, recognised, acknowledged, admitted; and when Christopher Columbus came, under a commission from Ferdinand and Isabella, King and Queen of Castile, Leon, and Aragon—when he came and made his discovery, which he did in October, 1492, in the next year, some time in the month of March or April, 1493, the Pope of Rome—at that time authorized, according to all international law between Christians to do it—gave to Ferdinand and Isabella the whole continents of North and South America. He authorized the drawing of a line from pole to pole 100 leagues west of the Azores islands and Cape de Verde; and he gave the whole 100 leagues beyond, from pole to pole, to Ferdinand and Isabella, King and Queen of Castile, Leon, and Aragon. Now, do I intend to say that that is one of our titles? I must say it, although I think, perhaps, as little of it as any member of this House. But it was a good title when it was given. It was the understanding, the faith, the belief of all the Christian nations of Europe, that the Pope had his power; and it was acquiesced in by them all for a time. That same Pope at that time was in the custom of giving away not only barbarous nations, but civilized nations. He dethroned sovereigns, put them under interdict, and excommunicated them from intercourse with all other Christians; and it was submitted to. And now, sir, the Government of Great Britain—the nation of Great Britain—holds the island of Ireland on no other title. Three hundred years before that time, Pope Adrian of Rome gave, by that same power, to Henry I of England the island of Ireland, and England has held it from that day to this under that title, and no other. That is, no other, unless by conquest; (for it has been in a continued state of rebellion ever since, and Great Britain has been obliged to conquer it half a dozen times since; and now the question is, whether Ireland shall ever become an independent kingdom. If we come to a war with Great Britain, she will find enough to do to maintain that island.) I do not think it of very great value; though I think it does not go for nothing. Now, that general authority given to man to increase, multiply, and replenish the earth, and subdue it, was a grant from the Creator to man as man; it was a grant to every individual of the human race in his individual capacity. But, then, the portion that belongs to the individual, and was given thereby, was a matter for the whole human race to accommodate among themselves. That is to say, in communities, communities were to agree together what should be the metes and bounds of that portion of the earth given them by the general grant from the Creator. When communities were formed, it became a matter of legislation among them to whom any particular property—e.g. a lot of land on which to build a house—should belong. Any territorial right whatever, as between individuals, was to be regulated by legislation; as between nations it was to be regulated by consent, by convention; and in that way the laws of nations, as they are called, (which are nothing more than the customs of nations,) and the treaties and conventions of nations, have regulated how every spot, every inch of land, shall be occupied. And among the rest, it is by these laws and regulations—internal among communities and international among nations—that you hold that seat, (referring to the Speaker's seat,) and I do not, because you have it, elevated to it by the laws of the country, and no other man can take, except by permission, so long as your right continues.

Well, sir, our title to Oregon stands on the same foundation. When this discovery of Columbus came to be a matter of great importance among the nations of the earth, other nations took into their heads to plant colonies on this continent, and then came the question of controversy between them, which never has been settled to this day. Our question now with Great

Britain is one of the consequences of that state of things. There never has been any agreement between the nations of the earth how these points shall be settled.

There have been titles derived from treaty, from agreement, from conquest; there have been sources from which they have derived title to territory. We have been told here that our title to Columbia river and all the territory that is drained by it, is in consequence of discovery and exploration. Well, sir, that has been partially an agreement between the nations that they will say they consider that where a nation discovers the mouth of a river, and explores that river to its source, then that nation is entitled, and has been generally allowed, to maintain their authority. But that is not the foundation of any of our titles. . . .

Coming down to this pretended principle, that the discovery of the mouth of a river gives title to all the land watered by that river and its tributaries—and this is the ground on which we contend that the Mississippi valley, among the rest, belongs to us—that title is a parcel of the rights by which you hold that seat, and by which all property is held. This charter of Charles I, to the colony of Massachusetts Bay, gives from 40 to 48 degrees of latitude, without reference to any rivers. The kings of England, following the example of the Pope of Rome, undertook to grant lands all over this continent, and upon such terms as they thought proper. When they found the mouth of a river, and it was for their interest to claim the territory watered by that river, they claimed it. Louis XIV gave to Crozart—and that is the title by which we still hold that country—he gave him no land, but gave him merely the power to trade with the Mississippi river and all its tributaries, because that river had been discovered by French subjects many years before coming from Canada.

All these titles are imperfect. Discovery is, therefore, no title of itself. The discovery of a river and of land is no title of itself. Exploration comes next. That gives something more of a title. Continuity and contiguity both concur to give a title. They are none of them perfect in themselves. There is nothing complete in the way of title, but actual possession; and that is the only thing we now want, to have a perfect, clear, indisputable, and undoubted right to the territory of Oregon. It is possession; it is occupation, if you please. . . .

. . . She herself [Great Britain] admits that she has no title there; she pretends that she has none. But what does she say? She says that it is an open country; that it is one of those countries occupied, as far as it is occupied at all, only by barbarous nations—that it is a country which is open to all parties. She does not claim exclusive jurisdiction. I promise you she will, if you suffer her to do it, before she has done, not only to what you choose to give her, but to the whole territory. But at this day she claims no exclusive jurisdiction over the whole country. She claims, and by virtue of this convention, to have the country free and open—that is, to keep it in a savage and barbarous state for her hunters—for the benefit of the Hudson Bay Company for hunting. Now, she knows that it would have no value to her at all from the day that it is settled by tillers of the ground. It is abolished from that time by the nature of things. And therein consists the difference between her claims and our claims. We claim that country—for what? To make the wilderness blossom as the rose, to establish laws, to increase, multiply, and subdue the earth, which we are commanded to do by the first behest of God Almighty. That is what we claim it for. She claims to keep it open for navigation, for her hunters to hunt wild beasts; and of course she claims for the benefit of the wild beasts, as well as of the savage nations. There is the difference between our claims.

14   Charles Goodyear

Manifest Destiny a "Robber's Title"

Conservative Whigs, as well as many Eastern and Southern Democrats, rushed to defend American diplomatic tradition which they felt was being defied by the limitless claims of higher law doctrines. These men accused the extremists on the Oregon question of undermining the established American tradition not only of limiting the nation's claims to the 49th parallel, but also of confining all United States objectives abroad to precise definitions of national interest. Representative Charles Goodyear of New York, speaking in the House of Representatives on January 16, 1846, termed manifest destiny nothing but a robber's right, which not only threatened the nation's moral position in the world but also threatened to involve the country in a series of potentially costly policies that had little relationship to its interests. Goodyear argued that the United States had a great destiny, but one that rested on the development of the resources it already possessed, not on further territorial aggrandizement. To expand by conquest, he warned, was to overreach and ultimately perish in the midst of victories. Goodyear believed that the interests of the United States would be satisfied by a compromise settlement with England along the 49th parallel, and that the government in Washington should accept such a proposal from London in the proper spirit. To demand anything more was to make war inevitable. What mattered in international affairs was not the legal right but the consequences of an action.

. . . I AM aware, sir, that a claim in our favor paramount to all others has been set up—that of manifest destiny. It runs thus: God hath given to this nation the western continent and the fulness thereof. This, as I understand it, overrides all titles, and sets at defiance all reasoning. This claim to universal dominion was put forth in the commencement of this debate, and has been frequently urged in the course of it. . . . I regretted to hear the sentiment avowed in an American Congress, because it implies a doubt of the validity of our own perfect title, and because it has ever been used to justify every act of wholesale violence and rapine that ever disgraced the history of the world. It is the

---

From *Congressional Globe* (29th Cong., 1st Sess., 1846), Appendix, pp. 110–111.

robber's title; but its record is accompanied by the instructive lesson that it ultimately meets the robber's doom. The Macedonian conqueror consulted the Delphic oracle, and having obtained from the priestess an equivocal answer, which, in his construction, gave him the right, by *manifest destiny,* to conquer the world, he pursued his career of victory amid sighs and tears and blood, over homes and hearths made desolate, cities wasted, and prostrate thrones, until, standing on the verge of the then habitable globe, he wept that he had not another world to conquer. Confident in the omnipotence of his fate, he drew around him his imperial robes and proudly boasted of the endless duration of his dynasty and his throne. But death struck the conqueror in a drunken revel, and his fated empire was broken into fragments, and disappeared from the earth, like the sand before the simoom of the desert. Rome, too, consulted her oracles, and sought in omens and signs her title by manifest destiny to universal empire. The response of the priest was propitious, and her legions proceeded to execute the decree. The title lost nothing of its force while there was wealth to plunder or nations to subdue; under it, the rapacity of the Roman praetor knew no bounds, his cruelty no remorse. She checked not her career of victory until the spoils of every nation, from the pillars of Hercules to the Indian ocean, swelled the triumph of her conquerors, and contributed to the luxuries and magnificence of what she fondly termed the Eternal City. "While the Colliseum stands Rome shall stand," was her proud boast. The Colliseum still stands, majestic in its ruins; but the Eternal City, long since despoiled of its glory and its power, is now only known to the traveller as the city of shattered columns and mighty recollections. The modern conqueror—the man of unbeating heart and iron nerve, who pursued his purposes with like unbending firmness upon the sands of Egypt and the snows of Russia—whose eye never quailed, and whose heart never faltered—who asserted and proved his title at that cannon's mouth, until victory, even, seemed the doomed minister of his stern and unrelenting will—he, too, pointed to his star and talked of destiny; but that bright luminary has set in perpetual night, and the eye that gazed upon its brightness was closed forever upon a barren rock in the steep Atlantic wave.

Who hath read the book of fate, or fathomed the purposes of the Almighty? Sir, we may read the future by the past. I have no doubt of our destiny, if we limit our ambition to the development of the human faculties and the cultivation of the arts of peace. With a territory capable of sustaining a larger population in comfort and opulence than any other country under one Government upon earth, the human mind can scarcely limit the progress of our dominion, either in duration or extent. But if, on the other hand, we should be stimulated to territorial aggrandizement by the prospect of successful war, I have as little doubt that the western continent would soon to be found too narrow a sphere for our conquests. But with this brilliant prospect before us, we should remember that all history comes burdened with the admonition, that the nation which is destined to extend its territory by conquest, is equally fated to perish in the midst of its victories. It is due, sir, to the American people to know that their title, in this instance, needs no such equivocal alliance. In the appropriate language of the gentleman from Tennessee, [Mr. Stanton,] our right is our destiny, not our destiny our right. But we are led to consider, in this connexion, the duty of our Government, in case England should propose to renew the negotiation upon the basis of the division of the territory in the spirit of amicable adjustment. I answer she should be met in the same spirit; and, in case she should offer the terms recently tendered and withdrawn by this Government, they should be unhesitatingly accepted. If it was consistent with the duties of Government to make the offer then, it is proper to accept it now. The interests and rights of the two countries have in no respect changed in regard to this territory. I do not say that the negotiation should be reopened at our instance, nor that any more favorable terms should be offered or accepted. On the contrary, I think our Government, in the manifestation of its disposition to adjust this difficulty, has approached the extremest limit which the rights, the interests, or the honor of our country will warrant; and if England should prefer to try the issue of a resort to arms, we shall then be restored to our belligerent rights, and may claim and take the whole. England well knows that war is a game which more than one can play at.

Sir, the inference I draw from this view of the matter is, that the notice being given, the joint occupancy terminated, and England remaining quiet, our rights to exclusive jurisdiction should be asserted only up to the 49th parallel of latitude. This being understood to be the policy and determination of our Government, the chances of war are entirely removed. England will not incur the hazards of a war for an inconsiderable tract of unproductive wilderness, the title to which she knows is clearly and unquestionably in us. This being known, the excitement upon this subject, as well in England as in this country, would entirely subside, and we should hear little more of Oregon.

But if the extreme policy, of the whole or none, urged by a few gentlemen upon this floor, is to be carried out, I cannot see how a war can be avoided. England cannot, consistently with her national honor, accept less, in the division of this territory, than has been repeatedly offered her; and, however reluctant she may be, I see not how she can escape a resort to this last dread alternative.

I proceed to consider for one moment whether it is our interest to drive her to this extremity.

Our national honor is no way concerned in the matter. By adopting the 49th parallel as our boundary we make our own terms, and dictate them, too, somewhat imperiously to the haughtiest and most powerful nation upon earth. It is, then, a mere matter of expediency, and as such I propose to consider it.

The value of the territory in dispute, compared with the

expenses, the sacrifices, the sufferings, bloodshed, and horrors of a war, is the question at issue. Sir, I address not my arguments to those sublimated gentlemen who assert that the existence of a right precludes the consideration of consequences in its assertion. The gentlemen have forgotten, or haply never learned, that a regard to consequences is the first duty of a statesman; that it is that alone for which impartial history will give him credit for sagacity and wisdom. . . .

15   Robert C. Winthrop

A Plea for Compromise

Representing the viewpoint of the New England Whigs whose primary interest was in adequate ports along the Pacific coast, Representative Robert C. Winthrop of Massachusetts reminded the House on January 3, 1846, "As to land, we have millions of acres of better land still unoccupied on this side of the mountains." Winthrop demanded negotiation with the London government, as he believed that the ports essential for the development of American commerce in the Pacific could be secured by a compromise settlement at 49°. War, he was convinced, could not be a rational solution. In addition, Winthrop ridiculed the concept of manifest destiny, maintaining that it could have no influence on people residing outside the United States. What was at issue in Oregon, he declared, was a boundary, not a title, and as a boundary question it had a long tradition in which the United States had repeatedly offered Britain a settlement at the 49th parallel. "With what face, then," he asked, "can we now turn round and declare that there is no boundary line to be run, nothing to negotiate about. . . ." If war came, ran Winthrop's conclusion, the administration must take responsibility "for all its guilt and all its disgrace." (Document 15.)

. . . I AM perfectly aware, Mr. Speaker, that, express the views which I entertain when I may, I shall not escape reproach and imputation from some quarters of the House. I know that there are those by whom the slightest syllable of dissent from the extreme views which the Administration would seem recently to have adopted, will be eagerly seized upon as evidence of a want of what they call patriotism and American spirit. I spurn all such imputations in advance. I spurn the notion that patriotism can only be manifested by plunging the nation into war, or that the love of one's own country can only be measured by one's hatred to any other country. Sir, the American spirit that is wanted at the present moment, wanted for our highest honor, wanted for our dearest interests, is that which dares to confront the mad impulses of a superficial popular sentiment, and to appeal to the sober second thoughts of moral and intelligent men. Every schoolboy can declaim about honor and war, the British lion and the American eagle; and it is a vice of our nature that the calmest of us have heartstrings which may vibrate for a moment even to such vulgar touches. But, (thanks to the institutions of education and religion which our fathers founded), the great mass of the American people have, also, an intelligence and a moral sense, which will sooner or later respond to appeals of a higher and nobler sort, if we will only have the firmness to make them. It was a remark of an old English courtier, a century and a half ago, to one who threatened to take the sense of the people on some important question, that he would take the nonsense of the people and beat him twenty to one. And it might have been something better than a good joke in relation to the people of England at the time it was uttered. But I am not ready to regard it as applicable to our own intelligent and educated American people at the present day. An appeal to the nonsense

---

From *Congressional Globe* (29th Cong., 1st Sess., 1846), Appendix, pp. 98–101.

of the American people may succeed for an hour; but the stern sense of the country will soon reassert itself, and will carry the day in the end. . . .

I honor the Administration, Mr. Speaker, for whatever spirit of conciliation, compromise, and peace, it has hitherto manifested on this subject, and have no hesitation in saying so. If I have anything to reproach them with, or taunt them for, it is for what appears to me as an unreasonable and precipitate abandonment of that spirit. And if anybody desires on this account, or any other account, to brand me as a member of the peace party, I bare my bosom, I hold out both my hands, to receive that brand. I am willing to take its first and deepest impression, while the iron is sharpest and hottest. If there be anything of shame in such a brand, I certainly glory in my shame. . . .

There are three distinct views in which this question may be presented, as one peculiarly for negotiation and compromise. In the first place, there is the character of the subject-matter of the controversy. Unquestionably there may be rights and claims not of a nature to admit of compromise, and as to which there must be absolute and unconditional relinquishment on one side or the other, or a conflict is inevitable. I may allude to the impressment of our seamen as an example—a practice which could not be renewed by Great Britain at any moment, or under any circumstances, without producing immediate hostilities. But here we have as the bone of our contention, a vast and vacant territory, thousands of miles distant from both countries, entirely capable of division, and the loss of any part, I had almost said of the whole, of which, would not be of the smallest practical moment to either of them—a territory the sovereignty of which might remain in abeyance for a half century longer without serious inconvenience or detriment to anybody, and in reference to which there is certainly not the slightest pretence of a necessity for summary or precipitate action. We need ports on the Pacific. As to land, we have millions of acres of better land still unoccupied on this side of the mountains. What a spectacle it would be, in the sight of men and angels, for the two countries which claim to have made the greatest advances in civilization and Christianity, and which are bound together by so many ties of nature and art, of kindred and of commerce, each of them with possessions so vast and various, to be seen engaging in a conflict of brute force for the immediate and exclusive occupation of the whole of Oregon! The annals of barbarism would afford no parallel to such a scene!

In the second place, sir, there is the character of the *title* to this territory on both sides. I shall attempt no analysis or history of this title. I am certainly not disposed to vindicate the British title; and as to the American, there is nothing to be added to the successive expositions of the eminent statesmen and diplomatists by whom it has been illustrated. But, after all, what a title it is to fight about! . . . Of what is the title made up? Vague traditions of settlement, musty records of old voyages, conflicting claims of discovery, disputed principles of public law, acknowledged violations of the rights of aboriginal occupants—these are the elements—I had almost said the beggarly elements—out of which our clear and indisputable title is compounded. I declare to you, sir, that as often as I thread the mazes of this controversy, it seems to me to be a dispute as to the relative rights of two parties to a territory, to which neither of them has any real right whatever; and I should hardly blame the other nations of the world for insisting on coming in for scot and lot in the partition of it. Certainly, if we should be so false to our character as civilized nations as to fight about it, the rest of Christendom would be justified, if they had the power, in treating us as we have always treated the savage tribes of our own continent, and turning us both out altogether. . . .

Let me not be misunderstood, Mr. Speaker. I have no hesitation in saying that I honestly think, upon as dispassionate a review of the correspondence as I am capable of, that the American title to Oregon is the best now in existence; but I honestly think, also, that the whole character of the title is too confused and complicated to justify any arbitrary and exclusive assertions of right, and that a compromise of the question is every way consistent with reason, interest, and honor.

There is one element in our title, however, which I confess that I have not named, and to which I may not have done entire justice. I mean that new revelation of right which has been designated as *the right of our manifest destiny to spread over this whole continent.* It has been openly avowed in a leading Administration journal that this, after all, is our best and strongest title—one so clear, so preeminent, and so indisputable, that if Great Britain had all our other titles in addition to her own, they would weigh nothing against it. The right of our manifest destiny! There is a right for a new chapter in the law of nations; or rather, in the special laws of our own country; for I suppose the right of a manifest destiny to spread will not be admitted to exist in any nation except the universal Yankee nation! This right of our manifest destiny, Mr. Speaker, reminds me of another source of title, which is worthy of being placed beside it. Spain and Portugal, we all know, in the early part of the sixteenth century, laid claim to the jurisdiction of this whole northern continent of America. Francis I is said to have replied to this pretension, that he should like to see the clause in *Adam's Will* in which their exclusive title was found. Now, sir, I look for an early reproduction of this idea. I have no doubt that, if due search be made, a copy of this primeval instrument, with a clause giving us the whole of Oregon, can be somewhere hunted up. Perhaps it may be found in that same Illinois cave in which the Mormon Testament has been discovered. I commend the subject to the attention of those in that neighborhood, and will promise to withdraw all my opposition to giving notice or taking possession, whenever the right of our manifest destiny can be fortified by the provisions of our great first parent's Will!

Mr. Speaker, there is a third, and, in my judgment, a still more conclusive reason, for regarding this question as one for negotiation and compromise. I refer to its history, and to the admissions on both sides which that history contains. For thirty years this question has been considered and treated as one not of title, but of boundary. To run a boundary line between Great Britain and the United States from the Rocky mountains to the Pacific ocean—this has been the avowed object of each successive negotiation. It has been so treated by Mr. Monroe, and Mr. Adams, and Mr. Gallatin, and Mr. Rush, and by all the other American statesmen who have treated of it at all. Offers of compromise and arrangement have been repeatedly made on both sides on this basis. Three times we have offered to Great Britain to divide with her on the 49th parallel of latitude, and to give her the navigation of the Columbia into the bargain. Mr. Polk and Mr. Buchanan themselves have acted upon the same principle up to the moment of the final abrupt termination of the negotiations. They have offered again to make the 49th parallel the boundary line between the possessions of Great Britain and the United States in the Northwestern Territory. With what face, then, can we now turn round and declare that there is no boundary line to be run, nothing to negotiate about, and that any such course would involve a cession and surrender of American soil! Such a course would be an impeachment of the conduct of the distinguished statesmen whose names I have mentioned. It implies an imputation upon the present President of the United States and his Secretary of State. And, explain it as we may, it would be regarded as an unwarrantable and offensive assumption by the whole civilized world.

. . . I deny that the rejection of the precise offer which was made to Great Britain last summer, has furnished satisfactory evidence that no compromise which the United States ought to accept can be effected. Certainly, I regret that Great Britain did not accept that offer. Certainly, I think that this question might fairly be settled on the basis of the 49th parallel; and I believe sincerely that, if precipitate and offensive steps be not taken on our part, the question will ultimately be settled on that basis. But there may be little deviations from that line required to make it acceptable to Great Britain; and, if so, we ought not to hesitate in making them. I deny that the precise offer of Mr. Buchanan is the only one which the United States ought to accept for the sake of peace. Such a suggestion is an impeachment of the wisdom and patriotism of men by no means his inferiors, who have made other and more liberal offers. I think that we ought to accept a compromise at least as favorable to Great Britain as the one which we have three times proposed to her. If we are unwilling to give her the navigation of the Columbia, we should provide some equivalent for it. If the question is to be amicably settled, it must be settled on terms consistent with the honor of both parties. And nobody can imagine that Great Britain will regard it as consistent with her honor, to take a line less favorable to her interests than that which she has three times declined within the last thirty years. . . .

But while I am thus opposed to war for Oregon, or to any measures which, in my judgment, are likely to lead to war, I shall withhold no vote from any measure which the friends of the Administration may bring forward for the defence of the country. Whether the bill be for two regiments or for twenty regiments, it shall pass for all men.To the last file, to the uttermost farthing, which they may require of us, they shall have men and money for the public protection. But the responsibility for bringing about such a state of things shall be theirs, and theirs only. They can prevent it if they please. The peace of the country and the honor of the country are still entirely compatible with each other. The Oregon question is still perfectly susceptible of an amicable adjustment, and I rejoice to believe that it may still be so adjusted. We have had omens of peace in the other end of the Capitol, if none in this. But if war comes, the Administration must take the responsibility for all its guilt and all its disgrace.

16

The Oregon Question
"A War Between Two Political Parties"

By January, 1846, it became clear that the movement within the nation for compromise on the Oregon question had challenged effectively the power of the extremists. It was already evident that any compromise treaty which established a boundary line along the 49th parallel would receive the overwhelming support of the Senate. It was equally certain that England had dropped her earlier demand for the Columbia River boundary and would, in time, accept a compromise at 49°. What stood in the path of this popular sentiment, therefore, was less the diplomatic position of the two nations (which were actually quite in agreement) than the internal pressures on the Polk administration which still demanded nothing less than the whole-of-Oregon. Polk, for political reasons, could not accept a compromise settlement until the movement for 54-40 had run its course both in Congress and out. Of the many articles which condemned the Western Democrats for perpetuating the Oregon dispute from purely partisan motives, none was more effective than a long essay which appeared in the January, 1846, issue of *The North American Review,* a leading American journal that, for over a quarter century, had been concerned with public affairs.

. . . THE country of Oregon, lying between the Rocky mountains and the Pacific Ocean, is bounded on the south by the parallel of

---

From "The Oregon Question," *The North American Review,* LXII (January, 1846), 220–221, 225, 227–230, 232–239, 243–244, 249, 251–252.

42° of latitude, and on the north by the parallel of 50° 40'. On a rough estimate, therefore, it occupies a space of about thirteen degrees of latitude, and fifteen of longitude, reckoning from the meridian of 110° to that of 125° west from Greenwich. Besides the great range of Rocky mountains, forming its eastern boundary, there are two other chains of mountains, one called the Far-West, or the Cascade range, and the other the Blue mountains, which run through the country from north to south, and separate it into three great divisions, differing from each other by marked peculiarities of soil and climate; these may be denominated for convenience as Western, Middle, and Eastern Oregon. . . .

To show what are the capacities of the country for agriculture and commerce, and what encouragements generally it offers for emigrants, we will begin with Eastern Oregon, which lies between the Blue and the Rocky mountains. A short quotation from Mr. Greenhow, whose work[1] is a very convenient and faithful summary of all the accessible information upon this subject, will place in a very clear light the true character of this region. His testimony, it may be observed, is unimpeachable, when used for this purpose, as the sole object of his book is to defend the American claim, and to advocate the retention of the country by the United States.

The country between the Blue mountains and the Rocky mountains appears to be, except in a very few, small, detached, spots, absolutely uninhabitable by those who depend on agriculture for subsistence. It is, in fact, a collection of bare, rocky mountain chains, separated by deep gorges, through which flow the streams produced by the melting of the snows on the summits; for in the lower grounds rain seldom falls at any time. On the borders of the Lewis, and of

[1] After the publication of his book, *The History of Oregon and California,* in 1844, Robert Greenhow was regarded both in and out of Washington as one of the nation's leading authorities on the Oregon country.

some of the streams falling into it, are valleys and prairies, producing grass for cattle; but all the attempts to cultivate the esculent
vegetables have failed, chiefly, as it is believed, from the great difference in the temperature between the day and the succeeding
night, especially in the summer, which is commonly not less than
thirty, and often exceeds fifty, degrees of Fahrenheit's thermome-
ter. . . .

This is bad enough, and Middle Oregon, according to the
same authority, is but little better. Here, the rain never falls
from April to November, and even during the remainder of the
year, which is called the wet season, the rains are neither
abundant nor frequent. It is impossible to form settlements,
then, except upon the borders of the streams, which are not
numerous, and the banks of which offer but few attractions in
other respects to the emigrant. There are but few trees, chiefly
sumach, cotton-wood, and other soft and useless woods. Fuel
and building materials can be obtained only from a great distance up the north branch of the Columbia, or from the Pacific
region, by few and difficult passes through the mountains. The
soil is very unpromising, consisting, in the northern part, generally, of a yellow, sandy clay, covered only with grass and small
shrubs. In the valleys farther south it is a little better, as there is
more vegetable mould, and a few trees are found of the species
above mentioned. Mr. Greenhow's conclusion is, "that little
encouragement is offered for the cultivation of this part of
Oregon," though cattle may be pastured to advantage, as grass
is abundant.

We cannot wonder, then, that emigrants from the United
States invariably pass through both the regions which we have
described, and seek a home only in Western Oregon. West of the
Cascade range is the only portion of this assumed El Dorado on
the Pacific which can ever be inhabited except by hunters and
their game. . . .

That the American settlers in the most promising part of
Oregon can raise enough from the soil for the supply of their

own wants is very certain; but it is impossible that they should ever become rich, owing to the want of a market. Of what use is it to raise more grain than they need for themselves, when they are separated from the United States by a desert two thousand miles broad, and from any other customers by thousands of leagues of ocean passage, to say nothing of the difficulty of reaching the seacoast, caused by the numerous falls and sandbanks which obstruct the navigation of the rivers? The mouth of the Columbia is closed by a bar which makes ingress and egress impossible for three-fourths of the year, and very dangerous at any other period. . . .

. . . In fine, it is hardly too much to say, that what Siberia is to Russia, Oregon is to the United States. The road thither is equally long and wearisome, and even less cheered by the sight of human habitations, though in the one case it is trodden only by the free backwoodsman and the sturdy emigrant, and in the other by the condemned exile who "drags at each remove a lengthening chain." . . .

The truth is, the extravagant notions entertained of Oregon have been nourished by the very cause which should have made men suspicious of all stories respecting it, and have entirely checked the tide of emigration that is now flowing thither. We mean the dispute respecting the ownership of the territory. Politicians and diplomatists, to make their services appear more meritorious, have striven to put a higher value upon the title they were defending. But for this reason, we should have heard little about the fertility of Oregon, the beauty of its climate, the ease of communicating with it, or its importance for commercial purposes. The statesman's shortest and surest road to popularity nowadays consists in an affected zeal and watchfulness for the interests of our country in its foreign relations. There is no risk here of offending one portion of the sovereign people while seeking to please another. There is no divergence, no contrariety, of interests here to care for; if but few are directly interested in the prosecution of a claim against France or En-

gland, none are injured by it. The good-will that is thus con-
ciliated is all clear gain. Not one in ten thousand of our vast
population would be immediately affected by the successful
assertion of our claim to the whole of Oregon. To the vast
majority of our people the matter is one of perfect indifference,
except so far as it is linked with the interests of a party. But to
this party it is of vital importance. Hence the warmth and
jealousy of each other which politicians manifest in combating
the pretensions of a foreign power. One party makes a merit of
having secured so much territory by a successful negotiation, as
in the case of the Ashburton treaty; and the other party imputes
to it as a fault that it did not obtain more. Lord Palmertson attacks Sir Robert Peel because Great Britain surrendered so
much by that treaty; Mr. Benton attacks Mr. Webster because
the United States surrendered so much. Both charges cannot be
true; but that is of no importance. If similar attacks were not
foreseen, the question about Oregon might be settled to-morrow.
If the two countries are finally plunged into a war respecting it,
it will not be because the bulk of the English or the American
people care a straw about the land; but because the dominant
party on both sides of the Atlantic wishes to preserve its as-
cendancy over its opponents. In its inception and fundamental
character, it will be, as usual, a war not between two nations, but
between two political parties. . . .

Since 1818, Oregon has been held under a convention,
avowedly temporary in its nature, which provides that the whole
country, with its rivers, bays, and harbours, shall remain free
and open to the vessels and subjects of both powers, without
prejudice to the claims of either to the entire and exclusive
sovereignty of the territory. Had it not been for the absurdly
exaggerated statements of its value, to which the circumstances
that we have mentioned have given currency in this country, the
land might have remained under this treaty of joint occupancy
for a century to come. Offering some facilities for trade in fur
and fish, but hardly any for permanent settlement, both nations

might have made free use of it for traffic, in open and manly competition with each other, and have left the land to its only proper owners, a few thousand miserably degraded Indians, who derive a wretched subsistence from it. But the evil is now done; these false reports, disseminated for political purposes, or to answer the private ends of a few persons, have caused an American colony to be established there, and the dominant party in the United States is so deeply pledged to support it by claiming the whole territory for its use, that a compromise seems hardly practicable. On the other hand, Great Britain is bound in honor not to recede so far as to sacrifice the interests of her subjects in that region. *The faith of the government is pledged to support the Hudson's Bay Company in its present location. . . .*

In conformity with this view of the case, the leaders of the two great parties in England, Lord John Russell and Sir Robert Peel, have formally declared in Parliament, that Great Britain has rights in Oregon which must be maintained at all hazards; and this declaration has been supported with the greatest unanimity by the voice of parliament and the public press. If the United States, then, insist upon the whole of the claim, war is inevitable. . . .

It may seem idle to discuss the merits of their respective titles, when it is evident that the parties cannot recede. It is useless to stand fencing with arguments, when every body can see that the affair must ultimately be decided by considerations of a totally different character. We have been arguing the question for thirty years, and stand precisely where we did when the discussion commenced. The resources of logic, then, are exhausted, even if it were possible that logic should ever settle a national dispute. We confess, that all the recent negotiations about Oregon seem to us very much like a solemn mummery. A series of well known facts, musty inferences, and venerable arguments are gravely adduced on both sides; each party repeats its conviction that it is entirely in the right, and its opponent is entirely wrong; reciprocal propositions for compromise, which had been made and rejected several times before, are again made and rejected; and the plenipotentiaries—so called because nothing is left to their power or discretion—then separate, repeating to each other "the assurances of their distinguished consideration," and leaving the matter precisely when it was before. Such conduct may be very proper for diplomatists, but it would be called very silly for children. . . .

To prevent misapprehension, we may as well repeat here the opinion that has often been expressed, and, as we think, proved, in our pages, that the United States title, though imperfect, is the better of the two. In fact, Great Britain has admitted by implication as much as this; for, while this country asserts its exclusive ownership of Oregon, she has expressly, in several official communications, limited her claim to a right of *joint occupancy* of the territory with the United States, leaving the question of *absolute dominion* in abeyance. . . .

The positive side of the British title may be very quickly discussed; it rests entirely on the Nootka convention of 1790. Up to that period, England and Spain were the only powers that had any claims to the possession of the North Pacific coast. The conflict of their respective claims was put at rest by the convention which Spain was bullied into making in this year, by the threat of a war which she was not prepared for. . . .

By this treaty, both Spain and England consented to forego all their previous claims and rights,—founded on alleged prior discoveries, contiguity of territory, or any other basis,—for the sake of this mutual guaranty of joint occupation. . . .

This is the whole positive side of Great Britain's pretensions to Oregon; the negative side consists in a refutation of the counter pretensions of the United States. By the Florida treaty of 1818, Spain made over all her right to the Pacific coast north of latitude 42°, whatever it might be, to the United States. Of course, she could not cede more than she possessed; she ceded it loaded with all the treaty stipulations and restrictions which she had made respecting it while it was in her possession. She did not *warrant* the goods sold; the purchaser took them for better or worse. Was Oregon, in 1818, still subject to the Nootka Convention of 1790? England maintains that it was, that the treaty was perpetual, that, as no limitation of time is mentioned in it, or even hinted at, it was to last for ever. The United States say that it was not, that Spain and England went to war with each other in 1796, and as war annuls all treaties, that the Nootka convention then ceased. . . .

It is also held, that the United States derive a claim from France, founded on the purchase of Louisiana from that power in 1803. The unquestioned possession of a territory extending to the eastern base of the Rocky mountains affords some title, it is thought, by contiguity at least, to the ownership of Oregon on the western side. To this it is replied, first, that France never pretended that Louisiana reached beyond the Rocky mountains; and secondly, that the same remark applies to this title which has just been made upon the title obtained from Spain; it is covered by the Nootka convention. France ceded Louisiana to Spain in 1762; and it was as the owner not only of California, but of Louisiana, that Spain signed a convention in 1790, which admitted the British to a right of joint occupancy of Oregon. Spain ceded Louisiana back to France in 1802, but not in such a perfect condition as it was when she received it. She returned it burdened with the treaty stipulations which she had made while it was in her hands. And it was with this incumbrance upon it that the United States purchased Louisiana in the following year.

Having considered two branches of the argument in favor of our pretensions to the whole of Oregon,—namely, the rights obtained by purchase from Spain and France,—we now come to the third and only remaining one, which is founded on the proceedings and discoveries of our own citizens. And here one remark is necessary respecting the effect of thus accumulating several distinct titles in the hands of one claimant. Some maintain, that these independent claims, being inconsistent one with

another, when united, destroy each other, and leave the claimant who has brought them together without any firm title.
Others say, that they mutually confirm and strengthen each
other, and in case of a division of the land, entitle the party
owning them to as many distinct shares as it possesses claims;
that is, that the United States in their own right, and in that of
France and of Spain, ought to have three fourths of the territory, while Great Britain, resting only on its own pretensions,
can demand but one fourth. Neither position is correct. The
United States, by purchasing the French and Spanish titles, gain
an advantage, though it is one only of a negative character, by
lessening the number of competitors; the agency of Frenchmen
or Spaniards in discovering or settling Oregon, or acquiring possessions bordering upon it, cannot be adduced to weaken our
claim, though it may be urged against the pretensions of the
English. On the other hand, this union of claims does not directly strengthen our title, for, if either of them be assumed to
be well founded, our own proper claim disappears entirely; and
conversely, if the claim in our own right be good, the French
and Spanish titles are of no worth. We cannot pile these pretensions one upon another; their force is not cumulative, but dis-
junctive. If Spain actually surveyed the coast of Oregon and
discovered the mouth of the Columbia in 1775, then Captain
Gray in 1792, and Lewis and Clarke in 1805, were only intruders; and on the other hand, if the discoveries of Gray, Lewis,
and Clarke make out a perfect right, if their explorations, in fact,
can be called *discoveries,* then Oregon was vacant and unappropriated,—a mere *terra incognita,* open to the first comer,—
down to 1792, and the antecedent claims of France and Spain
are mere nonentities. We may, it is true, elect the strongest out
of the three claims, and rest the whole of our title upon that,
reserving the other two to be urged against the English, and
thereby may weaken or break down their claim, though without demonstrating our own. . . .

We have but one other remark to make upon this subject,

but it is applicable to all the grounds upon which the American claim to Oregon is supported. A disputed title, whether it rests on discovery, settlement, or contiguity, is entirely indefinite in respect to the limits of the country claimed. If the subject of dispute be an island, indeed, of moderate magnitude, then discovery or settlement of any portion of it constitutes a good title to the whole. But when the land in question is only a small part of a vast continent, it is impossible to tell where the title ends. Discoveries and settlements are usually made on the seacoast; how far do they extend inland? Not, surely, over the whole breadth of the continent. . . .

But enough of this dry discussion of claims, which has been drawn out much longer than we had intended. We have not sought to disprove the American title to Oregon, but only to show that it is necessarily qualified, indeterminate, and imperfect; and this has been proved so conclusively, that any statesman who shall hereafter declare that this title is perfect and unquestionable will afford good reason to doubt either his soundness of mind or his honesty. That the United States have rights in Oregon, equal in every respect to the British rights, is known by the full and explicit admission of England herself; and thus we have all the needed ground for a compromise, and an equitable division of the territory. . . .

. . . The bulk of the population of either country care nothing about Oregon; why should they? Not one in ten thousand of them would be made richer or poorer, happier or sadder, by a gain of the whole territory. But where shall we put a limit, even in imagination, to the sufferings, the disasters, the horrors, which must follow in the train of an obstinate and protracted, though it be a successful, war? To what fireside, either in England or the United States, will not bring distress, if not a feeling of desolation and despair? . . .

It behooves those who have the power to act at a conjuncture pregnant with such awful consequences to look with a heedful eye to the measure of their own responsibility. . . . If the careless and the unthinking still speak recklessly about a war, it is only because war is not definitely connected in their minds with any idea of the shedding of blood. . . . The news of a great victory, of the old-fashioned kind, attended with the slaughter of thousands on both sides, instead of being received with exultation, as we verily believe, would excite in their minds only the mingled feelings of grief, humiliation, and repentance. Above all, they would hold to a fearful accountability the politicians whose policy had become so deeply stained with blood. Then let the English ministry and the American government look to it; they may carry on this war of words for a while longer, and it will harm no one; they will even deserve and obtain what is the sole object of their ambition, the applause of their countrymen for being so valiant and steadfast in defence of their country's rights. But the outbreak of actual hostilities between England and America about such a contemptible possession will be followed by a storm of popular indignation, that will not only hurl them from their pride of place, but will cover the history of their administration with disgrace, and leave an indelible blot upon their names.

PART FOUR

CALIFORNIA AND
THE MEXICAN WAR

17   John L. O'Sullivan

The Advancing March
of Our Civilization

California as well as Oregon was a growing consideration on the expansionist horizon in 1845. Still, it required more than the logic of geography to bring that region into the American expansionist crusade. Early in 1845 the metropolitan press called the attention of the nation to a new revolution in California. The ease whereby the Californians defeated the forces despatched from Mexico was encouraging. The weakness and inefficiency of Mexican rule had apparently cast the province adrift. American editors warned their readers that if British diplomacy failed to prevent the American annexation of Texas, England would accelerate her efforts to acquire California. On February 2, 1845, the New York *Herald* issued a word of advice to the officials in Washington: "Should Texas be annexed, the next movement of Great Britain will probably be to negotiate with Mexico for the purchase of California. . . . In this she will be successful unless anticipated by our government." As in the case of Oregon, however, the rapid flow of American pioneers into California served as a warning to the British that the province's destiny would be settled by courageous and independent men. Declared the *Herald* on July 30, 1845: "The pioneers and hunters of the West . . . have said that California is *theirs*—and the word they have said with the tongue, they will make good with the rifle."

During the summer of 1845 expansionist writers elaborated on this new manifest destiny theme. In July the *Democratic Review* rejoiced that the United States, in annexing Texas, had at last taught the great

European empires that they would not succeed in their objective of "thwarting our policy and hampering our power, limiting our greatness and checking the fulfillment of our manifest destiny to overspread the continent. . . ." Texas annexation, if not always handled judiciously, demonstrated the weakness of Mexico, a weakness too patient to forestall for long the loss of California to American pioneers already transforming California's society and institutions. Europe, the *Review* warned, could do nothing to stay the momentum of the American people.

By October, 1845, the *Democratic Review* contemplated the eventual annexation of Mexico itself. This circumstance, it predicted, could result either from a war against the United States, which might terminate in the subjugation of Mexico, or from some future revolution similar to that which occurred in Texas, followed by a request of the Mexican people to enter the United States. To O'Sullivan the prospect was pleasing, for he regarded the American governmental system capable of indefinite extension. Until the Mexican people became fit for self-government they could be governed from without by officials of the United States.

THE rapidity with which public opinion matures in this country, is one of the most extraordinary results of our peculiar political system. With our infinite newspaper circulation and with party-organizations singularly complete and penetrating the uttermost recesses of the nation, a new doctrine can be suggested, discussed and determined on with as much, nay, more promptness than an ordinary suit at law can be begun and concluded. We are impressed especially with this peculiarity, in observing the present state of the public mind upon the subject of our relations with Mexico and Texas. A short year ago the whole nation was occupied by the simple prospect of annexing Texas, and the consequence of such an alliance upon our na-

---

From "Territorial Aggrandizement," *The United States Magazine and Democratic Review,* XVII (October, 1845), 243–248.

tional welfare. More recently—that subject having been fully exhausted and disposed of—the chances, the dangers and the advantages of a war with Mexico, became the questions paramount. Even these have subsequently passed away. The impotence of the Mexican Government has been already discovered to be only less than its folly, and all apprehension from the quarter is giving place to speculations upon the probable consequences of annexing Mexico or some portion of her territory to our Republic. That that country is destined to become an integral portion of these United States at some future period, is a pretty universal conviction. Whether such an event is at hand, and the probable consequences of it, are now the chief points left in debate of all that have been provoked in one form or another and at divers times by the Texas Revolution of 1836. Certain it is, that the question whether we would accept Mexico into our Union, if it could be done consistently with our national honor and international duties, is no longer premature.

It is thought by some that it will be impossible permanently to compose our difficulties with her government without a war; that no permanent peace can be established while she has the power to vex this country, which she charges with having robbed her of her possessions, and that we shall be compelled to subjugate and extend over her our government, in self-defence. It is thought by others that the internal dissensions of the Mexican States will continue to become more violent when the weakness of their present administration becomes known, and that the departments conterminous with Texas will be tempted to follow her example, declare their independence, receive aid from Texas as she did formerly from the United States, and finally, like her, ask to join our confederacy.

With regard to the first point, we entertain little apprehension from any cause of quarrel at present subsisting, though we are free to admit that the state of feeling between our Western people and the Mexicans does not promise a very long continu-

ance of peaceful relations between their respective governments unless the most rigid police be established along our
western border. If through any fatuous impulse Mexico should
elevate existing difficulties above the dignity of a mere border
warfare, and should provoke our government to make a retalia-
tory invasion, it is impossible to foresee any limit to the contest
short of an absolute subjugation of Mexico or of such a prostration of her national independence as to lead at no remote period to a revolution like, both in processes and consequences, to
that which threw Texas into our arms. The feelings of the outraged Texans and of our Western citizens, who sympathise
most warmly with them, are such that we are assured no half-
way measures will content them if occasion be given our armies
once to pass the Rio Grande. The moment that event shall
transpire, the young men at least, of this generation might expect to see the termination of Mexico's independent national
existence, and the Congress of the United States of America
proclaiming its laws to the Pacific.

But as we stated before, the prospect of a war with Mexico
for the recovery of Texas, or to revenge her loss, is too remote
to awaken any apprehension, or to deserve further discussion.
The other suggestion deserves more consideration, and if we
were disposed to wreak upon our readers our own conjectures,
we would prophecy the rebellion, revolution and independence
of New Mexico, Chihuahua, California and Yucatan, at no very
distant period. Such a result is certainly more probable than
was the ascertained destiny of Texas ten years ago. Should such
a separation take place, it would doubtless be followed with a
speedy application on the part of those States for admission to
our Union. In view of these considerations, we hope it will not
be esteemed out of time or place in us to offer a few reflections
upon our duty in such a contingency, and therein to consider
briefly the subject of territorial aggrandizement under our form
of government.

At the outset, we will remark, that in our judgment, the representative system as practically enjoyed in this country, will admit of an indefinite extension of territory, without weakening or impairing the political guaranties of any of its inhabitants. That the theory so popular among Europeans, that a democratic government can only be successfully administered upon a limited territory, is absurd. Indeed, it is our firm conviction, for reasons which, on a fitting occasion, we are prepared to render, that a democratic is the only form of government which, over a territory relatively large, can endure and furnish adequate security to the rights of its people. . . .

There are other questions, however, to be disposed of in determining upon the expediency of enlarging the territories of a nation which are not so clear. In a representative government, the laws embody the average political intelligence of the electors; that is, their average knowledge of the true functions and processes of government. As that knowledge advances, will their capacity to govern themselves advance, and the necessity for legislative interference be superseded. According to their knowledge of, and respect for, the rights of a citizen, shall their freedom from governmental restraints be measured out to them, and every privilege which they learn to exercise wisely, government will be forced to relinquish, until each man becomes a law unto himself. If our view be correct, and the whole theory of popular sovereignty depends upon its correctness, every new man admitted to the enjoyment of our political privileges, either abates or exalts the average of which we have spoken, as he is more or less acquainted with, and respectful of, the rights and duties of an American citizen, than the average previous to his admission. . . .

In view of these considerations, how should we estimate the fitness of the Mexican people to enter into the enjoyment of our political institutions. Taking that people as they are, and are likely to continue for the period within which the integrality of Mexico will probably continue, are they, or will they become, a valuable acquisition to us in any respect? Are there probably as

many men in the whole Mexican Republic competent to exercise
the elective franchise with the intelligence of the average American citizen as there were righteous men in Sodom when she
was destroyed? If so, the number of the righteous in that fated
city must have been exaggerated. Beyond a question the entire
Mexican vote would be substantially below our national average
both in purity and intelligence. The Mexican people are unaccustomed to the duties of self-government, and for years to come
must travel up through numberless processes of political emancipation before they can dispense with restraints which the
Saxon family threw off more than three hundred years ago. To
enfranchise them, therefore, and give their representatives a
voice in our legislature, would doubtless have the double effect
of producing anarchy within their own borders, and of embar-
rassing our own interests to a most disastrous extent. Disregard-
ing entirely the confusion which might result from such a step
to the Mexicans themselves, how should we be able to exercise
over them that federal supremacy which is necessary to the
proper consolidation of the Union. Though that people were
allowed to vote, it is doubtful if they could represent such a
public sentiment as we would respect. They would be under
influences which would deprive their political determinations of
all claim to our confidence. But the Federal government of a
democracy must be advised by the constituency which is most
interested in its action. Offices must be filled; protections and
guaranties, both civil and military, must be furnished, according
to the necessity and preferences of the people for whose benefit
chiefly they are designed. In our own country at present it is
comparatively easy to learn what these requirements are. Our
people are accustomed to deliberate upon political measures,
and know how to convey the fair result of their deliberations to
the understanding of the central government. It is about as easy
for Congress to know the political sentiments of a township in
Louisiana or in Maine, or in Missouri, as in Maryland. But it
would be far otherwise if its inhabitants were *Gachupins, Gam-*

bucinos, and *Mestizoes.* We should be obligated to disregard
the apparent wishes of such a people, and govern them instead
of permitting them to govern themselves, or else submit them
and ourselves to difficulties, the extent of which it is impossible
to divine. But in any case a consequence would follow which of
all others it is most desirable for this country, in our judgment,
to avoid—a greater centralization of power. This consequence
must be inevitable. To protect the Mexican citizen in the enjoyment of his property and rights, would require the arm of a
much more vigorous and centralized government than ours is
at present, or than its true friends wish it to become. We can
make no distinction among the States of the Union when once
they are incorporated, and if the mountain won't go to Mahomet,
Mahomet must go to the mountain. If Mexico can't be qualified
by the annexation to enjoy the privileges of the other States of
the Union, the other States must consent to abandon those privileges until the constitution which is necessary to protect the
rights of all, shall bear equally upon the privileges of all. For,
as we stated before, the nation must be governed by its average
intelligence. Now we submit that this will be earning the glories
of successful war or negociation, and of enlarged dominion at
too great expense; nay, at a price which, when we should come
to pay it, would disgust us with our bargain. We believe no
American is willing that we should suspend the advancing
march of our civilisation, and return upon our steps, or motion-
less abide the coming of this semi-barbarous people, who are
yet ignorant of the very elements of the science of political government, because the fortunes of war or successful revolution
had made them subject to our laws; which leads us to consider
the means by which free institutions may rightfully be propagated. Maintaining as we do, that a government in which the
whole people are fairly represented, developes political science
and advances national prosperity more rapidly than any other;
and believing as we do, that the American people are more adequately represented in their laws than any other, we are bound

to conclude that the distance between our political institutions and those of other nations is constantly increasing. This might seem to authorize the inference that we could never extend their beneficial influences to people less mature in political science than ourselves. The impropriety of such an inference will appear upon the slightest reflection. Democracies must make their conquests by moral agencies. If these are not sufficient, the conquest is robbery. By allowing to our people every inducement and opportunity for the utmost freedom of industry, we make them missionaries of our political science to every quarter of the globe. In establishing commercial and other business relations with and in the territories of our neighbors, they beget a community of interest between us; they obtain a confidence and respect for our institutions and spread an acquaintance with many of their merits which in time work influences far more efficacious and permanent than were experienced from all the arbitrary codes ever proclaimed by the renowned lawgivers of antiquity. . . .

We may seem to be taking a great deal for granted, in discussing thus early the consequences of extending our territorial limits further to the westward than the boundaries of Texas, and to be unmindful of Mrs. Glass's instructions in cooking a fish—first catch it. We believe, however, that our word, if wise in itself, is not premature. It is an opinion dangerously prevalent among some of our over-wise politicians that the events of the late presidential election was determined entirely by the views which the successful candidates entertained in favor of the Annexation of Texas to this Union. The enthusiasm which this alliance has since awakened throughout the country they have ascribed to a prevailing appetite among our people for territorial acquisition. Misled by this conviction, every engine is likely to be employed in enlisting public favor by endeavoring to anticipate its tendency in this direction. If our party prevailed by annexing Texas, why cannot another by annexing Mexico, and a third by annexing Canada, and a fourth, when our neighbors are all absorbed, by crossing the seas and annexing Ireland? This misapprehension of the true feeling which disposed this country to look with such favor upon the annexation of Texas is very likely to produce the very state of public opinion which is erroneously supposed already to exist, and which would lead to that very result, the consequences of which we have endeavored to consider, much sooner than is dreamed of by those who are most reckless in giving the impulse. The feeling upon our western border, we are pained to think anything but healthy upon this subject; and if, as there is certainly *some* reason to fear, we should be obliged, in self-defence, to assume an aggressive attitude towards Mexico, and our armies should once enter her territories, wise must be the statesman that can forsee an end short of absolute subjugation at once, or by fomenting a spirit of national hostility between us, which must ultimately lead to such a result.

18

California "must pass into the hands of another race"

Although California had never been an issue in American politics, it had become, by 1846, a significant topic for editorial opinion in the nation's great metropolitan newspapers. California, with its magnificent harbor of San Francisco, had become a vital interest to the United States which intended to make the territory an integral part of the country by whatever means came to hand. Why the question of California's future could no longer escape the American nation was revealed clearly by a long essay on California that appeared in *The American Review* of January, 1846. This important journal, published in New York, was the official mouthpiece of the Whig Party.

LETTERS from Washington, on which we rely, render it probable that Mr. Slidell, our newly appointed minister to Mexico, goes clothed with power to treat with that government for the cession of California to the United States. The intelligence is vague, but we trust it is true, and that the negotiation may prove successful. The natural progress of events will undoubtedly give us that province just as it gave us Texas. Already American emigrants thither are to be numbered by thousands, and we may, at almost any moment, look for a declaration, which shall dissolve the slight bonds that now link the province to Mexico, and prepare the way for its ultimate annexation to the United States.

Regarding, therefore, the accession of California as an event which present tendencies, if not checked or counteracted, must render inevitable, we should prefer to see it accomplished by an agency, at once more direct and less questionable in point of national morality. It cannot be disguised that we stand open to the charge of having colonized Texas, and recognized her independence, for the express purpose of seizing her soil—that we wrested her territory from Mexico, peacefully and by a gradual process, to be sure, but as really and as wrongfully as if we had conquered her by arms in the field of battle. . . .

. . . Texas, it seems not at all unlikely, may yet cost us more than would in the beginning have bought it outright; and California, it may fairly be presumed, may now be purchased, at least *nemine contradicente*, for a sum which the country will deem small for so valuable an acquisition.

For, certainly, we do regard it as extremely desirable that California—a part, at least, of the province known by that name

---

From "California," *The American Review: A Whig Journal of Politics, Literature, Art and Science,* III (January, 1846), 82–99.

—should become the property, and remain forever under the exclusive jurisdiction, of the United States. Lower California, as it is called, embracing the long, narrow peninsula between the Gulf and the Pacific, stretching from the 21st to the 33d degree of latitude, a distance of above eight hundred miles, with an average breadth of about sixty, is universally represented by travelers as sterile and hopelessly desolate. It consists, indeed, of a chain of volcanic, treeless, barren mountains of rock, broken only by still more dreary plains of sand, destitute of streams, swept by fierce tornadoes, and of necessity abandoned almost entirely to sterility and desolation. . . .

With Upper California the case is different. The southern and eastern portions—indeed nearly the whole province except that part bordering on the Pacific—is scarcely more valuable than the lower province. Through the eastern section extends the chain of the Rocky Mountains, broken into fragments, and converting a wide space of the country, through its entire length, into a waste perfectly uninhabitable, producing very little difficulty, finds a casual and precarious path. West of this chain lies a vast, sandy plain, nearly seven hundred miles in length, with a width of one hundred miles at its southern, and two hundred at its northern, extremity. The whole valley of the Colorado is utterly barren, and is described by an American traveler as a great burial-place of former fertility, which can never return. Like its branches the river is not navigable. . . .

The remaining part of Upper California—that which lies nearest the Pacific Coast—is not only by far the best portion of the province, but one of the most beautiful regions on the face of the earth. It embraces the whole country drained by the waters which empty into the Bay of San Francisco. . . .

Although agriculture, throughout this vast and fertile region, is of the rudest and most unskillful character, nearly all kinds of grain have been readily raised. In the immediate neighborhood of San Francisco Bay the most extraordinary crops are easily produced. Dr. Marsh, long a resident on the banks of the Sacramento, informed Mr. Farnham[1] that from ten bushels of wheat he had known to be harvested a crop of 3652: though he says that the average yield is from 30 to 50 bushels from one that is sown. The first part of this statement is incredible; but Commodore Wilkes mentions an instance in which 3600 bushels were harvested from 30 sown; and he places the average crop at 80 fold. The most moderate of these statements exhibits a degree of fertility seldom found in the most favored regions of the earth. Indian corn is said to return about 150 fold. The potato thrives; hemp, flax, oats, barley, peas, fruits of all kinds, and indeed all the productions of the temperate zone, are produced in great abundance, and with the greatest ease; while in the southern portion, cotton, tobacco, figs, lemons, olives, oranges, and especially grapes, seem to find a native and most propitious soil; and the marshes about the mouths of the San Joaquin and Sacramento, may easily be turned into some of the richest and most beautiful rice fields in the world.

Here, then, lies upon the Pacific coast, adjoining our western border, included between the parallels which embrace the southern sections of the United States, and stretching northward to the southern boundary of Oregon, a region of country capable of sustaining a greater population than now inhabits the entire American Union. Traversed, through its entire length, and from its most remote corners, by noble rivers all concentrating their waters, and forming at their common mouth, the finest harbor perhaps in the world;—abounding in timber of the best quality for ship-building and all naval purposes, easily floated to a common point, and that the beautiful and capacious harbor of San Francisco;—containing measureless water power, immense agricultural resources, and all the elements which nature can furnish of national wealth and national consequence—it is yet

[1] Thomas J. Farnham was a noted traveler who visited the Pacific coast during the early forties and, shortly after that, published several volumes on his travels.

shut out from the influences of Christian civilization and abandoned to a people who neither know its capacities, nor feel the pressure of any obligation to develop and expand them. The aggregate population is probably to develop and expand them. The aggregate population is probably below 20,000; the harvested crops in 1839 amounted to 69,000 bushels of wheat, 22,000 of maize, and 15,000 of barley; and the whole annual merchantable production of the country, including cattle and furs, its staple commodities, is estimated by Capt. Wilkes at less than a million of dollars. Nor is there anything in the history of the country, to induce the hope that, under its present control, it will ever attain that position, and serve those ends, in the great scheme of the world's civilization, for which Providence has so clearly designed it.

For more than three hundred years it has been under exclusive Spanish dominion. Yet up to the present time, notwithstanding its immense advantages for trade, it has no commerce; in spite of its fertility, it has no agriculture; its water power and ability to yield a bountiful supply of every raw material, have not erected a solitary manufacturing establishment within its borders; and the whole country is even now as far removed from that high and palmy state of wealth, cultivation and power of which it is susceptible, as it was before the Spaniard Cobrillo, in 1542, first explored its coast and landed upon its shore. . . .

. . . While California remains in possession of its present inhabitants, and under control of its present government, there is no hope of its regeneration. . . .

California, to become the seat of wealth and power for which Nature has marked it, must pass into the hands of another race. . . .

This point, then, being conceded, it remains only to inquire, into whose hands shall California pass? What nation of the earth shall succeed to Mexico, whenever the sovereignty shall pass from her grasp?

There are, we believe, but two powers to whom the design

of acquiring California is ever ascribed. One of these is Great Britain; the other is the United States. . . .

. . . There has sprung up of late a very general demand from all sides of the British press, for the prompt accomplishment of these designs. The Foreign Quarterly Review closes some speculations upon the probable destiny of California, with the remark that "an active minister, who had a forecast of the future, might secure it as an appendage to Oregon, our unquestionable right to which is too clear to be surrendered. The Mexicans," it is added, "would not be sorry to part with it to us upon fair terms." . . .

With this evidence before us, it is impossible, or at least unwise, to doubt that Great Britain is striving to secure from Mexico sovereignty in California, absolute, it may be, or perhaps "somewhat in the manner of the East India Company."

The next question naturally suggested relates to the probability of her success. This must be simply a matter of opinion. It would be useless to disguise our fear that, so far as Mexico is concerned, she may accomplish her purpose. We have less confidence than perhaps is just, in the good faith of the friendly disposition towards the Government and people of the United States, which Mexico is said of late to have evinced. Our acquisition of Texas as yet too recent—our port towards Mexico has been too commanding—our exactions have been too rigorous, for the wound they inflicted upon this sensitive and resentful race to have yet fully healed. . . .

It seems to us improbable that a government marked and swayed by Mexican temper, which persisted against the advice and example of the leading nations of the earth, in refusing to recognize the independence of Texas, for a long series of years of enforced inaction, which has, from first to last, charged upon the United States the robbery and despoilment of the fairest of her possessions, should now, so soon after the obnoxious deed is finally and fully accomplished, manifest even an intemperate eagerness to resume with us friendly relations, and to negotiate for a boundary upon so liberal a basis as she is said to have proposed. We fear these measures are but the fair-seeming dictates of a "necessity of present life." They have already relieved her seaboard from the presence of our squadron, and her Texan frontier from the pressure of our troops. They have averted, or at least deferred, a blow against which she had found it impossible to interpose the shield of British power, and have released her from the fatal necessity of engaging single-handed, the power of the United States. Of such a struggle the result has repeatedly been predicted in Europe. The French *Journal des Debats* has declared that "the conquest of Mexico would be a wide step towards the enslavement of the world by the United States, and a levy of bucklers by the Mexicans at this moment would lead the way to this subjection." The London *Times* remarks that Mexico has had the sagacity to perceive that a declaration of war would enable the United States to seize upon and retain the Mexican territory. . . . "Between the autocracy of Russia on the East, and the democracy of America, aggrandized by the conquest of Mexico, on the West," says the *Journal des Debats*, the official paper of the French government, *"Europe may find herself more compressed than she may one day think consistent with her independence and dignity."* It cannot be disguised that apprehensions of the future power of the American people are arousing the fears, and influencing the policy of the principal nations of Europe. The leading journal of Great Britain but a few days since, declared that "no European politician can look forward to the power of the United States, within the present century, but with the most appalling prospects." And so the Paris *Debats* remarks, that "for the political balance of the world, the conquest of Mexico by the United States may create eventual dangers, which, although distant, it may not be superfluous to *guard against*." And so again, upon another occasion, the same official journal employed this still more emphatic language:

"A cry of war between America and Mexico has been raised: although it is not believed that the threats will be followed by acts, yet it would be well for us to be prepared for anything.

North America presents her ambitious plans for conquering all the American continent. She began by the annexation of Texas, by which she divides Mexico, and a war will give her a welcome pretence for possessing herself of all Mexico. Soon the smaller states will follow, and the Isthmus of Panama fall into the hands of North America. *Europe should not tolerate this,* NOR SUFFER NORTH AMERICA TO INCREASE, or the independence of Europe might sooner or later be wedged in by the two colossuses of Russia and North America, and suffer from their oppression." . . .

The existence of this feeling among the sovereigns of Europe towards this country, cannot be cloaked by honied diplomatic assurances of distinguished consideration, nor disproved by angry or contemptuous denial. We look upon it as a fact—a *"fixed fact,"* which must have weight in any speculations, that claim to be intelligent, concerning our present and future foreign relations. We have introduced it here for the purpose of saying that Mexico cannot be ignorant of its existence, and that, in our judgment, she intends, with more of wisdom than we have given her credit for, to make it serviceable in "feeding fat the grudge" she bears us. She cannot lack the sagacity to perceive that, with Great Britain firmly fixed in California, she could not engage in war with the United States without a certainty, or, at the least, a very strong probability of having Great Britain for an active ally. . . .

. . . A glance at a globe, or a Mercator's map, will convince any one that the occupation of that province by Great Britain would give to that power, for all time to come, absolute dominion of the Pacific Ocean, with all its islands, coasts and commerce, and place her in a position which might at any moment become infinitely dangerous to our safety and prosperity. In an individual, self-defence is an instinct. In a nation it becomes a *duty*—one, too, of paramount obligation, far superior in binding force to any other, inasmuch as it lies at the foundation of all others, and as obedience to it is the sole condition upon which other duties can be discharged. As in individual cases, too, the obligation of national self-preservation comprises more than resistance to imminent and actual assault. It enforces in peace preparation for war—that is to say, the adoption of such measures as shall, in the event of war, put the national existence and safety beyond the hazards of any contest, and out of reach of any hostile blow. Though it neither sanctions nor requires injustice or wrong, it often supersedes the common rules of international law and, where clear and undeniable, justifies acts for which no public law exists. This broad but fundamental and essential principle, though it cannot invalidate existing rights, wherever they may exist, will most certainly forbid the extension of European dominion over at least this portion of the American Continent. And upon these grounds, sufficiently broad and perfectly tenable as we believe them to be, we have ventured the assertion that England cannot expect to occupy California with the acquiescence or indifference of the United States.

We have left ourselves but small space for reference to the efforts of the United States to become possessed, by purchase from Mexico, of this portion of her territory; but, fortunately, little is required. . . .

With regard to Mr. Slidell's negotiation, we must repeat, we have misgivings of his success. England stands ready, we doubt not, to give a larger sum for California than our government is likely to offer. If, as she seems to believe her paramount and imperative policy must be to check the further growth of the American Union, and to make perfect her net-work of military posts and stations, from which, at any moment, she may strike with most effect upon every side, her interest certainly lies in the acquisition of the bay and harbor of San Francisco. Nor can we escape the fear that Mexico would greatly prefer such an arrangement to that which we propose. She has not yet abandoned her project of reconquering Texas; and she must feel the need of a powerful ally. . . .

. . . We hope and trust that a timely purchase of California by the United States, and the adjustment of pending questions of difference between our government and those of Great Britain and Mexico, will avert the necessity of an appeal to the terrible arbiter of irreconcilable international disputes. Should such an appeal, through the madness or selfish ambition of any of the contestant parties, be finally taken, the struggle, as has been re-marked by a distinguished Senator of the United States, will involve far more than the questions out of which, as a pretext, it may grow: and not only will the entire territory bordering on the Pacific coast, from the Gulf of California to the Russian frontier, extending over *twenty-three* degrees of latitude, and embracing a region capable of becoming more populous and powerful than is France or the United States at the present day, become the prize of contending nations, but a contest will ensue between opposite systems of political existence—systems in their nature essentially hostile, and between which, in the judgment of many men of foresight and wisdom, there is yet to be a final, and for one or the other a fatal, collision. Most earnestly and sincerely do we hope the prophecy may prove fallacious, and the contest be forever averted. Should, however, the irresistible progress of events throw its tremendous weight upon us, it will not become the American nation, as the only republic of mark on the face of the earth, with timid shrinking or unmanly fear, to decline it, or to tremble for the result. . . .

19   James K. Polk

"We must obtain Upper California
and New Mexico
in any Treaty of Peace"

Relations between the United States and Mexico were tense in the late spring of 1846. Mexico had refused to reestablish formal diplomatic intercourse with Washington following her decision, a year earlier, to recall her minister. Polk had dispatched John Slidell to Mexico City in November, 1845, to establish contact with the Mexican government again and negotiate a boundary settlement along the Rio Grande. Mexico had always refused to accept this boundary, claimed by Texas, and had insisted rather on the Nueces. There is much evidence that the Polk administration hoped Texas would occupy the disputed area and thus enter the Union in a state of war —a war which the United States might inherit.

Having failed to achieve any settlement with Mexico through the activity of the Slidell mission, Polk dispatched General Zachary Taylor, during January, 1846, to the region of the Rio Grande where, at this point, any skirmish would set off a war. However, by May the President had decided on war with Mexico whatever happened along the Rio Grande. He would rationalize the war on the basis of Mexico's refusal to pay the claims demanded by American citizens and that country's obvious hostile attitude toward the United States. Polk made his decision clear in his diary entry of May 9, 1846 (included in this document). Once Polk received word that Taylor had at last suffered attack, he shifted the rationale for war. In his message to Congress, requesting that body's recognition of the war, he accused the Mexicans of "shedding American blood on American soil."

What remained for the administration thereafter was not only the successful conduct of the war but also the determination of its precise objectives. Polk's diary entry for June 30, 1846 (also included in this document) describes a cabinet discussion early in the war which was concerned with the question of war aims.

SATURDAY, *9th May, 1846.*—The Cabinet held a regular meeting to-day; all the members present. I brought up the Mexican question, and the question of what was the duty of the administration in the present state of our relations with that country. The subject was very fully discussed. All agreed that if the Mexican forces at Matamoras committed any act of hostility on Gen'l Taylor's forces I should immediately send a message to Con-

---

From Milo Milton Quaife, ed., *The Diary of James K. Polk During His Presidency, 1845 to 1849* (Chicago, 1910), I, 384–386, 495–497.

gress recommending an immediate declaration of War. I stated
to the Cabinet that up to this time, as they knew, we had heard
of no open act of aggression by the Mexican army, but that the
danger was imminent that such acts would be committed. I said
that in my opinion we had ample cause of war, and that it was
impossible that we could stand in *statu quo,* or that I could
remain silent much longer; that I thought it was my duty to
send a message to Congress very soon & recommend definitive
measures. I told them that I thought I ought to make such a
message by tuesday next, that the country was excited and impatient on the subject, and if I failed to do so I would not be
doing my duty. I then propounded the distinct question to the
Cabinet and took their opinions individually, whether I should
make a message to Congress on tuesday, and whether in that
message I should recommend a declaration of War against
Mexico. All except the Secretary of the Navy gave their advice
in the affirmative. Mr. Bancroft dissented but said if any act of
hostility should be committed by the Mexican forces he was
then in favour of immediate war. . . .

About 6 o'clock P.M. Gen'l R. Jones, the Adjutant General of
the army, called and handed to me despatches received from
Gen'l Taylor by the Southern mail which has just arrived, giving
information that a part of [the] Mexican army had crossed to
the Del Norte, [crossed the Del Norte] and attacked and killed
and captured two companies of dragoons of Gen'l Taylor's army
consisting of 63 officers & men. . . . I immediately summoned
the Cabinet to meet at 7½ o'Clock this evening. The Cabinet
accordingly assembled at that hour; all the members present.
The subject of the despatch received this evening from Gen'l
Taylor, as well as the state of our relations with Mexico, were
fully considered. The Cabinet were unanimously of opinion, and
it was so agreed, that a message should be sent to Congress on
Monday laying all the information in my possession before them
and recommending vigorous & prompt measure[s] to enable the
Executive to prosecute the War. . . .

TUESDAY, *30th June, 1846.*—This was the Regular day of meeting of the Cabinet. All the members attended except the attorney General, who, it was understood, was detained in consequence of indisposition. The Mexican War became the subject of discussion in the Cabinet. It was brought up by a question propounded by the Secretary of the Navy in regard to the policy of our blockading squadron seizing and holding Tampico. A discussion arose between Mr. Buchanan and Mr. Walker [Secretary of the Treasury] in regard to the objects of the War against Mexico, in the course of which Mr. Buchanan expressed himself in favour of acquiring the Rio Grande as our Western boundary as high up as the Passo in about latitude 32° of North Latitude & thence West to the Pacific. He expressed himself as being opposed to acquiring any territory of Treaty with Mexico South of 32° of North Latitude. He spoke of the unwillingness of the North to acquire so large a Country that would probably become a slave-holding country if attached to the U.S. Mr. Walker warmly resisted Mr. B.'s views, and insisted that we should if practicable acquire by Treaty, all the country North of a line drawn from the mouth of the Rio Grande in Latitude about 26° West to the Pacific. Mr. Buchanan said it was necessary to know what the objects of the war were, that it might be conducted accordingly; that if it was the object of the President to acquire all the country North of 26°, the line indicated by Mr. Walker, including all of the Department of Tamaulapas, it should be known, and added that if we attempted to acquire all this territory the opinion of the world would be against [us], and especially as it would become a slave-holding country, whereas while it was in possession of Mexico slavery did not exist in it. Mr. Walker remarked that he would be willing to fight the whole world sooner than suffer other Powers to interfere in the matter. I remained silent until the discussion had proceeded to a considerable length, when I spoke, and said in substance that the causes and objects of the war were as I supposed well understood, and that when we came to make peace the terms of the peace would be a subject for consideration. As to the boundary which we should establish by a Treaty of Peace, I remarked that I preferred the 26° to any boundary North of it, but that if it was found that that boundary could not be obtained I was willing to take 32°, but that in any event we must obtain Upper California and New Mexico in any Treaty of Peace we would make.

20   Lewis Cass

Expansion as "our safety valve"

Lewis Cass, Michigan's influential Senator and one of the Democratic Party's leading expansionists, assumed much of the responsibility for convincing Congress of the close relationship between the expanding power and interests of the United States, and the need for ample frontage on the Pacific to meet the demands of American commerce, between the availability of sufficient land and the requirements of American democracy, and between the obligation to regenerate the soil of Mexico and the right to territorial indemnity in the form of the permanent acquisition of California. Such themes as these he developed in his speech to the Senate, February 10, 1847.

. . . WE have grown with our growth and strengthened with our strength till the approach of physical infirmities, the kindly warnings of nature, bid us prepare for another and an untried world. And the Constitution, too, has grown with its growth and strengthened with its strength till from three millions it governs twenty million people, and has made them the happiest com-

From *Congressional Globe* (29th Cong., 2nd Sess., 1847), Appendix, p. 213.

munity upon the face of the globe. But it is yet fresh in its strength. No infirmity has come to tell us that its dissolution is near. It is no longer an experiment, but experience; no longer a promise, but performance. It has fulfilled all, and more than all, its most sanguine advocates dared predict. It is at this moment stronger in the affections of the American people than at any other period of its existence. Like the cliff of eternal granite which overlooks the ocean and drives back the ceaseless waves that assail its base, so will this Constitution resist the assaults that may be made upon it, come how or when or whence they may. In the providence of God no such lot as ours was ever conferred upon a people. What we have been and are the past and the present have told and are telling us; what we are to be the future will tell to those who are to come after us, to their joy or sorrow, as we cherish or reject the blessings we enjoy. If we are not stuck with judicial blindness, as were God's chosen people of old, and punished for national offenses by national punishments, we shall cling to this Constitution as the mariner clings to the last plank when night and the tempest close around him; and we shall cling to it the stronger as the danger is greater. . . .

A strong desire pervades this country that a region extending west of our present possessions to the Pacific ocean should be acquired and become part of our Confederacy. The attempt to purchase it was made during the administration of General Jackson, and the hope of succeeding has never since been wholly abandoned. I will not detain the Senate by spreading out the reasons which render such a measure desirable. It would give to us a large territory, a great deal of it calculated for American settlement and cultivation, and it would connect us with the great western ocean, giving us a front along its shores in connection with Oregon of perhaps thirteen or fourteen degrees of latitude. It would give us also the magnificent Bay of San Francisco, one of the noblest anchorages in the world, capable of holding all the navies of the earth, and from its commanding position controlling in some measure the trade of the northern

Pacific. But, sir, beside these advantages, commercial and geographical, there are important political considerations which point to extension as one of the great measures of safety for our institutions.

In Europe one of the social evils is concentration. Men are brought too much and kept too much in contact. There is not room for expansion. Minds of the highest order are pressed down by adverse circumstances without the power of free exertion. There is no starting-point for them. Hence the struggles that are ever going on in our crowded communities; and hence the *emeutes* which disturb and alarm the Governments of the Old World, and which must one day or other shake them to their center. Questions of existence are involved in them as well as questions of freedom. I trust we are far removed from all this; but to remove us further yet we want almost unlimited power of expansion. That is our safety-valve. The mightiest intellects which when compressed in thronged cities and hopeless of their future are ready to break the barriers around them the moment they enter the new world of the West feel their freedom and turn their energies to contend with the works of creation; converting the woods and the forests into towns and villages and cultivated fields, and extending the dominion of civilization and improvement over the domain of nature. This process has been going on since the first settlement of our country; and while it continues, whatever other evils betide us, we shall be free from the evils of a dense population with scanty means of subsistence and with no hope of advancement.

. . . There are those yet living who will live to see our Confederacy numbering a population equal to the Chinese empire. This stupendous progress outstrips the imagination. The mind cannot keep up with the fact; it toils after it in vain; and as we increase in numbers and extend in space our power of communication is still more augmented. The telegraph has come with its wonderful process to bind still closer the portions of this empire as these recede from its capital. It is the most admirable invention of modern days. We can now answer the sublime interrogatory put to Job: "Canst thou send lightnings that they may go and say unto thee, here we are?" Yes, the corruscations of Heaven man has reduced to obedience, and they say unto him here we are. It is yet in its infancy, an experiment rather than an arrangement. Who can tell where future improvements may conduct it, or what sway it may hereafter exercise over the social and political condition of the world; what people it may bring together and keep by the power of instantaneous communication; or how the events of distant nations, told almost to the other side of the globe the very moment of their occurrence, may affect the future destiny of mankind? I have been industriously engaged seventeen days in coming from Detroit to Washington, and the journey between here and Baltimore once cost me two days. We have now a process within our reach by which we can send to California and receive answers from there more than twenty times a day. I shall not pursue these investigations; they are sufficiently obvious in their general bearing, though the practical result of this great measure is beyond the reach of human vision.

We are at war with Mexico, brought on by her injustice. Before peace is established we have a right to require a reasonable indemnity, either pecuniary or territorial, or both, for its injuries we have sustained. Such a compensation is just in itself and in strict accordance with the usages of nations. . . . In the condition of Mexico there is no disposition in this country to ask of her an unreasonable sacrifice. On the contrary, the wish is everywhere prevalent, and I am sure the Government participates in it, that we should demand less than we are entitled to. No one proposes a rigid standard by which the indemnity shall be measured; but there are certain territorial acquisitions which are important to us, and whose cession cannot injure Mexico, as she never can hold them permanently. We are willing, after settling the indemnity satisfactorily, to pay for the excess in money. . . .

21   Thomas Corwin

"Show Mexico you are sincere
when you say you desire
nothing by conquest"

Whig criticism of Democratic policy toward Mexico culminated in Thomas Corwin's reply to Cass, delivered in the Senate on February 11, 1847. This speech, by the popular Whig orator from Ohio, voiced the standard Whig conservatism in matters of external affairs. It revealed as well the close relationship between American attitudes toward the Mexican War and American attitudes toward territorial extension as the fruit of that war. Corwin condemned the war, with considerable success, as had few members of the Senate. Corwin went on to ridicule Cass's notions of expansion and destiny as the excuse of every conqueror in pursuit of "more room." Not only did he oppose expansion on moral grounds, but he was heartily against it on grounds of national unity. Corwin, like other thoughtful Americans, understood that the North and South had entered an irrepressible conflict over the expansion of slavery into any new territories that the United States might acquire. With clear insight Corwin predicted that the nation would pay dearly in the form of intense civil strife for any territorial acquisitions from Mexico.

. . . MR. PRESIDENT, it is a fearful responsibility we have assumed; engaged in flagrant, desolating war with a neighboring republic, to us thirty millions of God's creatures look up for that moderated wisdom which, if possible, may stay the march of misery

From *Congressional Globe* (29th Cong., 2nd Sess., 1847), Appendix, pp. 238–246.

and restore to them, if it may be so, mutual feelings of good will with all the best blessings of peace.

I sincerely wish it were in my power to cherish those placid convictions of security which have settled upon the mind of the Senator from Michigan [Lewis Cass]. So far from this, I have been, in common with the Senator from South Carolina [John C. Calhoun], oppressed with melancholy forebodings of evils to come, and not unfrequently by a conviction that each step we take in this unjust war may be the last in our career, that each chapter we write in Mexican blood may close the volume of our history as a free people. Sir, I am the less inclined to listen to the siren song the Senator from Michigan sings to his own soul because I have heard its notes before. I know the country is at this moment suffering from the fatal apathy into which it was lulled a few years ago. Every one must recall to his mind with pleasing regret the happy condition of the country in 1843 when the other question, the prelude to this, the annexation of Texas, was agitated here; we remember how it attracted the attention of the whole Union; we remember that the two great leaders of the two great parties, agreeing in scarcely any other opinion, were agreed in that; they both predicted that if Texas were annexed war with Mexico would be the probable result. We were told then by others, as now by the Senator from Michigan, that all was well, that all was calm, that Mexico would not fight, or if she would she was too weak to wage the struggle with any effect upon us. . . .

Every one can feel, if he will examine himself for a moment, what must have been the mingled emotions of pride, humiliation, and bitter indignation which raged in the bosoms of the Mexican people when they saw one of their fairest provinces torn from them by a revolution moved by foreign people; and that province by our act and our consent annexed to the already enormous expanse of our territory. It is idle, Mr. President, to suppose that the Mexican people would not feel as deeply for the dismemberment and disgrace of their country as you would for the dismemberment of this Union of ours. Sir, there is not a race nor tribe nor people on earth who have an organized, social, or political existence who have clung with more obstinate affection to every inch of soil they could call their own than this very Spanish, this Mexican, this Indian race in that country. So strong and deep is this sentiment in the heart of that half savage, half-civilized race that it has become not merely an opinion, a principle, but with them an unreasoning fanaticism. So radically deep and strong has this idea rooted itself into the Mexican mind that I learn recently it has been made a part of the new fundamental law that not an inch of Mexican soil shall ever be alienated to a foreign power; that her territory shall remain entire as long as her republic endures; that if one of her limbs be forcibly severed from her death shall ensue unless that limb shall be reunited to the parent trunk. With such a people, not like you, as you fondly and I fear vainly boast yourselves, a highly civilized, reasoning, and philosophical race, but a people who upon the fierce barbarism of the old age have ingrafted the holy sentiments of patriotism of a later birth; with just such a people the pride of independence and the love of country combine to inflame and sublimate patriotic attachment into a feeling dearer than life, stronger than death.

What were the sentiments of such a people toward us when they learned that at the battle of San Jacinto there were only seventy-five men of their own country out of the seven hundred and fifty who conquered them on that day, and that every man of that conquering army who fought that battle and dismembered their republic of one fourth part of its territory had but recently gone there from this country, was fed by our people, and armed and equipped in the United States to do that very deed? . . .

The President has now to deal with a people thus humbled, thus irritated. It was his duty to concede much to Mexico; everything but his country's honor or her rights. Was this done? Not at all. Mexico and her minister were alike spurned as weak and trivial things, whose complaints you would not hear or heed; and when she humbly implored you not to take this province, declared that it might disturb the peace subsisting between us, you were still inexorable. During this time she was forcing loans from her citizens to pay the debt she owed yours, fulfilling her treaties with you by painful exactions from her own people. She begged of you to let Texas alone. If she were independent let her enjoy her independence; if free, let her revel in her new-born liberty in defiance of Mexico, as she alleged she would and could. Your stern reply was, no; we will, at your expense, strengthen our own arm by uniting to ourselves that which has been severed from you by our own citizens; we will take Texas, we will throw the shield of our Constitution over her rights, and the sword of our power shall gleam like that at Eden, "turning every way," to guard her against further attack. . . .

While the American President can command the Army, thank Heaven I can command the purse. While the President, under the penalty of death, can command your officers to proceed, I can tell them to come back, or the President can supply them as he may. He shall have no funds from me in the prosecution of a war which I cannot approve. That I conceive to be the duty of a Senator. I am not mistaken in that. If it be my duty to grant whatever the President demands for what am I here? Have I no will upon the subject; is it not placed at my discretion, understanding, judgment; have an American Senate and House of Representatives nothing to do but obey the bidding of the President, as the Army he commands is compelled to obey under penalty of death? No! The representatives of the sovereign people and sovereign States were never elected for such purposes as that.

. . . Here we are told we must not look to the objects of the war; being in the war made by the President, we must help him to fight it out, should it even please him to carry it to the utter extermination of the Mexican race. Sir, I believe it must proceed to this shocking extreme if you are by war "to conquer a peace."

Here, then, is your condition. The President involves you in war without your consent. Being in such a war it is demanded as a duty that we grant men and money to carry it on. The President tells us he shall prosecute this war till Mexico pays us or agrees to pay us all its expenses. I am not willing to scourge Mexico thus; and the only means left me is to say to the Commander-in-Chief, "Call home your Army, I will feed and clothe it no longer; you have whipped Mexico in three pitched battles; this is revenge enough; this is punishment enough."

The President has said he does not expect to hold Mexican territory by conquest. Why, then, conquer it? Why waste thousands of lives and millions of money fortifying towns and creating governments, if at the end of the war you retire from the graves of your soldiers and the desolated country of your foes only to get money from Mexico for the expense of all your toil and sacrifice? Who ever heard since Christianity was propagated among men of a nation taxing its people, enlisting its young men, and marching off two thousand miles to fight a people merely to be paid for it in money? What is this but hunting a market for blood, selling the lives of your young men, marching them in regiments to be slaughtered and paid for like oxen and brute beasts? Sir, this is when stripped naked that atrocious idea first promulgated in the President's message, and now advocated here, of fighting on till we can get our indemnity for the past as well as the present slaughter. We have chastised Mexico, and if it were worth while to do so we have I dare say satisfied the world that we can fight. What now? Why the mothers of America are asked to send another of their sons to blow out the brains of Mexicans because they refuse to pay the price of the first who fell there fighting for glory! And what if the second fall, too? The Executive, the parental reply is, "We shall have him paid for; we shall get full indemnity!" Sir, I have no patience with this flagitious notion of fighting for indemnity, and this under the equally absurd and hypocritical pretense of securing an honorable peace. An honorable peace? If you have accomplished the objects of the war, (if, indeed, you had an object which you dare avow,) cease to fight and you will have peace; conquer your insane love of false glory, and you will "conquer a peace."

Sir, if your Commander-in-Chief will not do this I will endeavor to compel him, and as I find no other means I shall refuse supplies; without the money of the people he cannot go further. He asks me for that money; I wish him to bring your armies home, to cease shedding blood for money; if he refuses I will refuse supplies, and then I know he must; he will cease his further sale of the lives of my countrymen. May we not, ought we not, now to do this? I can hear no reason why we should not except this: it is said that we are in war, wrongfully it may be; but being in, the President is responsible, and we must give him the means he requires. He responsible! Sir, we, we are responsible if, having power to stay this plague, we refuse to do so. When it shall be so, when the American Senate and the American House of Representatives can stoop from their high position and yield a dumb compliance with the behests of a President who is for the time being commander of your Army; when they will open the Treasury with one hand and the veins of all the soldiers in the land with the other merely because the President commands, then, sir, it matters little how soon some Cromwell shall come into this Hall and say, "The Lord hath no further need of you here." When we fail to do the work "whereunto we were sent" we shall be, we ought to be, removed and give place to others who will. The fate of the barren fig-tree will be ours; Christ cursed it and it withered. . . . ,

Sir, look at this pretense of want of room. With twenty million people you have about one thousand million acres of land, inviting settlement by every conceivable argument, bringing them down to a quarter of a dollar an acre, and allowing every man to squat where he pleases. But the Senator from Michigan says we will be two hundred millions in a few years, and we want room. If I were a Mexican I would tell you, "Have you not room in your own country to bury your dead men? If you come into mine we will greet you with bloody hands and welcome you to hospitable graves."

Why, says the chairman of this Committee on Foreign Relations [Ambrose H. Sevier of Arkansas], it is the most reasonable thing in the world. We ought to have the Bay of San Francisco. Why? Because it is the best harbor on the Pacific! It has been my fortune, Mr. President, to have practised a good deal in criminal courts in the course of my life, but I never yet heard a thief arraigned for stealing a horse plead that it was the best horse that he could find in the country! We want California? What for? Why, says the Senator from Michigan, we will have it; and the Senator from South Carolina, with a very mistaken view, I think, of policy, says you cannot keep our people from going there. I do not desire to prevent them. Let them go and seek their happiness in whatever country or clime it pleases them. All I ask of them is not to require this Government to protect them with that banner consecrated to war waged for principles; eternal, enduring truth. Sir, it is not meet that our old flag should throw its protecting folds over expeditions for lucre or for land. But you will say you want room for your people. This has been the plea of every robber chief from Nimrod to the present hour. I dare say when Tamerlane descended from his throne built of seventy thousand human skulls and marched his ferocious battalions to further slaughter, I dare say he said, "I want room." Bajazet was another gentleman of kindred tastes and wants with us Anglo-Saxons; he "wanted room." Alexander, too, the mighty "Macedonian madman," when he wandered with his Greeks to the plains of India, and fought a bloody battle on the very ground where recently England and the Sikhs engaged in strife for "room" was, no doubt, in quest of some California there. Many a Monterey had he to storm to get "room." Sir, he made quite as much of that sort of history as you ever will. Mr. President, do you remember the last chapter in that history? It is soon read. Oh, I wish we could but understand its moral. Ammon's son, (so was Alexander named,) after all his victories, died drunk in Babylon! The vast empire he conquered to "get room" became the prey of the generals he had trained; it was disparted, torn to pieces, and so ended. Sir, there is a very significant appendix; it is this: the descendants of the Greeks, of Alexander's Greeks, are now governed by a descendant of Attila! Mr. President, while we are fighting for room let us ponder deeply this appendix. I was somewhat amazed the other day to hear the Senator from Michigan declare that Europe had quite forgotten us till these battles waked them up. I suppose the Senator feels grateful to the President for "waking up" Europe. Does the President, who is I hope, read in civic as well as military lore, remember the saying of one who had pondered upon history long; long, too, upon man, his nature and true destiny. Montesquieu did not think highly of this way of "waking up." "Happy," says he, "is that nation whose annals are tiresome."

The Senator from Michigan has a different view of this. He thinks that a nation is not distinguished until it is distinguished in war; he fears that the slumbering faculties of Europe have not been able to ascertain that there are twenty million Anglo-Saxons here making railroads and canals and speeding all the arts of peace to the utmost accomplishment of the most refined civilization. They do not know it. And what is the wonderful expedient which this Democratic method of making history would adopt in order to make us known? Storming cities, desolating, peaceful, happy homes, shooting men—ay, sir, such is war—and shooting women, too. . . .

Why is it, sir, that we of the United States, a people of yesterday compared with the older nations of the world, should be waging war for territory, for "room?" Look at your country, extending from the Allegheny mountains to the Pacific ocean, capable itself of sustaining in comfort a larger population that will be in the whole Union for one hundred years to come. Over this vast expanse of territory your population is now so sparse that I believe we provided at the last session a regiment of mounted men to guard the mail from the frontier of Missouri to the mouth of the Columbia; and yet you persist in the ridiculous assertion "I want room." One would imagine from the frequent reiteration of the complaint that you had a bursting, teeming population, whose energy was paralyzed, whose enterprise was crushed for want of space. Why should we be so weak or wicked as to offer this idle apology for ravaging a neighboring republic? It will impose on no one, at home or abroad. . . .

Mr. President, this uneasy desire to augment our territory has depraved the moral sense and blighted the otherwise keen sagacity of our people. What has been the fate of all nations who have acted upon the idea that they must advance? Our young orators cherish this notion with fervid but fatally mistaken zeal. They call it by the mysterious name of "destiny." "Our destiny," they say, is onward; and hence they argue with ready sophistry the propriety of seizing upon any territory and any people that may lie in the way of our "fated" advance. Recently these progressives have grown classical; some assiduous student of antiquities has helped them to a patron saint. They have wandered back into the desolated Pantheon, and there, among the Polytheistic relics of that "pale mother of dead empires," they have found a god whom these Romans centuries gone by baptized "Terminus."

Sir, I have heard much and read somewhere of this gentleman Terminus. Alexander, of whom I have spoken, was a devotee of this divinity. We have seen the end of his empire. It was said to be an attribute of this god that he must always advance and never recede. So both republican and imperial Rome believed. It was, as they said, their destiny. And for a while it did seem to be even so. Roman Terminus did advance. Under the eagles of Rome he was carried from his home on the Tiber to the furthest East, on the one hand, and to the far West, among the then barbarous tribes of Western Europe, on the other. But at length the time came when retributive justice had become "a destiny."

The despised Gaul calls out to the condemned Goth, and Attila, with his Huns, answers back to the battle-shout to both. The "blue-eyed nations of the North," in succession or united, pour forth their countless hosts of warriors upon Rome and Rome's always advancing god Terminus. And now the battle-ax of the barbarian strikes down the conquering eagle of Rome. Terminus at last recedes, slowly at first, but finally he is driven to Rome, and from Rome to Byzantium. Whoever would know the further fate of this Roman diety, so recently taken under the patronage of American Democracy, may find ample gratification of his curiosity in the luminous pages of Gibbon's "Decline and Fall." Such will find that Rome thought as you now think, that it was her destiny to conquer provinces and nations, and no doubt she sometimes said, as you say, "I will conquer a peace." And where now is she, the mistress of the World? . . .

But, Mr. President, if further acquisition of territory is to be the result either of conquest or treaty then I scarcely know which should be preferred, eternal war with Mexico or the hazards of internal commotion at home, which last I fear may come if another province is to be added to our territory. There is one topic connected with this subject which I tremble when I approach, and yet I cannot forbear to notice it. It meets you in every step you take; it threatens you which way soever you go in the prosecution of this war. I allude to the question of slavery. Opposition to its further extension, it must be obvious to every one, is a deeply rooted determination with men of all parties in what we call the non-slaveholding States. New York, Pennsylvania, and Ohio, three of the most powerful, have already sent their legislative instructions here. So it will be, I doubt not, in all the rest. It is vain now to speculate about the reasons for this. Gentlemen of the South may call it prejudice, passion, hypocrisy, fanaticism. I shall not dispute with them now on that point. The great fact that it is so and not otherwise is what it concerns us to know. You nor I cannot alter or change this opinion if we would. These people only say we will not, cannot consent that you shall carry slavery where it does not already exist. They do not seek to disturb you in that institution as it exists in your States. Enjoy it if you will and as you will. This is their language, this their determination. How is it in the South? Can it be expected that they should expend in common their blood and their treasure in the acquisition of immense territory, and then willingly forego the right to carry thither their slaves and inhabit the conquered country if they please to do so?

Sir, I know the feelings and opinions of the South too well to calculate on this. Nay, I believe they would even contend to any extremity for the mere right had they no wish to exert it. I believe, and I confess I tremble when the conviction presses upon me, that there is equal obstinacy on both sides of this fearful question. If then, we persist in war, which, if it terminate in anything short of a mere wanton waste of blood as well as money, must end as this bill proposes in the acquisition of territory, to which at once this controversy must attach, this bill would seem to be nothing less than a bill to produce internal commotion. Should we prosecute this war another moment or expend one dollar in the purchase or conquest of a single acre of Mexican land the North and the South are brought into collision on a point where neither will yield. Who can foresee or foretell the result? Who so bold or reckless as to look such a conflict in the face unmoved? I do not envy the heart of him who can realize the possibility of such a conflict without emotions too painful to be endured. Why, then, shall we, the representatives of the sovereign States of this Union, the chosen guardians of this confederated Republic, why should we precipitate this fearful struggle by continuing a war the results of which must be to force us at once upon it? Sir, rightly considered, this is treason, treason to the Union, treason to the dearest interests, the loftiest aspirations, the most cherished hopes of our constituents; it is a crime to risk the possibility of such a contest; it is a crime of such infernal hue that every other in the catalogue of iniquity when compared with it whitens into virtue.

. . . We stand this day on the crumbling brink of that gulf; we see its bloody eddies wheeling and boiling before us; shall we not pause before it be too late? How plain again is here the path, I may add the only way of duty, of prudence, of true patriotism. Let us abandon all idea of acquiring further territory and by consequence cease at once to prosecute this war. Let us call home our armies and bring them at once within our own acknowledged limits. Show Mexico that you are sincere when you say you desire nothing by conquest. She has learned that she cannot encounter you in war, and if she had not she is too weak to disturb you here. Tender her peace, and my life on it she will then accept it. But whether she shall or not you will have peace without her consent. It is your invasion that has made war; your retreat will restore peace. Let us, then, close forever the approaches of internal feud, and so return to the ancient concord and the old ways of national prosperity and permanent glory. Let us here in this temple consecrated to the Union perform a solemn illustration; let us wash Mexican blood from our hands, and on these altars, in the presence of that image of the Father of his Country that looks down upon us, swear to preserve honorable peace with all the world and eternal brotherhood with each other.

22

The Whig Accusation

"A War of Conquest and Spoliation"

When the Mexican War openly evolved into an agency for expansion, it created a variety of internal and external problems which the Polk administration had not foreseen when it dispatched United States armed forces into Mexican territory. At the outbreak of war Polk confidently anticipated not only a series of easy military victories but also the rapid progress of diplomacy which would bring the war to a satisfactory conclusion and secure for him his territorial war aims. Instead, by the spring of 1847 he discovered that for the United States, a nation overwhelmingly powerful when contrasted to the enemy of the moment, military policy was far less demanding than diplomacy. Somehow the easy military victories of the United States did not assure a satisfactory conclusion of the war at all. As the conflict dragged on, the President demanded of Congress larger military appropriations to conduct a war against an ephemeral enemy that would not treat. The administration's critics—and they were legion—vigorously questioned both the President's decisions which led to war and his military strategy of dispatching armies into a country as politically chaotic as Mexico.

Now that the United States had a conquering army in the heart of Mexico, it was no longer clear what ultimate intentions the administration had in mind. Why, asked *The American Review* in the following article, dated October, 1847, was there no peace? What terms was the United States government exacting that ruled out a decent diplomatic arrangement that might conclude the struggle? The explanation for the nation's dilemma seemed clear enough. The administration was seeking a vast accession of Mexican territory. American military and naval policy in California pointed to the acquisition of no less than all that province. The *Review* ridiculed the entire concept of manifest destiny which now threatened to embark the United States on a career of conquest and acquisition. What would become of American policy in Mexico if the Mexican government continued to avoid a diplomatic confrontation? The choices were narrowing. Either the United States would be obligated to subjugate and hold the entire country or it would be forced to withdraw its forces to defensible positions and hold the line against future counter-offensives. At least, at the level of argumentation, the Whig Party favored the latter course.

THERE is very little difference of opinion, we believe, among Whigs—very little certainly among all intelligent and impartial

From "The Whigs and the War," *The American Review*, VI (October, 1847), 331–346.

observers of events—in regard to the origin of our war upon Mexico. There are, perhaps, a few who choose to go no further than insist that the war was wholly unnecessary, however begun, and that it might have been, and ought to have been avoided. The responsibility of the President and his administration in permitting the country to become involved in a war which could and should have been avoided, is fearfully great. Among a virtuous and wise people, this condemnation alone should be enough to overwhelm those who have been guilty of so great a crime. A civilized and Christian people engaged in an unnecessary war, in the middle of the nineteenth century, is a spectacle of backsliding and crime over which angels may weep. So far, at least, the Administration at Washington is guilty, in the deliberate estimation, we do not doubt, of four-fifths of the whole body of intelligent persons throughout the country. . . .

Looking at the war in this aspect—as a war of conquest and spoliation—we are well assured that there is one predominant sentiment among the Whigs of the United States, in whatever quarter of the Union they are found, and that is a sentiment of disgust and unqualified condemnation. We do not say that there may not be those among us, and of our number, and some of them persons of consideration, who are not averse to extending still further the limits of the republic, provided it can be done by fair and just means, and an honest purchase, and in a way to comport with our own honor and magnanimity, as a powerful nation dealing with another, all of whose rights are as sacred as our own, while it has less ability to maintain and defend them. But we are sure we are safe in saying that there is not a Whig in the United States who does not, with all honest and ingenuous minds, reject with scorn the very thought that his country should be engaged in war with a sister republic far below ourselves in every element of strength and greatness, for the real purpose, however sought to be disguised by plausible pretences, of effecting a forcible dismemberment of that republic, and of profiting ourselves by the spoils. . . .

But we turn to consider, first of all, the great leading question in our Mexican relations. What have we been fighting for in this Mexican war? Or rather, the question is, What has the Administration proposed to accomplish by sending a conquering army to the heart of the Mexican empire, and holding one half of the entire country under military subjection? And why has it been, after all our battles and victories, long ago fought and won, and so vast a country overrun, that peace was not long ago obtained? What terms and conditions has the Administration persisted in its purpose of exacting, that have put a peace between the two countries, and even a negotiation for peace, notwithstanding our successive and overwhelming triumphs, all the while, or for so long a period, out of the question?

In our view, but one general answer can be given to all this significant interrogation. The Administration has looked from the beginning for a vast accession of foreign territory to the United States, as the result of this onslaught upon Mexico. This war has been quite an anomalous proceeding from the beginning. The Constitution constitutes Congress the war-making power of this government; but in this case, as we have read events and transactions, the President made the war. The Constitution contemplates that before deliberate hostilities shall be undertaken in any case, a declaration of war shall be made; but in this case, a hostile aggressive movement was made under the personal orders of the President, resulting in a conflict of arms and in actual war, as must have been calculated on with entire certainty. No declaration of war has *ever* been made. The war has been *recognized* by Congress—that is all. . . .

. . . The President thought to glorify his reign by pushing the limits of the Progressive Republic in one direction or another, far beyond any serious dream of any Anglo-American land-robber of preceding times. He first tried his hand with England, by protesting that he would have the whole of Oregon, every minute of it, up to "fifty-four forty." He would not submit to take anything less; and but for the unwearied and sleepless efforts of men quite as patriotic as himself, and, under favor, we believe, a good deal wiser, this folly of his would have cost us a war with England. Disappointed in not being able to carry the nominal line of our national jurisdiction quite as far into the hyperborean regions as his unmeaning ambition had prompted him to desire, he turned his regards to the opposite quarter of North America, and there, stretching away in the sunny south, and towards the placid west, he saw New Mexico and the Californias, and how much more of the goodly possessions of the Republic of Mexico Heaven only knows, which he thought he would be the happiest man alive if he could clutch, and dedicate, as his official offering, to the progressive spirit of his country. It is to the influence of this motive on his mind, that we attribute the daring resolution which he took originally to precipitate this war. He counted on a weak enemy, an easy conquest, and a speedy accomplishment of his purpose. Just as before he had claimed that our Oregon ran up to "fifty-four forty," so now he claimed that our Texas ran down to the Rio Grande; and, in this case, seeing nothing in the character of Mexico to make him pause, he ordered Taylor to march upon that river, and occupy it as our rightful boundary.

As he began, so he went on. Battle after battle was fought, and victory after victory won, and still the Mexican seemed as much unconquered as before. He showed a disposition to defend his fields and firesides on this side the Rio Grande; whereupon the President asked for a great army, and a well-filled military chest, believing, as he declared, that "the immediate appearance in arms of a large and overpowering force" would be "the most certain means of bringing the existing collision with Mexico to a speedy and successful termination." Everything he asked for was accorded to him, and his first campaign presented truly a magnificent plan of operations. The forces of the United States were to enter Mexico in three grand divisions. Kearney in the west was to invade and subdue New Mexico, and then push for the Californias, where he should be met and aided by a naval force, and by a regiment sent round by sea. Wool, with the army of the centre, was to penetrate to Chihuahua; and Taylor, with the main army, moving by the Rio Grande, and passing through the States of Tamaulipas and New Leon, and into Coahuila, taking the only practicable route in this direction, from the coast to the table-lands of Mexico, was to make a demonstration towards the capital. Napoleon never undertook the invasion of a foreign country with a more manifest purpose of making a thorough conquest of his enemy, dictating his own terms of peace, and bearing off the spoils of victory. . . .

Long before General Kearney arrived in California, another governor has established civil sway, in the name of the United States, in that remote country. Instructions from the Secretary of the Navy, of the 12th of July, informed the commander of the naval forces in the Pacific, very explicitly, that *the object of the United States is, under its rights as a belligerent nation, to possess itself entirely of Upper California.* In other words, the object was, to seize and hold California by conquest, and as an acquest of war. "This will bring with it," says this letter, "the necessity of a civil administration;" and instructions are given for establishing such a government, for the appointment of officers, and taking from them *an oath of allegiance* to the United States. In another letter from the Secretary of the Navy, to the officer commanding our naval forces in the Pacific, we have this significant declaration and avowal: "Without being animated by any ambitious spirit of conquest! our naval and military forces must *hold* the ports and territory of the enemy, of which possession has been obtained by their arms. You will, therefore, *under no circumstances, voluntarily lower the flag of the United States, or relinquish the actual possession of Upper California.* Of *other* points of the Mexican territory, which the forces under your command may occupy, you may maintain the possession, or withdraw, as in your judgment may be most advantageous in prosecuting the war."

Commodore Sloat was the first naval commander who found

himself, under instructions from Washington, bearing military and civil sway in California. He issued his proclamation to the people of that country, declaring that, "henceforward California will be a portion of the United States, and its peaceable inhabitants will enjoy the same rights and privileges they now enjoy, together with the privilege of choosing their own magistrates and other officers, for the administration of justice among themselves; and the same protection will be extended to them as to any other State in the Union." His successor in authority in this region, Commodore Stockton, did not, to say the least of it, in his exercise of power, lower the pretensions of the United States. He promptly declared to the people, on arriving at the city of the Angels, that "the territory of California now belongs to the United States, and will be governed, as soon as circumstances will permit, by officers and laws similar to those by which the other territories of the United States are regulated and protected.". . .

Nothing, certainly, could be plainer than what appears by the showing of these documents: that it was, from the beginning, a settled purpose of the Administration, to make this war the means of forcibly dismembering the Mexican empire, and bringing large portions of that country into permanent connection and incorporation with the United States. Nothing short of the Rio Grande as a boundary for Texas, the whole of New Mexico "on both sides of the Del Norte," and the whole of Upper California, was thought of, for a moment, as sufficient to satisfy the pestilent craving of the President for "the vast extension of our territorial limits." New Mexico and Upper California, alone, comprise one third of the entire territorial possessions of Mexico, since Texas was cut off from her dominion. With Texas and these two provinces together, we should about divide equally with Mexico, leaving her one half of her original empire, and appropriating the other half to ourselves. We do not suppose that this would fully satisfy the Administration. So much they were resolved to have, and beyond this they would take all they could get. Mr. Sevier, chairman of the Committee of Foreign Affairs in the Senate of the United States, when advocating the Three Million Bill, said in debate: "He was not authorized *to state precisely what territory this Government would require,* but he supposed no Senator would think they ought to get less than New Mexico and Upper California." They would take up with these two provinces if they could not get more; but they had a decided hankering after more. Any one who will read attentively the correspondence of the Department of War with General Taylor, will not fail to discover that the Administration, at one time at least, entertained strong hopes of some of the northern States of Mexico—those bordering on the Rio Grande. . . .

The country is not ignorant that the more thorough-paced friends of the Administration, the progressives, in speeches and newspapers, have for some time been accustomed to speak, with high gratification and delight, of "a good time coming," and not far off, when all Mexico shall be absorbed in our own progressive Republic. They call it our "manifest destiny." We are not sure that this "manifest destiny" of our Republic stops short—in their imaginings—of absorbing the whole of North America. We are not sure that even South America is to escape. Their notion is that the Spanish race on this continent, and all others, must fade away before the face of the Anglo-Saxons, or rather of the Yankees, as shadows fly before the coming light. The Indians have receded and wasted at our approach, and so must all the rest of the dwellers on this side of the globe, except, perhaps, so far as we may see fit to embrace them and inoculate them with our blood. It is evident that this idea of our "manifest destiny," is not an unpleasing one to the Administration, and they are not unwilling to be the instrument of furnishing to the world the first substantial proof of its reality. They are willing to show the faith they have in the sublimities of Progressive Democracy, by employing the awful agency of war, at least by using the occasion of the present war, to dismember and despoil

Mexico, if they can, of one third of her empire, and annex so much at once to the United States, as a kind of first fruits offered up to the present god of democratic worship—our Manifest Destiny. We had observed lately that an English newspaper, The London News, had deemed it a cunning stroke of policy to talk as if they had themselves, on that side of the water, discovered this "manifest destiny" of ours, and were prepared to yield gracefully to what they could not prevent. Considering what England is doing in the East, she might well afford to look with some degree of complacency on any career of conquest upon which we might seem disposed to enter in this quarter of the world—provided, of course, we did not touch any peculiar interest of her own. . . . And England is wise enough to know also, whether we know it or not, that the shortest possible way of bringing down our power and our pride, is to allow us to outgrow our strength—to become long-limbed and loose-jointed—to go on with our plan of ingrafting innumerable new shoots from strange stocks, not on the stem of the tree, but away off on the ends of the distant branches, to be fed with its vital sap, until the heart, and root, and trunk, robbed of their proper nutriment and support, fall into premature decay, and the brave old oak, under whose broad shadow successive and growing generations might have reposed and flourished, crushed by its own weight, comes suddenly down in one wide-spread ruin to the ground. . . .

. . . In the judgment of the Administration, then, we are engaged in making conquests in Mexico, which it is impossible for us to avoid. It is admitted that the design is to make these conquests, and the excuse for it is, that it is impossible to avoid making them—it is our "manifest destiny." It is right in spirit, that even England should bend before this "manifest destiny;" should forswear hostility to it, and even any ill humor at it, and learn to think and speak of our conquests under it—at least, of our conquests *southwestward*—as something impossible for us to avoid, or for her to prevent. In our view of the matter, no more complete manifestation could well be made, of the temper and determination with which the Administration entered into this war, and with which it has, all along, been prosecuted, than is here exhibited—albeit very unconsciously exhibited, perhaps. We do not know, indeed, that the powers at Washington care any longer seriously to disguise the fact, that their main purpose in this war has been to draw to the United States, in some way, and in any way they could, large and extensive portions of the Mexican territory. Certainly, it is very useless any longer, after all that has transpired, to set up any pretence to the contrary. One thing is indisputable, and that is, that they do desire their own party and partisans in the country so to understand their policy, and they count the more confidently—and no doubt justly—on their support, because they so understand it.

To us, therefore, it seems clear—and this approaches the point to which this article is mainly intended to direct attention —that the Whigs in the next Congress will have no difficulty in settling it definitively in their own minds, and with perfect unanimity, with what principal intent it has been from the beginning, that the Administration has been for sixteen months prosecuting what it calls a "vigorous war" in Mexico, and has made such a vast sacrifice of the lives of our citizens, and such an immense waste of the national treasures. They will believe, what every active, intelligent friend and supporter of the Administration undoubtedly believes, that the grand object has been the acquisition of territory. The fact has become too plain and palpable to be doubted by anybody. It may be, and probably is true, and events transpiring, perhaps, while we are writing, may show, that the Administration is willing to pay very liberally and largely for any territory that Mexico will agree to yield up to us. It has not, we believe, always been so disposed. . . .

We are well aware that the Administration has entertained only one idea, and has seemed incapable of entertaining any other, about the way we are to deal with Mexico, till she shall consent to make peace with us. That idea is summed up in the phrase, a thousand times repeated from Administration sources

—a vigorous prosecution of the war. They have conducted what they call a vigorous war from the beginning, and very likely they will be for conducting just *such* a vigorous war to the end. We shall not be surprised to find the President announcing to Congress, at the opening of the next session in December, not only that such is still the policy of his Administration, but that now, since Mexico refuses to make peace with us, after her capital has fallen, we must occupy the whole country, if need be, with our military forces, and bring the whole nation under complete subjugation. Possibly he may so far yield to Mexican obstinacy as to conclude that the military occupation and subjugation of one half, or one third, of the country, may, after all, answer every useful purpose of the war. In either case, we shall find the President calling on Congress, at its next session, by every appeal which can be made to the passions or the pride of his countrymen, to furnish him with large supplies of men and money for the war; heartily hoping, as we believe it is very likely he may, at the same time, if that branch of the National Legislature which more immediately holds the purse strings, shall be in the hands of the Whigs, that his demands may be met, in that quarter, by a flat refusal. . . .

The President has undertaken to conduct this war from the beginning, in his own way, without any other reliance upon Congress, or reference to it, than to ask that body, first to recognize the war after it was begun, and next to supply him with the men and money he required, as necessary to his plan of operations. He has, all the while, thus far, had his own party in majority, in both Houses, and everything has been accorded to him as he desired. And so long as Congress is content to leave the whole conduct of the war in his hands, we do not see how it could well refuse to continue to meet his wishes in the matter of the supplies. Certainly it would never refuse to grant anything and everything necessary or proper for the support and succor of our brave troops, placed, without any fault of theirs, in the heart of a distant country, and struggling with every peril, discomfort and difficulty. And though we are of the number of those who believe that Congress, as the war-making power, has a right, and it may be its imperative duty, to prescribe and limit the operations and general mode of conducting any war—as, for example, to limit its operations to defence merely, or, in its discretion, to fit out expeditions for the invasion of a foreign country, and for offensive war—yet, in the present instance, and especially if the two Houses in the next Congress could not be brought to agree on any measure or plan, either for conducting the war, or for bringing it to an immediate close, we do not see that the Whigs, being in a majority in one House only, will be in any condition, if they were so disposed, to take the management of the war out of the President's hands. It will be time enough for them to dispose of the war when the people shall give them the full power of the Government. They may yet have that high service to perform for the country. . . .

. . . It is easy to express the legitimate objects of the war on our part, and for which alone the money of the nation ought to be granted: First, the security of our frontier State of Texas, by the establishment of a definite boundary between it and Mexico, and in the adjustment of which the whole question of annexation, and all its incidentals, should be quieted forever; and next, a proper and secure provision for the payment of the just claims of our citizens on Mexico. These objects attained, the war ought to cease; and if the President were authoritatively restricted to these objects, in its prosecution, it is quite probable that he would think it best to change his plan of belligerent operations —if, indeed, it should be found necessary to carry them on at all, which we greatly doubt, for another day. At least we Whigs know very well, that if such a restriction had been imposed on him from the beginning, no war of invasion would ever have been undertaken—just as we know that no war at all would have been undertaken, if he had known before it was begun, that he was to be limited to the naked justice of our own cause, and would not be permitted to go farther and perpetrate a great wrong on Mexico. . . .

We believe, if there is any one proposition on which the

people of this country would rise in their might to sustain their faithful representatives, it is this—"That the war now existing with Mexico ought not to be prosecuted for the acquisition of territory, to form new States to be added to this Union." We have not a doubt that the time has come when the people, in all sections of the Union, are ready to unite on such a sentiment as this, with a strength which has not been exhibited on any other great public question in the last quarter of a century. We want no more territory; we want no more accessions of new States from newly-acquired territory; the country is ample enough; the people have room enough. There can be no mistake, or danger of mistake, in asserting that this is becoming the common and prevalent sentiment of the reflecting portion of our people. Especially, and above all things, they are against acquiring more territory by war and conquest.

. . . By no stretch of our imagination can we fancy the Administration, after all its bold pretensions, concluding a treaty with Mexico, dictated by itself from the Mexican capital, which shall not cede to the United States at least a couple of provinces—New Mexico and California. Of course, this would only be done, if at all, on condition of the direct payment by us of a very large sum of money as a consideration for the cession. The question arises—What would the Senate do with such a treaty? We answer, in our opinion, it would be rejected; and for ourselves we say, we should rejoice to see it rejected by Whig votes.

23   James Russell Lowell

A War "to lug new slave states in"

Because Texas entered the Union as a slave state in 1845 and because President Polk was a Southerner, many antislavery spokesmen of the North, especially those in New England, assumed, however erroneously, that the Mexican War was a Southern plot to extend the area of slavery to the Pacific coast. For this reason, much of the most bitter condemnation of the Mexican War came from Northern abolitionists such as Joshua Giddings. Of all the abolitionist writings against the war none was more satirical than James Russell Lowell's *Biglow Papers*. The following excerpt from this small volume comprises Lowell's best-known attack on the war.

> THRASH away, you'll *hev* to rattle
>   On them kittle drums o' yourn,—
> 'Taint a knowin' kind o' cattle
>   Thet is ketched with mouldy corn;
> Put in stiff, you fifer feller,
>   Let folks see how spry you be,—
> Guess you'll toot till you are yeller
>   'Fore you git ahold o' me! . . .
>
> 'T would n't suit them Southern fellers,
>   They're a dreffle graspin' set,
> We must ollers blow the bellers
>   Wen they want their irons het;
> May be it 's all right ez preachin',
>   But *my* narves it kind o' grates,
> When I see the overreachin'
>   O' them nigger-drivin' States.
>
> Them thet rule us, them slave-traders,
>   Haint they cut a thunderin' swarth,
> (Helped by Yankee renegaders,)
>   Thru the vartu o' the North!
> We begin to think it 's nater
>   To take sarse an' not be riled;—
> Who 'd expect to see a tater
>   All on eend at bein' biled?

From James Russell Lowell, *The Biglow Papers* (Cambridge, Mass., 1848), pp. 3–11.

Ez fer war, I call it murder,—
    There you hev it plain an' flat;
I don't want to go no furder
    Than my Testyment fer that;
God hez sed so plump an' fairly,
    It 's ez long ez it is broad,
An' you 've gut to git up airly
    Ef you want to take in God. . . .

Wut 's use o' meetin-goin'
    Every Sabbath, wet or dry,
Ef it 's right to go amowin'
    Feller-men like oats an' rye?
I dunno but ut it's pooty
    Trainin' round in bobtail coats,—
But it 's curus Christian dooty
    This ere cuttin' folks's throats.

They may talk o' Freedom's airy
    Tell they 're pupple in the face,—
It 's a grand gret cemetary
    Fer the barthrights of our race;
They jest want this Californy
    So's to lug new slave-states in
To abuse ye, an' to scorn ye,
    An' to plunder ye like sin.

Aint it cute to see a Yankee
    Take sech everlastin' pains,
All to git the Devil's thankee,
    Helpin' on 'em weld their chains?
Wy, it 's jest ez clear ez figgers,
    Clear ez one an' one make two,
Chaps thet make black slaves o' niggers
    Want to make wite slaves o' you. . . .

Massachusetts, God forgive her,
  She 's akneelin' with the rest,
She, thet ough' to ha' clung fer ever
  To her grand old eagle-nest;
She thet ough' to stand so fearless
  Wile the wracks are round her hurled,
Holdin' up a beacon peerless
  To the oppressed of all the world! . . .

Clang the bells in every steeple,
  Call all rue men to disown
The tradoocers of our people,
  The enslavers o' their own;
Let our dear old Bay State proudly
  Put the trumpet to her mouth,
Let her ring this messidge loudly
  In the ears of all the South:—

"I'll return ye good fer evil
  Much ez we frail mortils can,
But I wun't go help the Devil
  Makin' man the cus o' man;
Call me coward, call me traiter,
  Jest ez suits your mean idees,—
Here I stand a tyrant-hater,
  An' the friend o' God an' Peace!" . . .

24   William Jay

"The Corruption of Public Opinion
impairs the moral sense"

Throughout the Mexican War the Polk administration faced a continuing attack from the American Peace Society. This organization, comprising as it did one powerful aspect of the reform urge of the period, was bitterly opposed to war in general. It became especially hostile toward the Mexican War because many of its leaders were abolitionists and accepted without question the notion that the war was a Southern plot. Perhaps the most penetrating denunciations of the war and the concept of manifest destiny were Elihu Burritt's writings in *Christian Citizen* and *Advocate of Peace*. But William Jay's *A Review of the Mexican War* offered not only an excellent summary of the American Peace Society's arguments against the Mexican War but also a penetrating analysis of the question of governmental honesty in time of war.

. . . IT is utterly impossible that Congress would have issued, or the people have tolerated, a declaration of war against Mexico, either to compel her to pay our alleged claims, or to withdraw her troops and magistrates from her villages on the Rio Grande. Hence, it was deemed necessary first to provoke a collision, and *then* to appeal to Congress to defend the country from invasion! The war, therefore, although recognized and prosecuted by Congress *after* its commencement, was in fact and in truth begun in consequence of orders issued by the President on his own responsibility, and not in pursuance of any constitutional or legal authority. He had, indeed, as Commander-in-Chief, a right to direct the movements of the troops, but not in such a manner as necessarily and designedly to involve the country in war. . . .

The course pursued by Congress has apparently been directed by the principle, that when the country has once been involved in war, no matter by what means, or for what objects, it is the duty of the representatives of the people to afford to the President every facility he demands for its prosecution, however wicked or injurious it may be. . . .

From William Jay, *A Review of the Mexican War* (Boston, 1849), pp. 245–266.

From the commencement of hostilities, the public was almost daily served by the newspapers with details of battles, and bombardments, and mangled corpses, and all the varieties of human suffering caused by war. . . . This constant familiarity with human suffering, instead of awakening sympathy, has roused into action the vilest passions of our nature. We have been taught to ring our bells, and illuminate our windows, and let off fireworks, as manifestations of our joy, when we have heard of great ruin, and devastation, and misery, and death, inflicted by our troops upon a people who never injured us, who never fired a shot on our soil, and who were utterly incapable of acting on the offensive against us. Nor was our exultation at the flow of Mexican blood repressed by the recollection that American blood flowed with it. . . . The nation had gained glory, and would gain land; and politicians seemed anxious to gain popularity by rivalling each other in exulting shouts. Alas, in very many instances those shouts proceeded from the same lips which denounced the war as unconstitutional, unjust, and a national crime!

The struggles between the convictions of conscience and the aspirations for popular favor, led others besides the Whigs into strange and almost ludicrous contradictions. . . .

That portion of the public press which supported the war has, in many instances, been instrumental in diffusing throughout the community most impious and ferocious sentiments. It was, of course, the policy of the dominant party to excite the passions of the people against Mexico, to encourage admiration for military prowess, and to repress all compassion for those we were slaughtering and plundering. . . . Mr. Polk's own organ, the official *Union,* declared: "Our work of subjugation and conquest must go on rapidly and with augmented force, and, as far as possible, at the expense of Mexico herself. Henceforth, we must seek PEACE, and compel it by inflicting on our enemies all the evils of war."

. . . Anecdotes of officers, which, if true, could not fail to disgust all who reverence the awful realities of Christianity, have been loudly trumpeted as instances of American patriotism and heroism. Thus we have had an account of a captain mortally wounded, and just expiring. ". . . He concluded an answer to some inquiries concerning the battle of the 9th, by writing *'We gave the Mexicans hell!'* " These words so peculiarly horrible as uttered by a dying man, became with a certain class a slang phrase, and to give the Mexicans *hell*, seemed to be the glorious privilege, as well as duty, of American Christians. . . .

The Church has, on some few cases, united in this unholy work, of corrupting public opinion. The pulpit has occasionally uttered its benefictions on the Mexican invasion; and ministers of Christ, by joining in military funeral pageants, have given the sanction of the religion they professed, to the cause in which the deceased perished. On some of these occasions sermons have been delivered, breathing little of the spirit of the Prince of Peace. Men who had lost their lives in the act of voluntarily carrying fire and sword into a foreign country, have been held forth to the admiration of their countrymen, as having fallen in the *discharge of duty*. But these reverend patriots omitted to instruct their audience, that the Mexicans who fell in the act of defending their wives and children, were no less obedient to the commands of duty than the American volunteer. . . .

The moral sense of the nation was, moreover, impaired by the sentiment industriously cultivated by the politicians of both parties—"Our country, right or wrong." This sentiment was of course intended to vindicate each party, for the support it gave to the war, by insinuating that devotion to country is more imperative than moral obligation.

The war has also had a most unhappy influence in familiarizing the public ear to *falsehood*, and under circumstances tending to divest the sin of much of its vileness. Falsehood was dignified, both by the magnitude and importance of the objects it was intended to promote, and by the elevated position of those who condescended to use it as an instrument.

It was one of the lamentations of the Prophet, that "truth has fallen in the streets;" and in our days, the Mexican War has caused her to be trampled in the dust, not only in the streets of Washington, but in every highway throughout the republic. The Message of Mr. Polk (Dec. 1846), in vindication of the war, has been termed "a pyramid of mendacity." . . . With a reckless consistency rarely paralleled, he announced to Congress on the 6th of July, 1848, that "the war in which our country was RELUCTANTLY involved in the NECESSARY vindication of the national rights and honor, has been terminated."

The fictions of Mr. Polk were reiterated by his party with all the gravity of sincere belief. The Whigs in Congress, with a few honorable exceptions, pursued a different policy. They fearlessly confessed that the war for which they voted was unnecessary and unjust, a war of aggression and not of defence; and that the assertion in behalf of which they enrolled their names in an enduring record, that the war existed "by the act of Mexico" was FALSE. To excuse their conduct, they also had *their* fiction. They voted to raise fifty thousand men, for the purpose of rescuing General Taylor and his little army from capture by the Mexicans!

The falsehoods respecting the Mexican War, coined in Washington, became a circulating medium throughout the country. They were found in almost every official despatch; they were uttered through the press; they were passed as genuine by Governors in their messages, and by Legislatures in their resolves. Who shall estimate the injury done to the morality of the nation by this widespread contempt for truth? The example of men conspicuous for talents, influence, and station, must be operative for good or for evil. . . . It has been well said that truth and the confidence it inspires, is the basis of human society, and that error is the source of every iniquity. How deplorable, then, that the love of truth and abhorrence of falsehood should be weakened by the authority and example of those in high places! . . .

Surely, among the awful responsibilities resting upon the authors and supporters of the Mexican War, will be included the corruption of public opinion and the depravation of public morals to which it has given birth.

25   Albert Gallatin

The Fathers favored "a model Republic"

not "unjust usurpation"

Albert Gallatin interpreted the Polk administration's tendency to ignore the limited American mission as conceived by the Founding Fathers as the disturbing element of America's conduct with the Mexican War. The Founding Fathers believed that the United States could improve the condition of all countries by becoming a "model republic." They hoped that other governments would take as a touch-stone America's government and civilization. That vision required, above all, policies of moderation which the Polk leadership had ap-parently abandoned in its relations with Mexico. Gallatin could dis-cover no traditional moderation in either Polk's policies which led to the war or his conduct of the war itself. Gallatin denied that the superiority of American power gave the United States any special rights over the people of Mexico. Nor, believed Gallatin, could the United States, whatever the superiority of its institutions, bring any salvation to the people of Mexico. To reestablish its traditions of diplomacy the nation had no choice but to withdraw its forces from Mexico and demand of that country only what was due the citizens of the United States.

THE people of the United States have been placed by Providence in a position never before enjoyed by any other nation. They

From Albert Gallatin, "The Mission of the United States," *Peace with Mexico* (New York, 1847), pp. 25–30.

are possessed of a most extensive territory, with a very fertile soil, a variety of climates and productions, and a capacity of sustaining a population greater, in proportion to its extent, than any other territory of the same size on the face of the globe.

By a concourse of various circumstances, they found themselves, at the epoch of their independence, in the full enjoyment of religious, civil, and political liberty, entire free from the hereditary monopoly of wealth or power. The people at large were in full and quiet possession of all those natural rights, for which the people of other countries have for a long time contended, and still do contend. They were, and you still are the supreme sovereigns, acknowledged as such by all. For the proper exercise of these uncontrolled powers and privileges, you are responsible to posterity, to the world at large, and to the Almighty Being who has poured on you such unparalleled blessings.

Your mission is, to improve the state of the world, to be the "Model Republic," to show that men are capable of governing themselves, and that this simple and natural form of government is that also which confers most happiness on all, is productive of the greatest development of the intellectual faculties, above all, that which is attended with the highest standard of private and political virtue and morality.

Your forefathers, the founders of the Republic, imbued with a deep feeling of their rights and duties, did not deviate from those principles. The sound sense, the wisdom, the probity, the respect for public faith, with which the internal concerns of the nation were managed, made our institutions an object of general admiration. Here, for the first time, was the experiment attempted with any prospect of success, and on a large scale, of a Representative Democratic Republic. If it failed, the last hope of the friends of mankind was lost or indefinitely postponed; and the eyes of the world were turned towards you. Whenever real, or pretended apprehensions of the imminent danger of trusting the people at large with power, were expressed, the answer ever was, "Look at America!"

In their external relations the United States, before this unfortunate war, had, whilst sustaining their just rights, ever acted in strict conformity with the dictates of justice, and displayed the utmost moderation. They never had voluntarily injured any other nation. Every acquisition of territory from Foreign Powers was honestly made, the result of Treaties, not imposed, but freely assented to by the other party. The preservation of peace was ever a primary object. The recourse to arms was always in self defence. On its expediency there may have been a difference of opinion; that, in the only two instances of conflict with civilized nations which occurred during a period of sixty three years, (1783 to 1846), the just rights of the United States had been invaded by a long continued series of aggressions, is undeniable. In the first instance, war was not declared; and there were only partial hostilities between France and England. The Congress of the United States, the only legitimate organ of the nation for that purpose, did, in 1812, declare war against Great Britain. Independent of depredations on our commerce, she had, for twenty years, carried on an actual war against the United States. I say, actual war, since there is now but one opinion on that subject; a renewal of the impressment of men sailing under the protection of our flag would be tantamount to a declaration of war. The partial opposition to the war of 1812, did not rest on a denial of the aggressions of England and of the justice of our cause, but on the fact that, with the exception of impressments, similar infractions of our just rights had been committed by France, and on the most erroneous belief, that the Administration was partial to that country, and insincere in their apparent efforts to restore peace.

At present, all these principles would seem to have been abandoned. The most just, a purely defensive war, and no other is justifiable, is necessarily attended with a train of great and unavoidable evils. What shall we say of one, iniquitous in its origin, and provoked by ourselves, of a war of aggression, which is now publicly avowed to be one of intended conquest.

If persisted in, its necessary consequences will be, a permanent increase of our military establishment and executive patronage: its general tendency, to make man hate man, to awaken his worst passions, to accustom him to the taste of blood. It has already demoralized no inconsiderable portion of the nation.

The general peace, which has been preserved between the great European powers during the last thirty years, may not be ascribed to the purest motives. Be these what they may, this long and unusual repose has been most beneficial to the cause of humanity. Nothing can be more injurious to it, more lamentable, more scandalous, than the war between two adjacent republics of North America.

Your mission was, to be a model for all other governments and for all other less favored nations, to adhere to the most elevated principles of political morality, to apply all your faculties to the gradual improvement of your own institutions and social state, and, by your example, to exert a moral influence most beneficial to mankind at large. Instead of this, an appeal has been made to your worst passions; to cupidity, to the thirst of unjust aggrandizement by brutal force; to the love of military fame and of false glory; and it has even been tried to pervert the noblest feelings of your nature. The attempt is made to make you abandon the lofty position which your fathers occupied, to substitute for it the political morality and heathen patriotism of the heroes and statesmen of antiquity.

I have said, that it was attempted to pervert even your virtues. Devotedness to country, or patriotism, is a most essential virtue, since the national existence of any society depends upon it. Unfortunately, our most virtuous dispositions are perverted, not only by our vices and selfishness, but also by their own excess. Even the most holy of our attributes, the religious feeling, may be perverted from that cause, as was but too lamentably exhibited in the persecutions, even unto death, of those who were deemed heretics. It is not, therefore, astonishing, that patriotism, carried to excess, should also be perverted. In the entire devotedness to their country, the people, everywhere and at all times, have been too apt to forget the duties imposed upon them by justice towards other nations. It is against this natural propensity that you should be specially on your guard. The blame does not attach to those who, led by their patriotic feelings, though erroneous, flock around the national standard. On the contrary, no men are more worthy of admiration, better entitled to the thanks of their country, than those who, after war has once taken place, actuated only by the purest motives, daily and with the utmost self-devotedness, brave death and stake their own lives in the conflict against the actual enemy. I must confess, that I do not extend the same charity to those civilians, who coolly and deliberately plunge the country into any unjust or unnecessary war.

We should have but one conscience; and most happy would it be for mankind, were statesmen and politicians only as honest, in their management of the internal or external national concerns, as they are in private life. The irreproachable private character of the President, and of all the members of his administration, is known and respected. There is not one of them who would not spurn with indignation the most remote hint that, on similar pretences to those alleged for dismembering Mexico, he might be capable of an attempt to appropriate to himself his neighbor's farm.

In the total absence of any argument that can justify the war in which we are now involved, resort has been had to a most extraordinary assertion. It is said, that the people of the United States have an hereditary superiority of race over the Mexicans, which gives them the right to subjugate and keep in bondage the inferior nation. This, it is also alleged, will be the means of enlightening the degraded Mexicans, of improving their social state, and of ultimately increasing the happiness of the masses.

Is it compatible with the principle of Democracy, which rejects every hereditary claim of individuals, to admit an hereditary superiority of races? You very properly deny, that the son can, independent of his own merit, derive any right or privilege whatever, from the merit or any other social superiority of his father. Can you for a moment suppose, that a very doubtful descent from men, who lived one thousand years ago, has transmitted to you a superiority over your fellow-men? But the Anglo-Saxons were inferior to the Goths, from whom the Spaniards claim to be descended; and they were in no respect superior to the Franks and to the Burgundians. It is not to their Anglo-Saxon descent, but to a variety of causes, among which the subsequent mixture of Frenchified Normans, Angevins and Gascons must not be forgotten, that the English are indebted for their superior institutions. In the progressive improvement of mankind, much more has been due to religious and political institutions, than to races. Whenever the European nations, which, from their language, are presumed to belong to the Latin or to the Sclavonian race, shall have conquered institutions similar to those of England, there will be no trace left of the pretended superiority of one of those races above the other. At this time, the claim is but a pretext for covering and justifying unjust usurpation and unbounded ambition.

But admitting, with respect to Mexico, the superiority of race, this confers no superiority of rights. Among ourselves, the most ignorant, the most inferior, either in physical or mental faculties, is recognized as having equal rights, and he has an equal vote with any one, however superior to him in all those respects. This is founded on the immutable principle that no one man is born with the right of governing another man. He may, indeed, acquire a moral influence over others, and no other is legitimate. The same principle will apply to nations. However superior the Anglo-American race may be to that of Mexico, this gives the Americans no right to infringe upon the rights of the inferior race. The people of the United States may rightfully, and will, if they use the proper means, exercise a most beneficial moral influence over the Mexicans, and other less enlightened nations of America. Beyond this they have no right to go.

The allegation that the subjugation of Mexico would be the means of enlightening the Mexicans, of improving their social state, and of increasing their happiness, is but the shallow attempt to disguise unbounded cupidity and ambition. Truth never was or can be propagated by fire, and sword, or by any other than purely moral means. By these, and by these alone, the Christian religion was propagated, and enabled, in less than three hundred years, to conquer idolatry. During the whole of that period, Christianity was tainted by no other blood than that of its martyrs.

The duties of the people of the United States towards other nations are obvious. Never losing sight of the divine precept, "Do to others as you would be done by," they have only to consult their own conscience. For our benevolent Creator has implanted in the hearts of men the moral sense of right and wrong, and that sympathy for other men, the evidences of which are of daily occurrence.

It seems unnecessary to add anything respecting that false glory which, from habit and the general tenor of our early education, we are taught to admire. The task has already been repeatedly performed, in a far more able and impressive manner, than anything I could say on the subject. It is sufficient to say that, at this time, neither the dignity or honor of the nation demand a further sacrifice of invaluable lives, or even of money. The very reverse is the case. The true honor and dignity of the nation are inseparable from justice. Pride and vanity alone demand the sacrifice. Though so dearly purchased, the astonishing successes of the American arms have at least put it in the power of the United States to grant any terms of peace, without incurring the imputation of being actuated by any but the most elevated motives. It would seem that the most proud and vain must be satiated with glory, and that the most reckless and bellicose should be sufficiently glutted with human gore.

A more truly glorious termination of the war, a more splendid spectacle, an example more highly useful to mankind at large, cannot well be conceived, than that of the victorious forces of the United States voluntarily abandoning all their conquests, without requiring anything else than that which was strictly due to our citizens.

PART FIVE

ALL OF MEXICO

26

Military Occupation
for the "Regeneration" of Mexico

By November, 1847, it appeared that Polk's wartime policies toward Mexico had reached a dead end. Instead of gaining a quick and satisfactory diplomatic settlement, American military victories had produced a state of absolute confusion in Mexican politics. Indeed, the actual existence of a legitimate government in Mexico had become a matter of serious doubt. The burgeoning conviction that the United States no longer had any course before it—except to occupy Mexico indefinitely—produced another violent clash of opinion over the future and purpose of American policy. This debate raged throughout the winter. As might have been anticipated, the expansionist *Democratic Review,* in November, 1847, demanded that the United States accept its destiny and, if necessary, regenerate with an ample infusion of its superior civilization not only California but all of Mexico. The entire history of Mexico seemed to point to the ultimate and perhaps inevitable absorption of that country by the United States. Now, as a by-product of the Mexican War, the occasion had arisen for fulfilling the southward thrust of American destiny.

IT is now two months since, in treating of the Mexican War as it then existed, we professed ourselves incredulous of any peace to

From "Occupation of Mexico," *The United States Magazine and Democratic Review,* XXI (November, 1847), 381–383, 388–390.

be arrived at by accommodation, and urged the necessity of a vigorous prosecution of the war, with a view to the occupation of the country by a sufficient force of United States troops. By the term "occupation," we do not understand the direct and permanent annexation of the country to the United States. For such a promotion in the scale of humanity, the Mexican race are by no means fitted. Great as is our reverence for the people at large, and respectful as all ought to be to their opinions, we may look in vain among the populace of the Mexican states, for that activity of intellect and vigilant intelligence necessary to those who would govern themselves. A people who are too proverbially indolent to pursue industrial employments, and too dishonestly envious to permit others to enjoy the fruit of their own industry, would make unprofitable and dangerous inmates of our political family. A long course of probation is necessary so to regenerate them in their habits and views, as to make them worthy of self-government. This process of regeneration they should go through on their own account, and under their own government. This government should be composed as far as possible of native Mexicans to the exclusion of the Spaniards; to guarantee which, an American army should occupy the country at its expense, until such time as a system of entire free trade, scrupulous administration of justice, and undoubted security to property, shall have developed the commercial principle to its fullest extent, and the whole race of military interests have become so strong as to rally round and support the government, the United States troops may be withdrawn, and Mexico for the first time become really a great and independent nation. . . .

No country on the face of the earth enjoys so many natural advantages as Mexico. Her mineral resources beyond doubt exceed those of any other nation, and are capable of being developed to any extent. Her soil is most fertile, and the climate presents every variety of temperature. To bring these into requisition for the service of the world, all that is required is a firm and liberal government; one that shall not meddle with individual enterprise, and shall have sufficient stability to ensure justice and protection to property. Such a government as we have intimated may doubtless be composed of such men as Almonte and Herrera, supported by a column of United States troops, the chief of which should have sole charge of military affairs—attack and crush every Mexican force, and suppress, with the utmost promptitude and severity, every insurrectionary movement or organized hostility. By these means ten years would not elapse before the commercial principle would have so developed itself, as to afford the civil government of Mexico sufficient strength to maintain itself against the rise of any new military interest. A strong infusion of the American race would impart energy and industry gradually to the indolent Mexicans, and give them such a consistency as a people, as would enable them to hold and occupy their territories in perfect independence. If, in after years, they should then as a whole people desire union with the Northern States, it would become a matter of discussion.

The difficulties of Mexico have grown out of the fact that they possess vast natural wealth, which they do not appreciate nor exert themselves to develope. It is not in the nature of things that a race of enterprising adventurers should permit rich mines and valuable lands to remain unoccupied, merely because they are within the limits of a government whose people are too imbecile to turn them to advantage. . . .

. . . Had the Mexicans in any degree possessed the industrial activity of the Americans, the nation would have been in no danger of losing her territory. Not only, however, have her people been incapable of enterprize, but her insane government has by every means obstructed the progress of trade. The flourishing commerce which existed in former years, and which enabled the merchants of Vera Cruz to construct the splendid road to the city of Mexico, perished under the misnamed independence of the country, and the last vestige perished when the suicidal government of 1827 banished the foreign merchants.

It is the mission of the United States to restore the march of commerce and trade in Mexico, and to do so by an armed force to support a just government. . . .

. . . Nevertheless, Mexico should be made to pay at least all the pecuniary expense to which she has subjected us. The precious lives she has sacrificed cannot be restored; nor can the dangers which must assail our institutions growing out of the circumstance, be avoided. All that she can repair she should be compelled to make good; and this can be done in the shape of full payment in money for past debts, and an annual payment over the expense of the occupying force sufficient to pay the interest in full, and to form a sinking fund for the ultimate discharge of the debt created by the war,—and this, in addition to the territory acquired. As a Mexican government under such circumstances would have no military of its own to pay, as none should be suffered to exist, the burden would not be heavy upon her.

Even this mode of settling the difficulty would be accompanied by great disadvantage to the United States, inasmuch as it would involve the continuance of a large standing army, and greatly extend the patronage of the federal executive, while it would foster that military spirit which has already been developed to so great an extent; but it apparently presents evils of a less magnitude than any other mode of arriving at a settlement. To withdraw troops to a line of defence, would be first to surrender the military reputation which has been so dearly bought, and which, in view of our relations with Europe, is invaluable, and still to require an immense standing army, fraught with all the evils which such an institution engenders; to surrender all the advantages which commercial intercourse with Mexico would confer on both nations and on the world; to leave our commerce in all parts of the world permanently exposed to Mexican privateers; and to impose a heavy and useless expense on the people of the United States—an expense of not less than

$20,000,000 per annum, or equal to the whole ordinary expenditure of the government—in addition to past expense, and all that Mexico owes us under treaty. Without the force, the frontier would be continually exposed to inroads. Such a scheme is practicable on the ground that Mexico would forever remain inert—abandon the project of reconquering Texas, which has been the instrument of revolution for ten years—and tacitly preserve the peace which she refuses to acknowledge. To subjugate with the view to annexation, is the greatest of evils: because it is impossible to confer equal rights on eight millions of vanquished people; and what could be done with such a race subject to the federal government? Unless those people held the same relation to the government as do all the existing states, the nature of the federal government would be changed, and in their form assume a monarchical character. . . .

An army of occupation auxiliary to a purely Mexican government, would present less of danger, because the federal executive could not get that hold of the Mexican people which an incorporation of the governments would effect. The soldiers succeeding each other for short terms would most of them, as they were discharged, remain in the country, and, gradually infusing vigor into the race, regenerate the whole nation. They would lay the foundation for that law-abiding population, on the growth of which the Mexican government would rely for its support when the United States army should be withdrawn. This mode of proceeding would involve no retrograde movement of our arms, which would promptly be construed, whatever might be its real motive, by all our European *friends* into weakness and inability to maintain a war, and color with a shade of truth those malignant predictions in which public men and writers, especially in England, have delighted to indulge in relation to this country.

The great problem is to inoculate Mexico with the commercial spirit, without awaking, to too great an extent, the military spirit of the Union. Most assuredly this proneness to martial enterprize has been powerfully stirred among us during the past eighteen months. The temper of the nation is now such, that were the northeastern boundary question still under discussion, the government would not feel safe in making large concessions for the sake of settlement. To allay this feeling, and yet find means to make Mexico pay in full the damage she has done, and promote her own interests by adopting a free-trade policy, are the objects most desired.

27   Walt Whitman

"Either back out entirely" or
establish "our permanent power"

In the absence of a political structure in Mexico capable either of making peace with the United States or of sustaining a semblance of political order thereafter, the Polk administration faced a narrowing choice in its relations with Mexico. It could either withdraw all American forces from the interior of the country and permit Mexico to create a government capable of ruling through an open struggle for power, or it could occupy that nation indefinitely to create, through the presence of American power, the basis of democratic government. Walt Whitman, the noted American poet and editor of the *Brooklyn Daily Eagle*, favored the latter course. In his editorial of September 23, 1847, he advocated a large commitment of United States forces to Mexico, for an indefinite period of time, to bring that nation the political and commercial progress which would stabilize the peace between the two countries.

WHEN WILL THE WAR BE ENDED? A question which any one may ask, but which no one can answer. Of this, however, we are sure, that ordering out ten thousand men at a time, won't do it. Let fifty thousand fresh troops be raised and sent forward with all possible despatch, and with those already there something may be done to show the Mexicans that we are in earnest. This talk about a peace party is all moonshine, until we are able to protect them from their own military tyrants; and secure their property from military seizure, or the plunder of guerrilla robbers. We must make our authority respectable—we must make our possession of the country safe to the people, and give them security in the pursuit of their lawful occupations, and in their trade and traffic with our Army. It is idle to garrison a town with ten or twenty or five hundred men while as many thousand of guerrillas, the finest horsemen riding the finest animals in the land, are sweeping around the place to pounce upon them, and having intercourse with them—whenever a dozen yards from the walls.

We do not know what is the expectation or purpose of the government; but we are persuaded that if the work is well done, it must be quickly done. —Every body knows we can take possession of the country. But this is not the thing. We must hold possession, and so manage that they must stay beat. This cannot be done with 12 or 30,000 men, in the midst of a population of seven or eight millions. It cannot be done by barely keeping open our lines of communication. We must protect the people, inspire them with confidence in our permanent power—power for the future as well as the present. We must clear the country

---

From Walt Whitman, *The Gathering of the Forces: Editorials, Essays, Literary and Dramatic Reviews and other Material Written by Walt Whitman as Editor of the Brooklyn Daily Eagle in 1846 and 1847*, Cleveland Rodgers and John Black, ed., (New York, 1920), I, 259–263.

of robbers and military usurpers; garrison the large towns with large and efficient forces, which shall make all the surrounding regions feel secure. We must make the intercourse and trade of the interior with ports of entry perfectly safe, so that the goods imported may find a market, without the purchasers fearing to be lassoed on their return, for having dealing with the "Yankee heretics and robbers"—The miserable cry of expenses and running the country in debt is too late now. Every copper saved in this way costs a dollar in the end, and only protracts the war. God knows we have no love for this or any other kind of war; but we know that this temporising, delaying, negotiating, peace-begging policy with an ignorant, prejudiced, and perfectly faithless people, is not the way to end the contest. There is no middle course—either we must back out of it entirely, or we must drive it through with a vigorous hand. . . .

Our prophecy from the beginning had been: place 30,000 disciplined troops at Mexico; and as many more on the lines of communication with Vera Cruz and the Rio Grande. Under the protection of these let the peace party (which embraces the best part of the citizens, though they dare not speak as matters stand now,) establish a government, whose efficiency and permanency shall be guaranteed by the United States. This will bring out enterprise, open the way for manufacturers and commerce, into which the immense dead capital of the country will find its way, as soon as its owners can be assured it will be free from seizure and forced loans. Agriculture will develop the natural resources of the country, really one of the finest in the world, after all; and the increase of products and of trade will react in the increase of enterprise and of an active and business population from abroad. Then at the end of this will come an increase of printing presses, papers, books, education and general intelligence, and lastly, the happiness of the masses, now so sunk in ignorance and superstition.

To accomplish this may require the force above named for years, though it may be gradually lessened as confidence and security are established. To accomplish this will cost millions, but it will abundantly pay. This is the best kind of conquest; and so doing, in the end we shall have a sister Republic, whose alliance will be both an honor and a source of strength.

28   Robert F. Stockton

"Redeem Mexico from misrule

and civil strife"

Among the recorded speeches of United States military and naval officers returning from Mexico, none has received more attention than that of Commodore Robert F. Stockton, commander, after July, 1846, of the United States fleet off California. The speech was delivered at a dinner held in his honor in Philadelphia on December 30, 1847. As could be expected, Stockton pointed to the unlimited success of American arms in Mexico. To meet the responsibility placed upon the nation by its free institutions, the United States now had no alternative but to fill the political and moral vacuum which existed in Mexican leadership by extending the blessings of American civilization to neighbors on the North American continent. Stockton no longer saw the issue as indemnity; rather it was that of "redeeming Mexico from misrule and civil strife." In this way the United States would fulfill what he interpreted as its great mission to humanity.

NO thoughtful observer of the progress of the U. States, can fail to be impressed with the conviction that we enjoy a degree of happiness and prosperity never heretofore vouchsafed to the nations of mankind. With an unexampled measure of political liberty; unbroken social order; extraordinary growth of the arts

From *Niles' National Register*, LXXIII (January 22, 1848), 335.

and sciences—philanthropic and benevolent institutions, the fair offspring of the Christian faith, extending their blessed agency, in all directions—unbounded religious toleration, heaven's best gift; for which our fathers risked and suffered most—with all these rich endowments, do we not indeed present an example of the beneficent care of Providence for which we can find no parallel in the history of man? And now when engaged in war, we find ourselves, followed by the same blessed influences. Wherever our soldiers have carried our arms, victory has awaited them. We see them rushing against walls, bristling with bayonets and artillery, and lined with legions of armed men—we see our youthful heroes precipitating themselves from parapet to parapet, and charging from bastion to bastion—we hear the crash of grape and canister, and amid the smoke and thunder of the battle, we behold the flag of our country, waiving—[the remainder of the sentence was lost in the tremendous cheering which here burst forth from the assemblage.] We behold the flag of civil and religious freedom waiving over what had been regarded as unpregnable fortresses and the remains of armies fleeing to the mountains.

Gentlemen, how has all this been accomplished? Whence those achievements? I speak to intellectual men. All in the hearing of my voice entertain, I doubt not, a just and abiding sense of their deep responsibility not only on this earth, but in time hereafter. I ask you, then, how has all this happened? Is it to be attributed exclusively to the wisdom of our cabinet and the powers of our armies? These are all well—admittably well. But our successes have overleaped the bounds of all human calculation and the most sanguine hope. Therefore we must look beyond all this for the secret of our successes and the source of our remarkable prosperity. It is because the spirit of our pilgrim fathers is with us.—It is because of the God of armies and Lord of hosts is with us. [Tremendous applause.] And how is it with poor, unfortunate, wretched Mexico? Ever since the day of the last of the Montezumas, intestine broils have disturbed her peace. Her whole territory has been drenched with the blood of her own children. Within the last quarter of a century revolution has succeeded revolution. Now in the encounter with us she has been beaten in every field. She has been driven from fortress to fortress—from town to town, until the scattered remnants of her broken armies are fleeing to the mountains and calling upon the rocks to hide them. [Applause.] Is it not, therefore, in this disposition of public affairs, proper to rise superior to the consideration of party influences, and in true philosophical spirit and patriotic fidelity, take an honest view of our condition, in the sight of God and beneath the scrutiny of the christian and civilized world?

What you may think of it, I know not; and you must permit me to add, I care not; but for myself I speak not to you as a party man. Remember, gentlemen, that I go for my country. I cannot be bound, I cannot be kept within the restraints of party discipline when my country calls me forth. [Tremendous cheering, which lasted several minutes.] I go for my country—my whole country and nothing but my country. I desire to address you now in the spirit of the father of a large family, desirous to transmit to his latest posterity the blessings of civil and religious liberty. I speak to you as a christian man—as a son, perhaps an unworthy son of this great republic, but one whose heart burns with an ardent desire to transmit, not only to his own immediate descendants, the blessings of which I speak, but to extend them to our neighbors on this continent. [Great applause.]

But do not mistake me. Do not misunderstand me. I am no propagandist in the common reception of the term. In my judgment, principles depend much upon relations and circumstances, and that which in the abstract may be well enough, often wastes itself in fanaticism. All things must bide their time.

I have no respect for the man or set of men who will recklessly disturb the social order of my community and produce civil war for the purpose of hastening such a result, no matter how beneficial in the abstract it may seem to be. [Cheers.] And I am bound to say farther, that I have quite as little respect for the man or set of men, who have in the Providence of God been placed in stations, when the great questions of civil and religious liberty are to be determined, who will shrink from the responsibilities of that station. [Cheers.] In the application of these principles to the future policy of this country, let it not be supposed for a moment that I would presume to censure the great men of this nation.—Nor would I attempt to instruct the most humble of my countrymen. I present these views merely for the purpose of rendering more distinct and clear the remarks which I have offered, and which I may not have stated with sufficient explicitness.

I suppose the war with Mexico was caused by the repeated insults which time after time had been heaped upon this nation. [Great applause.] I regard this much talked of indemnity as merely collateral or incidental, arising out of the circumstances of the war. In my opinion, that question will be set aside, if not wholly lost sight of in the pressure of the great considerations which are to grow out of the high responsibilities and delicate duties crowding upon us, and the unexampled victories which have attended our arms. [Cheers.] In pursuing a legitimate object of war—in the providence of God we are placed, or are likely to be placed, in a position where by a fair and legitimate construction of the law of nations, the fate of Mexico and the peace of this continent, to a greater or less extent, will devolve upon the virtue, the wisdom, and the humanity of our rulers. [Applause.] In these rulers I have the greatest confidence, and for them I entertain the most profound respect. [Applause.]

I tell you again gentlemen, this matter of indemnity, in money or any thing else, will be secondary, altogether secondary, in comparison with the considerations which I have no doubt will be presented to this nation in the farther prosecution of this war. The insults have been resented—nobly resented—they have been wiped out—they have been washed out with blood. [Enthusiastic applause.] If, then, indemnity, mean money, any financier will tell you that if *that* is what you seek as the only object of the war, you had better withdraw your troops as soon as possible, and you will save money. [A laugh.]

But indemnity is not the object of the war. No man here or elsewhere will consent to weigh blood against money. [Great applause.] I do not care who presents the proposition—when it is presented; or to whom it is presented, whig or democrat, no man will weigh blood for money. (Loud applause.) But this is not, I repeat, our condition. Higher and nobler objects present themselves for the attainment of which you must increase your armies in Mexico, cost what it may. [Great applause.] Fifty thousand men must go to Mexico. [Renewed applause.] Let me then state the objects for the attainment of which, in my judgment, this augmentation of our force in Mexico is required.

Mexico is poor and wretched. Why? Misgovernment—insatiable avarice—unintermitted wrong unsparing cruelty and unbending insolence—these have inflicted their curse on the unhappy country, and made her what she is. But as the darkest hour is that which just precedes the advent of the morning sun, so let us hope that a better and happier day is now about to dawn upon fortunate Mexico. Be it ours, now to forgive her all her trespasses, and returning good for evil, make her free and happy!—

If I were now the sovereign authority as I was once the viceroy—[laughter]—I would prosecute this war for the express purpose of redeeming Mexico from misrule and civil strife. If, however, such a treaty were offered me as that offered to the government of the United States, before God, I would consider it my bounden duty to reject it. [Loud applause.]—I would say to them, we can pay the indemnity ourselves. But we have a duty before God which we cannot—we must not evade. The priceless bond of civil and religious liberty has been confided to us as trustees—[cheers]—I would insist, if the war were to be prolonged for fifty years, and cost money enough to demand from us each year the half of all that we possess, I would still insist that the inestimable blessings of civil and religious liberty should be guaranteed to Mexico. We must not shrink from the solemn duty. We dare not shrink from it. We cannot lose sight of the great truth that nations are accountable as well as individuals, and that they too must meet the stern responsibilities of their moral character—they too must encounter the penalty of violated law in the more extended sphere adapted to their physical condition.

Let the solemn question come home to the bosom and business of every citizen of this great republic: "What have I done—what has this generation done for the advancement of civil and religious liberty!—[Applause.]

It is in view of this responsibility—of our obligations to the infinite source of all our peace, prosperity and happiness—of our duty to fulfil the great mission of liberty committed to our hands, that I would insist, cost what it may, on the establishment of a permanent, independent republic in Mexico—[Cheers.] I would insist that the great principle of religious toleration should be secured to all—that the Protestant in Mexico should be guaranteed the enjoyment of all the immunities and privileges enjoyed by Mexicans in the United States: [Loud cheers.] These great and benevolent objects I would accomplish by sending into Mexico a force adequate to maintain all the posts which we now occupy, to defend them against any assaults that might be made against them, and to keep open our communications. I would seize upon Paredes, Arista, and other military chieftains, and send them to St. Helena, if you please. [Laughter and applause.] I would declare an armistice; and the executive should be called upon to issue a proclamation, and send six or more commissioners to meet Mexico in a liberal and generous spirit.

We have vanquished Mexico. She is prostrate at our feet—we can afford to be magnaminous. Let us act so that we need not fear the strictest scrutiny of the Christian and civilized world. I would with a magnanimous and kindly hand gather these wretched people within the fold of republicanism. [Loud applause.] This I would accomplish at any cost.—"Oh!" but it is said, this will bring us to direct taxation." Well, let it come. We must not shrink from our responsibility. We have ample means. —Throwing aside long financial reports which nobody understands, [Laughter.] let us in a manly, upright and philanthropic spirit meet every emergency which we may be called upon to encounter in the discharge of duty. . . .

29   Sidney Breese

"Let us expand to our true and proper dimensions"

Few Congressmen revealed as much optimism over the prospects of annexing all Mexico and so continuing to fulfill the continental destiny of the United States than did Senator Sidney Breese of Illinois. In his speech of February 14, 1848, he declared that the Mexican population, backward as it was, possessed nevertheless the capacity for development. He observed, furthermore, that the American system was admirably designed to manage an empire of any size —that past expansion had strengthened the nation's institutions. The idea of liberty had grown with the extension of the United States across the continent. "Our form of government," his Senate speech concluded, "is peculiarly fitted for this—it has a peculiar aptitude for expansion, a principle which no other Government ever did possess. . . ." Breese as a Democratic expansionist favored the annexation of all Mexico for the good it would render not only to the Mexican and the American people but also to the general cause of humanity.

. . . THE avowed objects of the war which we declared to exist by the Act of Mexico was to obtain redress of wrongs, a permanent

---

From *Congressional Globe* (30th Cong., 1st Sess., 1848), Appendix, pp. 349–350.

and honorable peace, and indemnity for the past and security for the future; and if they cannot be obtained in any other way than by the conquest of Mexico, and incorporating it into the Union, or holding it as a province, such a result would be in harmony with those objects. Nor would it be contrary to the spirit and genius of our Government, nor against its settled policy, to conquer, in a defensive war, any country, and annex it, which might be thought, from its contiguity, to be necessary to our own safety. The power "to declare war" carries with it all its consequences, of which territorial conquest is one; and our policy in 1812 was to conquer Canada, and if we had been successful, after having made the most strenuous efforts to that end, and on the return of peace, it had been relinquished to us, no doubt it would have been annexed to us, and I think the day is not distant when that event shall transpire.

How the annexation of Mexico to our Union would tend to subvert our free institutions, I cannot discover. . . . I have taken a different view of the people of that country, and I think I see in them attributes and elements quite susceptible, by proper appliances, of high improvement. Could they be brought under the happy influences of such a Government as our own, having all their rights, civil and religious, protected, what might we not hope from them? The Indian population, numbering about four millions, are reputed to be very gentle and quiet in their dispositions, apt to learn, and willing to improve, and, if not possessed of all the manlier virtues, have at least those which fully ensure their cheerful acquiescence to our control and rapid advancement under it. Take the population as a whole, and there is not a people on the globe more capable of advancement in the arts and sciences, and of assuming all the forms of the highest civilization. They came out of their revolution with a reputation only excelled by our own; and with the same advantages we have possessed, who can say they would not now rival us in all that contributes to national renown? But [it is said that] no instance can be found of any race, save the Caucasian, which has established and enjoyed self-government and free institutions; but [this] does not say no other race can be prepared for it. All other races have always been oppressed—are generally ignorant—have no just appreciation of liberty, and are for the most part uncivilized.

I do not suppose, sir, the Mexicans are at this time fitted for an equal union with us; and much is to be done before they will be. By the infusion of our own population among them . . . together with emigrants from Europe, who will not be slow to avail themselves of the unsurpassed advantages such a country enjoys, a gradual change in their manners, customs, and language, will ensue. Education will be diffused among the masses; speech, the press, and religion will be free, and high opinions of themselves speedily generated; and considering the rapidity of past events, the aids to knowledge, and for its rapid spread, which the world now possesses, the period of their pupilage will be of short duration. Sir, it has been alike our pride and boast, that our institutions were better calculated to elevate the masses than any others which have yet existed, and we feel it to be true; and it cannot be that it is the decree of Heaven that none but the white race shall enjoy them. It has been the abiding hope of the philanthropist, that in God's good time all nations should enjoy them, and the down-trodden millions of both hemispheres be exalted by their agency. There is nothing, sir, in the history of that beautiful country, or in the character of its people, to discourage the belief that they can, in a very short time, be brought to a condition qualifying them for admission into this great American family, adorning and strengthening it by a commingling and full development of all those grand and mighty elements they possess, and thus fulfill her own and our happy destiny. And, sir, it is her own and our happy destiny. And, sir, it is the fervent wish and hope of her most eminent citizens and patriots, that this war may accelerate it; and, if "coming events cast their shadows before," may it not be regarded as its certain precursor?

In my musings upon this subject, Mr. President, I have been cheered by the hope, that if I did not, my children would live to see that day when our institutions shall extend over the whole of this portion of our continent, all to be bound by one common ligament, and all to run one common career of honor, happiness, and renown? And, sir, why should we be alarmed at this contemplation? History, it is said, admonishes us that extension of dominion by territorial acquisition proved the downfall of the ancient republics; but, sir, were they fashioned like ours? Were they not, from their very nature, incapable of extension? And is there no difference of condition between us and them? They had not the press, nor the compass, nor the steam-engine—none of these great instrumentalities which, wielded by freemen, are to revolutionize the world. They worshipped Liberty, and sacrificed to her as to an idol. We regard her as an active, moving spirit, penetrating all the avenues of life, and cheering and stimulating man in his progress. Sir, our liberty can be preserved only by progress. Being stationary it stagnates, and in that condition the flame will expire. It is by action alone—by ceaseless, constant action—we can preserve it. Let us expand to our true and proper dimensions, and our liberty will be eternal; for, in the process, it will increase in strength, and the flame grow brighter, whilst it lights a more extensive field. Does any Senator believe our attachment to liberty would have been any stronger than it is now, or that we would have been more powerful and happy, had our Confederacy been confined within the Atlantic coast and the range of the Allegenies? Would any one of them willingly restore to their former owners Louisiana, Florida, and Texas, or surrender either without a deathly struggle? I apprehend not. Our history shows, thus far, that there is no danger in our extension. Our form of government is peculiarly fitted for this—it has a peculiar aptitude for expansion, a principle which no other Government ever did possess, and it is one of its greatest excellencies. Will any Senator deny that the new States have contributed new vigor to our system, and increased strength to our circle? Have any symptoms of disaffection to the Union been observed in any of them? Has any spirit of insubordination or of restlessness under the ties which bind them, ever been manifested by any of them? No, sir, it is not in them where man enjoys the largest liberty, only restrained by laws he makes himself, that *emeutes,* riots, and rebellions occur, but it is among a crowded population, in pent up masses, easily excited by collision, with no extended field of action to arouse their energies, and no attainable objects before them to guide them aright.

Let but Congress confine itself to its own proper functions, each State exercising its own undoubted powers within its own limits, managing its own legitimate concerns in its own way, without the unauthorized interference of Congress, no reason can be given why our Union should not be co-extensive with this portion of the American continent. We want no rival republics here, for they may become inimical, rendering it necessary to maintain standing armies to defend against their aggressions. If all was united in one harmonious whole, such defences would not be required. . . .

. . . Our credit was never in a better condition than it now is, and promises to continue to be. Our six per cent stocks are above par; and if we enter the market for more money, we will find the loanable capital, so far from being exhausted, at our command in abundance. The debt of the last war, was soon discharged, without affecting injuriously any of the great interests of the country; and so will this be.

In this view, sir, the acquisition of Mexico, with its unparalleled powers of production, yielding every article of luxury and necessity, save one, that ministers to the wants or pride of man— whose revenues can be made, under wholesome laws, and with proper management, to produce annually one hundred millions of dollars, and with mineral wealth from which the world now draws a great part of its supply, and those resources to be further developed by our enterprise and skill—what can we not expect when time shall have performed upon her its gentle yet potent and effective office?

As I believe, sir, there are but two alternatives—either to flee the country, or to hold on to our acquisitions, the result of which may be the final absorption of Mexico, I have not hesitated to declare for the latter, being well satisfied that great ultimate good to us, to her, and to humanity, is to flow from it. . . .

30   John C. Calhoun

"Draw a Defensive Line"

Calhoun's historic conservatism was never more apparent than in his speeches on foreign affairs. Always more concerned with means than with ends, he invariably sought to limit the nation's commitments abroad to clearly-defined issues of national interest. His opposition to the Mexican War reflected his conviction that Polk had, by his military policies in Texas, made an unnecessary war inevitable. Calhoun favored the acquisition of San Francisco Bay, but did not want to take it by conquest. The acquisition of all of Mexico, however, he regarded a thoughtless and potentially disastrous overcommitment. To head off that movement he introduced the following resolutions into the Senate on December 15, 1847:

Resolved, That to conquer Mexico and to hold it, either as a province or to incorporate it into the Union, would be inconsistent with the avowed object for which the war has been prosecuted; a departure from the settled policy of the Government; in conflict with its character and genius; and in the end subversive of our free and popular institutions.

Resolved, That no line of policy in the further prosecution of the war should be adopted which may lead to consequences so disastrous.

Then on January 4, 1848, he rose in the Senate to explain and defend his resolutions. The result was a thoughtful and impressive definition of the conservative tradition of American foreign policy that had held a place in the government since the days of Washington and Hamilton. Calhoun saw the problem of creating self-determination for Mexico. He believed that any government established by the United States would require the continued support of an American army—and endless and largely unremunerative commitment. He suggested rather that the United States withdraw from Mexico to a defense line which would not only protect the territory of the United States but also comprise a fair indemnity from Mexico. No indemnity from Mexico, Calhoun warned, would ever pay the cost of an American occupation. Such policy would always remain a burden, far transcending any American economic or security interest in Mexico. For the United States the chief task in January, 1848 was to disengage itself from Mexican affairs.

IN offering, Senators, these resolutions for your consideration, I have been governed by the reasons which induced me to oppose the war, and by the same considerations I have been ever since guided. In alluding to my opposition to the war, I do not intend to notice the reasons which governed me on that occasion, further than is necessary to explain my motives upon the present. I opposed the war then, not only because I considered it unnecessary, and that it might have been easily avoided; not only because I thought the President had no authority to order a portion of the territory in dispute and in possession of the Mexicans, to be occupied by our troops; not only because I believed the allegations upon which it was sanctioned by Congress, were unfounded in truth; but from high considerations of reason and policy, because I believed it would lead to great and serious evils to the country, and greatly endanger its free institutions.

But after the war was declared, and had received the sanction of the Government, I acquiesced in what I could not prevent, and which it was impossible for me to arrest; and I then felt it to

From *Congressional Globe* (30th Cong., 1st Sess., 1848), pp. 96–97, 99.

be my duty to limit my course so as to give that direction to the conduct of the war as would, as far as possible, prevent the evil and danger with which, in my opinion, it threatened the country and its institutions. For this purpose, at the last session, I suggested to the Senate a defensive line, and for that purpose I now offer these resolutions. This, and this only, is the motive which governs me. I am moved by no personal nor party considerations. My object is neither to sustain the Executive, nor to strengthen the Opposition, but simply to discharge an important duty to the country. . . .

I protest utterly against this Government undertaking to build up any government in Mexico with the pledge of protection. The party placed in power must be inevitably overthrown, and we will be under the solemn obligation to return and reinstate them in power; and that would occur again and again, till the country would fall into our hands precisely as Hindostan fell into the hands of the English. This very conquest of Hindostan, which we have been censuring for years and years, ever since I recollect, was the result of mistaken policy, leading on from step to step, each one deeper and deeper—scarcely any design of conquest being entertained; but ultimately conquest became unavoidable, and it was necessary not only to hold the country, but to conquer the adjacent territory.

Well, sir, if this contingency follows—if the Executive fails in establishing another government there under our encouragement and protection, and if the Government itself shall refuse to make a treaty with us on such terms as we will accept in regard to indemnity, then the President himself agrees that he must take the very course which I have said would be the inevitable consequence of a vigorous prosecution of the war. The President says in substance, after having attempted to build up such a government—after having employed the best efforts to secure peace upon the most liberal terms, if all fail—I now give his own words—if all fail, we must hold on to the occupation of the country; we must take the measure of indemnity into our own hands, and enforce such terms as the honor of the country demands. Now, sir, what is this? Is it not an acknowledgment, that if this factitious government, which is aimed at, cannot be built up, we must make a conquest of the whole country and occupy it—can words be stronger?—"Occupy the country." Take the full measure of indemnity—no defensive line—no treaty; and enforce terms—terms on whom? on the government? No—no—no. It is to enforce the terms on the people individually; that is to say, to establish a government over them in the form of provinces.

Well, the President is right. If, in the vigorous prosecution of the war, as the President proposes, the contingency should fail—and the chances of its failure are many—there will be no retreating. Every argument against calling back the army, as they designate it—against taking a defensive line—which is now advanced, will have double force after you have spent sixty millions of dollars, and have acquired possession of the whole of Mexico. The interests in favor of keeping us there will be much more influential then than now. The army itself will be larger. Those who live by the war—a large and powerful body: the numerous contractors, the sutlers, the merchants, the speculators in the lands and mines, of Mexico, and all engaged every way, directly or indirectly, in the progress of the war, and absorbing the whole expenditures—will be all adverse to retiring, and will swell the cry in favor of continuing and extending conquest. The President talks, sir, of taking indemnity into our hands then; but why not take indemnity now? We are much nearer indemnity now than we will be at the end of the next campaign, when we shall have sixty millions added to the expenditure of the last forty. What will you then have to indemnify you? Nothing but a Mexican population, on whom you are to impose taxation in all forms and shapes, and amongst which you will have to maintain an army of at least forty thousand men—according to the Senator from Mississippi, [Mr. Davis,] not a very large number, for he says that the seventy-three thousand men now there are in danger. That, then, is no indemnity at all. You will never get enough in that way to meet your expenditures. It will all have to come out of the pockets of the people of the United States; and, after all the talk of indemnity—of pushing on this war vigorously to success—at the end of the next campaign, instead of indemnity, you will have a heavy pecuniary burden imposed upon the present and succeeding generation.

Well, Mr. President, we have now come to the solemn question proposed by these resolutions. I have shown where this line of policy will, in all probability, lead you—I may say, will inevitably land you, unless some unexpected contingency should prevent. It will lead to the blotting out of the nationality of Mexico, and the throwing of eight or nine millions of people without a government, on your hands. It will compel you, in all probability, to assume the government, for I think there will be very little prospect of your retiring. You must either hold the country as a province, or incorporate it into your Union. Shall we do either? That's the question. Far from us be such an act, and for the reasons contained in the resolutions.

The first of these reasons is this: it would be inconsistent with the avowed object for which the war has been prosecuted. That needs no argument, after what has been said. Since the commencement of the war till this moment, every man has disavowed the intention of conquest—of extinguishing the existence of Mexico as a people. It has been constantly proclaimed that the only object was indemnity. And yet, sir, as events are moving on, what we disavow may be accomplished, and what we have avowed may be defeated. Sir, this result will be a dark and lasting imputation on either the sincerity of the intelligence of this country: on its sincerity, because so opposite to your own avowals; on your intelligence, for the want of a clear foresight in so plain a case as not to discern the consequences.

Sir, we have heard how much glory our country has acquired

in this war. I acknowledge it to the full amount, Mr. President, so far as military glory is concerned. The army has done nobly, chivalrously; they have conferred honor on the country, for which I sincerely thank them.

Mr. President, I believe all our thanks will be confined to our army. So far as I know, in the civilized world there is no approbation of the conduct of the civil portion of our power. On the contrary, everywhere the declaration is made that we are an ambitious, unjust, hard people, more given to war than any people of modern times. Whether this be true or not, it is not for me to inquire. I am speaking now merely of the reputation which we bear abroad—everywhere, I believe; for as much as we have gained in military reputation abroad, I regret to perceive, we have lost in our political and civil reputation. Now, sir, much as I regard military glory; much as I rejoice to behold our people in possession of the indomitable energy and courage which surmount all difficulties, and which class them amongst the first military people of the age, I would be very sorry indeed that our Government should lose any reputation for wisdom, moderation, discretion, justice, and those other high qualities which have distinguished us in the early stages of our history.

The next reason which my resolutions assign, is, that it is without example or precedent, either to hold Mexico as a province, or to incorporate her into our Union. No example of such a line of policy can be found. We have conquered many of the neighboring tribes of Indians, but we never thought of holding them in subjection—never of incorporating them into our Union. They have either been left as an independent people amongst us, or been driven into the forests.

I know further, sir, that we have never dreamt of incorporating into our Union any but the Caucasian race—the free white men. To incorporate Mexico, would be the very first instance of the kind of incorporating an Indian race; for more than half of the Mexicans are Indians, and the other is composed chiefly of mixed tribes. I protest against such a union as that! Ours, sir, is the Government of a white race. The greatest misfortunes of Spanish America are to be traced to the fatal error of placing these colored races on an equality with the white race. That error destroyed the social arrangement which formed the basis of society. The Portuguese and ourselves have escaped—the Portuguese at least to some extent—and we are the only people on this continent which have made revolutions without being followed by anarchy. And yet it is professed and talked about to erect these Mexicans into a Territorial Government, and place them on an equality with the people of the United States. I protest utterly against such a project.

Sir, it is a remarkable fact, that in the whole history of man, as far as my knowledge extends, there is no instance whatever of any civilized colored races being found equal to the establishment of free popular government, although by far the largest portion of the human family is composed of these races. And even in the savage state we scarcely find them anywhere with such government, except it be our noble savages—for noble I will call them. They, for the most part, had free institutions, but they are easily sustained amongst a savage people. Are we to overlook this fact? Are we to associate with ourselves as equals, companions, and fellow-citizens, the Indians and mixed race of Mexico? Sir, I should consider such a thing as fatal to our institutions.

The next two reasons which I assigned, were, that it would be in conflict with the genius and character of our institutions, and subversive of our free government. I take these two together, as they are so intimately connected; and now of the first—to hold Mexico in subjection.

Mr. President, there are some propositions too clear for argument; and before such a body as the Senate, I should consider it a loss of time to undertake to prove that to hold Mexico as a subjected province would be hostile, and in conflict with our free popular institutions, and in the end subversive of them. Sir, he who knows the American Constitution well—he who has duly studied its character—he who has looked at history, and knows what has been the effect of conquests of free States invariably, will require no proof at my hands to show that it would be entirely hostile to the institutions of the country to hold Mexico as a province. There is not an example on record of any free State even having attempted the conquest of any territory approaching the extent of Mexico without disastrous consequences. The nation conquered have in time conquered the conquerors by destroying their liberty. That will be our case, sir. The conquest of Mexico would add so vast an amount to the patronage of this Government, that it would absorb the whole power of the States in the Union. This Union would become imperial, and the States mere subordinate corporations. But the evil will not end there. The process will go on. The same process by which the power would be transferred from the States to the Union, will transfer the whole from this department of the Government (I speak of the Legislature) to the Executive. All the added power and added patronage which conquest will create, will pass to the Executive. In the end, you put in the hands of the Executive the power of conquering you. You give to it, sir, such splendor, such ample means, that, with the principle of proscription which unfortunately prevails in our country, the struggle will be greater at every Presidential election than our institutions can possibly endure. The end of it will be, that that branch of the Government will become all-powerful, and the result is inevitable—anarchy and despotism. It is as certain as that I am this day addressing the Senate.

Sir, let it not be said that Great Britain furnishes an example to the contrary—that she holds provinces of vast extent of population without materially impairing the liberty of the citizens, or exposing her to anarchy, confusion, or corruption. It is so. But what is the explanation? Of all Governments that ever existed, affording any protection whatever to liberty, the English Government far transcends them all in that respect. She can bear more patronage in proportion to her population and wealth, than any Government of that form that ever existed; nay, to go farther, than can despotism in its most absolute form. I will not go into the philosophy of this. That would take me farther from the track than I desire. But I will say in a very few words, it results from the fact that her Executive and the House of Peers, the conservative branch of her Government, are both hereditary. The Roman Government may have exceeded, and did exceed the British Government in its power for conquest; but no people ever did exist, and probably never will exist, with such a capacity for conquest as that people. But the capacity of Rome to hold subjected provinces, was as nothing compared to that of Great Britain, and hence, as soon as the Roman power passed from Italy beyond the Adriatic on one side, and the Alps on the other, and the Mediterranean, their liberty fell prostrate —the Roman people became a rabble—corruption penetrated everywhere, and violence and anarchy ruled the day. Now, we see England with dependant provinces of vastly greater territorial extent, and probably not less in population—I have not examined—we see her going on without impairing personal liberty or exposing the Government to violence or anarchy. Yet the English have not wholly escaped. Although they have retained their liberty, and have not fallen into anarchy and despotism, yet we behold the population of England crushed to the earth by the superincumbent weight of debt. Reflecting on that Government, I have often thought that there was only one way in which it could come to an end—that was the weight of the superstructure would crush the foundation—that the wealth accumulated in part by these very conquests by the higher classes, would crush the laboring masses below. But has she obtained indemnity from all her subjected prinvinces? On the contrary, instead of drawing the means of supporting herself from them, has she not been compelled to resort to the labor of her own population to hold them in subjection? And has she not thrown a burden upon them, which, with all their industry and skill—with all their vast accumulation of capital and power of machinery, they are incapable of bearing without being reduced to poverty? Take even her earliest and nearest conquest—the neighboring island of Ireland—is it not to this day a source of heavy expense, and a burden to her, instead of a source of revenue?

But while the English Government has such vast power of holding subjected provinces in subjection without impairing her liberty, without the evils incident to it, our Government, of all free Governments that ever existed, has the least capacity to bear patronage proportionate to its wealth and power. In this respect, the genius of the two Governments is precisely the opposite, however much alike in their exterior forms, and their laws and customs. The cause of this difference I cannot undertake to explain on the present occasion, but must content myself by saying that it results from its Federal character, and the nature of its conservative principles. Shall we, then, with these certain and inevitable consequences in a Government better calculated to resist them than any other, adopt such a ruinous policy, and reject the lessons of experience? So much, then, Mr. President, for holding Mexico as a province.

I come now to the proposition of incorporating her into our Union. Well, as far as law is concerned, that is easy. You can establish a Territorial Government for every State in Mexico, and there are some twenty of them. You can appoint governors, judges, and magistrates. You can give the people a subordinate government, allowing them to legislate for themselves, whilst you defray the cost. So far as law goes, the thing is done. There is no analogy between this and our Territorial Governments. Our Territories are only an offset of our own people, of foreigners from the same regions from which we came. They are small in number. They are incapable of forming a government. It would be convenient for them to sustain a government, if it were formed; and they are very much obliged to the United States for undertaking the trouble, knowing that, on the attainment of their majority—when they come to manhood—at twenty-one—they will be introduced to an equality with all the other members of the Union. It is entirely different with Mexico. You have no need of armies to keep your Territories in subjection. But when you incorporate Mexico, you must have powerful armies to keep them in subjection. You may call it annexation, but it is a forced annexation, which is a contradiction in terms, according to my conception. You will be involved, in one word, in all the evils which I attribute to holding Mexico as a province. In fact, it will be but a Provincial Government, under the name of a Territorial Government. How long will that last? How long will it be before Mexico will be capable of incorporation into our Union? Why, if we judge from the examples before us, it will be a very long time. Ireland has been held in subjection by England for seven or eight hundred years, and yet still remains hostile, although her people are of kindred race with the conquerors. A few French Canadians on this continent yet maintain the attitude of hostile people; and never will the time come, in my opinion, Mr. President, that these Mexicans will be heartily reconciled to your authority. They have Castilian blood in their veins—the old Gothic quite equal to the Anglo-Saxon in many respects—in some respects superior. Of all nations of the earth they are the most pertinacious—have the highest sense of nationality—hold out longest, and often even with the least prospect of effecting their object. On this subject also I have conversed with officers of the army, and they all entertain the same opinion, that these people are now hostile, and will continue so.

But, Mr. President, suppose all these difficulties removed; suppose these people attached to our Union, and desirous of incorporating with us, ought we to bring them in? Are they fit to be connected with us? Are they fit for self-government and for governing you? Are you, any of you, willing that your States should be governed by these twenty-odd Mexican States, with a population of about only one million of your blood, and two or three millions of mixed blood, better informed, all the rest pure Indians, a mixed blood equally ignorant and unfit for liberty, impure races, not as good as the Cherokees or Choctaws?

We make a great mistake, sir, when we suppose that all people are capable of self-government. We are anxious to force free government on all; and I see that it has been urged in a very respectable quarter, that it is the mission of this country to spread civil and religious liberty over all the world, especially over this continent. It is a great mistake. None but people advanced to a very high state of moral and intellectual improvement are capable, in a civilized state, of maintaining free government; and amongst those who are so purified, very few, indeed, have had the good fortune of forming a constitution capable of endurance. It is a remarkable fact in the history of man, that scarcely ever have free popular institutions been formed by wisdom alone that have endured.

It has been the work of fortunate circumstances, or a combination of circumstances—a succession of fortunate incidents of some kind—which give to any people a free government. It is a very difficult task to make a constitution to last, though it may be supposed by some that they can be made to order, and furnished at the shortest notice. Sir, this admirable Constitution of our own was the result of a fortunate combination of circumstances. It was superior to the wisdom of the men who made it. It was the force of circumstances which induced them to adopt most of its wise provisions. Well, sir, of the few nations who have the good fortune to adopt self-government, few have had the good fortune long to preserve that government; for it is harder to preserve than to form it. Few people, after years of prosperity, remember the tenure by which their liberty is held; and I fear, Senators, that is our own condition. I fear that we shall continue to involve ourselves until our own system becomes a ruin. Sir, there is no solicitude now for liberty. Who talks of liberty when any great question comes up? Here is a question of the first magnitude as to the conduct of this war; do you hear anybody talk about its effect upon our liberties and our free institutions?

No, sir. That was not the case formerly. In the early stages of our Government, the great anxiety was how to preserve liberty; the great anxiety now is for the attainment of mere military glory. In the one, we are forgetting the other. The maxim of former times was, that power is always stealing from the many to the few; the price of liberty was perpetual vigilance. They were constantly looking out and watching for danger. Then, when any great question came up, the first inquiry was, how it could affect our free institutions—how it could affect our liberty. Not so now. Is it because there has been any decay of the spirit of liberty among the people? Not at all. I believe the love of liberty was never more ardent, but they have forgotten the tenure of liberty by which alone it is preserved.

We think we may now indulge in everything with impunity, as if we held our charter of liberty by "right divine"—from Heaven itself. Under these impressions, we plunge into war, we contract heavy debts, we increase the patronage of the Executive, and we even talk of a crusade to force our institutions, our liberty, upon all people. There is no species of extravagance which our people imagine will endanger their liberty in any degree. But it is a great and fatal mistake. The day of retribution will come. It will come as certainly as I am now addressing the Senate; and when it does come, awful will be the reckoning—heavy the responsibility somewhere!

Mr. President, with these impressions I cannot approve of the policy recommended by the Executive, nor can I, with my present views, support it. The question is now, what shall be done? It is a great and difficult question, and it is daily becoming more and more difficult. What is to done? Sir, that question ought not to be for me to answer—I, who have used every effort in my power to prevent this war, and after its commencement have done everything in my power to diminish the evil to the smallest possible amount. But I will not shrink from any responsibility, whether it properly belongs to me or not. After saying that I cannot support the course recommended by the Executive, I will proceed to state that which I would propose as the best to be pursued. Well, then, I will say that there is not the smallest chance of our disentangling ourselves from the Mexican concern, which threatens us so much—there has not been, in my opinion, the smallest chance, from the commencement of the war until this time—but by taking a defensive line; doing that now which the President recommends should be done finally after the conquest, and taking indemnity into our own hands. To do this depends on our own volition, and not on the fleeting consent of Mexico. Sir, if time had been allowed to the Senate when the message of the President recommending war was before them; if time had been allowed to the Senate, I would have announced the course of policy which I thought right; but time was not permitted. My opinion was, that we should have simply voted Taylor the means of defending himself. That ought to have been done. There then should have been a solemn report from the proper committee, going into all the circumstances, showing that the Republic of Mexico had not yet recognized these hostilities, recommending a provisional army to be directed to a proper point, giving time to the Mexican Congress and Mexican people to have considered whether they would avow or disavow the attacks upon us; and if no satisfaction were obtained, not to make war in this set form, but seize upon the portions of the country contiguous and most convenient to us, and then have assumed the defensive line. These are my views; but unfortunately, we were all acting here under an urgency, without time to reflect. We were pushed on, and told, If you do not act to-day, nothing can be done.

Well now, sir, as to where the defensive line should be at the present time, I do not presume to offer an opinion. I suggested a line at the last session. I am not prepared to say what would be the proper one at the present time; but I do say that we must vacate the central parts of Mexico. We must fall back, if you choose to use that word, or take a line that shall cover ample territory for indemnity.

For my part, I am not for charging Mexico with the whole expense of the war; but I would take ample territory and hold it subject to negotiation. Now, sir, I know it will be said that this will be as expensive as the war. I think I have said enough to show that that cannot be; that it will fall far short of it; but I will not repeat the argument. But admitting it should: admitting that, by no means concludes the argument; for the sacrifice of men would be infinitely less, and, what is more important, you will thereby be able to disentangle yourselves. That is the only way by which it can be done. You are tied at present, as it were, to a corpse. My object is to get rid of it as soon as possible.

I look not to Mexico; I look to our own country and her institutions. I look to the liberty of this country, and nothing else. Mr. President, if we but preserve our liberty by a proper course of moderation, acting justly towards our neighbor, and wisely in regard to ourselves—if we remain quiet, resting in idle and masterly inactivity, and let our destinies work out their own results, we shall do more for liberty, not only for ourselves, but for the example of mankind, than can be done by a thousand victories. . . .

31   Frederick Douglass
For "the instant recall
of our forces"

Many Americans favored the complete withdrawal of American forces from Mexican territory and, unlike Calhoun, they did not base their arguments on prudence. Instead, they insisted that the United States has no moral right to bring death and destruction to a helpless people in the name of abstract principles. One American who believed United States policy in Mexico immoral and dishonest was the Negro leader, Frederick Douglass. This distinguished observer and critic was born a slave in 1817. At the age of twenty he arranged to hire himself out as a laborer in Baltimore with the provision that he would give his master three dollars per week. Soon he escaped to New York City where he joined the abolitionist ranks, and he quickly developed into an outstanding orator, writer, and journalist. In the mid-forties he established an antislavery paper, *The North Star*, published in Rochester, New York. The following editorial appeared in his paper on January 21, 1848.

FROM aught that appears in the present position and movements of the executive and cabinet—the proceedings of either branch of the national Congress—the several State Legislatures, North and South—the spirit of the public press—the conduct of leading men, and the general views and feeling of the people of the United States at large, slight hope can rationally be predicated of a very speedy termination of the present disgraceful, cruel, and iniquitous war with our sister republic. Mexico seems a doomed victim to Anglo Saxon cupidity and love of dominion. The determination of our slaveholding President to prosecute the war, and the probability of his success in wringing from the people men and money to carry it on, is made evident, rather than doubtful, by the puny opposition arrayed against him. No politician of any considerable distinction or eminence, seems willing to hazard his popularity with his party, or stem the fierce current of executive influence, by an open and unqualified disapprobation of the war. None seem willing to take their stand for peace at all risks; and all seem willing that the war should be carried on, in some form or other. . . .

From "The War with Mexico," in Philip S. Foner, ed., *The Life and Writings of Frederick Douglass* (New York: International Publishers, 1950), I, 291–296. Reprinted by permission of International Publishers Co. Inc.

Meanwhile, "the plot thickens"; the evil spreads. Large demands are made on the national treasury, (to wit: the poor man's pockets). Eloquent and patriotic speeches are made in the Senate, House of Representatives and State Assemblies: Whig as well as Democratic governors stand stoutly up for the war: experienced and hoary-headed statesmen tax their declining strength and ingenuity in devising ways and means for advancing the infernal work: recruiting sergeants and corporals perambulate the land in search of victims for the sword and food for powder. Wherever there is a sink of iniquity, or a den of pollution, these buzzards may be found in search of their filthy prey. They dive into the rum shop, and gambling house, and other sinks too infamous to name, with swine-like avidity, in pursuit of degraded men to vindicate the insulted honor of our Christian country. Military chieftians and heroes multiply, and towering high above the level of common men, are glorified, if not deified, by the people. The whole nation seems to "wonder after these [bloody] beasts." Grasping ambition, tyrannic usurpation, atrocious aggression, cruel and haughty pride, spread, and prevade the land. The curse is upon us. The plague is abroad. No part of the country can claim entire exemption from its evils. They may be seen as well in the State of New York, as in South Carolina; on the Penobscot, as on the Sabine. The people appear to be completely in the hands of office seekers, demagogues, and political gamblers. Within the bewildering meshes of their political nets, they are worried, confused, and confounded so that a general outcry is heard—"Vigorous prosecution of the war!"—"Mexico must be humbled!"—"Conquer a peace!"—"Indemnity!"—"War forced upon us!"—"National honor!"—"The whole of Mexico!"—"Our destiny!"—"This continent!"—"Anglo Saxon blood!"—"More territory!"—"Free institutions!"—"Our country!" till it seems indeed "that justice has fled to brutish beasts, and men have lost their reason." The taste of human blood and the smell of power seem to have extinguished the senses, seared the conscience, and subverted the reason of the people to a degree that may well induce the gloomy apprehension that our nation has fully entered on her downward career, and yielded herself up to the revolting idea of battle and blood. . . . The civilization of the age, the voice of the world, the sacredness of human life, the tremendous expense, the dangers, hardships, and the deep disgrace which must forever attach to our inhuman course, seem to oppose no availing check to the mad spirit of proud ambition, blood, and carnage, let loose in the land. . . .

Of the settled determination to prosecute the war, there can be no doubt: Polk has avowed it; his organs have published it; his supporters have rallied round him; all their actions bend in that direction; and every effort is made to establish their purpose firmly in the hearts of the people, and to harden their hearts for the conflict. All danger must be defied; all suffering despised; all honor eschewed; all mercy dried up; and all the better promptings of the human soul blunted, silenced and repudiated, while all the furies of hell are invoked to guide our hired assassins,—our man-killing machines,—now in and out of Mexico, to the infernal consummation. Qualities of head and heart, principles and maxims, counsels and warnings, which once commanded respect, and secured a nation's reverence, must all now be scouted; sense of decency must be utterly drowned: age nor sex must exercise any humanizing effect upon our gallant soldiers, or restrain their satanic designs. The groans of slaughtered men, the screams of violated women, and the cries of orphan children, must bring no throb of pity from our national heart, but must rather serve as music to inspire our gallant troops to deeds of atrocious cruelty, lust, and blood. The work is thus laid out, commenced, and is to be continued. Where it will end is known only to the Great Ruler of the Universe; but where the responsibility rests, and upon whom retribution will fall, is sure and certain.

In watching the effects of the war spirit, prominent among them, will be seen, not only the subversion of the great prin-

ciples of Christian morality, but the most horrid blasphemy.
. . . We are, in the hands of the great God, a rod to chastise this
rebellious people! What say our evangelical clergy to this
blasphemy? That clergy seem as silent as the grave; and their
silence is the greatest sanction of the crime. They have seen the
blood of the innocent poured out like water, and are dumb;
they have seen the truth trampled in the dust—right sought by
pursuing the wrong—peace sought by prosecuting the war—
honor sought by dishonorable means,—and have not raised a
whisper against it; they float down with the multitude in the
filthy current of crime, and are hand in hand with the guilty.
Had the pulpit been faithful, we might have been saved from
this withering curse. We sometimes fear, that now our case as
a nation is hopeless. May God grant otherwise! Our nation seems
resolved to rush on in her wicked career, though the road be
ditched with human blood, and paved with human skulls. Well,
be it so. But, humble as we are, and unavailing as our voice
may be, we wish to warn our fellow countrymen, that they may
follow the course which they have marked out for themselves;
no barrier may be sufficient to obstruct them; they may accomplish all they desire; Mexico may fall before them; she may be
conquered and subdued; her government may be annihilated—
her name among the great sisterhood of nations blotted out;
her separate existence annihilated; her rights and powers
usurped; her condition little better than that endured by the
Saxons when vanquished by their Norman invaders; but, so
sure as there is a God of justice, we shall not go unpunished;
the penalty is certain; we cannot escape; a terrible retribution
awaits us. We beseech our countrymen to leave off this horrid
conflict, abandon their murderous plans, and forsake the way
of blood. Peradventure our country may yet be saved. Let the
press, the pulpit, the church, the people at large, unite at once;
and let petitions flood the halls of Congress by the millions,
asking for the instant recall of our forces from Mexico. This
may not save us, but it is our only hope.

32

A Whig Indictment

"Manifest Destiny" as

"Political clap-trap"

Among the most bitter critics of President Polk and the Mexican War was the powerful *National Intelligencer*, a Whig newspaper published in Washington. As the debate on the future of American policy toward Mexico circulated around the capital, the editors, in the following editorial, condemned the administration and its supporters for basing American foreign and military policy on phrases that claimed either special powers or special privileges for the United States in its relations with other nations. This editorial, then, is more a criticism of the entire notion of manifest destiny than a direct attack on Polk's specific policies. Above all, the editorial claims the right of Americans to criticize the foreign policies of their government even in time of war.

THERE are certain things that it has become necessary we should say, if we would not, in the midst of all that summons the country to a decisive effort of its whole sense and spirit, quietly allow all appeals to the common sense and common honesty of our countrymen to be thwarted by the force of a few preverted phrases, the captivation of which is to hold and lead this whole land, as completely spellbound as if the lies of magic were realities, and a syllable or two of gibberish could

From "Political Clap-Trap," *The National Intelligencer*, January 15, 1848.

reverse all the laws of Nature and turn human intelligence into brutishness. . . .

There are still, as much as ever, sounds that bewitch multitudes of people, and have, by their mere senseless utterance, some secret strength, some mystical virtue, that subdues the understandings of many and sinks them into irrational animals. There are mere forms of speech which, set for some men, catch them like gudgeons. There is a small fry of political minnows whom thus any boy can catch with a string and a pin-hook; there are shoals besides whom mere authority and its pleasure can make game of and dip up unbaited, like sprats or shrimps, in any drag-net it chooses to use.

To come, however, to instances of these easy dupes of a sentence, these human gudgeons of a word: Among the famous and fatal absurdities which darken the history of mankind, the Crusades for the "recovery of the Holy Land" are, perhaps, held to be the most remarkable. . . . Monarchs laid down the care of their dominions, and great feudatories sold their vassals to run to Palestine; *our* Prince can do nothing good at home, lest the means for foreign mischief would be lacking. And, finally, above all, as then, while Peter the Hermit preached to superstitious throngs desolation in the name of Religion, a cry from some fool in the crowd arose, "It is the will of God!" and was instantly caught up and resounded through all Christendom, as an authentic voice of the Most High; so now, some equally respectable confidant of the Divine decrees has bellowed to the prudent populace that to conquer all this continent is *"our Manifest Destiny;"* and, behold! that shallow and impious phrase passes for a received decree of Fate! "Manifest," forsooth! What is manifest, and to whom? What prophet or saint hath spoken? To whom have the dark decrees of Heaven been made "manifest," in the visions of some new Apocalypse? Verily, no prophet at all, by any of the old marks of prophecy; for, among all the high messengers of God to men, where is one who came to flatter the bad passions of either the Jews or their Kings! God's servants came, of old, with no such smooth speeches; but to threaten wicked princes and rebuke a corrupt people. Has some Angel descended, then? Hardly; for the last that appeared came down to bring glad tidings of "Peace on earth and good will to men;" and we must doubt if he would come back again with so different a commission. If, in short, any such message of Fate has come to us, who shall assure us that it is not of the devil's fetching, like that other in Peter Hermit's time? One thing at least is certain: no wise man will own, since no wise man can see, our "destiny" or its "manifestness."' What sort of manifestness is that, unpreceived of the able and far-seeing, which none but the weak and ignorant can discern?

Much like and akin to this first word-snare for national vanity and presumption is that second, baited with the talkingness of another riddling phrase, "*Anglo-Saxonism.*" This again, has the genuine stamp of the Heathen oracle; which stamp was its ambiguity, its enigmaticalness. We are, it appears, of the "Anglo-Saxon race"—of a lineage of "land-stealers," a progeny of plunderers! Oh, pious genealogy! How we "honor our father and mother, that our days may be long in the land which the Lord our God hath given us!" which land is to be all that, with carnage and devastation and enslavement, we can wrest (without wanting a foot of it) from weak and wretched neighbors! . . . And for what are we, leaping over the kindred and the example of WASHINGTONS, HENRYS, FRANKLINS, and all our own genuine heroes of honest policy and defensive valor, to seek a forged lineage of the pagans who came as friends among an unarmed people and fell to butchering them? It is, of course, that we may imitate the ruthless deeds of Anglo-Saxons, not their subsequent glory of founding wise and free laws, resistance to bad kings, and a true and stable popular liberty. . . .

Another great and mischievous phrase for captivating and misleading word-victims is that of "*Our country, right or wrong.*" . . .

Concurring, evidently, in all the views of the *Intelligencer,* as to the origin and conduct of the war on the part of the President . . . the *Evening Journal* [Whig] yet thinks we are entirely wrong in opposing the war. We beg to know, then, in *what* case there ought to be opposition to an Administration; or *when before* such a case of opposition as the *Journal* itself admits was *ever* made out? Is there *any* war which ought to be opposed? Clearly none. But a war being, at best, one of the greatest ills which a Government can inflict upon a people, and an unnecessary war being the greatest of all national crimes, *what* is it permitted to oppose, if not a war which, besides being unjust abroad, was unconstitutional at home, and, in addition to visiting carnage and devastation on Mexico, visits upon ourselves so much that is mournful or guilty or suicidal in the present, with nothing of probable in the future but what is still darker and more appalling! If (we repeat) an abandoned and foolish war, *terminable at our pleasure,* is not, though the greatest of all public misdeeds and follies, to be opposed *by all who so view it,* then we beg to know what it can be right or expedient to oppose, in the measures of an Administration? . . . When the country has been betrayed into all that is ruinous as well as wicked, we must be mute—nay, applaud, soothing our souls with the wise and righteous sentence, "Our country, right or wrong;" and we must reserve our patriotic indignation for those things which commit or threaten no sin and no harm! These are to us new politics, new morals, and a new logic. . . .

PART SIX

CUBA

33

A Southern View
Cuba is "indispensable
for American Security"

For a generation the possibility of acquiring Cuba had never been far beneath the surface of public attention and concern, and after the Mexican War, the Democratic expansionists singled out the island as the next legitimate and inescapable objective of American manifest destiny. Spain still retained her possession of Cuba, but the rapid decline of Spanish power in the Atlantic and the general uneasiness in the political world, convinced Europeans and Americans that the days of Spanish rule in Cuba were numbered. Cognizant of the rapid changes in the Spanish government and the chaotic conditions on the island of Cuba, President Polk concluded by 1848 that the Spanish government might be induced to liquidate its imperial obligations by selling Cuba to the United States. On June 17, 1848, Secretary Buchanan instructed Minister R. M. Saunders at Madrid to offer the Spanish government 100 million dollars for the island as a maximum price. Spain's prompt rejection of the United States offer scarcely dimmed the American vision of expansion into the Caribbean.

DeBow's Review took up the issue of Cuba in 1848 with the passion that might have been expected of a leading mouthpiece for Southern causes. In July it adopted new goals for American destiny:

The North Americans *will* spread out far beyond their present bounds. They *will* encroach again and again upon their neighbors. New territories *will* be planted, declare their independence, and be annexed! We have New Mexico and California! We *will* have old Mexico and Cuba! The isthmus cannot arrest—nor even the Saint Lawrence!! Time has all of this in her womb.

Some Americans were prepared to push destiny hard on the question of Cuba. As Cuba was so desirable and so weakly defended, its acquisition appeared well within the capabilities of even a mere filibustering expedition. A leader appeared in the person of General Narciso López, a Venezuelan adventurer who was convinced that an American landing on Cuba would ignite a general revolution against Spanish rule. López first landed on Cuban shores in May 1850 with a tiny army. He returned again in August 1851 only to be captured and executed with fifty of his followers. Such gallantry in the name of destiny was too appealing to be ignored by *DeBow's Review*. In August, 1850, following the first fiasco, it defended López' right to attack Cuba. The Mexican War, noted the writer, had set the stage for further American advances by creating a martial spirit in the country and demonstrating the nation's power of conquest. Anticipating a violent European reaction when annexation occurred, however, *DeBow's* suggested that the United States, because it had many interests from which it did not want to be eliminated, forego the concept of American exclusiveness in the Western Hemisphere as embodied in the Monroe Doctrine.

THE history of the world furnishes no instance of a great and growing power intent to pursue its career of progress and improvement without encroaching upon the right and dominions of its weaker neighbors. In all ages, and under all circumstances, the nature of man is identical. Dependent, he is subservient and cringing; strong and powerful, his ambition and his arrogance tower aloft and are without practical limit. Give him power to oppress, and he will assuredly do it. Wielding the thunders of Jupiter, he will, without any of the discretion of the god, battle and rage, and storm, and be found beating ever against the barriers around him, and leveling them

From "The Late Cuban Expedition," *DeBow's Review*, IX (August, 1850), 165–169, 172–177.

all in the mere joy and consciousness of irresistible might. . . .

Whoever has followed the course of the United States, for the last half century, without noting the growth of a *military spirit*, diffusing itself through all classes of society, and ready, at any moment, to develop itself in every form of action, has observed to very little purpose. It was this spirit which almost defied the vigilance of Washington, when Genet would have precipitated the West upon New Orleans—this, which dictated the schemes of Burr, clamored for a part in the wars of Napoleon, and received with huzzas the proclamation of Mr. Madison's government of hostilities with England. Emboldened by the results of this brilliant war, the American eagle has plumed its pinions for a flight still nearer to the sun. Miniature West Points have sprung up in every State and on every hill top, indurating young sinews for the toils of the camp and the battle field, counseling discipline and strategy, and inspiring admiration for "nodding plumes" and "dazzling crests." The sports of boyhood have even assumed this form, as we find the cannon among the earliest playthings of the child, Napoleon. The tender heart of girlhood looks on and smiles, and, fashioning the stars and the stripes of the beautiful banner, presents it, all eloquent with blushes as with words, and yields her young affections irresistibly captive to the embroidery and the epaulette! How otherwise, in such a school, could American militia bayonets have else than bristled along the Maine frontier, when the occupation of disputed territory was threatened by British soldiery?—how otherwise, but the genius of the wisest and the greatest statesman should be sorely taxed in preventing the execution, by force of arms, of the threat, "the whole of Oregon or none"?—how otherwise, the call of Texas attracts legions of soldiers to her standard from our midst, and the proclamation of war with Mexico received with illuminations and bon-fires, and the tender, in a few months, as Mr. Polk is said to have admitted, of the *voluntary* services in the field of 200,000 men!

What have been the results of this Mexican war? They are but of yesterday, and we remember the intense excitement, from the Aroostook to the Columbia valley—the illuminations, the bon-fires, the banners, the shouts, the processions; the returning heroes, drawn in chariots over multitudes of heads, as great cities move from their foundations, in the figure of Cicero, to receive them on their triumphant advances; the muffled drum, the reversed arms, the toll of bells, the stiffled sobs, the somber pageant, the eloquent Periclesian eulogiums, the insignia and the reward of the dead warrior, "from the field of his fame, fresh and gory." The people, in a delirium of joy, welcome the return of their champions, and deem no chaplets of fame too glittering for their brows. The warrior captain becomes the civil chief of the great nation—his immediate compatriots, crown congressional, diplomatic, gubernatorial and legislative seats; the subaltern and verriest soldiery have a potency at the ballot box, and distance all competition in the race for office! Shall not they who have borne the heat and burden of the day reap the greater reward? and the arm which was mighty to protect and defend in the hour of danger, must it not be guided by a heart pure and incurrupt, and earnestly solicitous of the public weal, in peace or in war? What higher *preparation* or fitness for office can be required than these?

"The curtain has fallen upon the first act of American history," said the great statesman, who, but the other day, went down into his grave, "and, for the first time, all before me is dark." With the Mexican war the nation entered upon a new career, which was predicted of her, and to which her institutions and position peculiarly inclined—one of *war and conquest!* Shall we essay to lift the curtain form the future?

The brilliant and unparalleled success of the field, and the high and distinguished honors and emoluments accorded to the warriors and soldiers at home, are not likely, soon, to be forgotten. . . .

The military spirit of the country has been aroused, and is

rife for anything, and woe to the power that shall endeavor to stay it. Administrations will fall to pieces at its blow—statesmen will not dare the ostracism of its voice. The cry of war is flattering to our pride and our power, and they are either of them equal to that of any other nation, ancient or modern. The field before us is boundless, and the power that broods over it, grows every day in energy, in resources and in magnitude, and will be as resistless, in time, as the whirlwind. Armed bands will sally from our ports, as in days of yore from the northern hive, covertly, often openly, in the service of every power that shall offer emolument and glory. Our sympathies with freedom, everywhere, are first the incentive; but there will, in time, be other and less honorable incentives. *We have a destiny to perform*, "a manifest destiny" over all Mexico, over South America, over the West Indies and Canada. The Sandwich Islands are as necessary to our eastern, as the isles of the gulf to our western commerce. The gates of the Chinese empire must be thrown down by the men from the Sacramento and the Oregon, and the haughty Japanese tramplers upon the cross be enlightened in the doctrines of republicanism and ballot box. The eagle of the republic shall poise itself over the field of Waterloo, after tracing its flight among the gorges of the Himalaya or the Ural mountains, and a successor of Washington ascend the chair of universal empire! These are the giddy dreams of the day. The martial spirit must have its employ. The people stand ready to hail to-morrow, with shouts and enthusiasm, a collision with the proudest and the mightiest empire upon earth. The valley of the Mississippi alone, will arm its half million, of stout woodsmen, hardy hunters, deadly rifles, for any field where the cause of liberty and glory shall call. Thus is it.

Have a care how we trifle with this tremendous power, or unduly excite it, and let us not cease to admire the foresight of the Spanish minister, the Count of Aranda, who said, in 1783, "the federal republic is a pigmy in its cradle; she has needed the support of two States, powerful like France and

Spain, to obtain independence. The day will come when she will be a giant—a formidable colossus even in these parts. She will forget the services received from those countries, and will only think of her own aggrandizement."

These reflections, rather too much extended, perhaps, have been induced by the late attempt upon the island of Cuba, by a party of adventurers under our flag and embarking from our ports. We are willing, at the outset, to accord, to the leader of the expedition, the highest motives of patriotism and honor, and to the hundreds who flocked around his standard many generous, though, perhaps, misdirected impulses and sympathies, without questioning there were others, at the same time, moved by the most sordid considerations.

The signal failure of the enterprise and all the attendant circumstances of it, have been such as to provoke derision rather than admiration or respect; and the parties having themselves braved the ordeal, must be content with that obloquy which the want of success will ever inspire. . . .

It is difficult to distinguish this case, *upon principle,* from that of the Texan revolution, when men, and arms, and amunition were continually being thrown into that country, from our ports, notwithstanding the loud protests of Mexico, with whom we were at peace, and with whom we were bound by all the solemnities of treaty stipulations. The Cubans were not in arms—but revolution may begin long before a standard is erected or a sword drawn from its scabbard. Contributing money, conducting correspondence, are as much overt acts of rebellion or treason as open revolt, and do not distinguish the parties, in the eye of the law and government, from those that are actually in the field. Were the Cubans so far committed? The evidences are not wanting that they were, and that contributions of money and the warmest protestations of sympathy, and vows of hearty cooperation, did emanate from the quarter to encourage and cheer the movement. The rebutting circumstance is the cold reception which they gave to the men at

Cardenas. We are bound, in our search after truth, to consider this of little weight. They must have been bold and hardy revolutionists, indeed—supposing that *external* aid was *indispensable* to their cause—to regard that which landed in the Creole as at all adequate to the exigence. A mere handful—where it is believed ten times the number had been expected—and a handful, too, whose movements had long before been known to the authorities of the island—who, with extraordinary vigilence, were throwing armies of disciplined soldiers upon every assailable point and scouring the Gulf with their fleets. The landing at Cardenas could only have been considered a piece of American Quixoticism, of which it seems we are capable when occasion requires. . . .

That this, the second unsuccessful attempt upon Cuba within a few months, is but the beginning of the end which looks to the acquisition of that island, by the United States, can hardly be a subject of debate. American and Spanish blood has been shed, and the bitter feelings of consequence, engendered upon both sides, will long survive the occasion, indulging itself in petty acts of jealousy—in ill-concealed hostility—in crimination and recrimination. Already the islanders loudly boast of their heroic onslaught upon the Buena Vista Yankees, and search their vocabulary for every term of opprobrium and contempt to heap upon their heads. Bravely, it must be admitted, almost chivalrously, as they did act, these glorifications are not likely to produce a pleasant tingle upon American ears, unaccustomed to such sounds from others than themselves. It is not improbable that our citizens, now or hereafter in the island, will be subjected to vexatious restrictions, growing out of these matters, and that, in the haughtiness of almost unexpected triumph, the authorities will be guilty of some infractions upon their rights and privileges. The taking of the Georgiana and the Loud, and unlawful detention of their crews and passengers, may already have furnished an instance. In the excited state of public mind, the least pretext would pave the way for other invasions of the island, for which, in a moment, any number of men could be enlisted—and an injury done to American citizens, however slight, would raise a war cry throughout the nation, which even the government could not resist. Besides, where a quarrel becomes, in any sense, desirable, it will not be hard to pick one, as the fable of the wolf and the lamb abundantly proves.

None can doubt, that, at this moment, there is a well fixed and almost universal conviction upon the minds of our people, that the possession of Cuba is indispensible to the proper development and security of the country. We state the fact, without entering into the reasons of it or justifying it, that such a conviction exists. Call it the lust of dominion—the restlesness of democracy—the passion for land and gold, or the desire to render our interior impregnable by commanding the keys of the gulf—possession of Cuba is still an American sentiment, not to be sure a late, but a growing and strengthening one. We trust, for the honor of humanity and the faith of treaties, it will lead us into nothing for which our history shall blush.

The path before us, in a state of things like this, is plain. There are honorable means of achieving our purpose, and, if these fail, the purpose itself becomes dishonorable. Let us negotiate with the Cabinet of Madrid, as we did with that of Versailles. Perchance the dangers which environ the island from *within* and from *without*—and those formed must not be underrated, if what is said about the restlesness and revolutionary spirit of the creoles requiring such armies and surveillance to keep them down be true (and the history of Cuba seems to make it probable), nor must the latter be from the considerations we have adverted to, and from the chances of unlawful invasion, or ultimate, open and direct hostilities—will induce the home government to entertain propositions of *purchase*. A liberal figure would undoubtedly be named by our countrymen. Spanish *pride*, to be sure, would be opposed (and this, we know, is without limit), and, to some extent, considering the revenues of the island, Spanish *interest;* but when that government shall have duly reflected how she has lost the whole of her American possessions but this, in most cases without any equivalent—how difficult the possession of colonies becomes now, even to the strongest maritime powers—how contrary to the spirit of the age, and likely to fall into pieces, is all government exercised over distant possessions, growing rich and powerful—how every other nation has been bound to yield to the times, while even the policy itself, of large colonial possessions, is being daily drawn sensibly into question, by those who claim the largest of such possessions—how impossible, in fine, it would be to retain Cuba, in the event of a general war—it seems, to us, a wise statesman might put off, like Bonaparte, all idle pride and close in, at once, with any terms that shall appear, in every respect, fair and just. Such terms would, undoubtedly, be offered. Should these negotiations fail, honor and preservation of national faith demand, that we give no countenance to any movements hostile to the cause of Spain. . . .

34   Edward Everett

No Diplomatic Curbs on
"the Law of American Growth"

It was only a matter of time before the vast dichotomy between the weakness of Spain's authority in Cuba and the potential commercial and agricultural value of the island would arouse the concern of Britain and France. Cuba, despite the futility of Spanish policy, attracted the trade of all the major maritime powers. To Europeans it seemed clear that Cuba possessed the wealth and maturity to establish and maintain an independent existence. What disturbed them, however, were the scarcely concealed ambitions of the United States regarding Cuba, as well as the activities of such adventurers as López. Consequently in April, 1852, the British and French governments pressed Secretary of State Daniel Webster for a tripartite convention of renunciation. Webster, on April 29, addressed the French Minister, Count Sartiges: "It has been stated, and often repeated to the government of Spain by this government, under various administrations, not only that the United States have no design upon Cuba themselves, but that if *Spain should refrain from a voluntary cession of the island to any other European power, she might rely on the countenance and friendship of the United States, to assist her in the defence and preservation of that island.*"[1] Sartiges and the British Minister, John Crampton, made clear in their response of July that the British and French interpreted Webster's letter as assurance that the United States would not support a Cuban revolution against Spanish authority.

The negotiation fell next to Edward Everett, the new Secretary of State. Like Webster, Everett was a New England conservative. Yet because of domestic expansionist sentiment he responded more forcefully than Webster and refused to accept the self-denying principle embodied in the Franco-British proposal. His letter to Count Sartiges of December 1, 1852, stated the principle of natural growth and explained that American destiny was not to be curtailed by pacts that might, at some future day, limit the national expansion of the United States.

YOU are well acquainted with the melancholy circumstances which have hitherto prevented a reply to the note which you addressed to my predecessor on the 8th of July.

From Everett to Count Sartiges, December 1, 1852, printed in John Bassett Moore, *A Digest of International Law* (Washington, 1906), VI, 460–470.

[1] Webster to M. de Sartiges, April 29, 1852, John Bassett Moore, *A Digest of International Law* (Washington: Government Printing Office, 1906), VI, 460.

That note, and the instruction of M. de Turgot [French Minister of Foreign Affairs] of the 31st March, with a similar communication from the English minister, and the *projet* of a convention between the three powers relative to Cuba, have been among the first subjects to which my attention has been called by the President.

The substantial portion of the proposed convention is expressed in a single article in the following terms:

"The high contracting parties hereby, severally and collectively, disclaim, now and for hereafter, all intention to obtain possession of the island of Cuba, and they respectively bind themselves to discountenance all attempt to that effect on the part of any power or individuals whatever."

"The high contracting parties declare, severally and collectively, that they will not obtain or maintain for themselves, or for any one of themselves, any exclusive control over the said island, nor assume nor exercise any dominion over the same."

The President has given the most serious attention to this proposal, to the notes of the French and British ministers accompanying it, and to the instructions of M. de Turgot and the Earl of Malmesbury, transmitted with the project of the convention, and he directs me to make known to you the view which he takes of this important and delicate subject.

The President fully concurs with his predecessors, who have on more than one occasion authorized the declaration referred to by M. de Turgot and Lord Malemsbury, that the United States could not see with indifference the island of Cuba fall into the possession of any other European Government than Spain; not, however, because we should be dissatisfied with any natural increase of territory and power on the part of France or England. France has, within twenty years, acquired a vast domain on the northern coast of Africa, with a fair prospect of indefinite extension. England, within half a century, has added very extensively to her Empire. These acquisitions have created no uneasiness on the part of the United States.

In like manner, the United States have, within the same period, greatly increased their territory. The largest addition was that of Louisiana, which was purchased from France. These accessions of territory have probably caused no uneasiness to the great European powers, as they have been brought about by the operation of natural causes, and without any disturbance of the international relations of the principal states. They have been followed, also, by a great increase of mutually beneficial commercial intercourse between the United States and Europe.

But the case would be different in reference to the transfer of Cuba from Spain to any other European power. That event could not take place without a serious derangement of the international system now existing, and it would indicate designs in reference to this hemisphere which could not but awaken alarm in the United States.

We should view it in somewhat the same light in which France and England would view the acquisition of some important island in the Mediterranean by the United States, with this difference, it is true; that the attempt of the United States to establish themselves in Europe would be a novelty, while the appearance of a European power in this part of the world is a familiar fact. But this difference in the two cases is merely historical, and would not diminish the anxiety which, on political grounds, would be caused by any great demonstration of European power in a new direction in America.

M. de Turgot states that France could never see with indifference the possession of Cuba by *any* power but Spain, and explicitly declares that she has no wish or intention of appropriating the island to herself; and the English minister makes the same avowal on behalf of his Government. M. de Turgot and Lord Malmesbury do the Government of the United States no more than justice in remarking that they have often pronounced themselves substantially in the same sense. The President does not covet the acquisition of Cuba for the United States; at the same time, he considers the condition of Cuba as mainly an American question. The proposed convention proceeds on a different principle. It assumes that the United States have no other or greater interest in the question than France or England; whereas it is necessary only to cast one's eye on the map to see how remote are the relations of Europe, and how intimate those of the United States, with this island. . . .

The convention would be of no value unless it were lasting: accordingly its terms express a perpetuity of purpose and obligation. Now, it may well be doubted whether the Constitution of the United States would allow the treaty-making power to impose a permanent disability on the American Government for all coming time, and prevent it, under any future change of circumstances, from doing what has been so often done in times past. In 1803 the United States purchased Louisiana of France; and in 1819 they purchased Florida of Spain. It is not within the competence of the treaty-making power of 1852 effectually to bind the Government in all its branches; and, for all coming time, not to make a similar purchase of Cuba. A like remark, I imagine, may be made even in reference both to France and England, where the treaty-making power is less subject than it is with us to the control of other branches of the Government.

There is another strong objection to the proposed agreement. Among the oldest traditions of the Federal Government is an aversion to political alliances with European powers. In his memorable farewell address, President Washington says: 'The great rule of conduct for us in regard to foreign nations is, in extending our commercial relations, to have with them as little political connexion as possible. So far as we have already formed engagements, let them be fulfilled with perfect good faith. Here let us stop.' President Jefferson, in his inaugural address in 1801, warned the country against 'entangling alliances.' This expression, now become proverbial, was unquestionably used by Mr. Jefferson in reference to the alliance with France of 1778—an alliance, at the time, of incalculable benefit to the United States;

but which, in less than twenty years, came near involving us in the wars of the French revolution, and laid the foundation of heavy claims upon Congress, not extinguished to the present day. It is a significant coincidence, that the particular provision of the alliance which occasioned these evils was that, under which France called upon us to aid her in defending her West Indian possessions against England. Nothing less than the unbounded influence of Washington rescued the Union from the perils of that crisis, and preserved our neutrality.

But the President has a graver objection to entering into the proposed convention. He has no wish to disguise the feeling that the compact, although equal in its terms, would be very unequal in substance. France and England, by entering into it, would disable themselves from obtaining possession of an island remote from their seats of government, belonging to another European power, whose natural right to possess it must always be as good as their own—a distant island in another hemisphere, and one which by no ordinary or peaceful course of things could ever belong to either of them. If the present balance of power in Europe should be broken up, if Spain should become unable to maintain the island in her possession, and France and England should be engaged in a death struggle with each other, Cuba might then be the prize of the victor. Till these events all take place, the President does not see how Cuba can belong to any European power but Spain.

The United States, on the other hand, would, by the proposed convention, disable themselves from making an acquisition which might take place without any disturbance of existing foreign relations, and in the natural order of things. The island of Cuba lies at our doors. It commands the approach to the Gulf of Mexico, which washes the shores of five of our States. It bars the entrance of that great river which drains half the North American continent, and with its tributaries forms the largest system of internal water-communication in the world. It keeps watch at the door-way of our intercourse with California by the

Isthmus route. If an island like Cuba, belonging to the Spanish Crown, guarded the entrance of the Thames and the Seine, and the United States should propose a convention like this to France and England, those powers would assuredly feel that the disability assumed by ourselves was far less serious than that which we asked them to assume.

The opinions of American statesmen, at different times, and under varying circumstances, have differed as to the desirableness of the acquisition of Cuba by the United States. Territorially and commercially it would, in our hands, be an extremely valuable possession. Under certain contingencies it might be almost essential to our safety. Still, for domestic reasons, on which, in a communication of this kind, it might not be proper to dwell, the President thinks that the incorporation of the island into the Union at the present time, although effected with the consent of Spain, would be a hazardous measure; and he would consider its acquisition by force, except in a just war with Spain, (should an event so greatly to be deprecated take place,) as a disgrace to the civilization of the age.

The President has given ample proof of the sincerity with which he holds these views. He has thrown the whole force of his constitutional power against all illegal attacks upon the island. It would have been perfectly easy for him, without any seeming neglect of duty, to allow projects of a formidable character to gather strength by connivance. No amount of obloquy at home, no embarrassments caused by the indiscretions of the colonial government of Cuba, have moved him from the path of duty in this respect. . . .

That a convention such as is proposed would be a transitory arrangement, sure to be swept away by the irresistible tide of affairs in a new country, is, to the apprehension of the President, too obvious to require a labored argument. The project rests on principles applicable, if at all, to Europe, where international relations are, in their basis, of great antiquity, slowly modified, for the most part, in the progress of time and events; and not applicable to America, which, but lately a waste, is filling up with intense rapidity, and adjusting on natural principles those territorial relations which, on the first discovery of the continent, were in a good degree fortuitous.

The comparative history of Europe and America, even for a single century, shows this. In 1752 France, England, and Spain were not materially different in their political position in Europe from what they are now. They were ancient, mature, consolidated states, established in their relations with each other and the rest of the world—the leading powers of western and southern Europe. Totally different was the state of things in America. The United States had no existence as a people; a line of English colonies, not numbering much over a million of inhabitants, stretched along the coast. France extended from the Bay of Saint Lawrence to the Gulf of Mexico, and from the Alleghanies to the Mississippi; beyond which, westward, the continent was a wilderness, occupied by wandering savages, and subject to a conflicting and nominal claim on the part of France and Spain. Everything in Europe was comparatively fixed; everything in America provisional, incipient, and temporary, except the law of progress, which is as organic and vital in the youth of states as of individual men. A struggle between the provincial authorities of France and England for the possession of a petty stockade at the confluence of the Monongahela and Alleghany, kindled the seven years' war; at the close of which, the great European powers, not materially affected in their relations at home, had undergone astonishing changes on this continent. France had disappeared from the map of America, whose inmost recesses had been penetrated by her zealous missionaries and her resolute and gallant adventurers; England had added the Canadas to her transatlantic dominions; Spain had become the mistress of Louisiana, so that, in the language of the archbishop of Mexico, in 1770, she claimed Siberia as the northern boundary of New Spain.

Twelve years only from the treaty of Paris elapsed, and another great change took place, fruitful of still greater changes to come. The American Revolution broke out. It involved France, England, and Spain in a tremendous struggle, and at its close the United States of America had taken their place in the family of nations. In Europe the ancient states were restored substantially to their former equilibrium; but a new element, of incalculable importance in reference to territorial arrangements, is henceforth to be recognized in America.

Just twenty years from the close of the war of the American Revolution, France, by a treaty with Spain—of which the provisions have never been disclosed—possessed herself of Louisiana, but did so only to cede it to the United States; and in the same year Lewis and Clark started on their expedition to plant the flag of the United States on the shores of the Pacific. In 1819 Florida was sold by Spain to the United States, whose territorial possessions in this way had been increased threefold in half a century. This last acquisition was so much a matter of course that it had been distinctly foreseen by the Count Aranda, then prime minister of Spain, as long ago as 1783.

But even these momentous events are but the forerunners of new territorial revolutions still more stupendous. A dynastic struggle between the Emperor Napoleon and Spain, commencing in 1808, convulsed the peninsula. The vast possessions of the Spanish Crown on this continent—vice-royalties and captain-generalships, filling the space between California and Cape Horn—one after another, asserted their independence. No friendly power in Europe, at that time, was able, or, if able, was willing, to succor Spain, or aid her to prop the crumbling buttresses of her colonial empire. . . .

Thus, in sixty years from the close of the seven years' war, Spain, like France, had lost the last remains of her once imperial possessions on this continent. The United States, meantime, were, by the arts of peace and the healthful progress of things, rapidly enlarging their dimensions and consolidating their power.

The great march of events still went on. Some of the new republics, from the effect of a mixture of races, or the want of training in liberal institutions, showed themselves incapable of self-government. The province of Texas revolted from Mexico by the same right by which Mexico revolted from Spain. At the memorable battle of San Jacinto, in 1836, she passed the great ordeal of nascent states, and her independence was recognized by this Government, by France, by England, and other European powers. Mainly peopled from the United States, she sought naturally to be incorporated into the Union. The offer was repeatedly rejected by Presidents Jackson and Van Buren, to avoid a collision with Mexico. At last the annexation took place. As a domestic question, it is no fit subject for comment in a communication to a foreign minister; as a question of public law, there never was an extension of territory more naturally or justifiably made.

It produced a disturbed relation with the Government of Mexico; war ensued, and in its results other extensive territories were for a large pecuniary compensation on the part of the United States, added to the Union. Without adverting to the divisions of opinion which arose in reference to this war, as must always happen in free countries in reference to great measures, no person surveying these events with the eye of a comprehensive statesmanship can fail to trace in the main result the undoubted operation of the law of our political existence. The consequences are before the world. Vast provinces, which had languished for three centuries under the leaden sway of a stationary system, are coming under the influences of an active civilization. Freedom of speech and the press, the trial by jury, religious equality, and representative government, have been carried by the Constitution of the United States into extensive regions in which they were unknown before. By the settlement of California, the great circuit of intelligence round the globe is completed. . . .

Such is the territorial development of the United States in the past century. Is it possible that Europe can contemplate it with an unfriendly or jealous eye? What would have been her condition in these trying years but for the outlet we have furnished for her starving millions?

Spain, meantime, has retained of her extensive dominions in this hemisphere but the two islands of Cuba and Porto Rico. A respectful sympathy with the fortunes of an ancient ally and a gallant people, with whom the United States have ever maintained the most friendly relations, would, if no other reason existed, make it our duty to leave her in the undisturbed possession of this little remnant of her mighty trans-Atlantic empire. The President desires to do so; no word or deed of his will ever question her title or shake her possession. But can it be expected to last very long? Can it resist this mighty current in the fortunes of the world? Is it desirable that it should do so? Can it be for the interest of Spain to cling to a possession that can only be maintained by a garrison of twenty-five or thirty thousand troops, a powerful naval force, and an annual expenditure for both arms of the service of at least twelve millions of dollars? Cuba, at this moment, costs more to Spain than the entire naval and military establishment of the United States costs the Federal Government. So far from being really injured by the loss of this island, there is no doubt that, were it peacefully transferred to the United States, a prosperous commerce between Cuba and Spain, resulting from ancient associations and common language and tastes, would be far more productive than the best contrived system of colonial taxation. Such, notoriously, has been the result to Great Britain of the establishment of the independence of the United States. The decline of Spain from the position which she held in the time of Charles the Fifth is coeval with the foundation of her colonial system; while within twenty-five years, and since the loss of most of her colonies, she has entered upon a course of rapid improvement unknown since the abdication of that Emperor.

I will but allude to an evil of the first magnitude: I mean the African slave-trade, in the suppression of which France and England take a lively interest—an evil which still forms a great reproach upon the civilization of Christendom, and perpetuates the barbarism of Africa, but for which it is to be feared there is no hope of a complete remedy while Cuba remains a Spanish colony.

But, whatever may be thought of these last suggestions, it would seem impossible for anyone who reflects upon the events glanced at in this note to mistake the law of American growth and progress, or think it can be ultimately arrested by a convention like that proposed. In the judgment of the President, it would be as easy to throw a dam from Cape Florida to Cuba, in the hope of stopping the flow of the Gulf Stream, as to attempt, by a compact like this, to fix the fortunes of Cuba 'now and for hereafter;' or, as expressed in the French text of the convention, 'for the present as for the future,' *(pour le présent comme pour l'avenir,)* that is, for all coming time. The history of the past—of the recent past—affords no assurance that twenty years hence France or England will even wish that Spain should retain Cuba; and a century hence, judging of what will be from what has been, the pages which record this proposition will, like the record of the family compact between France and Spain, have no interest but for the antiquary.

Even now the President can not doubt that both France and England would prefer any change in the condition of Cuba to that which is most to be apprehended, viz: An internal convulsion which should renew the horrors and the fate of San Domingo.

I will intimate a final objection to the proposed convention. M. de Turgot and Lord Malmesbury put forward, as the reason for entering into such a compact, 'the attacks which have lately been made on the island of Cuba by lawless bands of adventurers from the United States, with the avowed design of taking possession of that island.' The President is convinced that the conclusion of such a treaty, instead of putting a stop to these lawless proceedings, would give a new and powerful impulse to them. It would strike a death-blow to the conservative policy hitherto pursued in this country toward Cuba. No administration of this Government, however strong in the public confidence in other respects, could stand a day under the odium of having stipulated with the great powers of Europe, that in no future time, under no change of circumstances, by no amicable arrangement with Spain, by no act of lawful war, (should that calamity unfortunately occur,) by no consent of the inhabitants of the island, should they, like the possessions of Spain on the American continent, succeed in rendering themselves independent: in fine, by no overruling necessity of self-preservation should the United States ever make the acquisition of Cuba.

For these reasons, which the President has thought it advisable, considering the importance of the subject, to direct me to unfold at some length, he feels constrained to decline respectfully the invitation of France and England to become a party to the proposed convention. He is persuaded that these friendly powers will not attribute this refusal to any insensibility on his part to the advantages of the utmost harmony between the great maritime states on a subject of such importance. As little will Spain draw any unfavorable inference from this refusal; the rather, as the emphatic disclaimer of any designs against Cuba on the part of this Government, contained in the present note, affords all the assurance which the President can constitutionally, or to any useful purpose, give of a practical concurrence with France and England in the wish not to disturb the possession of that island by Spain.

35   Hiram Bell
No sanction to "schemes
of unlimited Annexation
under the plea of destiny"

Conservatives commenced their opposition to the notion that American policies should reflect the dictates of manifest destiny as early as the debates over Texas annexation. Throughout the fifties they continued to argue against such doctrines, for they understood clearly that the phraseology of manifest destiny could have no meaning within the context of actual policy formulation. They were concerned, as were the Founding Fathers, with the quality of American civilization, not with boasts of American superiority which would allegedly prompt other nations to give way. A writer for *DeBow's Review* saw the futility, if not the danger and dishonesty, in the constant references to destiny. In December, 1853 he observed:

Much nonsense has been said of our manifest destiny. Every folly is to be covered by this manifest destiny. The thief thinks it his destiny when he picks your pocket or steals your horse. Others may think it his destiny to be hung. Our true destiny, we cannot doubt, is to do justice to others, and to see that justice is done to us. Our institutions suit us, and no foreign power has the right to interfere with them, or do anything that will endanger them; nor have we any right to interfere with the institutions of other people, or to attempt to force ours upon them, any more than they have to force theirs upon us. Propagandism is not the business of our sort of constitutional, representative democracy. Let us leave that to socialists, communists, abolitionists, and all other such mad men, and bad men; it is enough that we are satisfied with our system. We no more believe that it would suit all other people, than that it would answer for the government of a drove of hogs or mules. Let the emperors, czars and sultans, these political pig-drivers, alone. They have their flock, and their mission to fill, and we have ours. It is enough that we have opened our doors to every one who may choose to abandon the mule-drivers, and place themselves under the protection of our institutions.

Even abolitionists such as Senator Gerrit Smith of New York, who spoke much of increasing the base of American liberty, denied that such objectives and rhetoric had any place in statements relative to foreign affairs. Claims to superiority in matters of liberty, he feared, could too easily lead a nation, in the name of liberty, to deny the liberties of others. In his speech before the Senate on June 27, 1854, Smith condemned the expansionist doctrines that, to his mind, distorted the name of liberty:

Never has there been so self-deceived a nation as our own. That we are a nation for liberty is among our wildest conceits. We are not a nation for liberty. I refer not, now, to the terrible blot of slavery upon our country.

I refer to our pride. No proud man is for liberty. No proud nation is for liberty. Liberty—precious boon of Heaven—is meek and reasonable. She admits, that she belongs to all—to the high and the low; the rich and the poor; the black and the white—and, that she belongs to them all equally. The liberty, for which a proud man contends, is a spurious liberty; and such is the liberty, for which a proud nation contends. It is tyranny; for it invades and strikes down equal rights. But true liberty acknowledges and defends the equal rights of all men, and all nations.

The Congressional arguments of Hiram Bell, Representative from Ohio, criticized manifest destiny's emphasis on ends rather than means. Bell demanded what policy expansionists might devise that would bring Cuba into the United States without the price of war. He questioned the tendency of Democratic leaders to insist that the country acquire peacefully what he thought it could acquire only through war. He stressed the fact that the nation could not pursue peace with Spain at the same time that it sought the annexation of Cuba. He insisted that the American people overwhelmingly preferred peace. In his speech of January 10, 1853, Bell offered a profound criticism of the Monroe Doctrine as the basis of American action in the Western Hemisphere. The nation had no choice, he said, but to pursue its concrete interests wherever they might be, not what some Americans would term its manifest destiny. Bell insisted that the United States enjoyed phenomenal success because it had followed the dictum of the Founding Fathers which limited objectives abroad largely to irreducible national interests. He even questioned the value Cuba would contribute to the United States and expressed doubt that the Cuban population, even, its white leadership, had any interest in American political principles. He concluded that if the United States embarked on expansion it should do so to the north—toward Canada—if it indeed could do so peacefully, where an Anglo-Saxon people had some knowledge and appreciation of democratic institutions.

. . . WE have been told by honorable members of this House, that the people of this country were for annexation of Cuba;

From *Congressional Globe* (32nd Cong., 2nd Sess., 1853), Appendix, pp. 58–60.

that they were for progress; and they were for the extension of the country; and even some have gone so far, without a limit as regards time, as to express themselves in favor of taking the balance of Mexico. That may all be right; but I would inquire of honorable gentlemen who entertain those sentiments, and send them abroad, upon what pretext are we to acquire this territory? Why are we talking about the conquest of Cuba? Perhaps some gentlemen may say that they are not in favor of a war; why, then, are we—the representatives of this nation—sending abroad to the world an expression of the legislative branch of this Government, that we are in favor of taking possession of territory to which we admit we have no right, and to the acquisition of which we have not the shadow of a pretext? I ask you, Mr. Chairman, if that is a portion of the present Democratic creed? Are we in a state of war with Spain? No, sir. On the contrary, we are at peace, and professing the most amicable relations toward that Government. How, then, are we to have an opportunity of accomplishing what it is said upon this floor the people of this country are in favor of? Are we to hatch up some pretext for disturbance with that country? Why, it would seem to look like it. And, sir, what effect would such a state of things have upon our national character, but to dishonor it in the opinion of all christendom? I stand here, as one of the Representatives of this House, of this nation, and especially of the State from whence I come, to protest against all such doctrines. I tell you, sir,—and in doing so, I would wish to send it abroad throughout the length and bredth of this and other lands,—that these are not the sentiments of the people of this country. They never have been the sentiments of our people, and I trust they never will.

We hear it said in high places that we are to acquire all this territory—that we are to aggrandize ourselves by the acquisition of that which does not now belong to us, and of which there is no possible evidence that we have any right to assume to claim. Why, they say it is our destiny as a nation—*our manifest*

destiny! Why, sir, I have heard of spiritual rappers, and I believe they affect to reveal destiny; but I would like to know if,
at this day, we are to risk the future policy of this Government
upon the pretended revelations of this class of impostors? If not,
shall we sanction these schemes of unlimited annexation of territory, under the plea of "destiny," which have at least as sandy
a foundation as those taught by the delusions of the class just
referred to? I hope not, sir. But, Mr. Chairman, if we were to
pursue and adopt this policy which is suggested as our interest
and as our *manifest destiny*—if we were to assume that we were
to become the possessors of Cuba, would it not be well to cast
about us before we settled down upon the fact that such is our
manifest destiny as a nation, and ascertain how we are going to
acquire it? Are we to acquire that island by conquest or by
treaty, or other peaceful arrangements? The consideration of
these questions requires us to look at the policy the Government
must adopt to accomplish the proposed object by either means.

The first is, is it the interest or the duty of this nation to
pursue the course of policy recommended by and carried out in
the administration of Washington, and the fathers of this country, and continued from the organization of this Government
down to the present time; or are we to change that course of
policy which has rendered us so prosperous as a nation, and
launch our boat upon the wide and boundless ocean of annexation and conquest? We must adopt one or the other. Why, sir,
what, in former times, was considered the republican, the democratic, the national doctrines and interests of this country?
Was a peaceful administration of the Government repudiated?
Where colonial possessions sought? Were entangling alliances
with any nations recommended as the policy beneficial to the
Republic? No, sir. The opposite policy was inculcated, and
practicaly carried out by the framers of the Government; and
in the pursuit of that policy, this nation has grown to be what
it is, where every citizen is proud to be known as an American
citizen, wherever he may be found. In whatever quarter of the

world he may be, those stars and stripes, with their ample folds, protect him, and secure to him his rights. I say the advocates of this new doctrine must adopt one of these two courses of policy. If they are in favor of abandoning the policy of Washington, and of changing the entire policy of the country, and seek by conquest the extension of our territorial limits, and as a consequence withholding the necessary protection and promotion of the interests of our people at home, who have the first claims upon our Government and its sympathies, and who are already under our control,—if they are prepared to say they are in favor of changing the policy, and abandoning the doctrines of Washington and Jefferson, and Madison and Monroe, Adams and Jackson, I trust they will be willing to abandon also all claim to the name they have so proudly heretofore sought to be known by, whether it be Whig or of the old line Democrat.

Again, I would request of those persons who advocate this new policy, to look a little at the results and effects of that policy. Will Cuba be acquired and annexed, and form a part of this Government, without a war? No, sir; the correspondence between the Ministers of France, England, and the Government of the United States has already settled that. . . .

Mr. Chairman. I would not pretend to say but what the time may come when it may be necessary for this country to hold Cuba; and not only Cuba, but other islands of the ocean, and other countries. I do not know why we should have our attention so exclusively turned to the Island of Cuba. Why, sir, what is there in that island that should absorb our whole attention? If we could have her peaceably, and at our own option, and take her to-day, would it be a blessing to us? I think not. I am bold to declare that I believe that if we could have Cuba without war, with all the advantages and disadvantages to this Government, it would be a curse—an injury, and prejudicial to our institutions.

But, sir, I wish to read the opinions of a southern man, the editor of the Charleston Mercury, as described in his own language, of his opposition to the acquisition of Cuba, even if it could be acquired peaceably. His language is as follows:

Besides, in what condition would Cuba be to justify her admission into the Union? There is a white population, native to the island, or permanently settled, amounting to near six hundred thousand, (double that of the white population of South Carolina, in a territory little larger than our State,) not one of whom ever exercised a political franchise, or ever took a share in public affairs, other than to submit to the power and shout around the chariot wheels of established authority. We proposed to drive out all those who have ever held rule; and of those who have heretofore only had experience of unquestioning submission, we propose to make a democratic republic, and this in the face of two hundred thousand free blacks, and four hundred thousand slaves, freshly imported from Africa. Among all the recent abortive attempts at free governments in Europe, was there a single one commenced under such desperate auspices as this? Is it not absolutely certain that to preserve order in such a community, an army would be necessary? And where there was an army for the purpose of domestic peace and civil rule, could there be a State? Would we admit into the Union a State which had no power of self government, but was in the hands of the United States Army and Navy? . . .

It is now proposed by the advocates of that measure, that we shall take that class of population, and make them a part and parcel of this country—a class of people worse than slaves, more vicious and less informed—and that is claimed by some to be democratic doctrine. What, attach a class of people, that so far as they have any knowledge, are antagonistic in their principles, their prejudices, and their feelings, to every principle of this republican Government! They come is as copartners! That, sir, may be the democracy of the present day, but it was not the doctrine of our forefathers.

But, sir, there is a country and there is a people competent for self-government, that are prepared to take upon themselves the responsibilities of free men, and which we may find for our interest to receive among us—I mean peaceably—and allow them to become a part and parcel of this country, and I care not how soon. I refer, Mr. Chairman, to the whole British possessions upon the north, containing an area of two millions two hundred and fifty-two thousand three hundred and ninety-five square miles. There is something worth looking at. There are two millions six hundred and fifty-two thousand people, bone, as it were, of our bone, flesh of our flesh, deriving their origin from the same Angle-Saxon source, a large class of them disciplined in that school which is calculated to train them up as independent freemen, and all anxious and ready to come into the possession of enjoyment of those great principles which we are now enjoying. I say it may be for our advantage to acquire that country and that people, if we can peaceably. They are near three millions, scattered over a large territory, sufficient in extent to make several States, and possessing as healthy a climate, and a large part of it as rich a soil as any in the world. Then, sir, by the accomplishment of that matter, and the attaching it as a part of this Union, you banish all the vast expense of maintaining fortifications upon your northern borders, and save the millions of dollars now thrown away in keeping up your customhouses upon the borders of the North; you give to yourself the free navigation of that mighty stream of the North, the St. Lawrence. You give to yourself the sole control and command of that channel, and of that bay at its mouth, with the great chain of lakes or inland seas which nature has formed for a ready and direct communication and navigation for the commerce of this northern territory to the ocean; and you welcome near three millions of people, who are like brethren, into this family, to form a part and parcel of this Republic, thereby adding strength and vigor to the body-politic.

Here, sir, is something worth turning the attention of this nation to. Great Britain can have no object in holding the rule over these northern colonies, except national pride.

Meet this question fairly frankly, and say to them, we are not going to war with you for this territory and these people; you have rights to all these. Would not the interests of these great nations be promoted and benefited by your withdrawing all claim to them, or over the territory, and permit these colonies, if they choose, to become a part and parcel of this Government, and link their destinies with this nation?

By the annexation of this territory on the north you would increase your navigation and commercial interest, and the value of every foot of soil in that country fourfold. It is a fact known to those who reside on our northern frontier, that land within Canada of the same quality as land within the United States, separated only by a line of the nature of the one which divides our townships, is only worth about one quarter as much as the land within the United States; and what portion of this Union has a greater interest in the accomplishment of that object than the States of Ohio, Indiana, Illinois, Michigan, Vermont, Maine, New Hampshire, Pennsylvania, and New York? Consider for a moment those great lakes to the north, inland seas, surrounded by territory under the control of our own Government, instead of the limit of a midway channel. The accomplishment of that object peacefully will strengthen this Union, and add to its power and influence. The annexation of that territory to this Union (to use terms of gentlemen) Destiny has ordained, and it will ere long take place.

Mr. Chairman, I hope the time will not arrive when it may become necessary for this nation to engage in a war for the acquistion or possession of Cuba, or any other island or territory, for the purpose of preserving and protecting our maritime interests or national rights. But, should that time ever come, whether brought about by European diplomacy or aggression upon our rights by any Power, whether upon this or other continents, I am free to declare that I should wish this Government to act under the circumstances as our national interests and honor should require; and if necessary to preserve these to acquire more territory—Cuba or other territory south or north, without regard to any local interests—I would say as an American citizen, let it be done. But now, we are at profound peace with all the nations of the world, and have no cause to quarrel about the possessions of Cuba, or any other territory. I am opposed to the agitation of this question at the present time, because I believe it will be a renewal of those exciting scenes witnessed within the past few years. I am well satisfied that no Union man, and especially no man who has felt that he was the advocate of those compromise measures which, it was said, were calculated to preserve the Union, can be in favor of the agitation of questions that will result in bringing about the sectional feeling that existed at the passage of those measures. The annexation, or the attempt to annex Cuba, must inevitably bring up those questions which were pending during the Congress preceding this one, and which were then intended to be settled by the series of measures called the compromise. It will not do to say or imagine that those questions will not arise again under similar circumstances. . . .

36 Milton S. Latham

Expansion "without

Noise and Bluster"

Milton S. Latham, Representative from California, harbored a quiet confidence regarding the nation's destiny. In a speech before the House on June 14, 1854, Latham noted the remarkable internal and external growth of the United States. He was convinced that the general decline of Spanish power in the New World destined Cuba for membership in the American Union. He believed that an adequate passage of time was the only element necessary to bring this about. Latham ridiculed the rhetoric of the spokesmen for manifest destiny in Congress. He accused them of relying on words in lieu of policy, and of employing a meaningless rhetoric to create objectives outside the country without assuming any responsibility for national action. He saw clearly that Congressional resolutions, reflecting as they did "a sort of rhetorical fillibusterism," were concerned less with influencing governments abroad than with influencing parties at home. The control of foreign policy, he said, belonged to the Executive. Those who propounded the doctrines of manifest destiny could lay no claim to statesmanship; they conveyed no great or lasting thought, but merely the folly uppermost at the time. The nation's real destiny, great as it was, worked quietly. It was founded, not on the power, but on the country's civilizing role, operating less through war and conquest than through the unfolding of time and opportunity.

MR. CHAIRMAN: In the midst of peace and general prosperity, while commerce and agriculture are flourishing, and every species of industry meeting its adequate reward, the apprehensions of the country have been excited, and our business community startled by various resolutions introduced into this House and the Senate, by gentlemen who seem to have paid especial attention to our foreign relations, and to whose peculiar keeping it would seem an overruling Providence had confided the destinies of this great Republic!

While we have been taught for years past to believe in manifest destiny, while historical events, which we all witnessed, have contributed to create and strengthen that belief, in which the present generation is now regularly educated, we are permitted to behold and admire in this House the instruments through which God's providence is to work out the problem of peopling and civilizing this great continent! The men who have received this special mission are before us, and their inspiration is manifest from their high resolve! Anticipating the future, and strong in the consciousness of the power to be

From *Congressional Globe* (33rd Cong., 1st Sess., 1854), Appendix, pp. 948–954.

acquired by us within the next two or three decades, they have, in a parliamentary way—the only one left open to their ambition and patriotism—laid down the principles which ought to guide our intercourse with foreign nations, and the policy which we ought to pursue at this particular crisis. It is not enough for the people of this country to believe in a particular doctrine; they must have faith also in the Apostles.

. . . We are a free, happy, prosperous people; we have from the beginning of our national existence increased in wealth, population, and territory; and this is steadily, without interruption, that not only ourselves but the world believes in our mission. Under the benign influence of our institutions, each State of our Federal galaxy is developing its gigantic resources, while the energy and enterprise of the whole people is constantly employed in discovering new sources of wealth and prosperity, and new scope for the exercise of their varied faculties. We have not only added vast possessions to our magnificent domain; but we have cultivated, peopled, and improved them without diminishing the rapid development of what was already ours by the labor and valor of our ancestors.

As a child outgrows its garments, we have outgrown our ancient metes and bounds, and are even now daily increasing in wealth and power. What we are too young to do to-day, we are ripe for tomorrow, and will accomplish, without extraordinary effort, the day after. We, of all the nations of the world, are best able to bide our time. We have a continent before us, and the future is ours without dispute. . . .

Spanish power in the Gulf of Mexico has only had a nominal existence: It cannot grow and expand while the mother country is declining in influence and power, and while the United States are constantly increasing in territory and population. Cuba is a mere Spanish farm, badly worked by tenants for its lazy and thriftless proprietors. It must, in due time, come under the hammer, and there is no party which can afford to pay as high a price for it as ourselves. In case of sale, we shall certainly be the most liberal purchaser, and pay enough for it to discourage all the mortgages and every other species of claim upon the estate. At the same time we cannot allow it to pass from its present properietors into other hands. We certainly cannot allow any one else to bid for it; and, in case of accident or death of the present holder, would feel ourselves called upon to administer upon the estate. But we have no desire to take forcible possession of it, by *expelling* the present owner, as long as we can live in peace with him; in other words, so long as we can preserve neighborly relations with him without inconvenience and injury to *our* property. Let Spain make the most of the island—let her dispose of that revenue as she pleases, we have no right or disposition to meddle with it; but if she choose to lay it waste, because she thinks we desire its acquisition, or makes a nuisance of it to spite us, then let us give her warning that we will not submit to so barbarous a course, and that, in case she persists in it, we will forcibly enter upon the farm and abate the nuisance. In doing this in a quiet, orderly, direct way, without noise or bluster, we shall preserve our own self-respect, and be justified in the eyes of the civilized world.

. . . I would not resort to force till all peaceable means are exhausted, and then I should only have recourse to force after being fully prepared to do so, and without leaving to Spain or any other Power the faintest hope of a protracted struggle. Success should not only be probable, it should be certain; and that not only in the end, but at the very outset. It is not my business here to enter into details to show that, in the present state of our Army and Navy, it would be rash, to use no stronger term, to expose our martial reputation to the chances and casualties of a war with a second-rate power; that it would be fatal to the prestige we have acquired during the brief period of our national existence, if obliged to declare war against Spain, for the possession of the Island of Cuba, our military and naval operations against the island were to meet with a check, and our forces were to be repulsed. . . .

Sir, when we strike a blow for Cuba, it must be but one, and when it is struck, Cuba must be irretrievably ours; it must be an "accomplished fact," and, as such, invite no interference on the part of other nations. This cannot be done by noisy and wordy diplomacy, or by resolutions in Congress which give the world warning of our intentions, our hopes, and prospects, and the pith and substance of our foreign policy. Nor can it be accomplished by long and formidable discussions in this or the other House, by an attitude of definance assumed by members or Senators, or by a display of patriotic eloquence whose thunder it is perhaps calculated shall shake the foundation of Moro Castle. These speeches may do a great deal of harm; but they can do no good. They do harm by revealing our position to those who are opposed to us, and by exciting our own people to acts of lawless violence, destructive to themselves, and disreputable to us as a nation. Sir, the power to make war is one of the highest attributes of sovereignty, which cannot be usurped by any body of men within the State; it belongs to the collective power of the Government, and a usurpation of it, even by a sovereign State of this Union, would be a revolution and an act of treason to the Confederacy. From these remarks you may infer, sir, that, though a "Cuban annexationist" *sub modo,* I am opposed to fillibusterism *in toto.* . . .

The President of the United States, by the Constitution, has the initiative in all matters belonging to our foreign relations, and it is necessary that it should be so. It is he who selects his Cabinet ministers, and who appoints our diplomatic agents abroad. Foreign ministers and diplomatic agents confer with him and the Secretary of State on all matters concerning their respective Governments, and there is no other way of making propositions to foreign Governments, or of receiving propositions from them except through the medium of the President of the United States and the agents and ministers of his choice.

Resolutions may be introduced into Congress for the purpose of attacking or defending the Administration, or with a view to stimulate public opinion, by a sort of rhetorical fillibusterism, as I have already remarked; but it cannot coerce the Administration into the adoption of a course which it deems unwise or inexpedient at a particular time. As a general rule, these resolutions can only embarrass negotiations, and render the position of our diplomatic agents abroad more difficult than before. They seldom leave sufficient margin for their discretion, and render diplomacy either entirely impossible or superfluous; while, at the same time, they accomplish nothing. Supposing the President and his Cabinet, from all the information at their command, judge that the time for action has not yet arrived, what, then, can possibly be the effect of a resolution introduced into this House, urging him to act, except to establish an antagonism between the Administration and Congress, that exposes our weakness to foreign powers, and our want of harmony to the opposition at home? But suppose the resolutions conform to the views and objects of the Administration, what good can they do it? In what respect will they render its acts more prompt, steady, and effective? Sir, these resolutions are not *intended* to affect parties abroad; they are intended to influence parties at home, and must necessarily fail of every other object. If some distinguished statesman, known and respected at home and abroad—a man of wide-spread reputation for ability and experience—were to introduce them, they might have some weight with European statesmen, carrying with them the assent and approbation of the American people; but if it were to appear, or be suspected, that these resolutions were introduced merely to afford members an opportunity of talking about our foreign affairs to Buncombe, then it is clear that no attention would be paid to them abroad, and that they could only lessen the dignity and importance which would otherwise attach to propositions made to foreign Powers, in the regular diplomatic way, by the responsible agents of the Government.

Congress cannot compel the Executive to make war, if the latter is unwilling to do it; nor can it compel him to make peace, except by refusing the supplies for the Army and Navy. When Congress shall judge that the President has done wrong, or that he neglects his duty to the country, then the Constitution prescribes the mode of impeaching him. I know no other official act by which Congress may interfere with the foreign policy of the Administration. This House is not even invested with the ratifying power, bestowed, from wise, considerations, on the Senate; it merely cooperates with the other branches of the Government in the execution of treaties which it has no power to originate. It is necessary for the preservation of our institutions that the powers vested in the different branches of our Government should be kept separate and distinct, and that neither branch should assume the duties and responsibilities of the other. That is the only way which they are sure to move in harmony with each other, and yet preserve that mutual independence of each other which is of the essence of republican government, and insures the greatest amount of efficiency.

But it is said, Mr. Chairman, that we are impelled to these things by "manifest destiny," and I more than half believe it. I believe there are men who, watching the current of popular opinion, are willing to be borne along by its waves, and called "*leaders;*" while there are others who have not the courage to resist it, even if the current were to carry them over a precipice. These men, whoever they may be, and whatever station they may occupy, can lay no claims to statesmanship; they are mere jobbers and journeymen politicians. Men of great mind and character impress their thoughts on the age in which they live; but our political jobbers bear the imprint of the popular passion of the hour, and follow the age in whatever folly may be uppermost at the time. Sir, destiny is nothing but the final result of all the tendencies of our moral and physical system; it is the effect of the laws of nature, whose operations, whenever they are most beneficent, are silent and secret, not boisterous and noisy, by fits and starts.

Sir, we have, no doubt, a proud mission to fulfill; but it does not merely consist of the acquisition of territory, and in the extension of power. Our calling is a far nobler one. We must cultivate, fertilize, regenerate the regions which become subject to our rule. It is not merely power, but our institutions and laws, and our higher civilization which we are bound, in the course of time, to carry to the most remote part of this continent and to its neighboring islands. Unless we can regenerate and Americanize what we acquire or annex, we shall not improve on former conquerors, but only add another page to the long catalogue of national crime in the world's history. Now, it appears to me that our Federal institutions are admirably calculated to promote the gradual process of assimilation, and to render that homogeneous for all practical purposes of government, which, from its foreign origin and other local causes, would forever remain separate and distinct, and, on that account incapable of producing great results. Our true expansive power consists in this power of assimilation. We do not conquer and coerce; we attract, assimilate, reorganize. The former is never accomplished without consuming power, and thereby producing waste; the latter is a natural process, combining elements for a new and higher purpose, and adding to the strength of all by giving them unity of direction.

. . . Born at an advanced stage in the history of the world, and conceived of strong and healthy parents, our confederacy of States gave, even at its birth, assurance of its future greatness. Like Hercules, we killed two serpents in our cradle, placed there by the ignorance of the world, not by the malice of a jealous goddess. We destroyed the wordly power of the established church by banishing it from the political arena, and reared in its place the temple of religious tolerance; and we expelled royalty as a useless and expensive political institution. But in assuming the supreme direction of our own affairs, we committed no injustice to others. We did not infringe on the rights of the church or the clergy, in religious matters; and in suppressing royalty, applied merely to our own use, what was already our own.

With the Declaration of Independence of the United States,

a new great historical era was ushered into the world, not only for individual freedom, but of liberal political *association,* insuring and guarantying that freedom. It is the peculiar *mode* of associating men for the exercise of power which constitutes American freedom and signalizes its superiority over all other Governments; and the distribution of power, under this new association, formed by our ancestors on the rubbish of the old association of church and State, marks as distinct a progress in the *art* of government as the Revolution itself manifested in men's ideas. True to the doctrine of the Revolution, that all Governments derive their just power from the consent of the governed, the framers of our Constitution had a care to interest all equally in its maintenance, and to let all share proportionally in its power. Not only were the different Colonies who had achieved their independence, united into a representative Confederacy, but individually elevated into sovereign and independent States; delegating to the Federal Government no other powers than those named in the Constitution. While all share in the power of the Federal Government through their representatives in Congress, each has supreme control over the administration of its own affairs, and enjoys, within its own limits, the privileges and immunities of sovereignty. Herein consists the immeasurable superiority of our Confederacy of States, over any system of government as yet recorded in history, and its adaptation to indefinite expansion without loss of power. We have, in less than a century, tripled the number of states composing our Federal Union, without suffering the least perturbation in our political system; and our population has increased from three to twenty-five millions, without complicating the system, or meeting with the least difficulty in the application of the principles which were laid down by our forefathers with so much vigor and simplicity.

Nor is this all. We have, during that brief period, received among us so large a portion of foreign immigrants that their number exceeds alone our whole population during the revolutionary war, and would in itself suffice to add a dozen States to our Confederacy. The monthly arrivals of immigrants from foreign countries average now fifty thousand for the single port of New York, and not less than a million in all the ports of the United States, *per annum.* All these men, and women, and children, or most of them, come here with the crudest political and social notions, with habits and customs not unfrequently repugnant to our own, and speaking languages which, until they become familiar with our idiom, prevent them from communicating freely with our people. Yet in a few years we absorb this whole vast accretion to our strength. The immigrants have become assimilated with us in labor and enterprise, in customs and manners, in thought and language, and in political ideas. What other people than our own, what other Government than ours, could thus invite all the political, social, and religious heretics of the world to come and sojourn among them, without fear of being ultimately contaminated and overwhelmed? This power of absorbing and assimilating foreign elements is the strongest proof of our historical mission; or, if gentlemen would rather have it, our "manifest destiny;" for it affords the strongest evidence of the superior energy of our people, and the practical advantages of our political institutions. We absorb to elevate; we rule by bestowing on the governed a share of political power. Sir, we are destined to expand by assimilation, and by elevating those who have been misgoverned and oppressed to the rank of free men; and if we have the power to do that with millions of Europeans who flock to our shores; if our example is constantly working revolutions and changes in the political and social condition of the Old World, why should we not possess the same faculty here, when less powerful States, and more misgoverned people are eager to share the blessings of our institutions and laws? Rome, and the people of Romanic origin, French, Spaniards, Portuguese, have never colonized; they merely planted or transplanted power; the people of England cultivated and improved, but held, and still hold, their colonies in subjection; the Americans alone, for the first time in the history of the world, elevate and regenerate those over whom they extend their sway. We conquer that we may raise the conquered to an equality with ourselves; we annex to assimilate others with us in a higher scale of humanity.

These faculties and purposes of ours constitute our patent right to extend our power and influence over the constituent; it is our mission to install new life into the feeble and misgoverned people grown on the *débris* of Spanish power in America, and of the colonies still subjected to the withering influence of her rule; but we must not expect to fulfill it in an age, or in a century. We must not be tempted to absorb faster than we can assimilate; and avoid convulsions, when the same object may be attained by the attractive force of our institutions, and the decomposing process now going on among our neighbors. Time, which is against them, operates in our favor; and there is no stride that any European Power can take, and no combination that any of those Powers can form, capable of thwarting our destiny. This country is destined to support a larger population than all Europe—a population of happy, thinking, self-relying men; not a mixture of beggers and princes. And it will, despite the heterogeneous elements which contribute to it, be a population full of national, American sentiments, energetic, free, martial; whose friendship and good will will be an object of solicitude with the different nations of Europe. The present war in Europe will excite a bitterness of feeling, and beget new national jealousies, which will continue long after the conclusion of peace, and be an effectual bar to all joint operations against our growing power. England, France, and Spain may yet sojourn in different parts of America. We are at home in it, and shall arrange our household as we please.

But while I have full faith in the mission of our country; while I have no apprehension of any successful interference of any European Power, or any combination of them, in the affairs of this continent; while I believe, if I may indulge in the expression, in the invincibility of the United States, I yet wish that, in our conduct as a great nation, we avoid everything like provocation to the weaker Powers. Let our mission be accomplished by as few collisions with our neighbors as possible. Let the world be convinced of our mission as we are, and let the world see that that mission is compatible with public justice. . . .

37

The Ostend Manifesto: The Case for "the immediate acquisition" of Cuba

When Franklin Pierce entered the White House in March, 1853, it marked a return of the Democratic Party to power. The new President reflected his party's enthusiasm for Cuba when he declared in his inaugural address:

The policy of my Administration will not be controlled by any timid forebodings of evil from expansion. Indeed . . . our attitude as a nation and our position on the globe render the acquisition of certain possessions not within our jurisdiction eminently important for our protection, if not in the future essential for preservation of the rights of commerce and the peace of the world.

Indeed, it seemed the President would quickly convert such purpose into policy, for he despatched Pierre Soulé to Madrid to negotiate for Cuba. The Louisiana Senator, known for his determination to see the island enter the empire of the United States, carried the nation's apparent intentions forward another step by making a number of proannexationist speeches before embarking for Spain. Yet the administration could formulate no genuine program for acquiring Cuba without committing the country to war against Spain, a course which, as representative Latham pointed out (Document 36) was not a legitimate or acceptable choice. In his instructions of July 23, 1853, Secretary of State Marcy warned Soulé that the administration favored continued peace with Spain but would oppose vigorously any transfer of Cuba to another European power.

Marcy instructed Soulé to make no effort to acquire Cuba as the Pierce administration understood that Spain would reject any offer of money for the island. However, the seizure of the *Black Warrior*, an American steamer, by Spanish officials in Cuba on February 28, 1854, gave the impatient Soulé an opportunity to fish in troubled waters. Jumping ahead of Marcy's instructions, the American Minister presented an ultimatum to the Spanish government—a demand for an indemnity of $300,000, the dismissal of all responsible for the *Black Warrior* affair, and an answer within forty-eight hours. The Spanish government, to avert a crisis, dealt directly and fairly with the owners of the ship. All but the ardent expansionists let the crisis pass quickly into history. However, using the *Black Warrior* incident as an excuse, the administration requested Soulé in April to offer Spain $130 million for Cuba. When Soulé failed to establish a negotiating position with the Madrid government, the Pierce administration suggested that he arrange a conference on the Cuban question with the American Ministers at London and Paris. The men met at Ostend, a seaport city in Belgium. The deliberations of this group produced the notorious Ostend Manifesto in October, 1854, one of the key manifest destiny documents of the fifties.

. . . WE have arrived at the conclusion, and are thoroughly convinced, that an immediate and earnest effort ought to be made by the government of the United States to purchase Cuba from Spain at any price for which it can be obtained, not exceeding the sum of $.

The proposal should, in our opinion, be made in such a manner as to be presented through the necessary diplomatic forms to the Supreme Constituent Cortes about to assemble. On this momentous question, in which the people both of Spain

From *House Ex. Doc. No. 93* (33rd Cong., 2nd Sess., 1854–1855), pp. 127–132.

and the United States are so deeply interested, all our proceedings ought to be open, frank, and public. They should be of such
a character as to challenge the approbation of the world.

We firmly believe that, in the progress of human events, the
time has arrived when the vital interests of Spain are as seriously
involved in the sale, as those of the United States in the purchase, of the island and that the transaction will prove equally
honorable to both nations.

Under these circumstances we cannot anticipate a failure,
unless possibly through the malign influence of foreign powers
who possess no right whatever to interfere in the matter.

We proceed to state some of the reasons which have brought
us to this conclusion, and, for the sake of clearness, we shall
specify them under two distinct heads:

1. The United States ought, if practicable, to purchase Cuba
with as little delay as possible.

2. The probability is great that the government and cortes of
Spain will prove willing to sell it, because this would essentially
promote the highest and best interests of the Spanish people.

Then, 1. It must be clear to every reflecting mind that, from
the peculiarity of its geographical position, and the considerations attendant on it, Cuba is as necessary to the North
American republic as any of its present members, and that it
belongs naturally to that great family of States of which the
Union is the providential nursery.

From its locality it commands the mouth of the Mississippi
and the immense annually increasing trade which must seek
this avenue to the ocean.

On the numerous navigable streams, measuring an aggregate
course of some thirty thousand miles, which disembogue themselves through this magnificent river into the Gulf of Mexico,
the increase of the population within the last ten years amounts
to more than that of the entire Union at the time Louisiana was
annexed to it.

The natural and main outlet to the products of this entire

population, the highway of their direct intercourse with the Atlantic and the Pacific States, can never be secure, but must ever be endangered whilst Cuba is a dependency of a distant power in whose possession it has proved to be a source of constant annoyance and embarrassment to their interests.

Indeed, the Union can never enjoy repose, nor possess reliable security, as long as Cuba is not embraced within its boundaries.

Its immediate acquisition by our government is of paramount importance, and we cannot doubt but that it is a consummation devoutly wished for by its inhabitants.

The intercourse which its proximity to our coasts begets and encourages between them and the citizens of the United States, has, in the progress of time, so united their interests and blended their fortunes that they now look upon each other as if they were one people and had but one destiny.

Considerations exist which render delay in the acquisition of this island exceedingly dangerous to the United States.

The system of immigration and labor lately organized within its limits, and the tyranny and oppression which characterize its immediate rulers, threaten an insurrection at every moment which may result in direful consequences to the American people.

Cuba has thus become to us an unceasing danger, and a permanent cause of anxiety and alarm.

But we need not enlarge on these topics. It can scarcely be apprehended that foreign powers, in violation of international law, would interpose their influence with Spain to prevent our acquisition of the island. Its inhabitants are now suffering under the worst of all possible governments, that of absolute despotism, delegated by a distant power to irresponsible agents, who are changed at short intervals, and who are tempted to improve the brief opportunity thus afforded to accumulate fortunes by the basest means.

As long as this system shall endure, humanity may in vain demand the suppression of the African slave trade in the island.

This is rendered impossible whilst that infamous traffic remains an irresistible temptation and a source of immense profit to needy and avaricious officials, who, to attain their ends, scruple not to trample the most sacred principle under foot.

The Spanish government at home may be well disposed, but experience has proved that it cannot control these remote depositaries of its power.

Besides, the commercial nations of the world cannot fail to perceive and appreciate the great advantages which would result to their people from a dissolution of the forced and unnatural connexion between Spain and Cuba, and the annexation of the latter to the United States. The trade of England and France with Cuba would, in that event, assume at once an important and profitable character, and rapidly extend with the increasing population and prosperity of the island.

2. But if the United States and every commercial nation would be benefited by this transfer, the interests of Spain would also be greatly and essentially promoted.

She cannot but see what such a sum of money as we are willing to pay for the island would effect in the development of her vast natural resources.

Two-thirds of this sum, if employed in the construction of a system of railroads, would ultimately prove a source of greater wealth to the Spanish people than that opened to their vision by Cortez. Their prosperity would date from the ratification of the treaty of cession . . . .

Whilst two-thirds of the price of the island would be ample for the completion of her most important public improvements, she might, with the remaining forty millions, satisfy the demands now pressing so heavily upon her credit, and create a sinking fund which would gradually relieve her from the overwhelming debt now paralyzing her energies.

Such is her present wretched financial condition, that her best bonds are sold upon her own Bourse at about one-third of their par value; whilst another class, on which she pays no interest, have but a nominal value, and are quoted at about one-sixth of the amount for which they were issued. Besides, these latter are held principally by British creditors who may, from day to day, obtain the effective interposition of their own government for the purpose of coercing payment. Intimations to that effect have been already thrown out from high quarters, and unless some new source of revenue shall enable Spain to provide for such exigencies, it is not improbable that they may be realized.

Should Spain reject the present golden opportunity for developing her resources, and removing her financial embarrassments, it may never again return.

Cuba, in its palmiest days, never yielded her exchequer, after deducting the expenses of its government, a clear annual income of more than a million and a half dollars. These expenses have increased to such a degree as to leave a deficit chargeable on the treasury of Spain to the amount of six hundred thousand dollars.

In a pecuniary point of view, therefore, the island is an incumbrance, instead of a source of profit, to the mother country.

Under no probable circumstances can Cuba ever yield to Spain one per cent. on the large amount which the United States are willing to pay for its acquisition. But Spain is in imminent danger of losing Cuba, without renumeration.

Extreme oppression, it is now universally admitted, justifies any people in endeavoring to relieve themselves from the yoke of their oppressors. The sufferings which the corrupt, arbitrary, and unrelenting local administration necessarily entails upon the inhabitants of Cuba, cannot fail to stimulate and keep alive that spirit of resistance and revolution against Spain, which has, of late years, been so often manifested. In this condition of affairs it is vain to expect that the sympathies of the people of the United States will be warmly enlisted in favor of their oppressed neighbors.

We know that the President is justly inflexible in his determination to execute the neutrality laws; but should the Cubans themselves rise in revolt against the oppression which they suffer, no human power could prevent citizens of the United States and liberal minded men of other countries from rushing to their assistance. Besides, the present is an age of adventure, in which restless and daring spirits abound in every portion of the world.

It is not improbable, therefore, that Cuba may be wrested from Spain by a successful revolution; and in that event she will lose both the island and the price which we are now willing to pay for it—a price far beyond what was ever paid by one people to another for any province.

It may also be remarked that the settlement of this vexed question, by the cession of Cuba to the United States, would forever prevent the dangerous complications between nations, to which it may otherwise give birth.

It is certain that, should the Cubans themselves organize an insurrection against the Spanish government, and should other independent nations come to the aid of Spain in the contest, no human power could, in our opinion, prevent the people and government of the United States from taking part in such a civil war in support of their neighbors and friends.

But if Spain, dead to the voice of her own interest, and actuated by stubborn pride and a false sense of honor, should refuse to sell Cuba to the United States, then the question will arise, What ought to be the course of the American government under such circumstances?

Self-preservation is the first law of nature, with States as well as with individuals. All nations have, at different periods, acted upon this maxim. Although it has been made the pretext for committing flagrant injustices, as in the partition of Poland and other similar cases which history records, yet the principle itself, though often abused, has always been recognized.

The United States have never acquired a foot of territory except by fair purchase, or, as in the case of Texas, upon the free and voluntary application of the people of that independent State, who desired to blend their destinies with our own.

Even our acquisitions from Mexico are no exception to this rule, because, although we might have claimed them by the right of conquest in a just war, yet we purchased them for what was then considered by both parties a full and ample equivalent.

Our past history forbids that we should acquire the island of Cuba without the consent of Spain, unless justified by the great law of self-preservation. We must, in any event, preserve our own conscious rectitude and our own self-respect.

Whilst pursuing this course we can afford to disregard the censures of the world, to which we have been so often and so unjustly exposed.

After we shall have offered Spain a price for Cuba far beyond its present value, and this shall have been refused, it will then be time to consider the question, does Cuba, in the possession of Spain, seriously endanger our internal peace and the existence of our cherished Union?

Should this question be answered in the affirmative, then by every law, human and divine, we shall be justified in wresting it from Spain if we possess the power; and this upon the very same principle that would justify an individual in tearing down the burning house of his neighbor if there were no other means of preventing the flames from destroying his own home.

Under the circumstances we ought neither to count the cost nor regard the odds which Spain might enlist against us. We forbear to enter into the question, whether the present condition of the island would justify such a measure? We should, however, be recreant to our duty, be unworthy of our gallant forefathers, and commit base treason against our posterity, should we permit Cuba to be Africanized and become a second St. Domingo, with all its attendant horrors to the white race, and suffer the flames to extend to our own neighboring shores, seriously to endanger or actually to consume the fair fabric of our Union.

We fear that the course and current of events are rapidly tending towards such a catastrophe. We, however, hope for the best, though we ought certainly to be prepared for the worst.

We also forbear to investigate the present condition of the questions at issue between the United States and Spain. A long series of injuries to our people have been committed in Cuba by Spanish officials and are unredressed. But recently a most flagrant outrage on the rights of American citizens and on the flag of the United States was perpetrated in the harbor of Havana under circumstances which, without immediate redress, would have justified a resort to measures of war in vindication of national honor. That outrage is not only unatoned, but the Spanish government has deliberately sanctioned the acts of its subordinates and assumed the responsibility attaching to them.

Nothing could more impressively teach us the danger to which those peaceful relations it has ever been the policy of the United States to cherish with foreign nations are constantly exposed than the circumstances of that case. Situated as Spain and the United States are, the latter have forborne to resort to extreme measures.

But this course cannot, with due regard to their own dignity as an independent nation, continue; and our recommendations, now submitted, are dictated by the firm belief that the cession of Cuba to the United States, with stipulations as beneficial to Spain as those suggested, is the only effective mode of settling all past differences and of securing the two countries against future collisions. . . .

38   John Slidell

"To cast the eye upon the map was sufficient to predict its destiny"

James Buchanan was one of the signers of the Ostend Manifesto, and his ambitions toward Cuba did not diminish with the acquisition of presidential responsibility. His second annual message of December, 1858, reminded Congress of the island's strategic and commercial importance to the United States. He found, in Spain's refusal to give redress for the alleged attacks of Cuban officials on the persons and property of the United States, the occasion for dwelling on the subject at great length. American claims against the Cuban government amounted to $128,635, of which Cuban officials agreed to pay one third. In Havana endless procrastination developed as a result of the Spanish regulation that compelled American citizens to present all complaints against Cuba through the United States Minister in Madrid. On previous occasions the United States had attempted to acquire Cuba through honorable negotiations; Buchanan had no desire to acquire the island by any other means. Before he would attempt another negotiation, however, Buchanan laid the issue before Congress to acquire the means to make an advance to the Spanish government immediately after signing the treaty.

In the following report, dated January 24, 1859, the Senate Committee on Foreign Relations viewed the ultimate acquisition of Cuba as the fixed policy of the United States. There existed differences of opinion only as to the time, mode, and conditions of obtaining it. "The law of our national existence is growth," ran the report. "We cannot, if we would, disobey it." If Spain could not hold the island much longer, three alternatives remained for its disposal: First, possession by a European power; second, independence (which it could never, in fact, maintain); and, third, annexation by the United States. But how was the United States to acquire it? Conquest would be expensive. The remaining alternative was to purchase it through negotiation, a procedure which the committee believed the United States could pursue with success. If the President could not negotiate for Cuba without the previous sanction of Congress, it was still not clear what either he or the Congress would do if Spain refused to sell Cuba to the United States.

IT is not considered necessary by your committee to enlarge upon the vast importance of the acquisition of the island of Cuba by the United States. To do so would be as much a work of

---

From *Senate Report*, No. 351 (35th Cong., 2nd Sess., 1858–1859), Serial 994, pp. 1–20.

supererogation as to demonstrate an elementary problem on mathematics, or one of those axioms of ethics or philosophy which have been universally received for ages. The ultimate acquisition of Cuba may be considered a fixed purpose of the United States, a purpose resulting from political and geographical necessities which have been recognized by all parties and all administrations, and in regard to which the popular voice has been expressed with a unanimity unsurpassed on any question of national policy that has heretofore engaged the public mind.

The purchase and annexation of Louisiana led, as a necessary corollary, to that of Florida, and both point with unerring certainty to the acquisition of Cuba. The sparse and feeble population of what is now the great west called in 1800 for the free navigation of the Mississippi, and the enforcement of the right of deposit at New Orleans. In three years not only were these privileges secured, but the whole of the magnificent domain of Louisiana was ours. Who now doubts the wisdom of a measure which at the time was denounced with a violence until then unparalleled in our political history?

From the day we acquired Louisiana the attention of our ablest statesmen was fixed on Cuba. What the possession of the mouth of the Mississippi had been to the people of the west that of Cuba became to the nation. To cast the eye upon the map was sufficient to predict its destiny. A brief reference will show the importance attached to the question by our leading statesmen, and the steadiness and perseverance with which they endeavored to hasten the consummation of so vital a measure. . . .

John Quincy Adams while Secretary of State under Mr. Monroe, in a despatch to Mr. Nelson, our minister at Madrid, of the 28th April, 1823, says:

"In the war between France and Spain, now commencing, other interests, peculiarly ours, will in all probability be deeply involved. Whatever may be the issue of this war as between those two European powers, it may be taken for granted that the dominion of Spain upon the American continents, north and south, is irrecoverably gone. But the islands of Cuba and Porto Rico still remain nominally and so far really dependent upon her, that she yet possesses the power of transferring her own dominion over them, together with the possession of them, to others. These islands, from their local position and natural appendages to the North American continent, and one of them, Cuba, almost in sight of our shores, from a multitude of considerations, has become an object of transcendent importance to the commercial and political interests of our Union. Its commanding position, with reference to the Gulf of Mexico and the West India seas, the character of its population, its situation midway between our southern coast and the island of St. Domingo, its safe and capacious harbor of the Havana, fronting a long line of our shores destitute of the same advantage, the nature of its productions and of its wants, furnishing the supplies and needing the returns of a commerce immensely profitable and mutually beneficial, give it an importance in the sum of our national interests with which that of no other foreign territory can be compared and little inferior to that which binds the different members of this Union together. Such, indeed, are, between the interests of that island and of this country, the geographical, commercial, moral, and political relations formed by nature, gathering in the process of time, and even now verging to maturity, that, in looking forward to the probable course of events, for the short period of half a century, it is scarcely possible to resist the conviction that the annexation of Cuba to our federal republic will be indispensable to the continuance and integrity of the Union itself. . . .

Mr. Buchanan, in his despatch to Mr. R. M. Saunders, of June 17, 1848, said: "With these considerations in view, the President believes that the crisis has arrived when an effort should be made to purchase the island of Cuba from Spain, and he has determined to intrust you with the performance of this most delicate and important duty. The attempt should be made, in the first instance, in a confidential conversation with the Spanish minister for foreign affairs; a written offer might produce an absolute refusal in writing, which would embarrass us hereafter in the acquisition of the island. Besides, from the incessant changes in the Spanish cabinet and policy, our desire to make the purchase might thus be made known in an official form to foreign governments, and arouse their jealousy and active opposition. Indeed, even if the present cabinet should think favorably of the proposition, they might be greatly embarrassed by having it placed on record; for in that event it would almost certainly, through some channel, reach the opposition and become the subject of discussion in the Cortes. Such delicate negotiations, at least in their incipient stages, ought always to be conducted in confidential conversation, and with the utmost secrecy and despatch."

"At your interview with the minister for foreign affairs you might introduce the subject by referring to the present distracted condition of Cuba, and the danger which exists that the population will make an attempt to accomplish a revolution. This must be well known to the Spanish government. In order to convince him of the good faith and friendship towards Spain with which this government has acted, you might read to him the first part of my despatch to General Campbell, and the order issued by the Secretary of War to the commanding general in Mexico and to the officer having charge of the embarkation of our troops at Vera Cruz. You may then touch delicately upon the danger that Spain may lose Cuba by a revolution in the island, or that it may be wrested from her by Great Britain, should a rupture take place between the two countries arising out of the dismissal of Sir Henry Bulwer, and be retained to pay the Spanish debt due to the British bond-holders. You might assure him that, whilst this government is entirely satisfied that Cuba shall remain under the dominion of Spain, we should in any event resist its acquisition by any other nation. And, finally, you might inform him that, under all these circumstances, the

President had arrived at the conclusion that Spain might be willing to transfer the island to the United States for a fair and full consideration. You might cite as a precedent the cession of Louisiana to this country by Napoleon, under somewhat similar circumstances, when he was at the zenith of his power and glory. I have merely presented these topics in their natural order, and you can fill up the outline from the information communicated in this despatch, as well as from your own knowledge of the subject. Should the minister for foreign affairs lend a favorable ear to your proposition, then the question of the consideration to be paid would arise, and you have been furnished with information in this despatch which will enable you to discuss that question.

"The President would be willing to stipulate for the payment of one hundred millions of dollars. This, however, is the maximum price; and if Spain should be willing to sell, you will use your best efforts to purchase it at a rate as much below that sum as practicable. In case you should be able to conclude a treaty, you may adopt as your model, so far as the same may be applicable, the two conventions of April 30, 1803, between France and the United States, for the sale and purchase of Louisiana. The seventh and eighth articles of the first of these conventions ought, if possible, to be omitted; still, if this should be indispensable to the accomplishment of the object, articles similar to them may be retained." . . .

From these and other extracts that might be presented it is manifest that the ultimate acquisition of Cuba has long been regarded as the fixed policy of the United States—necessary to the progressive development of our system. All agree that the end is not only desirable but inevitable. The only difference of opinion is as to the time, mode, and conditions of obtaining it.

The law of our national existence is growth. We cannot, if we would, disobey it. While we should do nothing to stimulate it unnaturally, we should be careful not to impose upon ourselves a regimen so strict as to prevent its healthful development. The tendency of the age is the expansion of the great powers of the world. England, France, and Russia, all demonstrate the existence of this pervading principle. Their growth, it is true, only operates by the absorption, partial or total, of weaker powers— generally, of inferior races. So long as this extension of territory is the result of geographical position, a higher civilization, and greater aptitude for government, and is not pursued in a direction to endanger our safety or impede our progress, we have neither the right nor the disposition to find fault with it. Let England pursue her march of conquest and annexation in India, France extend her dominions on the southern shores of the Mediterranean, and advance her frontiers to the Rhine, or Russia subjugate her barbarous neighbors in Asia; we shall look upon their progress, if not with favor, at least with indifference. We claim on this hemisphere the same privilege that they exercise on the other—

"Hanc veniam petimusque damusque vicissim."

In this they are but obeying the laws of their organization. When they cease to grow they will soon commence that period of decadence which is the fate of all nations as of individual man.

The question of the annexation of Cuba to the United States, we repeat, is a question but of time. The fruit that was not ripe when John Quincy Adams penned his despatch to Mr. Forsyth, (it has not yet been severed by violence from its native tree, as he anticipated,) is now mature. Shall it be plucked by a friendly hand, prepared to compensate its proprietor with a princely guerdon? or shall it fall decaying to the ground?

As Spain cannot long maintain her grasp on this distant colony, there are but three possible alternatives in the future of Cuba: First, possession by one of the great European powers. This we have declared to be incompatible with our safety, and have announced to the world that any attempt to consummate it will be resisted by all the means in our power. When first we made this declaration we were comparatively feeble. The struggle would have been fearful and unequal; but we were prepared to make it at whatever hazard. That declaration has often been repeated since. With a population nearly tripled, our financial resources and our means, offensive and defensive, increased in an infinitely larger proportion, we cannot now shrink from an issue that all were then ready to meet.

The second alternative is the independence of the island. This independence could only be nominal; it never could be maintained in fact. It would eventually fall under some protectorate, open or disguised. If under ours, annexation would soon follow as certainly as the shadow follows the substance. An European protectorate could not be tolerated. The closet philanthropists of England and France would, as the price of their protection, insist upon introducing their schemes of emancipation. Civil and servile war would soon follow, and Cuba would present, as Hayti now does, no traces of its former prosperity, but the ruins of its once noble mansions. Its uncontrolled possession by either France or England would be less dangerous and offensive to our southern States than a pretended independent black empire or republic.

The third and last alternative is annexation to the United States. How and when is this to be effected? By conquest or negotiation? Conquest, even without the hostile interference of another European power than Spain, would be expensive, but with such interference would probably involve the whole civilized world in war, entail upon us the interruption, if not the loss, of our foreign trade, and an expenditure far exceeding any sum which it has ever been contemplated to offer for the purchase of Cuba. It would, besides, in all probability, lead to servile insurrection, and to the great injury or even total destruction of the industry of the island. Purchase, then, by negotiation seems to be the only practicable course; and, in the opinion of the committee, that cannot be attempted with any reasonable prospect of success, unless the President be furnished with the means which he has suggested in his annual message, and which the bill proposes to give him. . . .

The act of 3d March, 1847, "making further appropriation to bring the existing war with Mexico to a speedy and honorable conclusion," has been adopted as the model on which the present bill is framed. Its preamble states that "whereas, in the adjustment of so many complicated questions as now exist between the two countries, it may possibly happen that an expenditure of money will be called for by the stipulations of any treaty which may be entered into, therefore the sum of three millions of dollars be, and the same is hereby, appropriated, to enable the President to conclude a treaty of peace, limits, and boundaries, with the republic of Mexico; to be used by him in the event said treaty, when signed by the authorized agents of the two governments and duly ratified by Mexico, shall call for the expenditure of the same, or any part thereof." The bill now reported, appropriates, under the same conditions, thirty millions of dollars to make a treaty with Spain for the purchase of the island of Cuba. . . .

Much has been said of the indelicacy of this mode of proceeding. That the offer to purchase will offend the Spanish pride, be regarded as an insult, and rejected with contempt. That instead of promoting a consummation that all admit to be desirable, it will have the opposite tendency. If this were true it would be a conclusive argument against the bill, but a brief consideration will show the fallacy of these views. For many years our desire to purchase Cuba has been known to the world. Seven years since President Fillmore communicated to Congress the instructions to our ministers on that subject, with all the correspondence connected with it. In that correspondence will be found three letters from Mr. Saunders, detailing conversations held with Narvaez and the minister of foreign relations, in which he notified them of his authority to treat for the purchase of Cuba, and while the reply was so decided as to preclude him from making any direct proposition, yet no intimation was given that the suggestion was offensive. And why should it be so? We simply say to Spain, you have a distant possession, held by a precarious tenure, which is almost indispensable to us for the protection of our commerce, and may, from its peculiar position, the character of its population, and the mode in which it is governed, lead, at any time, to a rupture which both nations would deprecate. This possession, rich though it be in all the elements of wealth, yields to your treasury a net revenue not amounting, on the average of a series of years, to the hundredth part of the price we are prepared to give you for it. True, you have heretofore refused to consider our proposition, but circumstances are changing daily. What may not have suited you in 1848 may now be more acceptable. Should a war break out in Europe, Spain can scarcely hope to escape being involved in it. The people of Cuba naturally desire to have a voice in the government of the island. They may seize the occasion to proclaim their independence, and you may regret not having accepted the rich indemnity we offer.

But even these arguments will not be pressed upon unwilling ears. Our minister will not broach the subject until he shall have good reason to believe that it will be favorably entertained. Such an opportunity may occur when least expected. Spain is the country of *coups-d'etat* and pronunciamentos. The all-powerful minister of today may be a fugitive to-morrow. With the forms of a representative government, it is, in fact, a despotism sustained by the bayonet. A despotism tempered only by frequent, violent, and bloody revolutions. Her financial condition is one of extreme embarrassment. A crisis may arise when even the dynasty may be overthrown unless a large sum of money can be raised forthwith. Spain will be in the position of the needy possessor of land he cannot cultivate, having all the pride of one to whom it has descended through a long line of ancestry, but his necessities are stronger than his will; he must have money. A thrifty neighbor whose domains it will round off is at hand to furnish it. He retains the old mansions, but sells what will relieve him from immediate ruin.

The President, in his annual message, has told us that we should not, if we could, acquire Cuba by any other means than honorable negotiation, unless circumstances which he does not anticipate render a departure from such a course justifiable, under the imperative and overruling law of self preservation. He also tells us that he desires to renew the negotiations, and it may become indispensable to success that he should be intrusted with the means for making an advance to the Spanish government immediately after the signing of the treaty, without awaiting the ratification of it by the Senate. This, in point of fact, is an appeal to Congress for an expression of its opinion on the propriety of renewing the negotiation. Should we fail to give him the means which may be indispensable to success, it may well be considered by the President as an intimation that we do not desire the acquisition of the island.

It has been asserted that the people of Cuba do not desire a transfer to the United States. If this were so it would present a very serious objection to the measure. The evidence on which it is based is, that on the receipt of the President's message, addresses were made by the municipal authorities of Havana, and other towns, protesting their devotion to the crown, and their hostility to the institutions of the United States. Any one who has had an opportunity of observing the persuasive influence of the bayonet in countries where it rules supreme will know how much value to attach to such demonstrations of popular sentiment. There can be no doubt that an immense majority of the people of Cuba are not only in favor, but ardently desirous of annexation to the United States. It would be strange indeed, if they were not so; deprived of all influence even in the local affairs of the island—unrepresented in the Cortes—governed by successive hordes of hungry officials sent from the mother country to acquire fortunes to be enjoyed at home, having no sympathy with the people among whom they are mere sojourners, and upon whom they look down as inferiors; liable to be arrested at any moment on the most trifling charges; tried by military courts or submissive judges, removable at pleasure, punished at the discretion of the captain general, they would be less than men if they were contented with their yoke. But we have the best authority from the most reliable sources, for asserting that nearly the entire native population of Cuba desires annexation. . . .

. . . There is good reason to suppose that the slaves considerably exceed the estimated number, it having been, until very recently, the interest of the proprietor to under state it. The feeling of caste or race, is as marked in Cuba as in the United States. The white creole is as free from all taint of African blood as the descendant of the Goth on the plains of Castile. There is a numerous white peasantry, brave, robust, sober, and honest, not yet perhaps prepared intelligently to discharge all the duties of the citizen of a free republic, but who, from his organization physical and mental, is capable of being elevated by culture to the same level with the educated Cubans, who, as a class, are as refined, well-informed, and fitted for self-government as men of any class of any nation can be who have not inhaled with their breath the atmosphere of freedom.

Many of them accompanied by their families are to be met with every summer at our cities and watering places, observing and appreciating the working of our form of government and its marvelous results; many seeking until the arrival of more auspicious days an asylum from the oppression that has driven them from their homes; while hundreds of their youths in our schools and colleges are acquiring our language and fitting themselves hereafter, it is to be hoped, at no distant day, to play a distinguished part in their own legislative halls, or in the counsels of the nation.

These men, who are the great proprietors of the soil, are opposed to the continuance of the African slave trade, which is carried on by Spaniards from the peninsula, renegade Americans, and other adventurers from every clime and country, tolerated and protected by the authorities of Cuba of every grade. . . .

There is another aspect in which this proposition may be viewed which is deserving of serious consideration. It is forcibly put in the President's annual message that the multiplied aggressions upon the persons and property of our citizens by the local authorities of Cuba for many years past present, in the person of the captain-general, the anomaly of absolute power to inflict injury without any corresponding faculty to redress it. He can, almost in sight of our shores, confiscate, without just cause, the property of an American citizen, or incarcerate his person; but if applied to for redress, we are told that he cannot act without consulting his royal mistress, at Madrid. There we are informed that it is necessary to await the return of a report of the case which is to be obtained from Cuba; and many years elapse before it is ripe for decision. These delays in most instances amount to an absolute denial of justice. And even when the obligation of indemnity is admitted, the state of the treasury or a change of ministry is pleaded as an excuse for withholding payment. This would long since have justified us in resorting to measures of reprisal that would have necessarily led to war and ultimately resulted in the conquest of the island. Indeed such is the acute sense of those wrongs prevailing among our people, that nothing but our rigid neutrality laws, which, so long as they remain unrepealed or unmodified, a chief magistrate, acting under the sanction of his official oath to see that the laws be faithfully executed, is bound to enforce, has prevented the success of organized individual enterprises that would long ere this have revolutionized the island. It is in part, probably, for this cause that the President has recommended the policy which this bill embodies, and the world cannot fail to recognize in its adoption by Congress a determination to maintain him in his efforts to preserve untarnished our national character for justice and fair dealing.

The effects of the acquisition of Cuba will be no less beneficial in its commercial, than in its political and moral aspects. The length of the Island is about seven hundred and seventy miles, with an average breadth of about forty miles, comprising an area of 31,468 square miles. The soil is fertile, climate genial, and its ports the finest in the world. Havana is more familiarly known to us, for apart from our extensive trade, which employs several hundred American vessels, thousands of our citizens have touched at that port in our steamers on their way to California or New Orleans. They have all carried away with them vivid recollections of its magnificent harbor, and have breathed ardent prayers that their next visit should be hailed by the stars and stripes floating from the Moro. And yet Cuba can boast of several other harbors equally safe and more extensive than that of Havana.

In 1855 the importations, by official custom-house returns, were $31,216,000, the exports $34,803,000. As duties are levied on exports as well as imports, there can be no exaggeration in these returns, and the real amount is undoubtedly considerably larger.

When we consider that more than two-thirds of the whole area of the island is susceptible of culture, and that not a tenth part of it is now cultivated, we may form some idea of the immense development which would be given to its industry by a change from a system of monopoly and despotism to free trade and free institutions. Whatever may be the enhanced cost of production, caused by the increased value of labor, it will be nearly if not quite compensated by the removal of export duties; and of those levied on articles produced in the United States, which are now by unjust discrimination virtually excluded from consumption. . . .

Since the reference of the bill to the committee, the President, in response to a resolution of the Senate requesting him, if not incompatible with the public interest, to communicate to the Senate any and all correspondence between the government of the United States and the government of her Catholic Majesty relating to any proposition for the purchase of the island of Cuba, which correspondence has not been furnished to either

House of Congress, informs us that no such correspondence has
taken place which has not already been communicated to Congress. He takes occasion to repeat what he said in his annual
message, that it is highly important, if not indispensable to the
success of any negotiation for the purchase, that the measure
should receive the previous sanction of Congress. . . .

PART SEVEN

CENTRAL AMERICA AND BEYOND

39   Stephen A. Douglas

Do not "prescribe Limits"
to the area of expansion

Edward Everett's letter of December, 1852 (Document 34), in-augurated a new burst of interest not only in Cuba but also in Central America. What anchored the question of Cuba to that of Central America in 1853 was the rebirth of anti-British feeling in the United States, especially among those Democratic expansionists who be-lieved that England and English policy were opposed to American expansion and progress on every front. The self-denial clause in the Clayton-Bulwer Treaty of 1850 merely exaggerated the dangers of British encroachment in the Caribbean and, as usual, exposed the Whig leadership to attack because of its alleged pro-British policies. Expansionists in 1853, focusing on the entire region of the Caribbean, could not be unmindful of the fact that John M. Clayton, as Whig Secretary of State in 1850, had agreed to a clause in his treaty with Sir Henry Lytton Bulwer, British Minister to the United States, which declared that neither Great Britain nor the United States "will ever . . . occupy or colonize either Nicaragua, Costa Rica, the Mosquito Coast, or any part of Central America. . . ."

For many Americans the acquisition of California in 1848 created an unprecedented interest in proposals for building an interoceanic canal through Central America that might speed and facilitate Amer-ican commerce and communication between the east and west coasts of the United States. At the moment, the Nicaragua route seemed the most promising, but this brought the United States into conflict with Britain along the Mosquito coast, which included the entire eastern shore of Nicaragua with the important port of San Juan del Norte. This city lay at the eastern terminus of the proposed canal route. Early in 1848 British forces took the port and renamed it Greytown.

In June, 1849, however, Elijah Hise, the diplomatic agent for the United States in Nicaragua, signed a treaty with the Nicaraguan government which gave the United States the exclusive right to build and control an interoceanic canal across the country. The treaty, if agreed to by the United States, would have brought the United States and Britain into direct conflict at the mouth of the San Juan River. Clayton, then Secretary of State, attempted to avoid a struggle for position with England by denying that the United States had any desire to acquire a canal monopoly in Central America. Next, Clayton made it clear that he desired British cooperation in protecting and maintaining a neutral canal. To guarantee the mutual interests of Britain and the United States in a Nicaraguan canal, Clayton suggested to the London government that both governments abandon all their claims to Nicaragua, Costa Rica, and the Kingdom of the Mosquito Indians. Lord Palmerston, the British Prime Minister, agreed to this proposal. In February, 1850, the Clayton-Bulwer Treaty, with the famous self-denying clause, was signed in Washington.

Clearly, the intensity of Democratic criticism toward the Clayton-Bulwer Treaty would have a direct relationship to the alleged American interest in acquiring territory in Central America. By 1853 Clayton had returned to the Senate. There he was called upon to defend his treaty, and he continued to deny that the United States had any territorial interests in Central America. Stephen A. Douglas, always an ardent expansionist, took up the question in his speech of March 10, 1853. He declared that he had no desire to annex any portion of Central America, but he reminded the Senate of the progress of the previous fifty years that had carried the United States across the continent. What the nation's ultimate destiny might be he could not predict, but he did not want it limited by self-denying clauses in treaties regarding the North American continent. Douglas's condemnation of Clayton's treaty revolved on the idea of the boundless future of the United States.

. . . THIS question of a canal in Nicaragua, when negotiations were pending to give it to us, was so much an American ques-

---

From *Congressional Globe* (32nd Cong., 3rd Sess., 1853), Appendix, pp. 261–262.

tion that the English Government was not entitled to be consulted. England not consent! She will consent to allow you to do that just so long as you consent to allow her to hold Canada, the Bermudas, Jamaica, and her other American possessions. I hope the time has arrived when we will not be told any more that Europe will not consent to this, and England will not consent to that. I heard that argument till I got tired of it when we were discussing the resolutions for the annexation of Texas. I heard it again on the Oregon question, and I heard it on the California question. It has been said on every occasion whenever we have had an issue about foreign relations, that England would not consent; yet she has acquiesced in whatever we have had the courage and the justice to do. And why? Because we kept ourselves in the right. England was so situated with her possessions on this continent, that she dare not fight in an unjust cause. We would have been in the right to have accepted the privilege of making this canal, and England would never have dared to provoke a controversy with us. I think the time has come when America should perform her duty according to our own judgment, and our own sense of justice, without regard to what European Powers might say with respect to it. I think this nation is about of age. I think we have a right to judge for ourselves. Let us always do right, and put the consequences behind us.

But, sir, I do not wish to detain the Senate upon this point, or to prolong the discussion. I have a word or two to say in reply to the remarks of the Senator from Delaware [John M. Clayton] upon so much of my speech as related to the pledge in the Clayton and Bulwer treaty, never to annex any portion of that country. I objected to that clause in the treaty, upon the ground that I was unwilling to enter into a treaty stipulation with any European Powers in respect to this continent, that we would not do, in the future, whatever our duty, interest, honor, and safety, might require in the course of events. The Senator infers that I desire to annex Central America because I was unwilling to give a pledge that we never would do it. He reminded me that there was a clause in the treaty with Mexico containing the stipulation, that in certain contingencies we would never annex any portion of Mexico. Sir, it was unnecessary that he should remind me of that provision. He has not forgotten how hard I struggled to get that clause out of the treaty where it was retained in opposition to my vote. Had the Senator given me his aid then to defeat that provision in the Mexican treaty, I would be better satisfied now with his excuse for having inserted a still stronger pledge in his treaty. But having advocated that pledge then, he should not attempt to avoid the responsibility of his own act by citing that as a precedent. I was unwilling to bind ourselves by treaty for all time to come never to annex any more territory. I am content for the present with the territory we have. I do not wish to annex any portion of Mexico now, I did not wish to annex any part of Central America then, nor do I at this time.

But I cannot close my eyes to the history of this country for the last half century. Fifty years ago the question was being debated in this Senate whether it was wise or not to acquire any territory on the west bank of the Mississippi river, and it was then contended that we could never, with safety, extend beyond that river. It was at that time seriously considered whether the Alleghany mountains should not be the barrier beyond which we should never pass. At a subsequent date, after we had acquired Louisiana and Florida, more liberal views began to prevail, and it was thought that perhaps we might venture to establish one tier of States west of the Mississippi; but in order to prevent the sad calamity of an undue expansion of our territory, the policy was adopted of establishing an Indian Territory, with titles in perpetuity, all along the western border of those States, so that no more new States could possibly be created in that direction. That barrier could not arrest the onward progress of our people. They burst through it, and passed the Rocky Mountains, and were only arrested by the waters of the Pacific. Who, then, is prepared to say that in the progress of events, having met with the barrier of the ocean in our western course, we may not be compelled to turn to the north and to the south for an outlet? . . .

. . . I have not forgotten that a respectable portion of this body, but a few years ago thought it would be preposterous to bring a country so far distant as California, and so little known, into the Union. But it has been done, and now since California has become a member of the Confederacy, with her immense commerce and inexhaustible resources, we are told that the time will never come when the territory lying half way between our Atlantic and Pacific possessions will be desirable. Central America is too far off, because it is half way to California, and on the main, direct route, on the very route upon which you pay your Senators and Representatives in Congress their mileage in coming to the capital of the nation. The usual route of travel, the public highway, the half-way house from one portion of the country to the other, is so far distant that the man who thinks the time will ever come when we will what it is deemed a madman.

. . . But I am not mistaken in saying that the Senator on yesterday did ridicule the idea that we were ever to want any portion of Central America. He was utterly amazed, and in his amazement inquired where were these boundaries ever to cease? He wanted to know how far we were going, and if we were going to spread over the entire continent. I do not think we will do it in our day, but I am not prepared to prescribe limits to the area over which Democratic principles may safely spread. I know not what our destiny may be. I try to keep up with the spirit of the age, to keep in view the history of the country, see what we have done, whither we are going, and with what velocity we are moving, in order to be prepared for those events which it is not in the power of man to thwart.

You may make as many treaties as you please to fetter the limits of this giant Republic, and she will burst them all from her, and her course will be onward to a limit which I will not venture to prescribe. Why the necessity of pledging your faith that you will never annex any more of Mexico? Do you not know that you will be compelled to do it; that you cannot help it; that your treaty will not prevent it, and that the only effect it will have will be to enable European Powers to accuse us of bad faith when the act is done, and associate American faith and Punic faith as synonymous terms? What is the use of your guarantee that you will never erect any fortifications in Central America; never annex, occupy, or colonize any portion of that country? How do you know that you can avoid doing it? If you make the canal, I ask you if American citizens will not settle along its line; whether they will not build up towns at each terminus; whether they will not spread over that country, and convert it into an American State; whether American principles and American institutions will not be firmly planted there? And I ask you how many years you think will pass away before you will find the same necessity to extend your laws over your own kindred that you found in the case of Texas? How long will it be before that day arrives? It may not occur in the Senator's day, nor mine. But so certain as this Republic exists, so certain as we remain a united people, so certain as the laws of progress which have raised us from a mere handful to a mighty nation, shall continue to govern our action, just so certain are these events to be worked out, and you will be compelled to extend your protection in that direction.

Sir, I am not desirous of hastening the day. I am not impatient of the time when it shall be realized. I do not wish to give any additional impulse to our progress. We are going fast enough. But I wish our public policy, our laws, our institutions, should keep up with the advance in science, in the mechanic arts, in agriculture, and in everything that tends to make us a great and powerful nation. Let us look the future in the face, and let us prepare to meet that which cannot be avoided. Hence I was unwilling to adopt that clause in the treaty guaranteeing that neither party would ever annex, colonize, or occupy any portion of Central America. I was opposed to it for another reason. It was not reciprocal. Great Britain had possession of the Island of Jamaica. Jamaica was the nearest armed and fortified point to the terminus of the canal. Jamaica at present commands the entrance of that canal; and all that Great Britain desired was, inasmuch as she had possession of the only place commanding the canal, to procure a stipulation that no other Power would ever erect a fortification nearer its terminus. That stipulation is equivalent to an agreement that England may fortify, but that we never shall. Sir, when you look at the whole history of that question, you will see that England, with her farseeing, sagacious policy, has attempted to circumscribe and restrict and restrain the free action of this Government. When was it that Great Britain seized the possession of the terminus of this canal? Just six days after the signing of the treaty which secured to us California! The moment that England saw that by the pending negotiations with Mexico, California was to be acquired, she collected her fleets, and made preparations for the seizure of the port of San Juan, in order that she might be gate-keeper on the public highway to our own possessions on the Pacific. Within six days from the time we signed the treaty, England seized by force and violence the very point now in controversy. Is not this fact conclusive as to her motives? Is it not clear that her object was to obstruct our passage to our new possessions? Hence I do not sympathize with that feeling which the Senator expressed yesterday, that it was a pity to have a difference with a nation so FRIENDLY TO US AS ENGLAND. Sir, I do not see the evidence of her friendship. It is not in the nature of things that she can be our friend. It is impossible she can love us. I do not blame her for not loving us. Sir, we have wounded her vanity and humbled her pride. She can never forgive us. But for us, she would be the first Power on the face of the earth. But for us, she would have the prospect of maintaining that proud position which she held for so long a period. We are in her way. She is jealous of us, and jealousy forbids the idea of friendship. England does not love us; she cannot love us, and we do not love her either. We have some things in the past to remember that are not agreeable. She has more in the present to humiliate her that she cannot forgive.

I do not wish to administer to the feeling of jealousy and rivalry that exists between us and England. I wish to soften and smooth it down as much as possible; but why close our eyes to the fact that friendship is impossible while jealousy exists? Hence England seizes every island in the sea and rock upon our coast where she can plant a gun to intimidate us or to annoy our commerce. Her policy has been to seize every military and naval station the world over. Why does she pay such enormous sums to keep her post at Gibraltar, except to keep it *"in terrorem"* over the commerce of the Mediterranean? Why her enormous expense to maintain a garrison at the Cape of Good Hope, except to command the great passage on the way to the Indies? Why is she at the expense to keep her position on the little barren island Bermuda, and the miserable Bahamas, and all the other islands along our coast, except as sentinels upon our actions? Does England hold Bermuda because of any profit it is to her? Has she any other motive for retaining it except jealousy which stimulates hostility to us? Is it not the case with all of her possessions along our coast? Why, then, talk about the friendly bearing of England towards us when she is extending that policy every day? New treaties of friendship, seizure of islands, and erection of new colonies in violation of her treaties, seem to be the order of the day. In view of this state of things, I am in favor of meeting England we meet a rival; meet her boldly, treat her justly and fairly, but make no humiliating concession even for the sake of Peace. She has as much reason to make concessions to us as we have to make them to her. I would not willingly disturb the peace of the world; but, sir, the Bay Island colony must be discontinued. It violates the treaty. . . .

40 Samuel S. Cox

"The Law of Growth" demands intervention in Mexico and Central America

Representative Samuel S. Cox of Ohio defined and defended America's destiny to the south with appeals to the doctrine of natural growth. The nation, he declared in the following speech, delivered in the House on January 18, 1859, was derelict in not living up to its expansionist potential. He declared that Cuba, Mexico, and Central America had emerged as proper objectives of American expansionism, for these countries, he believed, must obey the law of political gravitation. "They must," he emphasized, "become confiscate to the decrees of Providence!" The United States, however, was marking time; it was not moving forward. Cox pointed specifically to the United States' interest in Cuban trade and the canal routes through Central America, all of which the country must control if it wished to guarantee its security and commerce in the Western Hemisphere. Only by intervening in the affairs of Cuba, Mexico, and Central America, Cox declared in this speech, would the United States "conform to the law of growth, by which alone we have become great, and by which alone we shall become greater."

. . . THERE is a logic in history which is as inexorable as fate. A writer in the time of the first Stuart, gave as the number of the kingdoms of Christendom, five-and-twenty. But there was no mention of three of the principal nations, Russia, Austria, and

From *Congressional Globe* (35th Cong., 2nd. Sess., 1859), pp. 430–434.

Prussia, in their present condition; nor of twelve other nations out of the twenty now enumerated in Europe; nor of the thirty petty sovereignties now extant in Germany. Within two centuries, the transatlantic continent has changed its territory and rulers beyond all the caprices of fancy; yet by a law as fixed as that which returns the seasons or rolls the starts.

The disquieting aspect of cisatlantic politics signifies the consummation of territorial changes on this continent, long predicted, long delayed, but as certain as the logic of history!

Some of these changes in Europe have been through decay, dissolution, and disintegration. Spain was once the Peru and Mexico of the Old World. The ancestors of the hidalgo were enslaved in the mines of Spain by Rome and Carthage. But now, Leon, Aragon, Castile, Navarre, Toledo, Galicia, and Granada, once separate kingdoms, have lost their isolated glory, and are only known as the props of the "worm-eaten throne of Spain." The stronger races of Europe have consolidated their power by extending its sphere and absorbing the weaker neighboring nations. England, Ireland, and Scotland, by union, have transplanted their colonies and multiplied their strength; and Russia has clasped the half of Europe and Asia in its strong embrace, until, from the furthest West we perceive the conflict of their civilization in the furthest East!

These are but illustrations of a law from which America is not exempt. Not more surely will northern Africa, and indeed the countries whose boundaries are coincident with the Mediterranean, become French; western and northern Asia become Russian; and southern and central Asia become English, than this continent-become American! The law which commands this is higher law than congressional enactment. If we do not work with it, it will work in spite of us. This law may be expressed thus:

That the weaker and disorganized nations must be absorbed by the strong and organized nation. Nationalities of inferior grade must surrender to those of superior civilization and polity!

Whether the races of this continent be in a tribal condition, as our Indians; in a semi-civilized and anarchical condition, as are the Central and South American and Mexican races, they must obey this law of political gravitation. This law drives them to the greater and more illustrious State for protection, happiness, and advancement? Whether the United States go and take them, or they come and ask to be taken, no matter. They must whirl in; throw off their nebulous and uncertain form, and become crystalized into the higher forms of civilization.

The largest expression of this law of annexation, is: That no nation has the right to hold soil, virgin and rich, yet unproducing; no nation has a right to hold great isthmean highways, or strong defenses, on this continent, without the desire, will, or power, to use them. They ought, and must, inure to the advancement of our commerce. They must become confiscate to the decrees of Providence!

In carrying out these designs, we have, from time to time, added territory from France, Spain, and Mexico. We have endeavored to add other territory, which the jealousy of France, Spain, and especially of England, has prevented. It is not my purpose now to rehearse our history in this regard. We may have kept step with our interests and our destiny; but at this juncture, standing on the threshold of this new year, we are only marking time, not moving forward! It is well to inquire whether there is not now upon us, as the assembled expression of this nation, a peculiar duty with respect to this element of our progress. My judgment is, that we are to-day, derelict. We are not up to the enterprise of the nation. If we consider just now the elements of our people, martial, mechanical, intellectual, agricultural, and political, who will doubt but that there are a dozen locomotive Republics already fired up and ready for movement?

The Executive has done his duty. He has boldly followed out his Ostend ideas. He has urged upon us a duty, which being undone, leaves him powerless, and leaves the national enthusiasm and expansion a prey to adventurous raids and seditious propagandists. Had the Thirty-Fourth Congress aided President Pierce in the Black Warrior matter, we should now have representatives from Cuba on this floor!

The President has called our attention to the territory upon our south. Not New Granada—she will come in time. Not Venezuela—she is even yet more vital than New Granada; but the country north of these, and lying between them and us, must be absorbed. For this absorption we must contend, not so much with the people, whose interests will be enhanced by the absorption, but with Spain, France, and England, who have no interests comparable with our own. These interests and antagonisms I propose to consider in this order: First, Cuba; second, Central America; third, Mexico.

As to Cuba, the reasons for its acquisition are well understood by the country. The message has succinctly and ably presented them. Its geographical position gives to the nation which holds it, unless that nation be very weak, a coign of vantage as to which self-preservation forbids us to be indifferent. Our Misssissippi, foreign, and coast-wise trade, now $200,000,000, and in ten years to be $500,000,000, are within its compass; while the island is of little use to Spain, save as a source of revenue, it is to us of incalculable advantage. The nature of the colonial office in Cuba—its power to harm us remedilessly, unless we go to Madrid for remedy; and the final stopping of the slave trade, are reasons well urged by the President. Our unsettled claims, and the many other difficulties growing out of our relations to Spain, demand settlement, but receive none.

How long shall we continue in this condition? During the pleasure of Spain? Is there no redress? Is our every attempt to be construed into a usurpation? What impediments have we to meet? There is one which has since Mr. Polk's time, proved insurmountable—Spanish pride. It is well said by an old poet, that

> Spain gives us pride, which Spain of all the earth
> May freely give, nor fear herself a dearth.

Since then, there has been no curtailment of that pride. True, Spain has now little to be proud of but her recollections. Poor, sensitive, corrupt, she holds to the punctillio of dignity without its substantial energy. If Spain will not sell Cuba to us, because she feels that she will thereby sell her honor, we must insist on her changing its policy. She should keep the island aloof from French intervention. She should preserve its independence. . . .

As to Central America, I do not desire to enter so fully into our relations with this region. . . . We know well the impediment existing in the way of our acquisition there. The Clayton-Bulwer treaty—the diplomatic blunder of the century—stands as a huge gorgon in our path. The policy of its abrogation is conceded; but "how not to do it," seems to have been the practice. The present Executive, in his message of December 8, 1857, bewailed this condition of things. He inherited, as did President Pierce, this treaty of peace, which has proved a treaty of offense. England and the United States have been quarreling over its construction, when its destruction was the most pacific course that could have been adopted. Collateral treaties may be made which will prevent the consequences of an abrupt abrogation of this treaty. Diplomacy is now, we are told, working to this end. . . .

Crampton and Webster tried in 1852 to unravel the web. Then Webster and Molina tried it with the aid of Costa Rica. Then Wheeler and Escobar, acting for Nicaragua, made an effort, which our Government failed to accept. Then Clarendon and Herran, for Honduras, sought to untie the knot; and thus led the way to the Cass-Yrisarri treaty in the fall of 1857, which began *de novo*. Then, a fair treaty was made, allowing us the protectorate of the transit; but through foreign influence it was so modified by Nicaragua as to be unacceptable to our Government. Now, Sir Gore Ouseley, having ceased to be a diplomatic myth here, has gone to the south, where, we trust, something may be done to cancel that part of the Clayton-Bulwer treaty by which we agreed with England to cut our throats, by never "occupying, fortifying, or colonizing, or assuming or exercising any dominion over Nicaragua, Costa Rica, the Mosquito coast, or any part of Central America." We trust that such an arrangement may be made to this end; but my reading of history is vain, if we do not find thrown about this abrogation some clog which the American people will not bear.

The truth is, that we have slept so long, and dreamed so transportingly of our destiny over these regions, that meanwhile Japan and China are opened; Frazer's river becomes an Eldorado; and English and French navies, quitting the attempt on Cronstadt, and tiring of the red storm of the Euxine, display their guns on this continent. Their entente cordiale, as Clarendon said it would be, is extended to this hemisphere; and here we have them! They are, by their presence, if not by their diplomacy, ignoring the far-famed doctrine of Mr. Monroe, which had, when first given, as general a meaning and as practical a use as it ought now to have a specific application. His doctrine was, that the American continents by the free and independent condition which they have assumed and maintain, are henceforth not to be considered as subjects for future colonization or influence by any European Power. . . .

Yet this doctrine is sneered at, as if Monroe's ghost were involved to do a kind of constable's duty, to warn all foreign intruders from this continent. So far as emigration is concerned, this continent is open as day; but no flag, no polity, no institutions, no colonies, no protectorates of Europe, can exist here, without endangering the peace, infringing the rights, or disturbing the order and prospective interests of this continent. Whatever may have been the occasion of the Monroe declaration, its cause is as eternal as liberty, and its consequences will be as progressive as our nation. I care not for its traditionary emphasis. Democrats, at least, can afford to let that go. Is it sound doctrine for the present? If so, it ought to be the enthusiastic sentiment and genius of this Government. If so, let it be no more the jeer of Europe, the swagger of America, but a fact as much a part of our historic life as the Declaration of Independence, which was its procreant source. That doctrine is the law of self-preservation. . . .

But it may be said, why so much risk of war with the combined powers of Europe; why so much anxiety for the Isthmus or Central American route? Not because we are in danger of being cut off from its dominion. That will come if these Central American States remain independent of European constraint. Not because it is the only feasible mode of transit for the great oriental trade between the oceans; for in time there will be rapid and safe transits on our own soil. Not so much because we ought to have and hold the hundred and fifty millions of trade with these Spanish American tropical lands, instead of but ten millions which we now have. But nature never made so narrow an obstacle; one so easily severed, and on which such great commercial and economical results depended, as that at Darien or Nicaragua. She buried mountains and valleys beneath the wave to narrow that neck, and thus expand the bounds of interchange, and encircle the earth with a white zone of argosies.

If New Granada shall be ours—as it should be within a twelvemonth, unless the Congress of Bogota show more honesty and wisdom in settling the claims of our Panama sufferers, than is likely; if New Granada would follow the advice of Gonzales, her attorney general, and enhance her interests by applying for admission to our Union; and if Venezuela would follow the wise inclinations of her patriot chief, General Paez, whose exile here has made him love the land of his home, the more for the prospect of uniting its fortunes with ours; then, indeed, these Central American States, now the football of European diplomacy, must either come to us, or be powdered into nothingness between the industrial movements of the surrounding States. Once let the agriculture of Venezuela be smiled upon by a protecting Government, and her magnificent ports would soon fill with the keels of her elder commerce. Let northern energy blend with her undirected labor, and the gold mines of Upata would gleam with their olden treasures. Let Panama break from her vassalage to her irresponsible rulers, and that mart of the golden age of Spain and her viceroys will teem with a wealth which no buccaneers in a thousand caravels can bear away. These accomplished, and the intermediate States of Nicaragua, Costa Rica, Salvador, Honduras, and Guatemala, will follow, as surely as the sheaf of the summer follows the seed of the spring. The trade of all tropical America would then fall to us naturally by our proximity, and by the variety of our productions with which to barter. These tropical wastes ought to give us coffee, indigo, and cocoa, which are failing in India, as well as the cabinet woods, so much in demand. In return, they will take our flour, pork, machinery, fabrics, and a thousand other articles which they need, and which every State of this Union produces. Our trade, which now counts its hundreds, will then count its millions.

If this Congress has optic nerve enough to look a few years ahead, it will at least start a policy which will secure all the isthmean highways which are so indispensable to our development and power. Its first duty is to repel every attempt of the remotest influence, come from what quarter it may, which may impede this procession of events or arrest our inevitable and legitimate aggrandizement. No nation with one harbor, much less a nation with a coast bestrewn with harbors like ours, can be long prosperous within, that does not prosper and grow without. When a State, which is commercial by situation, forgets the work of outbuilding its empire, it loses its inner vitality. The day that marks its failure to meet every rising opportunity of advancement abroad, marks its sure decline at home. As with the individual, so with the State; if its ambition be dead and its hopes of expansion smoulder, its dissolution is speedy and sure. While its intellectual and physical energies are tense and grasp a large range; its internal and foreign empire will become consummate because it has the everlasting law of GROWTH!

We have illustrated that law with reference to our southern neighbor, Mexico. The effete and wasted portions of Mexico, being one half of her area, lying next to us, became nutriment to our stalwart strength. . . . It was once objected that the soil of California, New Mexico, and Arizona, was poor; a land of sand and centipedes; that there was no homogeneity in the people.

True, she has six million Indians, with Spaniards in plenty and pride, and of mixed people not a few. But are they worse than the Indians of our own soil? On the contrary, they are far better. They are tractable, stout, and laborious. Spain managed them with but a handful of soldiers for three hundred years. She managed them, too, under every provocation to revolt. Had an American protectorate been the sequence of Scott's occupation, a few months of protection would have given their industry its reward and peace its blessing. Then, too, we should have no apprehension to disturb our present relations with Mexico. . . .

This constitution [of February, 1857,] is the rallying cry of the Liberals; to its defense the nation is committed; by it alone is order possible. To sustain its upholders is clearly the duty, as it is the interest and desire, of the United States. President Buchanan has well considered these facts. In the success of the constitutional party he places all his hopes of redress for the innumerable outrages to our citizens. If this party fail, and there "being abundant cause for a resort to hostilities against the Government now holding possession of the capital," I am ready, for one, to vote for any system of reprisal, or to grant the Executive the necessary power to take possession of any portion of Mexico, as a pledge for the settlement of our claims. . . .

Wisdom, interest, the law of American progress, and the predominance of our Union on this continent, all urge the course I have indicated. Juarez waits our action. Shall we miss the golden opportunity?

If we fail in our efforts with him, then I am willing at once to take Sonora and Chihuahua, whichever party succeeds.

I believe that the list of American claims and cruelties, which has even provoked the English press to wonder at our forbearance, is warrant enough for such possession. There are even yet higher grounds for such seizure. The French Minister, De Gabriac, rules in the Miramon councils. A French fleet rides before Sacrificios. The French admiral was very ready to back Spain in her demands. To break this French power is our imperative duty. If it be not broken, our line of extension southward to Central America will be broken irrevocably.

Such is the condition of parties in Mexico. I need not discuss it further. The contest now is between the democratic element and the conservative element. The latter has its eye ever on Europe, and averse to the United States. Its rule has proved the most distracting and disastrous ever yet known in the annals of the South American Republics, where the earthquake and the revolution alike awake the same sad cry of anguish, and receive the same defiant, destructive answer. . . .

This duty of intervention becomes at once imperative and dignified, when we remember that, by such an act, we not only protect our citizens, but we save Mexico. We not only save her from Spain, France, and England, but from herself. This is no conquest of Cortez. It is the salvation of a people whose interests will be bettered by our aid. Without such aid, the fairest part of this continent will be a ruin—only the worse because like the Parthenon, its fragments will remain to show the beauty and richness of her former condition.

In conclusion, the policy I have indicated with respect to this continent, and the application of which to Cuba, Central America, and Mexico, will be of such benefits to them, will enable us to conform to that law of growth by which alone we have become great, and by which alone we shall become greater. This is the policy of other nations, and they have met obstacles to accomplish it. We shall accomplish it, but we shall have them as our obstacles. England has swept with her power from the Shannon to the Indus. She is content, and so are we, to see her greatness repeated in the offspring of her loins. Yet she daily calls our attempt to expand by the rudest terms. France has twice threatened Europe with continental conquest, and now organizes the Arabs of Northern Africa, the granary of the Roman world, for her march upon Egypt and her domination of the Mediterranean. Russia, the great land animal, is piercing Asia at every vulnerable point with her lances, and is pressing for an empire of which there is no adequate prophecy in the Scriptures. Even Spain joins her arms and her priesthood with France, and is waging against Cochin China a war which her journals call the civilizing spirit of the age, impelling the force of Europe to break down the barriers which divide that race from humanity. . . .

41 William H. Seward

Freedom, Union, and

National Destiny in Expansion

It was a tragedy for the nation that the question of American territorial expansion entered the life and thought of the United States at a time when countless Americans regarded expansion only as an agency in the struggle for moral prestige and political power between the North and the South, between the slaveholding and the nonslaveholding states. Indeed, such conservatives as Thomas Corwin and John Bell opposed expansion entirely because of the fear that the slavery issue would destroy the nation's unity and thus curtail its possible destiny. Their attacks on Polk's expansionist policies, were prompted by the very success of the country's democratic mission which rested in the image it created abroad—an image that could be easily damaged by civil strife.

It was left for William H. Seward of New York to discover in a dividing nation the continuing sources of a great national destiny. Seward, as a Whig spokesman, had not supported the policies of the Polk administration. However, he accepted the general conviction that the United States possessed a boundless future. Its population, he predicted in 1846, was "destined to roll its resistless waves to the icy barrier of the North, and to encounter oriental civilization on the shores of the Pacific." He never doubted that the country's power and influence would survive any civil war. Even in the speech that follows, delivered at St. Paul, Minnesota, on September 18, 1860, during a decisive presidential campaign, Seward could appreciate the nation's expansive energy as revealed especially in the remarkable development of the Middle West. He could still predict freely the ultimate extension of the United States to the north and the northwest as well as into the border regions once dominated by Spain. Nor, did he believe, would the great sectional quarrel then tearing the nation apart stay its destiny, for nothing could long disturb the harmony and stability of the Union. Yet the persistence of slavery in the United States marred and threatened the American commitment to the political redemption of humanity and the concept of equality. The Founding Fathers, declared Seward, unable to eradicate slavery from American soil, had sought to limit it, and those states of the North which had abandoned the institution now revealed their superiority as the true agents of American destiny. It was for the Northwest, with its wealth and power, to decide whether the United States would be a land of slavery or freedom.

Destiny was an illusive concept. Some Americans interpreted it as the nation's intrinsic greatness—the power of its economy, the wisdom of its thought and public policies, the benefits which it might render mankind. To such notions the more characteristic proponents of manifest destiny added the necessity of territorial expansion. Seward represented both schools. His intense concern for the Union, yet a Union of free men, reflected his conviction that the future course of the nation lay in almost limitless internal improvement. Yet as Secretary of State under Abraham Lincoln and Andrew Johnson, he accepted the gift of Midway Island and acquired Alaska by purchase. What is more, his public statements as Secretary at times included vague references to destiny. Seward's acquisitions, however, were not the products of expansionist sentiment; they were isolated decisions responding to special opportunities and special needs, much as was Franklin Pierce's acquisition of the Gadsden Purchase. The Civil War opened a new age for the nation. The era of the forties and fifties, when Americans spoke so freely of the nation's destiny, proved to be a unique episode in the history of the United States.

. . . I FIND myself now, for the first time, on the highlands in the center of the continent of North America, equidistant from the waters of Hudson's bay and the gulf of Mexico, from the Atlantic ocean to the ocean in which the sun sets—here on the spot where spring up, almost side by side, and so near that they may kiss each other, the two great rivers of the continent, the one of which pursuing its strange, capricious, majestic, vivacious course through rapids and cascade, lake after lake, bay after bay, and river after river, till, at last, after a course of two thousand five hundred miles, it brings your commerce into the ocean midway to the ports of Europe, and the other, which meandering through woodland and prairie a like distance of two thousand five hundred miles, taking in tributary after tributary from the east and from the west, bringing together the waters from the western declivity of the Alleghanies and the torrents which roll down the eastern sides of the Rocky mountains, finds the Atlantic ocean in the gulf of Mexico. Here is the central place where the agriculture of the richest regions of North America must begin its magnificent supplies to the whole world. On the east, all along the shore of lake Superior, and on the west, stretching in one broad plain, in a belt across the continent, is a country where state after state is yet to rise, and whence the productions for the support of human society in other crowded states must forever go forth. This is then a commanding field; but it is as commanding in regard to the commercial future, for power is not to reside permanently on the eastern slope of the Alleghany mountains, nor in the seaports of the Pacific. Seaports have always been controlled at last by the people of the interior.

From George E. Baker, ed., *The Works of William H. Seward* (Boston, 1884), IV, 331–347.

The people of the inland and of the upland, those who inhabit the sources of the mighty waters, are they who supply all states with the materials of wealth and power. The seaports will be the mouths by which we shall communicate and correspond with Europe, but the power that shall speak and shall communicate and express the will of men on this continent, is to be located in the Mississippi valley, and at the source of the Mississippi and the St. Lawrence. . . .

. . . I seem to myself to stand here on this eminence as the traveler who climbs the dome of St. Peter's in Rome. There, through the opening of that dome, he seems to himself to be in almost direct and immediate communication with the Almighty Power that directs and controls the actions and the wills of men, and he looks down with pity on the priests and votaries below who vainly try, by poring over beads and rituals, to study out and influence the mind of the Eternal. Standing here and looking far off into the northwest, I see the Russian as he busily occupies himself in establishing seaports and towns and fortifications, on the verge of this continent, as the outposts of St. Petersburg, and I can say, "Go on, and build up your outposts all along the coast up even to the Arctic ocean—they will yet become the outposts of my own country—monuments of the civilization of the United States in the northwest." So I look off on Prince Rupert's land and Canada, and see there an ingenious, enterprising and ambitious people, occupied with bridging rivers and constructing canals, railroads and telegraphs, to organize and preserve great British provinces north of the great lakes, the St. Lawrence, and around the shores of Hudson bay, and I am able to say, "It is very well, you are building excellent states to be hereafter admitted into the American Union." I can look southwest and see, amid all the convulsions that are breaking the Spanish American republics, and in their rapid decay and dissolution, the preparatory stage for their reörganization in free, equal and self-governing members of the United States of America. In the same high range of vision I can look down on the states and the people of the Atlantic coast of Maine and Massachusetts, of New York and Pennsylvania, of Virginia and the Carolinas, and Georgia, and Louisiana, and Texas, and round by the Pacific coast to California and Oregon. I can hear their disputes, their fretful controversies, their threats that if their own separate interests are not gratified and consulted by the federal government they will separate from this Union. I am able to say, "peace, be still." These subjects of contention and dispute that so irritate and anger and provoke and alienate you, are but temporary and ephemeral. These institutions which you so much desire to conserve, and for which you think you would sacrifice the welfare of the people of the continent, are almost as ephemeral as yourselves. The man is born to-day who will live to see the American Union, the American people, coming into the harmonious understanding that this is the land for the white man, and that whatever elements there are to disturb its present peace or irritate the passions of its possessors, will in the end, and that end will come before long, pass away, ineffectual in any way to disturb the harmony of, or endanger the stability of this great Union.

It is under the influence of reflections like these that I thank God here to-day, more fervently than ever, that I live in so great a country as this, and that my lot has been cast in it, not before the period when political society was to be organized, nor yet in that distant period when it is to collapse and fall into ruin, but that I live in the very day and hour when political society is to be effectually organized throughout the entire continent. We seem here, and now for the first time, to be conscious of that high necessity which compels every state in the Union to be, not separate and isolated, but one part of the American republic. We see and feel more than ever, when we come up here, that fervent heat of love and attachment to the region in which our lot is cast, that will not suffer the citizens of Maine, the citizens of South Carolina, the citizens of Texas, or the citizens of Wisconsin or Minnesota to be aliens to, or enemies of, each other, but which, on the other hand, compels them all to be members of one great political family. Aye, and we see now how it is that while society is convulsed with rivalries and jealousies between native and foreign born in our Atlantic cities and on our Pacific coast, and tormented with the rivalries and jealousies produced by difference of birth, of language, and of religion, here, in the central point of the republic, the German, and the Irishman, and the Italian, and the Frenchman, the Hollander and the Norwegian, becomes in spite of himself, almost completely in his own day, and entirely in his own children, an American citizen. We see the unity, in other words, that constitutes, and compels us to constitute, not many nations, not many peoples, but one nation and one people only.

. . . Providence set apart this continent for the work, and, as I think, set apart and designated this particular locality for the place whence shall go forth continually the ever-renewing spirit which shall bring the people of all other portions of the continent up to a continual advance in the establishment of the system. I may make myself better understood by saying, that until the beginning of the present century, men had lived the involuntary subjects of political government, and that the time had come when mankind could no longer consent to be so governed by force. The time had come when men were to live voluntary citizens and sovereigns themselves of the states which they possessed, and that is the principle of the government established here. It has only one vital principle. All others are resolved into it. That one principle—what is it? It is the equality of every man who is a member of the state to be governed. If there be not absolute political equality then some portion of the people are governed by force, then you are carried so far backward again toward the old system of involuntary citizenship, or a government by kings, lords, and standing armies. This was the great necessity, not of the people of the United States alone— it was not even the original conception of the people of the United States that a republican government was to be established for themselves alone, but the establishment of the republican system of the United States of America was only bringing out and reducing to actual practice the ideas and opinions which men had already formed, all over the civilized world. . . .

. . . But it was not the good fortune of our fathers to be able to find full and ample materials, all of the right kind, for the erection of the temple of liberty, which they constructed. Providence has so ordered it that uniformly perfect materials for any edifice which the human mind is required to devise, and the human hand to construct, cannot be found anywhere. . . . Even the founders of a great republic like this, wishing and intending to place it on the principle of the equality of man, had to take such materials as they found. They had to take society as it was, in which some were free and some were slaves, and to form a Union in which some were free states and some were slave states. They had the ideal before them, but they were unable to perfect it all at once. What did they do? . . . Seeing this element of slavery, which they could not eliminate, they said, "We will take care that it shall not weaken the edifice and bring it down. We will take care that although we cannot get rid of slaves now, the number of slaves hereafter shall diminish and the number of white men shall increase, and that ultimately the element of free white men shall be so strong that the element of slavery shall be inadequate to produce any serious danger, calamity, or disaster." How did they do this? They did it in a simple way by authorizing congress to prohibit, and practically by prohibiting, the African slave trade after the expiration of twenty years from the establishment of the constitution; supposing that if no more slaves were imported, the American people, then almost unanimously in favor of emancipation, would be able to eliminate from the country the small amount of slavery which would be left to decay and decline for want of invigoration by the African slave trade. They did another thing. They set apart the territory northwest of the Ohio river, nearly all of the unoccupied domain of the United States, for freemen only, declaring that neither slavery nor involuntary servitude should ever enter on its soil. They did one thing more. They declared that congress should pass uniform laws of naturalization, so that when the importation of African slaves should cease, voluntary immigration of freemen from all other lands should be encouraged and stimulated. Thus, while unable to exclude slavery from the system, they provided for the rapid development and perfection of the principle that all men are born free and equal.

And now, fellow citizens, we see all around us the results of that wise policy. Certain of the states concurred partially in the policy of the fathers. I hardly need tell you what states they were. They were Massachusetts, Rhode Island, Vermont, Connecticut, New York, New Jersey and Pennsylvania. Some other states did not. It is scarcely necessary to name them. They were the six southern states of the Union. The six southern states said, although the constitution has arrested the slave trade and invited emigration, and adopted the policy of making all the men of the new states free and equal, yet we will adhere to the system of slavery. You see how it has worked in the cities of Boston, New York and Philadelphia. You see it in the wheat fields of New York, of Ohio, of Indiana, of Illinois, of Wisconsin. You see it in the flocks and herds of Vermont and New Hampshire; you see it in the cattle that multiply upon ten thousand hills; you see it in the million of spindles in the manufactories of the east, and in the forges and furnaces of Pennsylvania; you see it in the crowded shipping of New York, and in her palaces and towers, emulating the magnificence of the old world, and grasping for itself the commerce of the globe. You see even in California and Oregon the same results; you see them in the copper ore dug out on the banks of lake Superior, the iron in Pennsylvania, the gypsum in New York, the salt in Ohio and New York, the lead in Illinois, and the silver and the gold in the free states of the Pacific coast. In all these you see the fruits of this policy. Neither in forest, nor in mines, nor in manufactories, nor in workshop, is there found one African slave that turns a wheel or supplies the oil which keeps the machinery in motion. On the other hand, you see millions of freemen crowding each other in perpetual waves, rolling over from Europe on the Atlantic coast, and flowing on and forming great states on the western base of the Alleghany mountains—still rolling on again perpetually until it constitutes new states, in which is built up here in Minnesota in nine years, a capital equal to the capital built in any slave state in the Union in two hundred years. . . .

There is one danger remaining—one only. Slavery can never more force itself, or be forced, from the stock that exists among us into the territories of the United States. But the cupidity of trade and the ambition of those whose interests are identified with slavery, are such that they may clandestinely and surreptitiously reöpen, either within the forms of law or without them, the African slave trade, and may bring in new cargoes of African slaves at one hundred dollars a head, and scatter them into the territories, and once getting possession of new domain they may again renew their operations against the patriotism of the American people. Therefore it is I enjoin upon you all to regard yourselves as men who, although you have achieved the victory and are entitled even now, it seems, to laurels, are nevertheless enlisted for the war and for your natural lives. You are committed to maintain the great policy until it shall have been so firmly established in the hearts and wills and affections of the American people, that there shall never be again a departure from it. We look to you of the northwest to finally decide whether this is to be a land of slavery or of freedom. The people of the northwest are to be the arbiters of its destiny; the virtue that is to save the nation must reside in the northwest, for the simple reason that it is not the people who live on the sidewalks and who deal in merchandise on the Atlantic or the Pacific coasts, that exercise the power of government, of sovereignty, in the United States. The political power of the United States resides in the owners of the land of the United States. The owners of workshops and of the banks are in the east, and the owners of the gold mines are in the far west; but the owners of the land of the United States are to be found along the shores of the Mississippi river, from New Orleans to the source of the great river and the great lakes. On both sides of the noble flood are the people who hold in their hands the destinies of the republic. . . .

Index